WordPerfect For Dummies

MW00836883

General Information

To start WordPerfect, click on the WordPerfect icon on your desktop or choose WordPerfect from the menus you see when you click the K, GNOME, or other "start" button. If you can't figure out how to start the program, see the appendix in back of this book.

To close a document window, choose File⇨Close from the menu bar or click on the Close button (usually an X) in the upper-right corner of the window.

To leave WordPerfect, choose Program from the menu bar of the program window and then choose Exit. Or click on the Close button (usually an X) in the upper-right corner of the WordPerfect program window.

When we say "press Alt+some key" or "press Ctrl+some key," we mean that you hold down the Alt or Ctrl key (like you hold down the Shift key) while you type another key and then release it.

To Do This While You're Typing	Press This
Get help	F1
Erase the character you just typed	Backspace (depending on your X Window configuration)
Erase the character to the right of your cursor (insertion point)	Delete
Start a new paragraph	Enter
Start a new page	Ctrl+Enter
Indent the first line of a paragraph	Tab
Indent all lines in a paragraph	F7 (after moving the cursor to the beginning of the paragraph)

Mouse Droppings

To Do This	Do This with Your Mouse
Select (highlight) text	Click in the text, hold down the mouse button, and drag
Select a word	Double-click on the word
Select a sentence	Click once in the left margin
Select a paragraph	Double-click in the left margin
Move text or graphics	Select it and then click on it and drag
See a QuickMenu	Move the mouse to the item you want to work with and click the right mouse button
Change the font	Click on the Font Face button on the Property Bar
Go somewhere	Double-click on the position area of the Application Bar
Close a file	Click on the Close box on the right end of the menu bar
Exit from WordPerfect	Click on the Close box on the right end of the title bar of the WordPerfect program window

WordPerfect® For Linux® For Dummies®

Cheat Sheet

Kommon Kwick Key Kombinations

These quick key combinations help you manage your files and text:

Press This	To Do This
Ctrl+C	Copy to Clipboard
Ctrl+X	Cut to Clipboard
Ctrl+V	Paste to Clipboard
Ctrl+S	Save document
F3	Save with new name
Ctrl+Shift+S	Save all open documents
Ctrl+P or F5	Print a document
Ctrl+O or F4	Open a document
Shift+F4 or Ctrl+N	Start a new document
Ctrl+B	Apply boldface
Ctrl+I	Apply italics
Ctrl+U	Apply underlining
Ctrl+F	Find or replace text or codes
F9	Open the Font dialog box
Ctrl+G	Go To
Ctrl+K	Change capitalization
Ctrl+W	Insert weird characters
Ctrl+D	Insert today's date
Ctrl+Shift+D	Insert a code that always displays the current date

Recovering from Errors

If you don't like what's going on	Press Esc a few times
If you have just deleted something and you want it back	Press Ctrl+Z
If you have just given a command and you want to undo it	Press Ctrl+Z

Helpful Tips

✔ Tell WordPerfect what you have in mind. Never type page numbers yourself, use lots of tabs to create a table, or type multiple columns of text yourself. Instead, use the multitude of WordPerfect features, such as page numbering, tables, and columns.

✔ Save your documents often by pressing Ctrl+S. To save all open documents, press Ctrl+Shift+S.

✔ To see (or delete) the secret codes WordPerfect puts in your documents, choose View➪Reveal Codes from the menu bar. Use the same command again to close the Reveal Codes window.

Getting Around in Your Document

The following keys move the cursor around on your screen:

This Keystroke	Moves You Here
↑	Up one line
↓	Down one line
←	Left one character
→	Right one character
Ctrl+←	Left one word
Ctrl+→	Right one word
Home	Beginning of the line
End	End of the line
PgUp	Top of the screen or up one screen
PgDn	Bottom of the screen or down one screen
Ctrl+Home	Beginning of the document
Ctrl+End	End of the document

IDG BOOKS WORLDWIDE

...For Dummies®: Bestselling Book Series for Beginners

™

References for the Rest of Us! ®

BESTSELLING BOOK SERIES

Are you intimidated and confused by computers? Do you find that traditional manuals are overloaded with technical details you'll never use? Do your friends and family always call you to fix simple problems on their PCs? Then the *...For Dummies*® computer book series from IDG Books Worldwide is for you.

...For Dummies books are written for those frustrated computer users who know they aren't really dumb but find that PC hardware, software, and indeed the unique vocabulary of computing make them feel helpless. *...For Dummies* books use a lighthearted approach, a down-to-earth style, and even cartoons and humorous icons to dispel computer novices' fears and build their confidence. Lighthearted but not lightweight, these books are a perfect survival guide for anyone forced to use a computer.

> *"I like my copy so much I told friends; now they bought copies."*
>
> — Irene C., Orwell, Ohio

> *"Quick, concise, nontechnical, and humorous."*
>
> — Jay A., Elburn, Illinois

> *"Thanks, I needed this book. Now I can sleep at night."*
>
> — Robin F., British Columbia, Canada

Already, millions of satisfied readers agree. They have made *...For Dummies* books the #1 introductory level computer book series and have written asking for more. So, if you're looking for the most fun and easy way to learn about computers, look to *...For Dummies* books to give you a helping hand.

® IDG BOOKS WORLDWIDE

by Margaret Levine Young, David C. Kay, David Guertin, and Kathy Warfel

IDG Books Worldwide, Inc.
An International Data Group Company

Foster City, CA ◆ Chicago, IL ◆ Indianapolis, IN ◆ New York, NY

WordPerfect® For Linux® For Dummies®

Published by
IDG Books Worldwide, Inc.
An International Data Group Company
919 E. Hillsdale Blvd.
Suite 400
Foster City, CA 94404
www.idgbooks.com (IDG Books Worldwide Web site)
www.dummies.com (Dummies Press Web site)

Library of Congress Catalog Card No.: 99-67155

ISBN: 0-7645-0657-9

Printed in the United States of America

10 9 8 7 6 5 4 3 2 1

1B/RS/RR/ZZ/IN

Distributed in the United States by IDG Books Worldwide, Inc.

Distributed by CDG Books Canada Inc. for Canada; by Transworld Publishers Limited in the United Kingdom; by IDG Norge Books for Norway; by IDG Sweden Books for Sweden; by IDG Books Australia Publishing Corporation Pty. Ltd. for Australia and New Zealand; by TransQuest Publishers Pte Ltd. for Singapore, Malaysia, Thailand, Indonesia, and Hong Kong; by Gotop Information Inc. for Taiwan; by ICG Muse, Inc. for Japan; by Intersoft for South Africa; by Eyrolles for France; by International Thomson Publishing for Germany, Austria and Switzerland; by Distribuidora Cuspide for Argentina; by LR International for Brazil; by Galileo Libros for Chile; by Ediciones ZETA S.C.R. Ltda. for Peru; by WS Computer Publishing Corporation, Inc., for the Philippines; by Contemporanea de Ediciones for Venezuela; by Express Computer Distributors for the Caribbean and West Indies; by Micronesia Media Distributor, Inc. for Micronesia; by Chips Computadoras S.A. de C.V. for Mexico; by Editorial Norma de Panama S.A. for Panama; by American Bookshops for Finland.

For general information on IDG Books Worldwide's books in the U.S., please call our Consumer Customer Service department at 800-762-2974. For reseller information, including discounts and premium sales, please call our Reseller Customer Service department at 800-434-3422.

For information on where to purchase IDG Books Worldwide's books outside the U.S., please contact our International Sales department at 317-596-5530 or fax 317-596-5692.

For consumer information on foreign language translations, please contact our Customer Service department at 1-800-434-3422, fax 317-596-5692, or e-mail rights@idgbooks.com.

For information on licensing foreign or domestic rights, please phone +1-650-655-3109.

For sales inquiries and special prices for bulk quantities, please contact our Sales department at 650-655-3200 or write to the address above.

For information on using IDG Books Worldwide's books in the classroom or for ordering examination copies, please contact our Educational Sales department at 800-434-2086 or fax 317-596-5499.

For press review copies, author interviews, or other publicity information, please contact our Public Relations department at 650-655-3000 or fax 650-655-3299.

For authorization to photocopy items for corporate, personal, or educational use, please contact Copyright Clearance Center, 222 Rosewood Drive, Danvers, MA 01923, or fax 978-750-4470.

About the Authors

Unlike most of her peers in that mid-30-something bracket, **Margaret Levine Young** was exposed to computers at an early age. In high school, she got into a computer club known as the R.E.S.I.S.T.O.R.S. "We were a group of kids who spent all day Saturday together in a barn fooling around on three computers that ran on vacuum tubes." Their goal, she admits, was to do language processing "so that the computers could make smart-aleck remarks back to us."

Although Margy got into computers "for fun" and because "my brother did," she stayed in the field through college, graduating from Yale with a degree in computer science. She was one of the first microcomputer managers in the early 1980s at Columbia Pictures Industries.

Since then, Margy has written more than 20 other computer books with various friends, including Dave Kay; her brother, John Levine; and her husband, Jordan Young. The books include *The Internet For Dummies,* 6th Edition, *MORE Internet For Dummies,* 4th Edition, *UNIX For Dummies,* 4th Edition, and *Dummies 101: Netscape Communicator 4,* all published by IDG Books Worldwide, Inc., as well as *Internet: The Complete Reference* and *Windows 98: The Complete Reference*, published by Osborne/McGraw-Hill.

Margy also met Jordan in the R.E.S.I.S.T.O.R.S., and her other passion is her children, Meg and Zac. She loves gardening, "anything to do with eating," Brazil, and Vermont, where she lives.

Dave Kay is a writer, engineer, wildlife tracker, and aspiring artist, combining professions with the same effectiveness as his favorite business establishment, Acton Muffler, Brake, and Ice Cream (now defunct). Dave's computer book efforts include *...For Dummies* titles on Dragon NaturallySpeaking, Microsoft Works, WordPerfect, Web publishing, and VRML (IDG Books Worldwide, Inc.) and *Internet: The Complete Reference,* and *Graphics File Formats* (McGraw-Hill). In his other life, Dave is the Poo-bah of Brightleaf Communications, where he writes and teaches. He spends his spare time in the woods, playing with molten glass, designing stage scenery, and singing Gilbert and Sullivan choruses in public. He lives in the boondocks of Massachusetts with his wife, Katy, and his golden retriever, Alex.

David Guertin, who helped convert this edition from a Windows book to a Linux book, came into the computer business via the back door. Unlike some other authors, he did not start playing with UNIX as a young nerd; instead, he waited until he was an older, established nerd. Dave began serious programming as a graduate student in zoology, writing programs that taxed the capabilities of the most powerful personal computer then available. To circumvent this problem, he ignored the skepticism of his peers and installed a fledgling system named Linux. With the enthusiasm of the converted, he has used UNIX and Linux in his work ever since. Dave is the Science Specialist in Instructional Technology at Middlebury College, where he supports UNIX computing in the sciences.

Kathy Warfel, who also helped update this book from the preceding Windows-based edition, is a technical writer who has been teaching people how to use computers and writing about computers for the past 15 years. She was hooked on the Internet from the first time she logged on and saw a 6 second news video of a politician giving a speech. She holds a B.S. degree in journalism from the University of Colorado and hopes one day to own a small-town online newspaper.

ABOUT IDG BOOKS WORLDWIDE

Welcome to the world of IDG Books Worldwide.

IDG Books Worldwide, Inc., is a subsidiary of International Data Group, the world's largest publisher of computer-related information and the leading global provider of information services on information technology. IDG was founded more than 30 years ago by Patrick J. McGovern and now employs more than 9,000 people worldwide. IDG publishes more than 290 computer publications in over 75 countries. More than 90 million people read one or more IDG publications each month.

Launched in 1990, IDG Books Worldwide is today the #1 publisher of best-selling computer books in the United States. We are proud to have received eight awards from the Computer Press Association in recognition of editorial excellence and three from Computer Currents' First Annual Readers' Choice Awards. Our best-selling ...For Dummies® series has more than 50 million copies in print with translations in 31 languages. IDG Books Worldwide, through a joint venture with IDG's Hi-Tech Beijing, became the first U.S. publisher to publish a computer book in the People's Republic of China. In record time, IDG Books Worldwide has become the first choice for millions of readers around the world who want to learn how to better manage their businesses.

Our mission is simple: Every one of our books is designed to bring extra value and skill-building instructions to the reader. Our books are written by experts who understand and care about our readers. The knowledge base of our editorial staff comes from years of experience in publishing, education, and journalism — experience we use to produce books to carry us into the new millennium. In short, we care about books, so we attract the best people. We devote special attention to details such as audience, interior design, use of icons, and illustrations. And because we use an efficient process of authoring, editing, and desktop publishing our books electronically, we can spend more time ensuring superior content and less time on the technicalities of making books.

You can count on our commitment to deliver high-quality books at competitive prices on topics you want to read about. At IDG Books Worldwide, we continue in the IDG tradition of delivering quality for more than 30 years. You'll find no better book on a subject than one from IDG Books Worldwide.

John Kilcullen
Chairman and CEO
IDG Books Worldwide, Inc.

Steven Berkowitz
President and Publisher
IDG Books Worldwide, Inc.

Eighth Annual Computer Press Awards ≥1992

Ninth Annual Computer Press Awards ≥1993

Tenth Annual Computer Press Awards ≥1994

Eleventh Annual Computer Press Awards ≥1995

Dedication

We would like to dedicate this book to the Open Source movement, without which the growing success of Linux would not have been possible.

Authors' Acknowledgments

We would like to thank Matt Wagner, for putting all the pieces in place; Katy Weeks, for keeping Dave Kay sane; Diane Guertin, for keeping Dave Guertin sane; Jordan Young, for making Margy a latté every morning and feeding the chickens; John Levine, for providing the Web-O-Matic Web site and Linux advice; Rebecca Whitney, our editor, for her patience and professionalism; and the folks at IDG Books Worldwide, for making this book happen.

Publisher's Acknowledgments

We're proud of this book; please register your comments through our IDG Books Worldwide Online Registration Form located at http://my2cents.dummies.com.

Some of the people who helped bring this book to market include the following:

Acquisitions, Editorial, and Media Development

Project Editor: Rebecca Whitney

Acquisitions Editor: David Mayhew

Technical Editor: Keith Underdahl

Media Development Editor: Marita Ellixson

Associate Permissions Editor: Carmen Krikorian

Media Development Coordinator: Megan Decraene

Editorial Manager: Mary C. Corder

Media Development Manager: Heather Heath Dismore

Editorial Assistant: Beth Parlon

Production

Project Coordinator: E. Shawn Aylsworth

Layout and Graphics: Amy M. Adrian, Kate Jenkins, Jill Piscitelli, Barry Offringa, Tracy Oliver, Brent Savage, Brian Torwelle, Maggie Ubertini, Dan Whetstine, Erin Zeltner

Proofreaders: Laura Albert, Beth Baugh, Marianne Santy, Charles Spencer

Indexer: Johnna VanHoose

Special Help
Constance Carlisle, Amanda Foxworth, Suzanne Thomas

General and Administrative

IDG Books Worldwide, Inc.: John Kilcullen, CEO; Steven Berkowitz, President and Publisher

IDG Books Technology Publishing Group: Richard Swadley, Senior Vice President and Publisher; Walter Bruce III, Vice President and Associate Publisher; Joseph Wikert, Associate Publisher; Mary Bednarek, Branded Product Development Director; Mary Corder, Editorial Director; Barry Pruett, Publishing Manager; Michelle Baxter, Publishing Manager

IDG Books Consumer Publishing Group: Roland Elgey, Senior Vice President and Publisher; Kathleen A. Welton, Vice President and Publisher; Kevin Thornton, Acquisitions Manager; Kristin A. Cocks, Editorial Director

IDG Books Internet Publishing Group: Brenda McLaughlin, Senior Vice President and Publisher; Diane Graves Steele, Vice President and Associate Publisher; Sofia Marchant, Online Marketing Manager

IDG Books Production for Dummies Press: Debbie Stailey, Associate Director of Production; Cindy L. Phipps, Manager of Project Coordination, Production Proofreading, and Indexing; Tony Augsburger, Manager of Prepress, Reprints, and Systems; Laura Carpenter, Production Control Manager; Shelley Lea, Supervisor of Graphics and Design; Debbie J. Gates, Production Systems Specialist; Robert Springer, Supervisor of Proofreading; Kathie Schutte, Production Supervisor

Dummies Packaging and Book Design: Patty Page, Manager, Promotions Marketing

◆

The publisher would like to give special thanks to Patrick J. McGovern, without whom this book would not have been possible.

◆

Contents at a Glance

Introduction 1

Part I: Introducing WordPerfect for Linux 9
Chapter 1: WordPerfect Basics 11
Chapter 2: Using the Mouse and Keyboard 31
Chapter 3: Cruising the Document...51
Chapter 4: Fooling with Blocks of Text 61
Chapter 5: Text Improvements 75

Part II: Prettying Up Your Text 95
Chapter 6: Charming Characters 97
Chapter 7: Sensational Sentences and Poignant Paragraphs 109
Chapter 8: Perfect Pages and Dashing Documents 129
Chapter 9: The WordPerfect Secret Decoder Ring 151
Chapter 10: Documents with Style 171

Part III: Things You Can Do with Documents 187
Chapter 11: On Paper at Last: Printing Stuff 189
Chapter 12: Juggling Documents on Your Screen...........................203
Chapter 13: Juggling Files on Your Disk.................................221

Part IV: Creating Documents That Don't Just Sit There 233
Chapter 14: Chasing Your Words Around on the Page 235
Chapter 15: Say It with Pictures 261
Chapter 16: Creating Your Own Junk Mail................................275
Chapter 17: Recipes and Templates for Popular Documents 293
Chapter 18: Spinning Web Pages 319

Part V: Oh, Help! 341
Chapter 19: Training WordPerfect to Act Your Way.......................343
Chapter 20: Don't Panic! Read This Chapter!............................359

Part VI: The Part of Tens 369
Chapter 21: The Ten Commandments of WordPerfect 371
Chapter 22: Ten Awesome Tricks 377

Appendix: About the CD 383

Index 391

IDG Books Worldwide End-User License Agreement 403

Installation Instructions 405

Book Registration Information ....Back of Book

Cartoons at a Glance

By Rich Tennant

page 187

page 369

page 233

page 9

page 95

page 341

Fax: 978-546-7747 • E-mail: the5wave@tiac.net

Table of Contents

Introduction *1*

What Goes On in This Book..1
How to Use This Book 2
Who Am Us, Anyway?..3
What You're Not Supposed to Read....................................4
How This Book Is Organized..4
    Part I: Introducing WordPerfect for Linux........................4
    Part II: Prettying Up Your Text 5
    Part III: Things You Can Do with Documents 5
    Part IV: Creating Documents That Don't Just Sit There 5
    Part V: Oh, Help! 5
    Part VI: The Part of Tens 6
What's on the CD-ROM 6
Icons Used in This Book...6
Where to Go from Here..7

Part I: Introducing WordPerfect for Linux.....................9

Chapter 1: WordPerfect Basics 11

Which Window Manager Do You Have? 11
Honey, I Shrunk the Program!..13
Starting WordPerfect 14
The Two Windows of WordPerfect 15
What's on the Application Bar?..18
Typing Something 19
Waxing Eloquent...20
What's in a Name?...20
    Saving your document 21
    Filename rules...23
    Save it again, Sam 24
Getting Some Help...25
Editing Another File 25
Making a New File...27
Printing Your Document...27
Leaving WordPerfect...28

Chapter 2: Using the Mouse and Keyboard **31**

   To Mouse or Not to Mouse 32
   Choosing Commands from Menus 33
      Clicking on the menu bar 34
      Choosing a command 35
   Using Dialog Boxes 36
      Those wacky dialog thingies 37
      Our favorite buttons 38
   Using QuickMenus for Even More Ways to Choose Commands 39
   Fooling with the Toolbar 40
   Lunching with the Proprietors at the Property Bar 42
   Using the Ruler 43
   Using the Keyboard 44
      Shift, Ctrl, and Alt 44
      Knowing when to press Enter 45
      The story of Tab and the spacebar 45
      Choosing commands by using keys 46
   Undoing Mistakes 47
   Help, Help-Help, and More Help 48
      Help 48
      Ask PerfectExpert 49
      Context-sensitive Help 50

Chapter 3: Cruising the Document **51**

   Two — Count 'Em, Two — Ways 51
   Mousing Around 52
      Moving to the far reaches of the document 53
      Scrolling to the right spot 54
   Sticking with the Keyboard 55
      Using Ctrl with the arrow keys 56
      Moving farther and faster 56
   Go To Where? 57
      Top o' the page to you! 58
      Getting unlost 59

Chapter 4: Fooling with Blocks of Text **61**

   Basic Blocks 61
   Selecting Text with Your Mouse 62
      The point-and-shoot approach 62
      Lots of clicking for selecting lots of text 64
      The QuickMenu approach 66
      The menu bar approach 66
   Selecting Text with the Keyboard 67
   Selecting Text with Your Nose and a Pickle 68
   Extending Selections 68

Doing Stuff with Selected Text...69
   Deleting text..70
   Moving text...70
   Copying text..70
Using the X Clipboard...70
   Copying and pasting with the X Clipboard 71
   Cutting and pasting with the X Clipboard....................................72
   Using the QuickMenu approach to Clipboarding..........................73

Chapter 5: Text Improvements **75**
Deleting Text..75
   Dealing with one character at a time: Delete and Backspace........76
   Deleting blocks of text..76
   Using Insert and Typeover modes 77
Just (Un)Do It...78
Finding What's Lost: The Search for Sanity 79
   Changing the way you search..80
   Searching for sanity and finding insanity.....................................81
   Getting picky about what you find 82
Finding and Replacing Text...83
Finding and Replacing Codes 85
Typing Misspelled Words..85
   "I see red under my words"..85
   "I see blue under my words"...86
   "I see my words change even as I type them!" 87
Flying the Spell Checker Yourself..89
   Spell checking your entire document 89
   Dealing with real words that WordPerfect doesn't know...............91
   Spell-checking tips 93
   Dealing with Grammy Grammatik...93
   Taming the roar of the mighty thesaurus......................................94

Part II: Prettying Up Your Text *95*

Chapter 6: Charming Characters **97**
Emphasizing Text with Boldface, Italics, and Underlining.................98
   Formatting as you type..98
   Is this part formatted? 99
   Yikes! Getting rid of formatting...99
Making Text Larger or Smaller..100
Fonts of Wisdom...101
   Changing the font for some text..101
   Changing the font for the rest of the document...........................102

The Master Control Panel for Character Formats 103
Using the options in the Font dialog box 104
Formatting an entire document..106
Copying Character Formatting...107
Changing Capitalization 108

Chapter 7: Sensational Sentences and Poignant Paragraphs **109**

Using the Ruler..110
What are all those little triangles?....................................111
What's the ruler for? 111
Setting Margins..112
Dragging the margin lines..112
Using the Margins dialog box..113
Changing the margins for the rest of the document.....114
Changing margins for a paragraph or two 115
Changing the Justification...116
Kinds of justification 117
Centering, right-aligning, and justifying text..................117
To Hyphenate or Not to Hyphenate...119
Playing with Tab Stops 121
Stop! Tab!...121
Setting tab stops..121
Moving tab stops around 123
Blowing away tab stops 124
Making a brand-new tab stop 124
Indenting the First Line of Each Paragraph 125
Changing the Line Spacing..127
Changing the Spacing Between Paragraphs 128

Chapter 8: Perfect Pages and Dashing Documents **129**

Setting the Page Size..129
Adjusting the Top and Bottom Margins 132
Starting a New Page 133
Keeping Text Together 134
Avoiding broken homes (widows and orphans) 134
Keeping your act together..135
Keeping your head together 136
Centering a Page, from Top to Bottom 137
Looking at Different Views of Your Document.........................138
Numbering Pages 139
For all you Roman-numeral fans...141
Starting over again at 1..142
Adding Heads and Feets...142
Making a header or footer...143
Typing the text in a header or footer................................145
Controlling where headers and footers are printed 147
"Don't print it here!"..147
Discontinuing headers and footers....................................148
Getting rid of a header or footer 149

Chapter 9: The WordPerfect Secret Decoder Ring **151**

What Are Secret Formatting Codes?..152
Seeing the Codes..152
    Understanding the Reveal Codes window 153
    Adjusting the size of windows 154
    Getting rid of the Reveal Codes window 154
Cracking the Codes 154
    Looking at codes 155
    Modifying codes 155
    Deleting codes 156
Using the Open Style Code..157
Using Character Codes..157
Dealing with Character-Formatting Codes..158
    Undoing character formatting 158
    Editing formatted text 158
Undoing Sentence and Paragraph Formatting 159
Undoing Page and Document Formatting 160
Finding Codes 161
    Finding all codes of one type 161
    Finding specific codes 164
    Knowing what to do after you find your code 165
Replacing Codes Automagically..165
    Replacing specific codes with other codes............................166
    Replacing codes with other codes 167
    Deleting all codes 168
A Summary of Mysterious Codes...169

Chapter 10: Documents with Style **171**

What Is a Style?...172
A Style By Any Other Name Would Smell As Sweet 172
Creating and Applying a Style..173
    Creating a style by using QuickStyle.......................................173
    Applying a character style 174
    Creating a paragraph style by using QuickStyle 175
    Applying a paragraph style 176
Built-In Styles 176
    Heading styles...176
    The InitialStyle style..177
    More built-in styles..177
The Master Control Panel for Styles: The Style List 178
Creating Styles from Scratch and Modifying Existing Styles 179
    Creating a style from scratch..181
    Modifying existing styles..182
    Creating a document style 183
    Applying a document style 184
Turning Off Styles and Chaining Styles 184

Recycling Styles..184
    Dragging in styles from another document 184
    Creating the Martha Stewart library of styles 185
Getting Rid of Styles...186

Part III: Things You Can Do with Documents..................187

Chapter 11: On Paper at Last: Printing Stuff 189

Ready to Print? 189
    The basics 189
    Do Linux and WordPerfect know that you have a printer? 190
Printing the Entire Document...192
Printing Part of a Document 194
    Printing selected text 194
    Printing a specific page...195
    Printing a bunch of pages, but not all of them 195
    Printing random pages 196
Printing on Both Sides of the Paper....................................197
    If your printer can do two-sided printing....................197
    If your printer doesn't know how to print on both sides...........198
    Printing several copies 199
Printing a Document on Disk..200
Canceling a Print Job...201
    Who ya gonna call? 201
    WordPerfect, stop printing!......................................201

Chapter 12: Juggling Documents on Your Screen 203

How Can You Work on Two Documents at a Time? 204
    Switching between open documents 205
    Making baby documents 205
    Closing the curtains 205
    Working with multiple documents 206
Windows on Top of Windows..207
    Seeing lots of windows 207
    "I want that one!"...209
    Sizing your windows 209
    Maximizing your documents.....................................210
    Minimizing your documents 210
    Saving all your open documents 211
Combining Documents 211
    Inserting one document into another one 211
    Saving a chunk of text as a separate document 212
What If the File Already Exists?..213

Using Foreign Files 214
    Which format should I use? 215
    Creating a foreign file..216
    Reading a foreign file...217
    Word processors versus food processors 219

Chapter 13: Juggling Files on Your Disk **221**

WordPerfect Versus Real File Managers.............................222
Exploring Your Directories...222
    Creating directories 224
Moving, Renaming, Copying, and Deleting Files 226
    Moving or renaming a file...226
    Copying a file..227
    Deleting a file...227
Two Helpful File-Management Tools for the Forgetful Author 228
    The viewer window 228
    The QuickList 229
Kinds of Files...231
Finding a File with a Forgotten Name 231

Part IV: Creating Documents
That Don't Just Sit There **233**

Chapter 14: Chasing Your Words Around on the Page **235**

Working with Borders and Backgrounds 236
    Basic borders 236
    Phil — for all that white space behind your text 238
    Some miscellaneous thoughts about borders 238
Working with Columns 239
    Creating columns..240
    Bad breaks and what to do about them 242
Working with Tables 243
    Making tables with Table QuickCreate 243
    Adding or deleting rows and columns......................245
    Changing the column width 246
    Choosing borders and backgrounds with SpeedFormat.............247
    Making incredibly complex spreadsheet-like tables.............248
    Formatting the numbers in your complex spreadsheet.............250
Working with Text Boxes..251
    Creating your first box..251
    Moving a box to more or less where you want it 252
    Making a box more or less the right size 252
    Changing everything else about a box 253
    Working with the Graphics menu..............................254
    Moving a box exactly where you want it...................254

Making a box exactly the right size..256
Adding captions to your boxes 257
Text wrapping 258
Scribbling on Your Document..259
Up and down and side to side 259
Lines that go any which way..260

Chapter 15: Say It with Pictures 261

Working with Graphics..262
Inserting some Corel clipart into your document.....................263
Fooling with your picture..264
Inserting a shape into your document 266
Inserting a picture from somewhere else into your document 266
Creating Your Own Graphics with WP Draw................................267
Creating a new picture..268
Editing a graphic..269
Whipping your drawings into shape, or
whipping shapes into your drawings..............................269
Putting text in your drawings 271
Creating Graphs and Charts 272
Making a new chart...272
Editing your chart 273
Putting the chart back into the document...................................274

Chapter 16: Creating Your Own Junk Mail 275

How Does the Junk-Mail Feature Work? 276
Creating a Data File...277
Turning a document full of text into a data file 278
Creating a data file from scratch 282
Entering the data at last 284
Making corrections 285
Creating a Form File...286
Merging Your Files...289
Printing Your Data File...292

Chapter 17: Recipes and Templates for Popular Documents 293

What Are Templates?..293
Not a Template but Just As Good: Making a Document Uneditable......294
Using Templates 295
Letters...297
Getting WordPerfect to write your letter for you......................297
Printing your own letterhead...298
Skipping space for the letterhead on stationery.........................299
Dating your letter 299
Numbering the pages..300
Saving your letter as a prototype document 300
Memos 300
Faxes 301

Envelopes 301
  Printing the address on the envelope 301
  Tips for printing envelopes 303
Mailing Labels 303
  Printing addresses on mailing labels 304
  Selecting which labels to print 305
  Tips for printing labels 306
Booklets 306
  Creating a booklet document 307
  Printing your booklet: The magic part 308
  Tips for creating booklets 309
Reports, Books, and Other Big Documents 309
  Creating a master document and its subdocuments 310
  Expanding a master document 311
  Saving a master document 313
  Editing a master document 314
  Creating a table of contents 315

Chapter 18: Spinning Web Pages **319**
Hypertext, the Internet, and the World Wide Web 320
  What is hypertext? 320
  The Internet 320
  The World Wide Web 321
Hypertext Links and Bookmarks 321
  Creating a bookmark: A place you jump to 322
  Jumping to a bookmark 324
  Creating a hyperlink — a way to jump somewhere 324
  The Hyperlink Tools Property Bar 325
Creating Your Own Web Pages 327
  Text formatting on Web pages 328
  Adding a picture to a Web page 330
  Creating a link to another Web page 333
  Changing the look of your page 335
Converting Your Documents to Web Pages 335
  Saving your Web page as a WordPerfect document 337
  Saving your Web page as an HTML document 337
Stuff You Can Do in WordPerfect That You Can't Do on a Web Page.....340

Part V: Oh, Help! *341*

Chapter 19: Training WordPerfect to Act Your Way **343**
Seeing Information About Your Documents 344
Setting Your Favorite Font 344
Zooming Around in Your Documents 345
Setting Your Preferences 347

Changing the Way WordPerfect Looks 348
   Zooming...349
   Displaying spaces, tabs, indents, and returns.....................350
   Changing your colors...351
Where Does WordPerfect Put Your Files? 352
   Telling WordPerfect about directories and backups 352
   Getting back your timed backups 354
Some Cool Environment Preferences 355
   Finding where you left off...356
   Controlling mouse selection 357
Assigning Different Meanings to Keys 357

Chapter 20: Don't Panic! Read This Chapter! 359

"Where's WordPerfect?" (Part I) 359
"Where's WordPerfect?" (Part II) 360
"Where's My Document?" (Part I)...360
"Where's My Document?" (Part II)..361
"Where Am I?"...362
"The Entire Document Is Boldface!" 362
"The Screen Looks Weird!"..363
"My Document Isn't Printing!" 363
"Yikes! I Didn't Mean to Delete That!"..364
"They Can't Open My Document!" 365
"WordPerfect's Not Listening to Me!" 366
"Timed Backup Files Exist?" 367

Part VI: The Part of Tens *369*

Chapter 21: The Ten Commandments of WordPerfect 371

Tell WordPerfect What You Have in Mind...371
Do Not Use Extra Spaces or Tabs...372
Do Not Keep Pressing Enter to Begin a New Page 372
Do Not Number Your Pages Manually 373
Save Early and Often..373
Save Before Using the Edit⇨Find and Replace Command....................373
Back Up Your Work 373
Do Not Turn Off Your PC Until You Exit Linux......................................374
Turn On the Printer Before Printing Documents 374
Always Keep Printer Supplies on Hand...375

Chapter 22: Ten Awesome Tricks 377

Dragging and Dropping Text...377
Returning to Where You Were 378
Going Back to the Old Same Place 378
Reopening an Earlier Document...378

Inserting the Date...378
Using Unbreakable Hyphens and Spaces 379
Chasing Speeding Bullets 379
Converting Tabs to Tables 380
Sending Your Document By E-Mail.......................................381
Type It Again, Sam!..382

Appendix: About the CD **383**
System Requirements 383
How to Use the CD 384
Installing WordPerfect 384
Running WordPerfect...387
Installing the language modules 387
Adding WordPerfect to your KDE menus, panel, and desktop.....388
If You Have Problems (Of the CD Kind).................................390

Index...**391**

IDG Books Worldwide End-User License Agreement......**403**

Installation Instructions...**405**

Book Registration Information ....*Back of Book*

Introduction

*I*f you thought that the idea of word processing was to write, not to do amazing things on a computer. . . .

If you ever secretly wondered who the heck uses all those features advertised on the box your software came in. . . .

If you ever had to humiliate yourself in front of some computer wizard just to get words on paper. . . .

Congratulations — you're a "dummy!" Dummies are an underground group of people smart enough to say, "Call me what you will — I just want to get some work done, please!" If you're that sort of person, this book is for you.

WordPerfect for Linux is an exciting program because it brings an easy-to-use, powerful word processing program to the world of Linux. As more good Linux programs become available, the popularity of Linux is soaring. Linux is an amazing phenomenon — an operating system written almost entirely by volunteers — and you're part of it!

What Goes On in This Book

In this book, we do the following:

- Start from the beginning, in case you're a beginner. We use genuine English words, not cryptic technobabble.
- Lead you through the maze of buttons, commands, icons, menus, mice, and windows that make up WordPerfect for Linux.
- Give you just enough of the fancy stuff to look good — or to convince your boss or spouse that WordPerfect was worth the big bucks you paid for it.

True to the *...For Dummies* philosophy, this book refuses to take software too seriously. What we do take seriously is helping you get your work done. When WordPerfect has something to watch out for, this book tells you about it. When something really isn't important, the book tells you that, too.

Probably just as important as what's in this book is what isn't in it. It has no long, technical explanations of underlying principles; no huge tables of the 47 things that feature X can do; and no charts of commands and keystrokes organized in some useless manner, such as alphabetically.

WordPerfect for Linux is based on WordPerfect 8 for Windows. If you've ever used WordPerfect 8, you're in for a pleasant surprise because most of the commands, menus, and dialog boxes will look very familiar!

How to Use This Book

Because this book is a reference book, whenever some feature in WordPerfect has you tying knots in your mouse cord, you can just look up what you want in the table of contents or the index.

If your brow is already furrowing while you're just looking at the pictures of WordPerfect on the box, check out the earlier chapters first. They speak of mice and menus and similar basics, so they're written for beginners. If you're new to Linux or even to computers, you probably should start at the beginning. Those chapters help you get used to the what, why, and how of giving commands to WordPerfect. After you understand the basics, though, you don't have to read the chapters in any sequence.

This book stands by itself. (No one else will get near it!) It does not, for example, require you to read the WordPerfect manual. The book occasionally refers you, however, to a companion book in the ...*For Dummies* series — usually *LINUX For Dummies,* 2nd Edition, by Jon "Maddog" Hall (published by IDG Books Worldwide, Inc.), available wherever books are sold, read, or generally left lying around. That's because there's more to say about many of the topics we touch on here, and we figure that, just maybe, you want to know more. If you don't, though, don't fret. Everything you need to get a bunch of real work done is right here.

Most of what you find in this book are full, robust sentences, not cryptic abbreviations or shortcut terminology. Unfortunately, one person's full, robust sentence is another's long-winded description.

If we always used sentences such as "Move the mouse so that the mouse pointer covers the word *Edit* on the menu bar and then press the left mouse button; a menu appears and contains the word *Cut;* move the mouse so that the mouse pointer covers the word *Cut,*" you would be comatose by Chapter 2, and this book would take on encyclopedic dimensions. So, we generally restrict this sort of thing to chapters on the basics. When we get around to less-basic stuff, we say such things as "Choose the Edit⇨Cut command" and hope that you forgive us.

When we want you to choose a command from the menu bar and then choose another command from the menu that appears, we separate the two commands with this cute little arrow: ⇨. See Chapter 2 for details.

When we want you to type something, it appears in **bold type**. Onscreen messages and filenames look like this. When we suggest pressing two keys at the same time, such as the Ctrl key and the C key, we use a plus sign like this: Ctrl+C. In Chapter 2, we tell you all about choosing commands from menus.

Who Am Us, Anyway?

This section explains what we assume about you, our esteemed (and, thanks to the joy of software, occasionally steamed) reader:

- ✔ You use some version of Linux. We used Red Hat Linux and the KDE window manager when we wrote this book, although you may use a different version of Linux and a different window manager, like GNOME. If so, your screen may look a little different from the pictures in this book.

- ✔ WordPerfect is already installed. (If it's not, take a look at the appendix in the back of this book to find out how to install WordPerfect from the CD.)

- ✔ You want to write stuff and make it look nice.

- ✔ You don't really give a bat's eyelash about Linux or computers except for what you absolutely need for your daily work.

- ✔ You have a Linux "guru" available — an expert, like one of those infuriatingly clever 10-year-olds born with a computer cable for an umbilical cord, whom you can call for the tough stuff and whom you can probably pay off in cookies, pizza, or Chinese food. Because Linux is almost infinitely configurable, you may need your local Linux wizard to configure your system if it doesn't act the way we say that it should.

- ✔ You don't have fabulous expertise with windowing systems, although you have a mouse and probably would know a window if it were pointed out to you.

- ✔ You or the person who installed WordPerfect installed it in the standard way. WordPerfect is accommodating almost to a fault and lets itself be twisted and restructured like a ball of Silly Putty. If buttons and things on your screen don't look like the buttons in our pictures or if your keyboard doesn't work as this book describes, be suspicious that someone got clever and changed things.

Although we assume that you have a computer guru at your disposal, we also know that gurus can be hard to coax from their rock on top of the mountain. So, we teach you a few of the important guru-type tricks where it's practical.

What You're Not Supposed to Read

Don't read anything with a picture of that nerdy-looking Mr. Science guy next to it (the Technical Stuff icons) unless you really feel a need to know why something is true rather than how to do something useful. (You know the Mr. Science type — full of brain-glazing explanations of how, for example, "User Preferences set under the XYZ dialog box are actually edits to the .cshrc file" when what you really need to know is "Press this key now.") The only good part about reading the stuff is that it can help you sound sufficiently informed to your computer wizard to induce her to do technical things for you.

How This Book Is Organized

Unlike the WordPerfect manual, which is organized alphabetically, this book is organized by what you may be trying to do. It doesn't explain, for example, all the commands on the Edit menu in one chapter. Our reasoning is that the Edit commands don't necessarily have anything to do with editing and that Edit is a foolish category because isn't almost everything you do in a word processor a sort of edit anyway?

No, what this book does is break things down into the following five useful categories.

Part I: Introducing WordPerfect for Linux

Part I discusses the basics: your keyboard, your mouse, and the WordPerfect screen and how they all work together to let you write stuff and make it come out of your printer. Part I is the place to go for some of the basics of using WordPerfect menus, keystrokes, and buttons. It also has information about some fancier basics, such as searching and replacing, working with blocks of text, and spell checking. Part I can even help you if you have never worked in Linux or never even used a computer.

Part II: Prettying Up Your Text

If you didn't care how your text looked, you wouldn't be using a word processor, would you? What? You say that all you want to do is put something in bold-face type or italics? And perhaps center a heading? And set the margins? *And* put in page numbers? It's all here.

Part III: Things You Can Do with Documents

You thought that you were just *word* processing, didn't you? Hah! You're really *creating entire documents.* And now you have to live with your creation, Dr. Frankenstein. Maybe you want to print your document, for example. Or, kill it off altogether by deleting it. Or, move it somewhere where it can do no harm. Part III talks all about this kind of stuff.

Part IV: Creating Documents That Don't Just Sit There

Your document could just be words on a page, but, hey — this is the age of magazines with layouts so fancy you can hardly read them. You may as well get into the act, too. You can start with borders and columns and move on to pictures and drawings. After you've created a perfectly illegible document, send it out as junk mail or put it on the World Wide Web. It's all in Part IV.

Part V: Oh, Help!

WordPerfect is big-time software that consumes vast portions of your computer's disk and memory space with lots of incredibly complex, sophisticated, and clever software. Unfortunately, sometimes it's a tad too complex, sophisticated, and clever for its own good — or yours.

Go to Part V when things don't work quite right — or at least, when they don't work the way you think that they should.

Part VI: The Part of Tens

In honor of the decimal system, the Ten Commandments, and the perfectly silly accident of fate that humans have ten fingers, Part VI is where we stick other useful stuff. We would have made this part an appendix, but appendixes have no fingers and — look — just check it out. Part VI is full of stuff that everyone who uses WordPerfect should know.

What's on the CD-ROM

The CD in the back of this book contains an entire, free, working copy of WordPerfect for Linux! The program is also available for free for downloading over the Internet; because the files that make up the program are rather large, however, downloading them can be daunting. Instead, you have them already!

For instructions for installing WordPerfect for Linux, if you don't already have the program installed, see the appendix in back of this book.

Icons Used in This Book

The 20th century will be considered The Age of Icons by future historians, who probably will analyze how humanity lost its ability to read actual words. But — because we're not inclined to buck the trend and we want you to get accustomed to all the icons you have to deal with in WordPerfect — we have put them in this book, too.

What are icons? They're pictures that are cuter than the words they represent. They also take up less space than do the words, which is why they're used on computer screens in such blinding profusion.

Alerts you to the sort of stuff that appeals to people who secretly like software. It's not required reading unless you're trying to date a person like that (or are already married to one).

Flags useful tips or shortcuts.

Suggests that we're presenting something useful to remember so that you don't wear out this book by looking up the info all the time.

Cheerfully denotes things that can cause trouble. (Why doesn't life come with these icons?)

Where to Go from Here

If WordPerfect is already installed on your computer, you probably have already tried to do something in WordPerfect. You're probably annoyed, perplexed, or intrigued by the promise of something you have seen, so look it up in the table of contents or the index and see what this book has to say about it. Or, peruse the table of contents and see what appeals to you. You may learn something, and it beats the heck out of working.

If you don't yet have WordPerfect installed, flip to the appendix to find out how to install the program.

We would love to hear from you! Send comments about this book to our Internet address: wplinux@gurus.com. And check our Web site for updates to the book, at http://net.gurus.com. If you want to get in touch with IDG Books Worldwide, Inc., the publishers of this and other ...*For Dummies* books, write to info@dummies.com or go to http://www.dummies.com, the IDGB Web site.

Part I

Introducing WordPerfect for Linux

The 5th Wave   By Rich Tennant

"OK, TECHNICALLY, THIS SHOULD WORK. JUDY, TYPE THE WORD 'GOODYEAR' IN ALL CAPS, BOLDFACE, AT 700-POINT TYPE SIZE."

In this part . . .

You're ready to employ the latest in word processing technology. You have the power to create tables, graphics, columns, fonts, borders, tables of contents, illustrations, sidebars, envelopes, junk mail — you name it! In short, you're ready to launch yourself into the blazing, glorious future of word processing — except for one teensy little problem. You were wondering, perhaps, just wondering: How do you start the silly thing? And, um, how do you print something? Or delete a sentence? Or save your work? Good questions, pilgrim — questions that deserve answers. Read on!

Chapter 1

WordPerfect Basics

- -

In This Chapter

▶ Determining which window manager you have

▶ Starting WordPerfect

▶ Looking at the WordPerfect windows

▶ Checking out the Application Bar

▶ Typing your text

▶ Naming files

▶ Getting help

▶ Editing a file that has already been created

▶ Creating a new file

▶ Printing a document

▶ Leaving the program

- -

*T*his chapter gets you started using WordPerfect by showing you how to perform the Big Five word processing operations: Get the program (WordPerfect) running, type some text, save the text in a file on disk, open the file again later, and print the file. If you read to the end of this chapter, you will know how to coax WordPerfect into performing these five operations. In later chapters, we get you into some refinements, such as editing the text after you type it or making it look a little spiffier.

First, the basics.

Which Window Manager Do You Have?

If you use a mouse with Linux, you're using the X Window System (also known as simply *X*) and a window manager. A *window manager* is the program that draws the borders, title bars, and buttons around all your windows. Strictly speaking, window managers don't have anything to do with WordPerfect.

Because those windows include WordPerfect windows, however, sooner or later you need to interact with your window manager in the course of working with WordPerfect.

Unlike some other operating systems we could name (like Windows or the Mac), Linux doesn't have a one-size-fits-all look and feel to its windows. Instead, your windows' colors, style, and buttons depend on which window manager happens to be running. (Whether this is a Good Thing is open to debate.) Although lots of different window managers run under Linux, you're likely to run into only a few.

Here are the four most common window managers:

✔ **KDE, or K Desktop Environment:** More than just a window manager; a desktop environment that includes its own window manager (see Figure 1-1).

✔ **Enlightenment:** The default window manager for the GNOME desktop environment (see Figure 1-2).

✔ **WindowMaker:** The alternative window manager for the GNOME desktop environment (see Figure 1-3).

✔ **FVWM:** Used to be the most common window manager for Linux; has now become scarcer in favor of newer, spiffier window managers (see Figure 1-4).

To tell the difference, compare the title bar and buttons that run along the top of the windows.

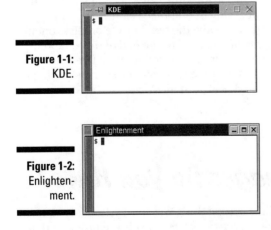

Figure 1-1: KDE.

Figure 1-2: Enlightenment.

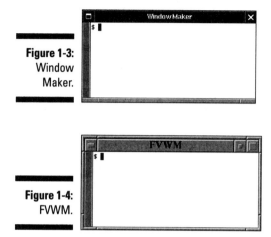

Figure 1-3:
Window
Maker.

Figure 1-4:
FVWM.

Throughout this book, we use KDE for examples (not because we think that it's any better than any of the other window managers, but rather because we did have to pick one and we think that it's a pretty good one). Corel Linux comes with KDE, which is another reason why you may be using it. All four window managers look strangely like Windows and Macs, so if you're comfortable with one of those systems, you'll find the switch to Linux easy! If your Linux system uses a window manager other than KDE, don't worry — they all work practically the same way.

Honey, I Shrunk the Program!

While WordPerfect is running, you can *minimize* (or *iconify*) it, which means that it shrinks into a little button on the taskbar or an icon on the desktop. You may want to minimize a program to get it out of the way temporarily while you do something else. Although the program's still running, ready to do your work, it's tiny. Minimizing is similar to freeze-drying your program: You can add water later to bring it back to life.

If you want to minimize WordPerfect (who wouldn't?), click on the little Minimize button for whatever window manager you have — the button is usually a little dot or underscore button near the upper-right corner of the window. Poof! The window disappears in a puff of bytes, to be replaced by a button on the taskbar or an icon on the desktop.

You get WordPerfect back by double-clicking on the WordPerfect icon on your desktop or by clicking on the WordPerfect button on the taskbar. WordPerfect not only jumps back into existence on the screen but also (if you were working on a document) is just the way you left it.

Okay, on to WordPerfect!

Starting WordPerfect

To begin using WordPerfect, you have to see it onscreen. Follow these steps:

1. **Get psyched.**

   Repeat to yourself three times, "I love using the computer! I love Linux! This is going to be great!" — whether you believe it or not.

2. **Look for WordPerfect.**

   If you're lucky, someone has installed a WordPerfect icon on your KDE or GNOME panel (that rectangle full of icons at the bottom of the screen) or on your desktop. If so, click on the icon. If no WordPerfect icon is in any of those places, try looking for it on a pop-up menu; in KDE and GNOME, look by clicking on the K icon or G footprint icon, respectively, in the lower-left corner of the screen, which work strangely similarly to the Start button on the Windows taskbar. Other window managers present you with pop-up menus if you left-click, right-click, or middle-click on the desktop background.

   Still no WordPerfect there? In that case, you have to start it from the (gasp!) command line. It's not that bad, really: Open an xterm or terminal window, the program that displays a plain, boring text-based window containing a command line. With this versatile command line, you can make your state-of-the-art graphics display act just like a 25-year-old dumb terminal.

3. **Start WordPerfect.**

   How you do this step depends on where you found the program. If you found a WordPerfect icon on a KDE or GNOME panel or if you found a menu listing for WordPerfect, single-click on it. If you found a WordPerfect icon on the desktop background, you probably need to double-click it.

   If you had to open a terminal window, type **xwp** at the command prompt and press Enter. You might first need to move to the directory in which you installed WordPerfect; see the appendix in the back of this book for more information.

WordPerfect begins to run. After a few seconds, you see the WordPerfect *splash* (opening) screen, followed quickly by the two main WordPerfect windows, which are described later in this chapter. Suffice it to say that the screen is a little more complicated than a nice blank piece of paper.

If WordPerfect doesn't appear on your desktop, panel, or menus, see this book's appendix to find out how to make icons and menu entries for WordPerfect by using KDE.

This list shows some things that may go wrong:

- ✔ If (heaven forbid!) WordPerfect crashed the last time you were running it, you may see a message that a timed backup document exists. If this message appears, see Chapter 20.

- ✔ If you have trouble getting WordPerfect to run or if you're wrestling with Linux, you may want to check out *LINUX For Dummies,* 2nd Edition, by Jon "Maddog" Hall (IDG Books Worldwide, Inc.) — a great book that clarifies a bunch of general Linux stuff.

If WordPerfect just refuses to run and if it reports a segmentation fault error if you try to run it from the command line, the chances are that some Linux libraries need updating. It's most definitely a job for a system administrator. Go get him and plead your case.

The Two Windows of WordPerfect

After WordPerfect is running, you see two WordPerfect windows. A cute little window has the WordPerfect logo and a menu, as shown in Figure 1-5. This window is the *program window.* The logo doesn't do anything other than sit there and look pretty; this window's reason for being there is its menu. A bigger window is the *document window,* as shown in Figure 1-6; you do all your typing there. The wide expanse of white screen corresponds to the white paper that sticks out of your old-fashioned typewriter and is probably no more inspirational.

Figure 1-5:
The
WordPerfect
program
window.

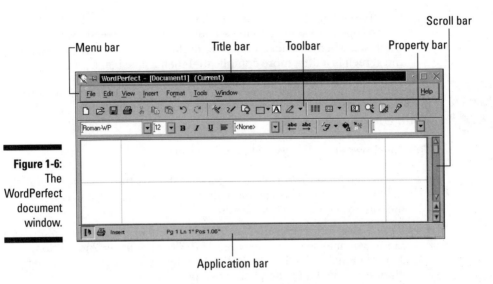

Figure 1-6:
The
WordPerfect
document
window.

Application bar

The following list describes lots of stuff around the edges that may not be familiar to you:

- ✔ **Title bar:** Displays this line at the top edge of the window: WordPerfect - [Document1 - unmodified] (Current). It tells you the name of the document you're editing and reminds you that you are, in fact, running WordPerfect (more about documents anon). The [unmodified] part tells you that you haven't typed anything yet, and the (Current) part means that this window is the one you're working in, which is useful information if you have more than one document open.

- ✔ **Menu bar:** The row of words just below the title bar. Each word is a command you can choose. Later in this chapter, we tell you how to use a command to close WordPerfect. We talk more about commands in Chapter 2.

- ✔ **Toolbar:** Made up of a row of *buttons* (the gray boxes) below the menu bar. The buttons usually have little pictures on them. Later in this chapter, you use some of these buttons to save and print a document. If you don't see the toolbar onscreen, use the following powerful incantation to make it appear: Click on the word *View* on the menu bar and then click on the word *Toolbar* on the menu that appears. When you see the Toolbars dialog box, make sure that the WordPerfect 8 box on the list that appears onscreen is selected (looks pushed in or contains a black dot) and click on OK. We explain more in Chapter 2 about using commands and in Chapter 19 about determining what you want to see onscreen.

✔ **Property Bar:** Contains a bunch of controls that let you change how things look in your document. The Truly Technical call how things look the *properties* of the things. Text (letters and numbers) has properties such as being **bold** or not or being in *italics* or not. Text in a table, however (lovingly described in Chapter 14), has properties such as whether the cells in the table have little outlines around them. Whatever you're doing in WordPerfect, the Property Bar changes to let you control all the characteristics (or properties) of what you're working with. It's pretty neat, actually.

✔ **Application Bar:** The bottom line of the WordPerfect window; shows you information about what's happening in WordPerfect. We talk about the controls on the Application Bar in the following section.

✔ **Scroll bars:** Along the right side of the window, the gray strip that helps you move around the document. You find out how to use scroll bars in Chapter 2. If a document is too wide to fit across the screen, WordPerfect displays a scroll bar along the bottom of the window too, right above the Application Bar. (Why does WordPerfect have so many bars? Maybe because Utah, where WordPerfect was originally written, doesn't have many bars.)

✔ **Mouse pointer and cursor:** (Mouse pointer) Usually a little arrow that shows where the mouse is pointing. The mouse pointer changes to other shapes, depending on what you're doing, as explained in Chapter 2. (Cursor, or insertion point) A blinking vertical line that indicates where you're typing. The *shadow* cursor is a WordPerfect innovation. It indicates where you *would* be typing if you clicked the mouse and started typing. It's a handy way of seeing where you're moving to in your document.

✔ **Dark edges:** Sometimes on either side of a document; represent your desktop under the "paper" on which you're typing. The WordPerfect folks seem to have gone overboard in the realism department here, although they might have gone a step further and displayed simulated wood grain with coffee mug rings.

Wow! You sure have lots of gizmos to look at while you're trying to type. Chapter 19 contains hints for controlling the things that clutter the WordPerfect window. Otherwise, you get used to all these little buttons and messages eventually — probably about the same time a new version of WordPerfect comes along, with a whole new concept in screen clutter.

When WordPerfect is busy, the mouse pointer, which is usually a little arrow, turns into a watch face. The seconds tick by while WordPerfect does something it considers to be more important than listening to your commands. The watch means, "Wait around until I'm finished. Consider warming up your coffee in the nuke." Sooner or later (usually within a few seconds), the mouse pointer turns back into its normal pointy self, and you can get back to work.

What's on the Application Bar?

The Application Bar displays vital information about a document. You can control the kind of information WordPerfect displays, although you're probably not interested in this rather arcane subject at the moment (see Chapter 19 if we're wrong about your insatiable curiosity). If you can't see your Applicaion Bar, your KDE or GNOME taskbar along the bottom of the screen might be covering it up. Starting from the left, here's what this gibberish means:

✔ The first picture looks like a very blurry cursor with a very blurry arrow next to it. Go ahead and squint, and while you're at it, use your imagination. The idea here is to tell you whether the shadow cursor is turned on and to let you turn it on and off. Think of it as a button. If it's pressed in (has a little square around it), it's on. If it doesn't have a little square around it, it's off. Click on the blurry picture, and you'll get the idea.

✔ Next to the blurry cursor is a picture of a printer. It sure would be nice if you could find out whether your printer is turned on by seeing whether the printer is pressed in (has the little square around it, although you've figured that out by now, right?), but, of course, that would be too simple. You can click on this picture of a printer to find out all about your printer. You'd better skip to Chapter 11 for the gory details, though. WordPerfect assumes that when you click on the Application Bar printer icon, you're interested in learning *about* your printer, and it displays the Select Printer dialog box, which describes your printer. When you click on the toolbar printer, WordPerfect assumes that you want to print your document and shows you the Print dialog box. In either case, you can click on the button you're really interested in.

✔ Next to the printer is the word Insert. *Insert mode* means that when you type, the letters are inserted wherever the cursor is positioned. In *Typeover mode*, the letters you type replace (or type over) the characters to the right of the cursor. You switch between Insert and Typeover modes by pressing the Insert (or Ins) key or by clicking on this box. When you're editing something fancy, such as a table or a merge file, other information may appear in this box. If you click on the information the Application Bar displays, you can change the info. (See Chapter 4 for more details.)

✔ Farther to the right, the Application Bar tells you where you are in a document, including the page number (Pg), how far down the page you are (Ln), and where you are across the page (Pos). For the most part, of course, who cares, unless you get paid to write by the inch? Every once in a while, however, you may want to know exactly where on the page your text will appear, and these measurements tell you.

Typing Something

WordPerfect is completely different from a typewriter in many ways, although in one way, it's the same: To enter some text, you just start typing.

If you make a mistake or change your mind about the wording, move the cursor (the slowly blinking vertical line that shows where you're typing) to the text you want to change; then change it. You can use either the mouse or the keyboard to get that cursor moving. (Chapter 2 explains ways to move the cursor around.)

All the regular keys on the keyboard — the letters, numbers, and punctuation keys — enter characters onscreen when you press them. The rest of the keys — the function keys (F1 and its friends), Enter, Insert, Delete, and all the keys with arrows on them — do not enter characters. Those keys do something else, and we tell you exactly what each key does as we get to it.

Normally, WordPerfect is in Insert mode, which means that whatever you type is inserted into the text. If the cursor is between two letters and you type a new letter, the new one is inserted between the two original letters.

To type a bunch of capital letters, press (but don't hold down) the Caps Lock key. Now whatever letters you type are capitalized. To turn off Caps Lock, press the Caps Lock key again. Unlike the Shift key, Caps Lock doesn't have the slightest effect on numbers or punctuation — only on letters.

If you want to type numbers, you can press the number keys just above the QWERTYUIOP row, or you can use the *numeric keypad,* which is the group of number keys on the right side of the keyboard. Watch out, though: You can also use the numeric keypad to move the cursor. (See Chapter 2 to learn how to determine when these keys do what.)

If you want to delete just a letter or two, you can usually move the cursor just after the letters and then press the Backspace key to wipe them out. Your Linux system may be set up so that the Backspace key works just like the Delete key: If so, move the cursor just in front of them and press the Delete key. Same difference — the letter disappears. See Chapter 5 to find out how to delete larger amounts of text.

Chapters 2 and 3 contain lots of information about using the keyboard and the mouse to do things in WordPerfect.

Waxing Eloquent

After you begin typing, you can go ahead and say what you have to say. What happens, however, when you get to the end of the line? Unlike a typewriter, WordPerfect doesn't go "Ding!" to tell you that you're about to type off the edge of the paper and get ink on the platen. Instead, WordPerfect (like all word processors) does something called *word wrap*. It figures out that you're almost at the right margin and moves down to the next line *all by itself.* What will they think of next?

Because of the miracle of word wrap (not to be confused with plastic wrap), you don't have to keep track of where you are on the line. You can just type away, knowing that WordPerfect will move you along to the next line as needed.

Not pressing the Enter key at the end of each line is important. WordPerfect, like all word processors, assumes that when you press Enter, you're at the end of a paragraph, not just at the end of a line within the paragraph.

If you change the margins later or use a larger font (character style), WordPerfect even moves the words around (keeping them in order, of course) so that your paragraphs fit within the new margins. This nice side effect of word wrap is called *reformatting.*

Press Enter only when you want to begin a new paragraph; otherwise, let WordPerfect handle the line endings. Pressing Enter at the end of every line is a sure sign of a word processing novice, and it makes computer nerds sigh and shake their heads sadly. Worse, keeping things looking right with this method eventually causes you a great deal of work and headaches.

If you want to split one paragraph into two, you can insert a paragraph mark by pressing Enter. Move the cursor just before the letter where you want the new paragraph to begin, and press Enter. Voilà! WordPerfect moves the rest of the line down to a new line and reformats the rest of the paragraph to fit.

What's in a Name?

When you type text in WordPerfect, you're making a *document,* the fancy WordPerfect name for anything that's typed. A letter, a memo, a laundry list, or the next great American novel — all these things are documents to WordPerfect.

To save your document so that you can look at it, edit it, or print it later, you save it in a *file* on the disk. Each document is in one file.

If you start with a new, blank window and type, your prose is in a document WordPerfect named `Document1`. Although the text is onscreen, it's not on disk (yet). Documents onscreen are ephemeral and disappear when you exit WordPerfect or log out of Linux — here today, gone tomorrow (or later this afternoon). Saving your documents on disk is important so that they're saved for good.

Document1 isn't a good name for a document because it doesn't give you a clue to what it's about; it's the best that WordPerfect can do, however. You should give the document a more descriptive name, which you can do when you save it.

Saving your document

You can save a document on disk and give it a name in at least three ways. Although we're sure that your insatiable curiosity will drive you to find out all three, this method is our favorite. Follow these steps:

1. **Click on the Save button on the toolbar.**

   The *toolbar* is the row of little buttons just below the title bar. (Refer to the section "The Two Windows of WordPerfect," earlier in this chapter, and Figure 1-6 if you can't find the toolbar.) The Save button is the one with a tiny picture of a floppy disk. (You probably are really saving your document on a hard disk; however, hard disks aren't as cute as floppy disks.) This button is probably the third from the left.

   When the mouse pointer points to a button on the toolbar, the name of the button appears in a little yellow box along with a description of the button. Thank goodness for that because many of those teeny little buttons look alike to us. (And don't tell us that it's time to break down and get reading glasses!) When the mouse pointer is on the Save button, for example, you see this helpful reminder: `Save the current document`. These messages tell you the name of the button and what the button does (as though you couldn't guess from the name). Chapter 2 has more information about this subject.

   As soon as you click on the Save button, a window appears onscreen, right on top of the WordPerfect window. The window is a *dialog box,* which WordPerfect displays when it wants to ask you some questions. Chapter 2 tells you more than you ever wanted to know about dialog boxes.

   This particular dialog box is labeled (not surprisingly) Save As, as shown in Figure 1-7. You use it to tell WordPerfect where to store the document on the disk and what to name it. We talk more in Chapter 13 about where you can store documents. For now, WordPerfect suggests that you store your document in your *home directory* — the directory to put files in unless someone says otherwise.

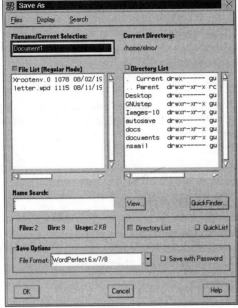

Figure 1-7:
The
WordPerfect
superduper
tell-it-
where-you-
want-your-
file-to-go
Save As
dialog box.

2. **In the box labeled Filename/Current Selection, enter a name for the document.**

   Feel free to name your document (almost) anything you want. You have to follow a couple of rules, which are listed in the next section in this chapter. If it's just a test document, you might name it test.wpd.

3. **Press Enter or click on the Save button.**

   WordPerfect saves the document in the file you named. You can tell that this procedure worked, because the title bar displays something like this:

   ```
   WordPerfect - [/home/myname/test.wpd - unmodified]
   ```

   When you save a document in a file, you can choose which directory the file should be in. See Chapter 13 to find out how to tell WordPerfect where to store it.

Save early and often. Save whenever you think of it and whenever you wonder when was the last time you saved. A save in time saves the loss of your document. You get the idea. If you kick the computer's cord out of the plug, if your 2-year-old presses the Reset button, or if you have a brain spasm that causes you to delete several paragraphs of perfectly good text, you will be happy if you know that the document is safe and sound on your disk. (See Chapter 20 to discover how to get your document back if these or other catastrophes occur.)

You can tell WordPerfect to save your document automatically every five or ten minutes, or at any interval you choose (for more info, see Chapter 19).

What if a file named `test.wpd` *already* exists? WordPerfect, which always watches out for your interests, tells you whenever that happens. A dialog box appears, telling you that the file already exists and asking whether you really want to replace it (irrevocably deleting the existing file in the process). You have two — count 'em — two options:

- ✔ **Yes:** Replace the existing file.
- ✔ **No:** Enter a different name for your new file.

If you're looking at the Save As dialog box and change your mind about saving the document, press the Escape (or Esc) key or click on the Cancel button. The dialog box disappears.

Chapter 13 describes everything you want to know about files, including how to delete, move, copy, and rename them.

Filename rules

When you enter a name for a new WordPerfect document, you must follow the rules for naming files. WordPerfect didn't make up these rules; Linux (or more generally, UNIX) did. Here are the rules:

- ✔ Letters are case-sensitive. That means that `Piffle`, `piffle`, and `PIFFLE`, for example, are all different filenames.
- ✔ You're not allowed to use any of the following special characters in a file-name: `<>{}[]()"`'*?|/\^!#$&~` — in other words, almost (but not quite) everything on the keyboard that's not a letter or a number. Any of these characters gets Linux hopelessly confused. (If you want to name a file after an expletive, you just have to spell it out.)
- ✔ You can use spaces and hyphens (-), although it's not a good idea. Some programs have trouble with them. In fact, forget that we even said you can use them.
- ✔ Rather than use spaces or hyphens, UNIX aficionados usually use either periods or underscores, so filenames frequently look like `directions.to.grandmas` or `chocolate_pickle_recipe`.

- ✔ A special use of periods is for a filename *extension*. In the world of Windows computers, a filename often ends with a period followed by (usually) three or four letters, such as `my_letter.wpd`. The group of three or four letters after the period is the extension and usually describes the type of file it is. (If you really care, look at the Technical Stuff sidebar "Doc, html, txt, and their friends," later in this chapter.) WordPerfect documents use the extensions `wpd` (word processing document), `frm` (mail merge forms, covered in Chapter 16), and `dat` (mail merge data files, also in Chapter 16). If you're used to Windows, you've seen extensions. Unlike Windows, however, Linux doesn't use the extension to automatically associate a filename with a program. Extensions are just a convenience to let you quickly locate files of a particular type, such as all your WordPerfect documents.

- ✔ You can omit the extension, if you want, although you cannot omit the name.

- ✔ You can use any extension you want, although using the `wpd`, `frm`, and `dat` extensions suggested by WordPerfect is more convenient. Use `wpd` for WordPerfect documents.

These three filenames, for example, are okay:

- ✔ `letter.wpd`
- ✔ `Chapter_1.-First_Draft.wpd`
- ✔ `SuperCaliFragiListicExpiAliDocious.Documents.Are.Fun.wpd`

These filenames aren't:

- ✔ `"Here's Johnny"` (has quotes and spaces)
- ✔ `Letter.to.\ /*!#<>|` (more punctuation characters you can't use in a filename)

Choose filenames that contain only letters, numbers, periods, and underscores and end with `.wpd`. Capitalization counts: Simplify your life and use only lowercase letters.

Save it again, Sam

After you save your document and give it a name, you don't have to tell WordPerfect the name again. If you enter some more text and want to save it, you can just click the Save button again. WordPerfect updates the file on the disk with the new version of your document, which replaces the old one.

Getting Some Help

Clearly, you have a great deal to remember about the basics of WordPerfect. And, you probably have better things to do than to memorize all this computer trivia. Luckily, WordPerfect can provide help when you need it — at least it can provide a description, in computerese, that may be of limited help.

Like most programs, WordPerfect has a *Help key:* the F1 function key. Pressing F1 runs the WordPerfect Help system, which contains most of the text in the WordPerfect reference manual. Finding information in the online Help system is usually easier than riffling through printed pages. Chapter 2 describes it in more detail.

Editing Another File

If you have followed along in this chapter, you have made a document from scratch. Frequently, though, you want to edit a document that's already stored on disk. It may be a document you made earlier and saved, a document someone else created, or a love note left on your disk by a secret admirer. (Secret admirers are getting more high-tech these days.) Whatever the document is, you can look at it in WordPerfect. This process is called *loading* (or *opening*) the document.

These steps show you the easiest way to open a document that has been stored on the disk:

1. **Click on the Open button on the toolbar.**

   It's the one with a tiny yellow folder on it — usually, the second button from the left.

   WordPerfect displays the Open dialog box, as shown in Figure 1-8. Displaying this dialog box is the program's subtle way of saying that it wants to know which file you want to open.

2. **Choose a file from the list that's displayed.**

   To choose one, click on a name on the list of displayed names. WordPerfect highlights the name by displaying it in another color to show that it knows the one you want.

3. **Click on the Open button (or double-click on the filename).**

   WordPerfect opens the file, reads the document, and displays it onscreen.

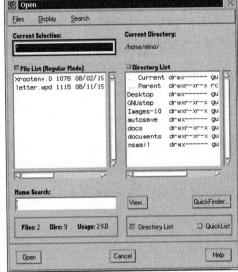

Figure 1-8:
Opening a
file you
made
earlier.

Now you can make changes in the document, save it again, print it, or whatever!

If the document is long, it doesn't all fit onscreen. Don't panic — it's still there. See Chapter 3 for information about how to move around in a document, including the parts that aren't visible.

You may want to open a file in a different directory from the one displayed in the Open dialog box. See Chapter 13 to find out how to use folders.

If the document was created by a word processor other than WordPerfect, see Chapter 12 to find out how to open it.

After you have opened a document in WordPerfect, you can see it onscreen, make changes in it, save the new version, and print it. We talk about how to print a document in a minute.

A brief diversion for conversion

When you open a document, you may see a little box with the message that a conversion is in progress. This message usually means that the document you're opening was created in a different version of WordPerfect, such as WordPerfect for Windows. Each version of WordPerfect stores documents in its own way.

Doc, html, txt, and their friends

The extension part of a filename usually indicates what kind of information the file contains. If a file contains an image, for example, its extension may be gif or jpg. Most people use the extension wpd for WordPerfect documents. You may run into the following file extensions:

doc: A Microsoft Word document (or a document created by another word processing program)

html: Sometimes shortened to just htm; a document from the World Wide Web (see Chapter 18 to find out how to create html files in WordPerfect)

txt: Just letters, with no fancy formatting or other fancy characters; usually created by a text editor

Even though these files may not have been created by WordPerfect or saved in WordPerfect's own format, WordPerfect can read some of them. See Chapter 12 for information about how to turn files from other word processing programs into WordPerfect documents.

Making a New File

What if you want to start with a new, blank file? Press Ctrl+N or click on the New Document icon (the leftmost icon on the toolbar in the document window). If you're in the WordPerfect program window (the one that displays the WordPerfect logo), click Program on the menu bar and click New Window on the menu that appears. Either way, WordPerfect opens a new window with a new, blank document. For more information about documents and windows, see Chapter 12.

Printing Your Document

After you type a document or edit it until it looks the way you want it, you probably will want to print it. The goal of most word processing is, after all, to produce — on paper — a letter, memo, report, or what have you. If you work in the Paperless Office of the Future (reputed to be just down the hall from the Paperless Bathroom of the Future), you may be able to send your memo or letter electronically at the touch of a button. For the rest of us, though, paper works well (typing paper, that is).

These steps show a fast way to print your document:

1. **Save the document first, just in case something goes wrong while you're trying to print it.**

To save, click on the Save button on the toolbar. (Refer to the section "Saving your document," earlier in this chapter, if you don't know what we're talking about.)

2. **Turn on your printer.**

   Good luck finding the switch!

3. **Make sure that some paper is in the printer.**

 4. **Click on the Print button on the toolbar.**

   Print is the button that shows a little printer with a piece of paper sticking out the top — usually, the fourth button from the left.

5. **Click on the OK button in the Print dialog box.**

   WordPerfect then prints the document in all its glory. Pretty simple, huh?

Chapter 11 contains lots more information about printing, including the care and feeding of your printer.

If you don't like the way your polished prose looks on the page, look in Chapter 6 to find out how to choose which typeface (or typefaces) to use for the text. Chapter 7 tells you how to center and justify text, and Chapter 8 shows you how to number pages and how to print page headers and footers.

Leaving WordPerfect

No matter how much fun you're having, sooner or later you may need to stop running WordPerfect. Because you use Linux, you can run other programs at the same time you run WordPerfect. You don't have to leave WordPerfect every time you want to check your e-mail, browse the Web, or play a little game of Solitaire. Although you may want to leave WordPerfect running all day so that you can switch back to it in a jiffy, you must exit WordPerfect (and Linux) before you turn off your computer.

To leave WordPerfect, you choose the Program⇨Exit command from the program window menu. (Remember the program window? Here's one of the places where you actually use it.) Or click the Close (X) button in the upper-right corner of the program window. Although we talk more in Chapter 2 about how to use commands, these steps show what you have to do:

1. **Click on the word Program on the program window menu bar.**

   The *program window* is the little window that displays the WordPerfect logo. The Program menu appears by dropping down from the word *Program.* (Wonder why they call it a pull-down menu when you don't have to pull on anything?)

2. Choose Exit near the bottom of the File menu.

If you have created or changed a document but haven't saved the document in a file, WordPerfect asks whether you want to save it now. Click on Yes to save the document, No to skip saving it, or Cancel to return to WordPerfect. Choose No only if you're sure that the document doesn't contain anything you ever want to see again.

WordPerfect packs up and goes home, and you're probably thinking about doing the same.

Never turn off your computer without exiting WordPerfect and Linux. Otherwise, you may catch these programs unawares (with their digital pants down, as it were), and they may not have saved everything on disk. When you start the computer again, you may get complaints. Consult your local Linux guru if Linux complains about your hard disk's not being "unmounted" properly before shutdown.

Chapter 2

Using the Mouse and Keyboard

● ●

In This Chapter

▶ Knowing when to mouse and when not to mouse

▶ Choosing commands from menus

▶ Dealing with dialog boxes

▶ Using QuickMenus for even more ways to choose commands

▶ Toying with the toolbar, the Property Bar, and the ruler

▶ Using the keyboard

▶ Knowing when to press Enter

▶ Using Tab and the spacebar

▶ Using the Undo button

▶ Getting help

▶ Letting PerfectExpert help

● ●

*U*sing WordPerfect for Linux is a little like dining at a fine restaurant in another country, or maybe on another planet. As anyone who has ever ordered in a foreign restaurant knows, you can tell the waiter what you want in three ways:

✔ The difficult, old-fashioned (but highly impressive) way: Speak the language.

✔ Order by the numbers (works mainly in Chinese-American restaurants).

✔ Point at the menu and grunt.

Originally, telling a computer what you wanted was also a matter of speaking the language: Type a command or "order by the numbers" by pressing a special key, such as F3. Now, however, with the advent of graphical window-filled interfaces, software is smart enough that you can just point and grunt.

That advance came just in time, too, because the menu of things that today's software can do is huge — so huge that to use the old-fashioned keyboard method, you have to hold down as many as three keys at a time and develop a keyboard method that would prostrate Paderewski.

That's why you have a mouse, trackball, or other pointing device next to your keyboard. To avoid disgruntling the folks who have already put a great deal of effort into refining their keyboard style (such as old UNIX users), WordPerfect for Linux also enables you to order it around the old-fashioned way: by using the keyboard.

The result of all this highly obliging, verging-on-sycophantic user-friendliness is that you now have three more or less alternative ways to order WordPerfect for Linux around:

- The regular keyboard, with letters, numbers, and stuff.
- The function keys, labeled F1 through F12.
- The mouse, which you can use by itself in about three ways to command WordPerfect. (Try not to think about this one for now.)

Another result of all this is that the keyboard and screen begin to resemble the cockpit of a jet fighter. As always when you face jet fighters, the important thing is not to let it intimidate you. It's a friendly jet fighter (oxymoronically speaking), and you can't crash and burn. You can't hurt any hardware on your computer, and it's hard to damage the software or data either unless you're willing to answer Yes to a number of intimidating questions. About the worst you can do is lose whatever work you have done since the last time you used WordPerfect, and even that's hard to do.

If you're already windows-familiar and keyboard-qualified, you can just skim the next two sections of this chapter to pick up the WordPerfect peculiarities. If you're switching to Linux from Windows or a Mac, follow along — you'll find everything very familiar.

To Mouse or Not to Mouse

Because of the popularity of the "point and grunt" method (hereafter called point-and-click, to be nice), mice are taking over the world. Accept this fact, and learn to love your mouse. WordPerfect for Linux is designed for the mouse, even though you can also do almost everything by using the keyboard.

Most people eventually find a particular combination of mousifying and keyboardification that suits them. Because mice are the cat's pajamas, this book generally emphasizes the mouse method and also lists the alternatives.

On most PCs, the mouse generally wears two buttons; UNIX systems have always used mice with three buttons. If your Linux system was set up from the beginning to be just like a Real Grownup UNIX Computer, it probably has a three-button mouse. If, like most Linux computers, it started out life as a PC running Windows, it probably has a two-button mouse. In that case, you can simulate the action of the middle button by pressing both buttons at the same time.

Here's how the three mouse buttons stack up:

- ✔ **Left:** Used for choosing commands from menus and for clicking on icons on the toolbar and the Property Bar. Most of your mouse-button clicking uses this button. When we tell you to click on something, we mean that you use the left mouse button.

- ✔ **Right:** Displays a *QuickMenu,* whose contents change depending on where the mouse pointer is pointing. This shortcut method, designed by the WordPerfect Department of Redundancy Department, provides commands you can do in about two other ways with the mouse. When we want you to click with the right mouse button, we tell you to right-click on something.

- ✔ **Middle:** Not used much in WordPerfect. You can use it to paste a copy of the highlighted word or phrase. (See the section in Chapter 4 about using the X Clipboard.)

If you're left-handed and really sensitive, you can ask your system guru to change the functions of the left button to the right button. (Be sure to motivate your computer expert as needed — this task is a one-cookie task, at current guru rates.)

Choosing Commands from Menus

Taking their cue from fine-dining establishments everywhere, most programs, including WordPerfect, have more than one menu of commands. They have the computer equivalent of an appetizer menu, an aperitif menu, a bread menu, a soup menu, a wine menu, an entrée menu, a choice-of-vegetable menu, a sorbet menu, and a dessert menu.

To help you sort out these menus, the next-to-topmost line (the one that displays all the words) in the WordPerfect window lists all available menus. This line is the *menu bar,* as shown in Figure 2-1.

Figure 2-1:
Not an
oyster bar,
not a sushi
bar — it's a
menu bar.

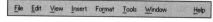

What's the function of all those keys with Fs on them?

Back in the old days, before mice, WordPerfect users did everything with function keys. *Function keys* are those keys with Fs on them above the number keys on the keyboard; their jobs change with every program you run. These keys are the second way of ordering around WordPerfect that we mention earlier in this chapter. Unless you happen to remember some of these function key combinations from earlier versions of WordPerfect, you'll have a dickens of a time figuring out what the function keys do now. Here are some you may find useful, though:

F1: Help. (We talk about this key later in this chapter.)

F2: Find and Replace (see Chapter 4).

F5: Print.

F10: Save.

Depending on how Linux and your X Window system are configured, all, some, or none of your function keys may work. (How's that for a vague statement?) Linux and X enable you to reassign the meaning of all the keys on the keyboard, and some X installations (particularly window managers) use the Ctrl and Alt keys for other purposes. Try pressing a few function keys and see what happens! (If a dialog box appears, press Esc to dismiss it. If the formatting of a document changes, press Ctrl+Z to undo whatever you did.) If your window manager usurps a function key that you really, absolutely must have for WordPerfect, talk to your local Linux guru about changing the window manager settings.

Clicking on the menu bar

To see what's on a menu, click on a word on the menu bar (with your left mouse button, if you were wondering). That word then gets highlighted, and a menu of commands drops down from it. Quite unreasonably (because you didn't pull anything), this menu is called a *pull-down menu*.

To try out this theory, start WordPerfect (refer to Chapter 1), make sure that you're working in the document window (the one that displays a blank document), and then click on the word *File*. The word *New* is highlighted (it has a box around it) as the WordPerfect waiter suggests the delightfully savory New command. Admire this screen, leave things as they are, and read on.

If you don't find anything you like, close the menu by clicking anywhere else in the WordPerfect window. If you click on another button or menu selection, however, you get whatever you clicked on.

How we talk about menus and commands in this book

Because darn near every command in WordPerfect appears on a menu, submenu, or sub-submenu, saying "Click on Edit on the menu bar and then on Select on that menu and then on Page on the next menu" gets tedious. We say it this way in the early chapters of this book so that you get used to the idea. After that, though, we just say "Choose Edit⇨Select⇨Page." It's a little terse, but if we don't do it that way, you would be comatose with boredom by the end of a paragraph. Also, think of all the trees we're saving by making this book shorter.

Choosing a command

To choose a command from a menu, click on the command. Related commands are clumped together and separated from other command clumps by a line.

You may find, in addition to the commands, other suggestive symbols — sort of like the little red dots next to the hot stuff on a Chinese menu. This list shows what a few of those symbols mean:

- **A little right-pointing triangle after the command:** If you click on one of these commands, you see a submenu. (The process is similar to choosing chicken and then being asked whether you want fried, roasted, or Szechuan.)

- **A box or diamond next to the command:** The box means that it's already turned on, whatever it is. In Windows, these boxes contain Xs or check marks; in Linux, the boxes usually contain dots or squares.

- **A key combination to the right of the command:** You can give some commands by pressing a key or combination of keys. If you do, WordPerfect gives you a hint about which keys you would use, by displaying the key combination on the menu, to the right of the command. On the File menu, for example, the Save As command has the notation *F3* to its right, which means that you can press F3 to issue the command, thereby avoiding using the menu bar! These key combinations are a carryover from the Windows version of WordPerfect, and not all of them work.

- **An ellipsis (. . .) after the command:** The ellipsis tells you that the command has more to say, if you ask. If you click on it, the command gift-wraps its thoughts in attractive little dialog boxes, which are discussed in the following section.

Using Dialog Boxes

If you click on a menu command that has an ellipsis (. . .) after it, either another menu or a *dialog box* is displayed. The dialog boxes shown in Figure 2-2 look like a cross between a tax form and a VCR remote control, although they're less painful to use than either one of those things.

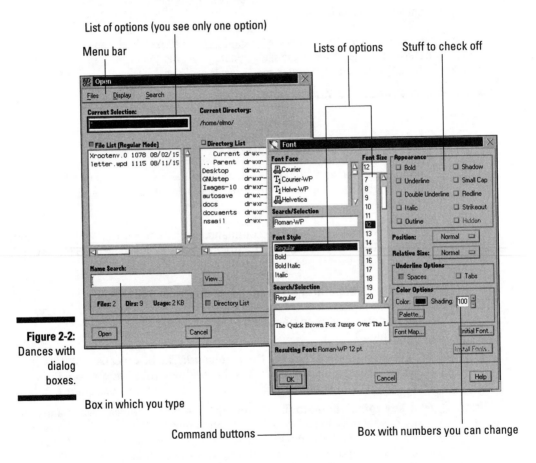

List of options (you see only one option)

Menu bar

Lists of options

Stuff to check off

Figure 2-2:
Dances with
dialog
boxes.

Box in which you type

Command buttons

Box with numbers you can change

If you want to follow along with our description of the stuff in the dialog boxes shown in Figure 2-2, you can display the dialog box shown on the left by choosing File⇨Open from the menu bar, and you can display the one shown on the right by choosing Format⇨Font.

What's with all these underlined characters on menus?

If you're already comfortable with computer keyboards, underlined characters designate the Alt+key combinations that choose the command. To save a file, for example, you can press Alt+F and then press S. If the preceding information is gibberish to you, read the section "Choosing commands by using keys," later in this chapter. *Warning:* Your Alt key may not work for issuing WordPerfect commands, depending on how your X Window System is configured.

Those wacky dialog thingies

This section shows some of the things (called *dialog thingies* herein) you may find in a dialog box:

- **Stuff to check off:** These items have a little square box or diamond to their left. Although these boxes and diamonds don't have actual check marks, in a typical display of software logic, they're called check boxes anyway. This type of item can be on (selected) or off (not selected). Click on the little box or diamond to select or deselect the item. The Font dialog box, for example, has a bunch of check boxes that tell WordPerfect how to decorate your fonts.

- **Lists of options:** You can tell which item is selected because it has a little box around it or is displayed in a different color. Click on the option you want. In the Font dialog box, Font Face and Font Style are examples of these kinds of lists.

- **Lists of options (although you see only one option):** On some lists of options, WordPerfect shows only the option that is selected. These options usually have a little rectangular button-looking thing near the right side of the option. To see all the options, click on the box containing the text. In the Font dialog box, for example, Position and Relative Size are examples of this kind of list.

- **Boxes in which you type:** Click on one of these boxes (a *text box*) to highlight it and then type stuff. For example, you can type a filename or specify a new font size.

  Don't press Enter when you finish typing in a text box. If you do, the dialog box closes and WordPerfect begins executing the command immediately, even if you aren't finished. When you're done typing, press Tab or click on another option.

✔ **Boxes with numbers you can change:** Some dialog boxes contain number settings, such as the width of a margin. To type a number, click on the existing number to highlight it and then type the new number. To increase or decrease the number a little at a time, click on the up or down arrows next to the box. Take a look at the Shading box in the Font dialog box.

✔ **Buttons you can "press" by clicking on them:** These buttons are called *command buttons* because you command WordPerfect to do stuff when you click on them with the left mouse button. If you see a button that has an ellipsis, guess what? When you click on it, you see another dialog box. If the button has a little triangle on it, clicking on it displays a menu. Both boxes shown in Figure 2-2 have a bunch of command buttons near the bottom, as do most dialog boxes in WordPerfect.

✔ **Menu bars:** Yes, sometimes a dialog box has its own menu bar, and you choose commands from it by using the same techniques you use to choose commands from the menu bar at the top of any other window.

Don't try to remember all this stuff. We talk about various instances of these dialog thingies as we go along, but you can refer to this list if you ever run into an unfamiliar one.

Our favorite buttons

Two common and important buttons in dialog boxes are the OK and Cancel buttons. Clicking on OK means "Do it — and do it the way this box says to do it." Clicking on Cancel means "Forget it — I didn't really want to do this. Get me outta here and ignore everything I said in this box."

"Forget it" apparently is a popular choice because WordPerfect lets you say the same thing in two other ways:

✔ Press the Esc key on the keyboard.

✔ Click on the Close box on the window border (usually the button with the X on it in the upper-right corner of the dialog box).

Pinky finger alert!

When you use dialog boxes, you should beware of two keyboard keys: Enter and Esc, which mean the same as the OK and Cancel buttons, respectively. This caution applies even if you're typing something in a dialog thingy. Keep a watchful eye on your pinky fingers, lest they unwittingly lead you astray by pressing Enter or Esc before you're truly finished with the dialog box.

We're talking overkill here. We just remember to click the Cancel button or press Esc — enough is enough.

You may also see a button labeled Close, which means basically the same thing as OK. Clicking on Close just closes the box without changing anything that hasn't already been changed.

Using QuickMenus for Even More Ways to Choose Commands

If you're beginning to get a headache just thinking about the regular, plain-vanilla menu bar, give this subject a miss.

As usual, in its quest to give you more options than you would have thought possible, WordPerfect provides another way to choose commands. This method involves the use of the right mouse button. Usually, whenever we tell you to click the mouse button, we always mean the left one.

The people who wrote WordPerfect, however, decided that because most mice have two or three buttons, ignoring the additional one or two buttons would be missing an opportunity for more menus, options, and (probably) confusion.

In many Windows programs, clicking on something with the right mouse button pops up a little menu. Those wacky WordPerfect for Linux people decided to have WordPerfect do the same, and they named their little menus QuickMenus. Throughout this book, whenever clicking on something with the right mouse button displays a QuickMenu, we tell you about it. We call it *right-clicking*. It's getting more and more popular, so try to remember it. The Application Bar (the bar at the bottom of the screen), for example, has a QuickMenu that includes an option to hide the Application Bar if you get tired of looking at it.

These steps show you how to see a QuickMenu:

1. **Point to the Application Bar with the mouse pointer.**

2. **Click once, using the right mouse button.**

   A little box pops up, right where the mouse pointer is.

Voilà! Now that you can see a QuickMenu — specifically, the one for the Application Bar — what good does it do you? This QuickMenu has only two options: Hide Application Bar and Settings.

Most QuickMenus have a Settings, Options, or Properties option that lets you customize the way WordPerfect works. We talk about customizing

WordPerfect much later in this book (in Chapter 19, when you may have read more of this book and be calmer about the idea of fooling around with the things that appear onscreen and how they work).

Each QuickMenu contains commands that have something to do with the thing you were pointing at (the Application Bar, in this case). This particular QuickMenu contains the command Hide Application Bar.

To choose a command, such as Hide Application Bar, from a QuickMenu, you have (as usual) a choice of methods:

✔ Point to the command with the mouse pointer, and click on it (either the left *or* the right mouse button will do).

✔ Press the underlined letter in the command (H, in this case).

Either way, WordPerfect leaps into action and performs the command. In this case, the Application Bar vanishes like M&Ms at a birthday party. (To get the command back, by the way, you can choose the View⇨Toolbars command and make sure that the little box beside the words *Application Bar* is pressed in or contains a black dot.)

Fooling with the Toolbar

As accustomed to bars as writers traditionally are, the number of bars in WordPerfect for Linux inspires even us. We're about to discuss two of these word processing watering holes: the toolbar and the Property Bar. As in real life (restaurants, that is), you can think of going to these bars as being a way to get quick service without a menu.

The *toolbar* is a line of buttons with pictures on them below the menu bar, as shown in Figure 2-3. The toolbar is one of those cool icon things that make graphical programs such as WordPerfect look impressive — like a VCR or CD player's remote control. Unlike a remote control, though, the toolbar is useful and simple after you get to know it.

Figure 2-3:
The toolbar. The tools at the hardware store never looked like this!

Sharpening your tools

Here's the cool thing about the toolbar: You can tell WordPerfect which buttons you want on the bar. You can even make your own buttons. Then you can make different sets of buttons for different kinds of documents you work on — one set of buttons for writing memos, perhaps, and a different set of buttons for writing reports.

Fortunately, we don't tell you how to do all this stuff right now. We want to warn you, though, in case someone else set up specialized toolbars on your computer, in which case the buttons on your toolbar change mysteriously when you use different documents. If you think that this feature sounds as cool as we think it does, check out Chapter 19 for details.

The first thing to know about the toolbar is that it's not always displayed. (This knowledge should be reassuring if you're now frantically looking for rectangular buttons with pictures on them.) The second thing to know is that the toolbar is not the same as the Property Bar, which has even more cryptic buttons. If you're not sure which bar you're looking at on the screen, check out Figure 1-6 in Chapter 1.

If you don't see the toolbar, you can display it by opening the View menu and clicking on Toolbars. Make sure that the box beside the words *WordPerfect 8 Toolbar* is selected and click on OK. Notice that you may not have the same buttons on your toolbar that we have on ours. If that's the case, the person who set up your software decided to change the buttons. If he went to all that trouble, he probably had a good reason, and you should ask him to explain what he had in mind.

Toolbar buttons are quick ways to do everyday things — things you can do with menus that take longer to do that way. To use a toolbar button, you click on it with the left mouse button. Some buttons are self-explanatory and simple, such as Print. If you want to print a document, you click the Print button. Thanks again to the Department of Redundancy Department (again), you can also print by choosing File⇨Print or pressing F5. Some toolbar buttons, such as Text Box, do things that are a little more complicated. If you want more explanation about a button, just move the pointer to it (don't click). A little birdie — ahem, we mean a little yellow box — delivers a brief one-liner about the button and lists the keyboard equivalent, if it has one.

If you decide that you don't like the adorable little pictures on the toolbar, open the View menu, click on Toolbars, and unselect the WordPerfect 8 Toolbar check box.

Throughout this book, we tell you when a button on the toolbar would be useful. In Chapter 1, for example, we use toolbar buttons to open, save, and print documents in one fell click.

Lunching with the Proprietors at the Property Bar

These days, everything's turning into private property. That includes things on your computer screen; even your words have property nowadays. The Property Bar is how you, the proprietor of those words, look into the property owned by your words. To put it in plain English, if some text is **bold**, for example, we might say that it's bold. This is too simple. Instead, the computer-geek types who write word processing programs say that the text has the bold property assigned to it. And (you guessed it), the Property Bar is where you find out which properties are assigned to the text.

If the Property Bar is displayed and you're looking at regular text you just typed in a document, the Property Bar looks something like Figure 2-4.

Figure 2-4:
Proprietary
buttons
on the
Property Bar.

Like the toolbar, the Property Bar has buttons that can be changed by the Very Knowledgeable, so yours may not look like ours. If the Property Bar isn't visible, open the View menu, click on Toolbars, and make sure that the check box beside Property Bar is selected. Then click on the OK button.

Also like the toolbar, the Property Bar is a quick, convenient way to do something that would take longer to do if you used the menus. If you place the mouse pointer on a Property Bar button, another little birdie — ahem, yellow box — provides a brief explanation of the button's function. Because some of the labels on the buttons can be a bit vague ("<None>"? None of what?), this explanation is quite useful.

Some Property Bar buttons have little down-pointing triangles on them. (A few toolbar buttons sport little triangles, too.) When you click on one of these triangles, a menu drops down from the button. If you click on the triangle next to the leftmost button, for example, you can choose the font to use for some text. This button usually starts out saying Courier, which is arguably the ugliest font on the entire list. By clicking on it, you can choose another, undoubtedly more attractive font from a long list of fonts that come with WordPerfect as well as other fonts that may be installed on your Linux system. (We talk more about fonts in Chapter 6.)

As with the toolbar, if you decide that you really don't like the Property Bar, click on View⇨Toolbars and deselect the Property Bar check box.

*Un*like the toolbar, however, the Property Bar changes on its own! When you start typing, the Property Bar looks like the one shown back in Figure 2-4. Suppose that you decide to add a little table to a document. (You've been reading Chapter 14, for example.) Suddenly, the Property Bar tells you about the table as well as about the text in those columns. If you add a picture, the Property Bar changes to include settings you can change for the picture. This feature is quite useful because you don't have to go searching through all the WordPerfect menus to find out exactly which commands might be relevant to what you're working on. Instead, WordPerfect puts right there on the Property Bar the things it thinks you might be interested in.

Using the Ruler

Okay, now you're on familiar ground. Everybody knows what a ruler is, right? Ummm, maybe. The WordPerfect ruler is not your ordinary tick-marks-along-the-edge sort of thing (although it has those, too). It's a behavior-controlling ruler (like the ones your grade-school teachers had), except that this ruler controls the behavior of your paragraphs. Specifically, it controls the indents and tabs of whichever paragraph you're working in (where the cursor — not the mouse pointer — is). The *cursor,* or *insertion point,* is a stationary, usually blinking vertical line after which text appears when you type. The mouse pointer is an arrow shape that moves when the mouse moves.

Like the various other bars, the ruler may or may not be displayed. Open the View menu and see whether the word *Ruler* has a box beside it. If it does and you can't find the ruler, keep searching around on the screen for something that looks like Figure 2-5 or get new glasses. Then click on the word *View* again to make the menu go away. If no box appears beside the word *Ruler,* click on the word *Ruler,* and the ruler appears, as shown in the figure.

Figure 2-5:
Pay homage
to your ruler.
He's picking
up your tab.

The top of the ruler shows the left and right margins, as well as the paragraph indents. In the little strip below the ruler, little triangles show the tab settings. The triangles take different shapes, according to which kind of tabs they represent. When you look at the ruler, you see that some tabs are already set. These settings are not your fault: They're default tabs, which you can change. You can add tabs, remove tabs, or move tabs around.

We discuss all this stuff in fascinating detail in Chapter 7, although the quick tour goes like this:

✔ To move a tab or paragraph margin around, you *drag* it. Point to it; press the mouse button and hold it down. Then move the mouse. Release the button when the selected item is where you want it.

✔ To change the type of tabs you're putting in, *right*-click on the tab you want to change. (Remember that we said this right-click stuff would come in handy.) WordPerfect displays a menu of tab types. Choose from the menu the kind of tab you want.

Make sure that the blinking cursor (the blinking vertical bar, not the mouse pointer) is in the correct paragraph before you set tab stops or indents with the ruler.

Using the Keyboard

With all these bars, windows, and buttons, the keyboard begins to seem rather old and dowdy. Still, it beats the heck out of trying to type with the mouse. For those of us who are reluctant to change our ways just because some software engineer decided to give us a mouse, the keyboard still provides a fairly fast way to give commands to WordPerfect.

Shift, Ctrl, and Alt

The shift keys — Shift, Ctrl, and Alt — work only in conjunction with other keys. All is well if you use them exactly like the Shift key on your beloved Periwinkle-Marmosette typewriter, as shown in these steps:

1. **Press a shift key (Shift, Alt, or Ctrl, as directed)** *first,* **and** *hold it down.*

   Don't crush it — just press it.

2. **Press the other key (F7, for example).**

3. **Release both keys.**

   If your fingers don't work well together, release the shift key last.

These types of key combinations are written as Shift+F7, for example, or Ctrl+F7 or Alt+F7.

Sometimes, you must press more than one shift key. Although this instruction is written as Ctrl+Shift+F3, it may as well be written Shift+Ctrl+F3 because it doesn't matter in which order you press the shift keys. Just get both of 'em down before you press the last key, and release 'em all at one time. (If you were brave and tried that, all sorts of stuff may have appeared on the screen. Don't panic. Just press Ctrl+Shift+F3 again.)

Depending on your Linux and X Window installation, WordPerfect may not be able to hear the Ctrl and Alt keys. If Ctrl and Alt combinations don't work for you, contact your Linux guru or use the menus instead.

Knowing when to press Enter

This section probably should be titled "Knowing when *not* to press Enter." In WordPerfect and any other word processor, you do *not* press the Enter key at the end of every line; you press Enter at the end of every *paragraph.* Failure to observe this rule causes you regular consternation and grief and marks you as a novice to all who observe your work.

Don't worry about the ends of the lines. WordPerfect takes care of most lines automatically and usually does it far better than you can (ragged right, justified — whatever you need). The *only* time you should press Enter at the end of a line is when you're typing a list and the line must end before it's full.

Because pressing the Enter key marks the end of a paragraph, WordPerfect inserts a little paragraph symbol, like this: ¶. Trouble is, the symbol is invisible. To make it visible, open the View menu and click on Show ¶. We highly recommend this technique; it gives you a good sense of what's going on in the document and serves as a reminder not to press the Enter key when you're not supposed to. You should see those little ¶s only at the ends of paragraphs.

Whether the ¶ symbol is visible or not, it's there. If you delete it — which you can do the same way you delete any normal, visible character — the paragraph gets merged with the one below it. That's another good reason to choose <u>V</u>iew⇨<u>S</u>how ¶. To make those symbols invisible again, choose View⇨Show ¶ again.

The story of Tab and the spacebar

This story sounds like an entertaining tale of Tab, the swinging Astro Kitty. Alas, although this story is about space, it's not about black holes and watering holes — it's about white space.

Like pressing Enter at the end of every line, another way to cause yourself no end of unnecessary grief is to overuse the Tab key and the spacebar to get your text where you want it. You generally have better ways to do this than the way you did it on your Stombrowski-Danglowicz steam-powered typing machine, which you fondly remember from the old days in the KGB.

The Tab and spacebar keys insert white-space characters. Like cockroaches in the Keys (Florida, that is), the characters are there even though you may not see them. A certain WordPerfect command is equivalent to snapping on the light switch to see these critters. It's the same command that shows the invisible paragraph mark: Choose <u>V</u>iew⇨<u>S</u>how ¶.

Whoa! Suddenly, all the spaces in the document appear as little black dots, all the tabs appear as arrows, and the little paragraph markers show up at the end of each paragraph. Don't worry — the document won't look like this when it's printed. This technique is just a useful way to see exactly which characters you have. If you're like us, seeing paragraph marks is one thing, but seeing those little dots where all the spaces are in the document really is a bit much. Here's the incantation to see only the paragraph marks and tabs: From the program window menu, choose Preferences, click on Display, click on Show ¶, and uncheck everything except Hard Return and Tab. Then click on OK and Close. Trust us; you'll be glad you did.

WordPerfect offers better ways to position text than to use a bunch of spaces and tabs, and we get into them in Chapter 7. This list tells you how to use these guys properly:

- ✔ Press the spacebar only between words or at the beginning of sentences.
- ✔ For the most part, you press the Tab key only to indent the *first line* of a paragraph or put white space in the middle of a sentence. (To indent an entire paragraph, choose the Fo<u>r</u>mat⇨Paragraph⇨Indent command or press the F7 key; see Chapter 7.)

If you want to create a table of words and numbers, you may have to use tabs too, or you can tell WordPerfect to help you make a table (see Chapter 14).

Choosing commands by using keys

As we intimate earlier in this chapter, you can use the keyboard rather than the mouse to choose commands from the menu bar. For touch typists, this method can be more efficient than mousing it, because you don't have to move your fingers from that all-important home row.

To choose a command without touching the mouse, follow these steps:

1. **Look at the menu bar, and notice which character in the command is underlined.**

The underlined character is always a letter or a number.

2. **Hold down the Alt key while you press the key; then release the Alt key.**

Aha! WordPerfect grasps your meaning and displays the menu associated with that command. If you press Alt+V, for example, WordPerfect rolls down the View menu.

3. **Again, check the command on this menu to see which character is underlined.**

Press the character *without* the Alt key. WordPerfect guesses that you're giving a command, so you don't have to press the Alt key to tip it off. If you do press the Alt key, do not pass go and do not collect $200; you're giving commands again to the menu that runs across the top of the screen.

If you choose a command that has a little triangle after it, such as the Format⇨Line command, WordPerfect displays another little menu. Repeat Step 3 to choose the command from this menu.

Your Linux and X Window installation may have the Alt key configured to pay attention to something other than WordPerfect. If WordPerfect doesn't display the File menu when you press Alt+F, check with your local Linux wizard.

For commands you use frequently, consider memorizing the letters that invoke the command because you can probably type them faster (even including pressing the Alt key) than you can choose the command with the mouse.

Here are some keyboard tips:

✔ To cancel a menu by using the keyboard, press the Esc key. Every time you press it, WordPerfect backs up one step. Keep pressing Esc until the menus go away and no command is highlighted on the menu bar.

✔ Computer-literate types may be tempted to think that the Break key also cancels commands, although WordPerfect ignores it.

Undoing Mistakes

Not that you're likely to make a mistake or anything, but for those of us who occasionally give the wrong command, the toolbar has a Highly Useful button named Undo. Actually, it's not named anything. The button doesn't say Undo — it just has an icon of an arrow doing a counterclockwise U-turn.

When you click on this button (or press Ctrl+Z or choose Edit⇨Undo), WordPerfect usually can undo whatever the last command did, including deleting a bunch of characters, whether you used the Delete key, the Backspace key (see Chapter 4), or both.

WordPerfect also has a Redo button (and a matching Edit⇨Redo command). This button undoes the last Undo you did. (Confused? We are!) Redo is the clockwise U-turn button on the toolbar.

Help, Help-Help, and More Help

Calling for help in a program such as WordPerfect for Linux is a little like calling for help at the Arnold Schwarzenegger–Leona Helmsley School of Lifeguard Training: Prepare to be a little overwhelmed. You don't just get information — you get an entire, muscle-bound information-retrieval and - management system designed to meet your assistance requirements (and leave a mint on your pillow).

We don't even try to explain everything this Dream Team of lifesavers can do; we just give you the simplest way to use Help. We recommend for all the fancy stuff that you play around in Help to your heart's content. You can't break anything, and you may learn a great deal.

Help

The simplest part is calling for Help: Click Help (way over at the right end) on the menu bar. At this point, it's a good thing that you're not literally drowning when you call for help in WordPerfect, because now you must decide precisely *how* you're going to ask for help. When you choose Help, you see a Help menu with three options at the top: Contents, Search for Help on, and PerfectExpert. Below these are three more options you probably won't use as much: Macros, Online Help, and About Corel WordPerfect. This list describes what all the Help buttons do:

- ✔ **Contents:** You see the Table of Contents page in the Corel WordPerfect Help window. Pages in the Help window work just like Web pages. You can click on one of the green hyperlinks to see the Help information for a particular topic.

- ✔ **Search for Help on:** WordPerfect Help opens the Help window and a separate Search window that displays a list of all topics, arranged alphabetically. As you type the first few letters of the topic you're interested in, WordPerfect displays the index entry that starts with what you typed.

- ✔ **PerfectExpert:** This tool helps you compose a document. Read the following section to help you decide how helpful this feature is.

- ✔ **Macros:** Macros are a way to combine a bunch of keystrokes into a sort of miniprogram. Although macros are helpful for complicated, repetitive tasks, discussing them is beyond the scope of this book. Click on this menu item to learn everything you always wanted to know about macros and more.

✔ **Online Help:** This option displays a submenu that includes the WP Online Manual and three useful Web sites. If you choose the WP Online Manual, WordPerfect runs the Acrobat Reader program to display the WordPerfect manual, an onscreen version of the printed manual you get if you buy Corel WordPerfect for Linux in a box. The other three options on the submenu open Web-based help documents in a Web browser window (usually Netscape Navigator). If you aren't running Netscape Navigator, selecting this option helpfully starts it for you.

✔ **About Corel WordPerfect:** This option opens a window full of obscure details about your version of WordPerfect, although it doesn't do anything very helpful. (Why is it on the Help menu? Because it's traditional!)

Whichever Help method you choose, you get a window full of information. Often, several areas of text are highlighted in green; each of these areas is itself a topic. These highlighted phrases are hyperlinks, just like the ones on the World Wide Web; when you click on one of these areas, you get information on that topic. If you get lost in this labyrinthine Hall of Help and want to find your way back, look for a Back button at the top of the Help window and click on it.

To make the Help window go away, the easiest thing to do is click on the window's Close button (usually the button with the X on it in the upper-right corner).

Ask PerfectExpert

Everyone's office usually has an expert WordPerfect user — in our experience, a really smart administrative assistant, someone in the technical-writing department, or someone who has way too much time on her hands and not enough work to do. In case your office doesn't have one of these people, those thoughtful WordPerfect folks included one in the WordPerfect program, and they call it PerfectExpert.

 You can have PerfectExpert sit by your side and help you get your work done. Imagine — Arnold and Leona right at your side. How? Choose Help⇨ PerfectExpert. Summoning PerfectExpert to your side adds a whole new component to the screen. You can also summon PerfectExpert by clicking on that little lightbulb button that's all the way at the right end of the toolbar. (Yes, we had trouble figuring that one out too, but that is a lightbulb.) If your WordPerfect window isn't wide enough, the PerfectExpert button may be right off the edge of the window.

PerfectExpert, as shown in Figure 2-6, contains a bunch of buttons corresponding to the steps in a writing project — at least what Corel thinks the steps in a writing project should be; your English teacher may disagree! Click on the button that describes what you want to do, and WordPerfect helps you do it.

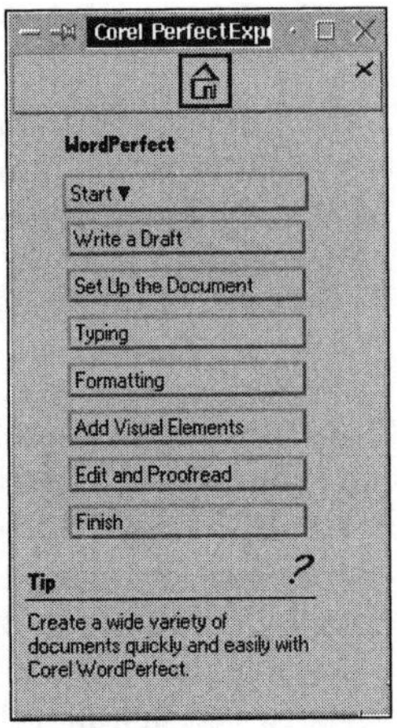

Figure 2-6:
Perfect
Expert at
your side.

PerfectExpert is a pretty cool idea. Although it gives you suggestions to look at when you're wondering what the heck to do next, it still doesn't write your document for you.

Context-sensitive Help

If you want the Help feature to pare the list of topics to things related to whatever you're doing right now, you can get context-sensitive Help by pressing F1. (Imagine Arnold and Leona trying to be sensitive to your personal needs, and you get the picture.) When you're in the middle of using a menu or a dialog box, press F1. Zap! Arnold figures out exactly which topic you ought to be interested in (whether you are or not). If you press F1 with the pointer in the middle of some text, you see the same window that appears when you choose Contents from the Help menu.

Chapter 3

Cruising the Document

• •

In This Chapter

▶ Moving around in a document

▶ Using the mouse

▶ Using the keyboard

▶ Going places with the Go To dialog box

• •

*A*fter you type some text in your document, you undoubtedly will want to do some editing. After all, that's what word processing is all about. When you use a regular typewriter, making changes involves splashing a viscous white liquid all over your paper, yourself, and the furniture — or slicing and dicing little slips of paper, only to reassemble them with glue or tape. Those days are over, however, now that you have entered the Age of Word Processing — you can slice and dice your text right on the screen, with no paper cuts or white-out stains.

To be able to edit, of course, you must move the cursor (the blinking vertical bar) to the text you want to change. The cursor is your pencil point on the page; the cursor's location determines where actions will happen. That's what this chapter is about: moving the cursor around in your document. In other chapters, we tell you what to do when you get there, such as deleting things (see Chapter 4), moving text around (see Chapter 5), and making the text look different (see Chapter 6).

Two — Count 'Em, Two — Ways

You have, of course, two ways of navigating around your document. (Computer people like to talk about *navigation* rather than just *moving;* we must be a group of frustrated sailors.) As you use WordPerfect, you find that two is the absolute minimum number of ways to do anything, and in many cases WordPerfect provides four or five ways. (Chapter 2 tells how many ways you can give a command.)

You can move the cursor in two general ways:

- ✔ Use the mouse to point to where you want to go.
- ✔ Use keys on the keyboard to move in the direction you indicate.

Two cursor-like things are also on the screen:

- ✔ **Mouse pointer:** Tells you where the mouse is pointing. It can change shapes and does so, depending on what WordPerfect thinks it's point-ing at. Usually in WordPerfect, the pointer is a little, black arrow. If WordPerfect is busy, the pointer turns into an hourglass. If the mouse is pointing to a place in WordPerfect where you can type, you may see a blue bar at the place where you would be typing if you clicked the mouse. If you don't see the mouse pointer, just move the mouse a little to make it appear.

- ✔ **Cursor:** Also called the *insertion point;* tells you where your typing will appear. (We hope you don't mind that we call this thing the cursor because it's the term we're used to.) The cursor is a slowly blinking ver-tical bar; you can't miss it.

The purpose of this chapter is to get the cursor into firing position so that you can take aim at some text. First, we talk about using the mouse; next, we talk about using the boring old keyboard; finally, we throw in a few other ways in which WordPerfect lets you cruise your document.

Mousing Around

If the place you want to go to is displayed onscreen, just position the mouse pointer there and click the left mouse button. Follow these steps:

1. **Move the mouse pointer to the position where you want to work.**

   When the mouse is pointing to your text, you can click to move the cursor there. If you move the mouse pointer off the text into some white space, you may see the *shadow cursor* (see the nearby sidebar "The shadow knows!" for information on how to use the shadow cursor). Move the mouse pointer to the beginning of the paragraph.

2. **Click the mouse button without moving the mouse.**

   This action tells WordPerfect to put the cursor right where the mouse pointer is.

3. **You may want to move the mouse pointer out of the way so that it doesn't obscure the text you're going to edit.**

   You don't have to, although the mouse pointer can be distracting.

The shadow knows!

When you move the mouse pointer into the white space in your document, a blue symbol (the *shadow cursor*) may appear on the same line as the mouse pointer. If the shadow cursor appears, it tells you where the cursor will go if you click the mouse where it is now. The exact appearance of the shadow cursor also tells you how the text you type will be formatted. (The shadow cursor may not appear, if your WordPerfect program isn't configured to display it.)

For example, if you move the mouse pointer to a blank area an inch or so in from the left margin,

the shadow cursor looks like a vertical line and a right-pointing arrow. This symbol tells you that, unlike most word processors, WordPerfect is happy for you to click on white space and that if you do, WordPerfect will obligingly stick in a Tab character or two so that the cursor will appear where you clicked. If the mouse pointer is near the center of the line, a vertical line with *two* arrows appears, indicating that WordPerfect will center the text you type there. Nice!

Moving to the far reaches of the document

If you cannot see the text you want to edit, don't panic. It's still there — it has just fallen off the edge of the screen. WordPerfect displays your document as though it were written on a long scroll. (Imagine medieval monks or Egyptian scribes.) The beginning and ending portions of the document are rolled up, and only the middle part is visible. If you want to see a different section of the text, WordPerfect unrolls the scroll for you and displays it onscreen.

You may have noticed a vertical gray bar running along the right side of the WordPerfect window. Figure 3-1 shows this *scroll bar* (which we mention in Chapter 1). You use it to tell WordPerfect to roll and unroll the metaphorical scroll that contains your document.

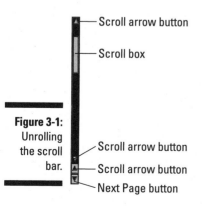

— Scroll arrow button

— Scroll box

Figure 3-1:
Unrolling
the scroll
bar.

— Scroll arrow button
— Scroll arrow button
— Next Page button

The scroll bar is similar to a little map of your document, with the full length of the scroll bar representing the entire document: The top end is the beginning of the document, and the bottom end is the end of it. The little gray box on the scroll bar (the *scroll box*) represents the part of the document you can see onscreen right now. The scroll box moves up and down the scroll bar the way an elevator moves up and down a shaft. By looking at the position of the scroll box on the scroll bar, you can tell where you are in a document — at the beginning, middle, or end.

Scrolling to the right spot

You can also move around the document by using the scroll bar, as you may have guessed already. This list shows the things you can do to the scroll bar with the mouse:

- ✔ **Move anywhere in a document in a big hurry.** Use the mouse to drag the scroll box up and down the scroll bar. As you move the scroll box, thus scrolleth the text of the document. To drag the scroll box, point to it with the mouse pointer, press and hold down the left mouse button, and move the mouse pointer up or down. The scroll box moves with the mouse pointer as long as you hold down the mouse button. When you release the button, the scroll box stays where you left it, and the document scrolls to match. If you let the mouse pointer stray too far into the text (that is, if you move the mouse to the left while you're trying to scroll up or down), the scroll box pops back to where it was when you started. Although this situation can be very annoying, don't panic: Continue to hold down the mouse button and move back to the right so that the mouse pointer is on the scroll bar again. The scroll box pops back to where it was before you made the mouse pointer wander into your text.

- ✔ **Move to the end of your document.** You can drag the scroll box down to the bottom of its elevator shaft.

- ✔ **Move to the beginning of the document.** Do the reverse: Drag the scroll box up to the tippy-top.

- ✔ **Move forward or backward one screen of text at a time.** Click on the scroll bar (not on the scroll box). To move to the next screen of text in a document, click on the scroll bar below the scroll box. To move to the preceding screen, click above the scroll box. The scroll box moves, and the document scrolls up (or down) one screen.

- ✔ **Scroll text one line at a time.** Click on the scroll-arrow buttons — the little buttons with arrows on them at either end of the scroll bar. The button with the up-pointing arrow (at the top of the scroll bar) moves you toward the beginning of the document, and the button with the down-pointing arrow moves you toward the end.

✔ **Move through the document page by page.** Click on the Next Page and Previous Page buttons. These buttons, which are at the bottom of the scroll bar, have little up and down arrows on them. When you click on the Next Page button, WordPerfect scrolls the document so that the top of the next page is at the top of the screen. The Previous Page button scrolls so that the top of the preceding page is at the top of the screen.

If a document is too wide to fit across the WordPerfect window, a scroll bar runs across the bottom of the window too, right above the Application Bar. This scroll bar works just like the vertical scroll bar we talk about, except that it moves sideways and has no Next Page and Previous Page buttons.

Sticking with the Keyboard

If you type like the wind, you probably don't want to have to move your hands from the home row of your keyboard — not even to have lunch. Your speedy fingers know where every key is, and they can hit them as fast as a 2-year-old can grab an Oreo. Faster, even.

After reading about all this mouse stuff, you're probably thinking, "Although the mouse is cute, it slows me down. I don't want to have to lift my hand, grope around for my mouse, and knock over my coffee cup just to see the next page of my letter." For you, dear friend, WordPerfect has navigation keys. Most of the time, you can forget about using the mouse; just press these keys to get where you want to go:

✔ The *arrow keys,* for moving the cursor up, down, left, and right.

✔ The keys labeled Home, End, Page Up (or PgUp), and Page Down (or PgDn).

✔ The numeric keypad, which contains duplicates of the arrow, Home, End, Page Up, and Page Down keys. If you want to use the numeric keypad for moving the cursor, make sure that Num Lock is on. (Press the Num Lock key on your keyboard to switch the numeric keypad between numbers and cursor motion.)

You can press the arrow keys — which have the little up-, down-, left-, and right-pointing arrows on them — to move up or down one line or to move left or right one character. These keys are great for positioning the cursor in an exact spot.

This list shows some of the finer points of using cursor-control keys:

✔ If the cursor is on the top line of the WordPerfect window and you press the up-arrow key, WordPerfect does your bidding. To move up a line, WordPerfect must display that line, so it scrolls the document down a tad. (If the cursor is already at the tippy-top of the document, it can't move upward, so nothing happens.)

✔ Ditto if the cursor is on the bottom line of the screen and you press the down-arrow key.

✔ Don't confuse the left-arrow key with the Backspace key, which usually also has a left-pointing arrow on it. The Backspace key *eats* text as it moves leftward. The left-arrow key just moves the cursor to the left and slides around below the letters like a hot knife through ice cream.

✔ As you move the cursor, it moves from letter to letter in your text. When you move rightward off the end of a line, the cursor moves to the left end of the next line. Unlike the mouse pointer, the cursor can go only where there is text. The cursor must have text to walk around on, as it were; you cannot move it off the text into the white void of the blank page.

Using Ctrl with the arrow keys

By pressing the Ctrl key while you press an arrow key, you can make the cursor move farther, as shown by these key combinations:

✔ **Ctrl+up arrow:** Moves the cursor to the beginning of the current paragraph; if you're already there, Ctrl+up-arrow moves the cursor to the beginning of the preceding paragraph.

✔ **Ctrl+down arrow:** Moves the cursor down to the beginning of the next paragraph.

✔ **Ctrl+left arrow:** Moves the cursor left one word.

✔ **Ctrl+right arrow:** Moves the cursor right one word.

To use the Ctrl key, press it while you press another key, as though it were the Shift key. Don't release it until you have released the other key.

Moving farther and faster

How about those other keys we mention earlier in this chapter — the Home, End, Page Down (or PgDn), and Page Up (or PgUp) keys? You can use them to range farther afield in your documents — an especially useful capability as they get larger (the documents, not the keys). As with the arrow keys, your keyboard probably has two sets of these keys, and you can use the ones on the numeric keypad only if the Num Lock key is turned off.

You can move to the beginning or end of the line by pressing one of these keys:

- **Home:** Moves the cursor to the beginning of the current line
- **End:** Moves the cursor to the end of the current line

We use the End key all the time to get back to the end of the line we're typing so that we can type some more.

You can move up or down one screen of information by pressing one of these keys:

- **Page Up:** Moves the cursor to the top of the screen. If you're already there, Page Up moves up one screen's worth of text and scrolls the document as it does so.
- **Page Down:** Moves the cursor to the bottom of the screen. If you're already there, Page Down moves down one screen of text and scrolls the document as it does so.

To move to the beginning or end of the document, press one of these keys:

- **Ctrl+Home:** Moves the cursor to the beginning of the document
- **Ctrl+End:** Moves the cursor to the end of the document

If you're wondering how long a document is, press Ctrl+End to get to the end of it. Then look at the Application Bar to see what page you're on (the number after Pg).

Go To Where?

WordPerfect has a Go To dialog box you can use to tell it where to go. Unfortunately, you cannot tell WordPerfect to go where you probably *want* to tell it to go, although this option is better than nothing. And, it's useful for moving around in really large documents.

You have three — count 'em, three — ways to display the Go To dialog box:

- Choose the Edit⇨Go To command from the menu.
- Press Ctrl+G.
- Click on the location section of the Application Bar (the part that gives you the page, line, and cursor position).

Actually, you have many more than four ways because you can use the keyboard or the mouse to choose commands, but you see our point. You see the Go To dialog box, shown in Figure 3-2.

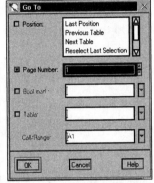

Figure 3-2:
Use the Go
To dialog
box to tell
WordPerfect
where to go.

The Go To dialog box has four settings to tell WordPerfect where to go: Position, Page Number, Bookmark, and Table. This section shows how to use the first two settings (the last two aren't useful unless you know about bookmarks and tables, which are more advanced items you can include in WordPerfect documents).

Top o' the page to you!

The following list shows you how to use the Go To dialog box to get to the top of any page in your document:

- ✔ **Move the cursor to the top of the current page:** Click on the list of possible positions (sounds indecent, doesn't it?), and then choose Top of Current Page from the list.

- ✔ **Move the cursor to the bottom of the current page:** Do the same thing you do to move to the top and choose Bottom of Current Page as the position. To bring that choice into view, scroll the list of positions downward.

- ✔ **Move the cursor to the top of a different page:** Choose Page number and either type the number of the page you want to go to or click the little up and down arrows until you find the page number you want.

When you click on OK or press Enter, WordPerfect transports you to the spot you wanted.

Getting unlost

If you use any of the mouse or keyboard methods described in this book to move the cursor or if you use the search commands described in Chapter 4, you may find that you made a dreadful error and you want to go back to where you started and try again. Amazingly enough, WordPerfect has a "go back to where I started" command. (These nice little surprises keep up our faith in computers.)

To return the cursor to its most recent location, use the Go To dialog box. Choose Position and then Last Position and click on OK or press Enter. The cursor flies back to its earlier location like a well-trained homing pigeon.

Chapter 4

Fooling with Blocks of Text

● ●

In This Chapter

▶ Building basic blocks

▶ Selecting text with the mouse

▶ Selecting text with the keyboard

▶ Extending a selection

▶ Deleting, moving, and copying selected text

▶ Copying and pasting with the Clipboard

▶ Cutting and pasting with the Clipboard

● ●

*E*ver since the first Egyptian hacked his papyrus scroll of *Pyramids For Dummies* into pages, the idea of blocks of text has progressed inexorably. The sentence. The paragraph. The page. The chapter. The volume. The CD. And now, WordPerfect text selection both embraces and transcends these classic ways of dividing text into blocks so that you can handle any lump of text.

Text selection enables you to choose precisely what you want to delete, capitalize, italicize, spell check, or otherwise word-process. Think of the power: You can surgically excise tedious text, rejuvenate a lackluster paragraph with screaming 26-point type, selectively subdue injudicious jargon with grammar- or spell-checking, and eliminate annoying alliteration.

WordPerfect gives you 60 quadjillion ways to select text and about as many things to do with it after it's selected. We stick to the simplest methods.

Basic Blocks

In WordPerfect, a *block* is a chunk of text in your document. Unlike the letter blocks your toddler friends play with, WordPerfect blocks can include a bunch of letters, words, lines, and even pages.

The WordPerfect program understands that humans are fond of blocks — not just arbitrarily defined blocks from "here" to "there" but also certain everyday blocks, such as sentences, words, and paragraphs. This list shows the main blocks of text that WordPerfect understands:

- Arbitrary blocks (as in "Begin with this word over here and end with that word over yonder")
- Individual words
- Sentences
- Paragraphs
- Pages

Like an overly fastidious nanny, WordPerfect allows you to play with only one block at a time. You cannot select a paragraph here, a paragraph there, and three words over there. Select a block. Have your way with it. Select another block. Do stuff to it. And so on.

Selecting Text with Your Mouse

For most people, the overall best and simplest way to select a block of text is with your buddy, the mouse.

The point-and-shoot approach

To select an arbitrary block of text (from any point to any other point), follow these steps:

1. **Put the mouse pointer at the beginning of the stuff you want to select.**

2. **Hold down the left mouse button, and drag the mouse pointer to the end of what you want to select.**

   Text is highlighted as you go, as shown in Figure 4-1.

3. **Release the mouse button.**

   The selected text remains highlighted, and you can do stuff to it (see the section "Doing Stuff with Selected Text," later in this chapter).

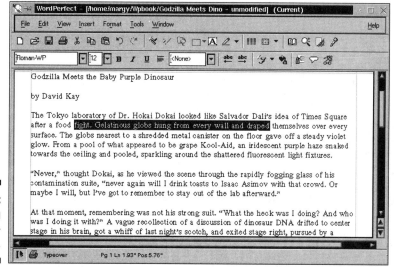

Figure 4-1:
Selecting
(highlight-
ing) text.

This clicking-and-dragging-along stuff makes perfect sense if all the text you want to select is on the screen. What if the text you want to select, however, starts, oh, three lines from the bottom of the screen and extends off the bottom for another couple of lines? Although dragging that mouse pointer off the bottom of the screen could take some doing, that's exactly what you need to do. To select text off the bottom of the screen (or the top, for that matter), slowly move the cursor toward the bottom of the screen. At some point, the text on the screen begins to move upward, bringing new text to the bottom of the screen. This new text arrives on the screen highlighted because that's what WordPerfect figures that you're trying to do.

Unless your reflexes are much better than ours (a depressingly real possibility), this text shoots by so fast that you end up highlighting more text than you want. *Don't panic!* More important, *keep holding down the mouse button.* Just move the mouse pointer up a little, and the text stops streaming by. You can find at your leisure the end of what you want to highlight, without having to chase it all over the screen.

Of course, if things really got going, the *end* of what you want to highlight has now disappeared off the *top* of the screen. You guessed it: *Don't panic!* More important, *keep holding down the mouse button.* This time, ever so gently move toward the top of the screen. Soon, text begins flowing to the screen from the top. When you see the place where you want to stop highlighting, move the cursor back down into the WordPerfect window. Now you can find the end of the text you want to highlight. At last, you can give your index finger a rest and let go of the mouse button.

If all this sounds too involved (and for selecting large amounts of text, it is), check out the following section to find faster ways to select words, sentences, and paragraphs.

Take my word for it

Take a close look at Figure 4-1. Notice that the highlighting starts at the word *fight* and ends at the word *draped*. We did not ever-so-carefully position the mouse right before *fight* and drag it ever-so-carefully just to the end of the word *draped*. Instead, we put the mouse pointer somewhere on the word *fight* and dragged the mouse until the word *draped* was highlighted. If you try this technique, you'll find that you can't select just a portion of the word *draped* (or any other word, for that matter). As soon as the mouse pointer hits a word, the whole word is highlighted.

Is that good or bad? It's up to you. This business about selecting words automatically arrived in WordPerfect 7. The folks at WordPerfect added this feature because many people found it hard to drag over exactly the selection they wanted and most of them wanted to select whole words anyway.

We find this feature to be incredibly annoying. Maybe it's because we have steady hands, or maybe we're just picky about what we select. Whatever.

If you also find automatic word selection to be annoying, you can turn it off. To do so, make sure that you don't have text selected in a document window, and then click on the WordPerfect program window. Choose Preferences and click the Environment button. Near the bottom of the Environment Preferences dialog box, you see a check box labeled Select whole words instead of characters. If you clear this check box and click on OK and then Close, you can select any characters you want to with the mouse, just as you could in older versions of WordPerfect.

If you're new to this sort of marking procedure, it can look weird. Here are a couple of tips:

- ✔ If the text you want covers several lines, don't bother to drag the mouse pointer to the end of the line and then back to the beginning of the next line and so on. This method wastes effort and looks funny. Like driving in Rome (or Boston), after you begin, you just have to close your eyes and go. Move boldly and directly toward your destination.

- ✔ You can go backward as well as forward (and up as well as down) — it makes no difference — but you cannot expand the selection in both directions. The place where you begin must be either a beginning or end point.

Lots of clicking for selecting lots of text

Clicking and dragging is the simple way to select text. Here are some faster ways to select words, sentences, and paragraphs:

✔ **To select a word:** Double-click on the word (position the mouse pointer anywhere within the word and then double-click the left mouse button).

✔ **To select a group of words:** Double-click on the first word in the group and hold down the mouse button on the second click. Drag the edge of the highlight (in either direction) to the other end of the group you want to select. This method works even if you turned off automatic word selection (see the sidebar "Take my word for it," earlier in this chapter). If you complete this maneuver successfully, you're eligible to receive your advanced mouse driver's license.

✔ **To select a sentence:** Triple-click on the sentence (move the mouse pointer anywhere in the sentence and triple-click the mouse button — it's similar to a double-click but with one more click). The WordPerfect idea of a sentence is anything that ends with a period and has a space before the next character. Therefore, the sentence "i write like e. e. cummings." contains three sentences as far as WordPerfect is concerned.

If you find triple-clicks to be a bit daunting, you can use another convenient way to select a sentence: Click in the left margin, next to the sentence.

✔ **To select a group of sentences:** This procedure is similar to selecting a group of words. Do the triple-click described in the preceding item (like the samba but faster), and hold down the mouse button on the last click. Then drag the highlight where you want it.

If you like the click-in-the-margin approach to selecting sentences, you can select a bunch of sentences by clicking in the margin and then dragging the mouse pointer up or down.

✔ **To select a paragraph:** Quadruple-click on the paragraph (move the mouse pointer anywhere within the paragraph and click four times in succession). Yes, the latté consumption in the WordPerfect engineering department must be at record levels if those people believe that you can quadruple-click without stuttering, but there it is: Four quick clicks of the mouse button nabs you a paragraph.

If you drink only decaf (such as New England hazelnut–acorn blend — our favorite), you may find the Alternative Paragraph Selection Method to be easier. Move the mouse pointer to the left of the paragraph (where the mouse pointer turns into an arrow) and double-click.

✔ **To select a group of paragraphs:** You guessed it: Hold down the mouse button on the fourth click and drag. Or click twice in the left margin and drag.

What about selecting a page? Logically, this procedure should consist of five clicks, although even the highly wired WordPerfect engineers decided that five clicks was beyond their motor skills. Instead, to select a page, try the QuickMenu approach, described in the next section.

The QuickMenu approach

You can select sentences, paragraphs, and pages by using a QuickMenu. First, click anywhere within the sentence, paragraph, or page you want to select. Then move the mouse pointer to the left margin (where the mouse pointer tips to the right rather than to the left). With a quick click of the right mouse button, you see the QuickMenu shown in Figure 4-2.

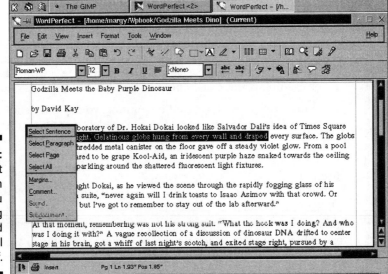

Figure 4-2:
The left margin QuickMenu for selecting text and other cool stuff.

The bottom of this QuickMenu has lots of really cool stuff, such as Sound and Subdocument. Don't play with that stuff now; show some restraint. This is serious business.

Now you get a chance to select a sentence, paragraph, page, or the ever-abundant All option. Just click (using either mouse button) on the menu option you want.

Notice that the menu has no Word option. You have to point and shoot with the mouse to select a word or group of words.

The menu bar approach

You can also select a sentence, a paragraph, a page, or an entire document by using the main menu. Just as you do with a QuickMenu, you begin by clicking anywhere within the text you want. Then choose the Edit⇨Select command, which has most of the same options as the left margin QuickMenu.

One additional option is on the Edit⇨Select menu, and we think that it's pretty cool. When you need it, it's a lifesaver; in all honesty, however, you need it only once in a blue moon. Notice that when you select text that extends over more than one line, the selection goes to the end of the first line and then starts at the beginning of the second line and so on until you get to the end of the selection. What if you just want to select a rectangle? Some day you will, and when you do, you'll be glad that you know about the Edit⇨ Select⇨Rectangle command. (For example, the rectangle approach would let you select the first five characters on each of ten contiguous lines.) Select the text first, with the beginning and end of the text where you want the upper-left and lower-right corners of the selected rectangle of text to be. Then give the command a try; WordPerfect changes the selected area into a rectangle with the corners you chose.

Selecting Text with the Keyboard

Some of us are still a little dubious about this business of taking our hands off the keyboard to use the mouse. We would just as soon use the keyboard, thank you.

Fortunately, many alternatives are available for the rodent-averse among us, whom we prefer to call Speedy Typists. All these alternatives involve the *navigation keys,* which are the arrow keys and the associated pad of keys that have such useful-looking names as Home and End. If you use the keyboard for selecting text, first read the section in Chapter 3 about sticking with the keyboard.

Finished reading Chapter 3? Okay, now you're briefed and ready for the highly complex secret of selecting text with the navigation keys:

Hold down the Shift key and press the navigation keys.

That's it — really. To be painstakingly specific, these steps show you what to do:

1. **Position the cursor at the beginning or end of the text you want to select.**

   Click the mouse at that position or press the navigation keys to move the cursor.

2. **Hold down the Shift key.**

3. **While you hold down the Shift key, press the navigation keys to stretch the selection area to the other end of the text.**

   The selected text is highlighted, and you can do stuff to it (see the section "Doing Stuff with Selected Text," later in this chapter).

Table 4-1 shows you how to select text from where the cursor is positioned.

Table 4-1	Selecting Text By Using the Shift Key
To Select Text Up to This Position	*Press*
Next character	Shift+→ (right arrow)
Preceding character	Shift+← (left arrow)
Same position, down one line	Shift+↓ (down arrow)
Same position, up one line	Shift+↑ (up arrow)
End of line	Shift+End
Beginning of line	Shift+Home
End of document	Shift+Ctrl+End
Beginning of document	Shift+Ctrl+Home
Bottom of screen	Shift+PgDn
Top of screen	Shift+PgUp
End of street	Accelerator pedal
Beginning of tape	Rewind button

Selecting Text with Your Nose and a Pickle

This approach to selecting text is rather unorthodox; it involves thinly sliced pickle spears and breathing through your mouth for a while. This method is not recommended for novices and is best reserved for cold and allergy seasons, when its decongestant effect is most welcome.

Extending Selections

Suppose that you have just finished carefully selecting text. With sudden shock, you see that you really should have selected more. You're consumed by regret and self-recrimination. Ah, how much like life itself is word processing. Unlike life, however, WordPerfect gladly lets you select more text — or less, for that matter. You don't even have to do it over again; simply extend your selection.

To extend a selection you have already made, follow these steps:

1. **Hold down the Shift key.**

2. **With the mouse pointer anywhere in the selected text, hold down the left mouse button.**

   The endpoint of the selection shrinks back to the point where you clicked, and you can drag it back and forth with the mouse.

Of course, you can do the same thing from the keyboard; follow these steps:

1. **Hold down the Shift key.**

2. **Press any of the navigation keys to move the endpoint — just as you did to make the original selection.**

Notice that WordPerfect doesn't allow you to change the original starting point of a selection; you can move only the end you moved the first time.

Doing Stuff with Selected Text

This section may as well be called "Doing Stuff with Molecules," for the breadth of discussion it opens. This list shows a few of the things you can change after you select text:

- ✔ Font
- ✔ Font size
- ✔ Font style
- ✔ Capitalization
- ✔ Paragraph layout
- ✔ Position
- ✔ Orientation
- ✔ Color

You can also delete, cut, copy, paste, move, replace, search, spell check, or grammar check the text; turn it into a bulleted or numbered list; or convert it to a subdocument. Because these topics are covered in most of the other chapters in this book, don't look for them here; find those topics in this book's index or table of contents.

Deleting text

The fastest, easiest, and (depending on how you feel about the document at hand) perhaps most useful thing you can do with selected text is delete it.

After you select text, just press the Delete key (or the Backspace key). The text goes away, never to return. It doesn't utterly, completely go away, however; it passes on to the next dimension, from which you can recall it with the Undo command (see Chapter 5, or just press Ctrl+Z to try it out).

Moving text

Another simple, useful task is moving text. Just select what you want to move; then click and drag the highlighted text where you want it.

As you perform this procedure, the mouse pointer has a shadowed rectangle added to it. You can move the mouse pointer anywhere in your document. If you move the mouse pointer into white space, the shadow cursor shows you where your text will end up. On the other hand, if you're just dragging some words around in your text, the regular cursor moves around in that text to tell you where all this dragging will take your words.

When you release the mouse button, the move is complete.

Copying text

You can copy text by using almost exactly the same technique you use to move it. To copy, hold down the Ctrl key while you drag. A second copy of the selected text is placed in the new location. The original, selected text stays put, just where it was.

Using the X Clipboard

Before we progress to cutting, pasting, and all those other functions that once were well within the capability of kindergartners but that now (thanks to the so-called magic of computers) take $2,000 worth of hardware and software and a library of books whose titles loudly proclaim your Dummyhood, in screaming yellow and black, to all who pass your office — whack! Ouch! Thanks, we needed that. Let's see, where were we?

Copying between documents with the X Clipboard

The X Clipboard is particularly useful for copying between documents. Because WordPerfect allows you to have more than one document open at a time, you can copy text in document A and paste it in document B. See Chapter 12 for more information about having more than one document open at a time.

A special place, the *X Clipboard*, can carry selected text and graphics when you copy, cut, and paste. The X Clipboard isn't a visible thing in WordPerfect; no cute little Clipboard icon moves around. It's just a sort of hidden storage area that is usable from many programs that run under the X Window System. If you're used to Windows or Macs, you'll be relieved to hear that the X Clipboard works much like the Windows and Mac Clipboards.

Copying and pasting with the X Clipboard

Suppose that you're writing a contract for the Dingelhausen-Schneitzenbaum Furniture Prefabrication Company and you're oddly averse to typing Dingelhausen-Schneitzenbaum Furniture Prefabrication Company more than once. Copying and pasting saves your fingers and your sanity by enabling you to make multiple copies of Dingelhausen-Schneitzenbaum Furniture Prefabrication Company all over your contract. (Guess which feature was useful in writing this paragraph?)

To copy some text, follow these steps:

1. **Select the text.**
2. **Press Ctrl+C or choose Edit⇨Copy.**
3. **Click where you want the new copy.**
4. **Press Ctrl+V or choose Edit⇨Paste.**

When you press Ctrl+C, WordPerfect copies your selection to the X Clipboard. Because the text stays in the X Clipboard, you can paste as many copies as you want until you exit WordPerfect.

WordPerfect is smart about including spaces after periods and commas when you cut or paste words and phrases. You may notice that it removes extra spaces after a comma and sometimes even inserts a space after a period. Way cool!

Don't destroy your cuttings

The X Clipboard can contain only one thing at a time. If you copy or cut something new, the old contents of the X Clipboard are wiped out, *unless* you add the new thing to what's already on the X Clipboard. To add the new thing, select whatever it is (it can be text or graphics or both) and choose Edit⇨Append. The new material is added at the end of the Clipboard, after whatever was already there.

On most Linux installations, you can use the middle key to paste a copy of highlighted material. Use any method to select some text in your document. With the text highlighted, move the cursor where you want a copy of that text and click the *middle* mouse button. A copy of the text appears!

Cutting and pasting with the X Clipboard

Cutting and pasting isn't much different from copying and pasting. The only difference is that the original selection gets deleted as soon as you cut it.

To cut and paste some text, follow these steps:

1. **Select the text.**

2. **Press Ctrl+X or choose Edit⇨Cut.**

   The selected text vanishes, although a copy is kept in the X Clipboard.

3. **Click at the location where you want to paste the text.**

4. **Press Ctrl+V or choose Edit⇨Paste.**

Keyboard skills to last a lifetime

The keyboard commands used for cutting, copying, and pasting in WordPerfect (Ctrl+X, Ctrl+C, and Ctrl+V, respectively) are used in some other programs (especially programs that were originally designed to work with Windows rather than with Linux). For this reason, memorizing and using these commands rather than the WordPerfect menu commands is slightly to your advantage. True, the keyboard names are not particularly mnemonic. We keep track of them by remembering that the X, C, and V keys form a little row on the bottom row of the keyboard in this order: cut, copy, and paste.

A handy list of helpful keystrokes

- Double-click to select a word.

- Triple-click to select a sentence.

- Quadruple-click to select a paragraph. (As an alternative, you can select a paragraph from a QuickMenu by clicking the right mouse button while the mouse pointer is in the left margin.)

- Press Ctrl+C to copy selected text.

- Press Ctrl+X to cut selected text.

- Press Ctrl+V to paste selected text. (As an alternative, you can copy, cut, and paste from a QuickMenu by selecting text and then clicking the right mouse button while the mouse pointer is in the text area.)

Just as you do with copying and pasting, you can paste as many copies as you want (Dingelhausen-Schneitzenbaum Furniture Prefabrication Company Dingelhausen-Schneitzenbaum Furniture Prefabrication Company).

As with copying, if you cut something new, it replaces the old stuff in the Clipboard, unless you use the Edit⇨Append command, described in the sidebar "Don't destroy your cuttings," earlier in this chapter.

Using the QuickMenu approach to Clipboarding

If you have trouble remembering Ctrl+C, Ctrl+X, and Ctrl+V or where the Copy, Cut, and Paste commands are on the Edit menu, the QuickMenu is just your cup of (instant) tea. To order from a QuickMenu, follow these steps:

1. **Select something.**

   Make sure that the mouse pointer is somewhere in the text area — not on a menu or in the margins.

2. **Click the right mouse button.**

   A QuickMenu appears.

3. **Choose Cut, Copy, or Paste from the QuickMenu.**

Chapter 5

Text Improvements

In This Chapter

▶ Deleting one character at a time: Backspace and Delete

▶ Deleting blocks of text

▶ Using Insert and Typeover modes

▶ Undoing

▶ Finding what's lost

▶ Searching for and replacing text

▶ Typing misspelled words

▶ Fixing misspelled words

▶ Checking your spelling throughout

*N*o one gets everything right the first time. We don't, anyway. After typing some text in your WordPerfect document, chances are that you'll look up at the text and see room for major improvement. The stuff at the beginning really belongs at the end, the weak jokes have to go (not that we deleted ours), and the spelling looks a bit misterious (mystereous?) in places.

Fixing up text is where word processing makes you glad that you're not typing on paper with an old-fashioned typewriter. Major revisions are easy on the screen — this chapter explains it all to you.

Deleting Text

The greatest boon to writers after the discovery of caffeine has been, arguably, correction fluid. It's therefore not surprising that the word processor's capability to do correction fluid one step better by absolutely, undetectably deleting text as though it had never been there — like really, really gone — is quite popular.

Dealing with one character at a time: Delete and Backspace

You can delete one character at a time in these two ways:

- ✔ The Delete key deletes the character *after* the cursor.
- ✔ The Backspace key usually deletes the character *before* the cursor. (Depending on how the X Window System is configured on your computer, the Backspace key may just act like the Delete key: if so, ask a Linux or X guru to change your keyboard mapping for you.)

In either case, the text closes up behind you as you go. It's surgery without scars.

Make sure that you don't have any text *selected* if you want to delete just one character at a time. (Refer to Chapter 4 for information on selecting text.) Both the Backspace and Delete keys delete whatever text is selected. Selected text is indicated by highlighting. (Actually, it's darklighting, but who's counting?)

Deleting blocks of text

The simplest way to delete a block of text is to *select* it (highlight it) with the mouse or keyboard and press the Delete or Backspace key. For the full details about selecting text, refer to Chapter 4.

Deleting secret codes

Feeling a tad paranoid? Can it be that everyone around you is, undetected by you, exchanging secret glances and signs? Just to add to your paranoia, be aware that WordPerfect is indeed using secret codes. As in your glory days in the CIA, if you lose the codes by accident, you may be in deep guacamole.

As we discuss in Chapter 9, lots of hidden, secret codes are sprinkled throughout every WordPerfect document. These codes are cryptic notes WordPerfect makes to itself to remember to, for example, "turn on boldface type here" and "turn off boldface type here."

While you're deleting text, you may also delete one or more of these secret codes. If you do, the appearance of a bunch of text then changes. Fortunately, in many cases, WordPerfect prevents you from accidentally deleting the secret codes.

If the formatting of a block of text changes while you're deleting, you probably deleted a secret code. If you catch your mistake soon enough, you may be able to undelete it with Edit➪Undo or its equivalent keyboard command, Ctrl+Z (see the section "Just (Un)Do It," later in this chapter); otherwise, just reformat it back to the way it was.

Typeovers and popovers

Sometimes, in the frenzy of typing, a flying finger mysteriously hits the Insert key and accidentally sends you into Typeover mode, which really messes things up. Or, sometimes you forget to switch back to Insert mode from Typeover mode.

If it looks as though you're typing over characters and you don't want to, follow these steps:

1. **Check out the Application Bar at the bottom of the WordPerfect window.**

   The Application Bar should tell you which mode you're in by displaying Insert or Typeover. If it doesn't and you use Typeover mode frequently, get your WordPerfect guru to add this feature to the Application Bar or see Chapter 19 to learn how to do it yourself.

2. **Undo your most recent typing by choosing Edit⇨Undo from the menu bar (or by pressing Ctrl+Z or by clicking the Undo button on the toolbar).**

   See the section "Just (Un)Do It," later in this chapter.

3. **Switch back to Insert mode by pressing the Insert key.**

   Check the Application Bar to make sure that you're in the right mode.

We recommend that you stay in Insert mode while you work in WordPerfect so that you don't delete stuff by mistake. Also, some keys (such as Tab and Backspace) work a little differently in Typeover mode — our descriptions in this book refer to the way things work in Insert mode.

If you think that you may be able to reuse the text you're deleting, you can cut it out rather than delete it and then paste it later (refer to Chapter 4).

Using Insert and Typeover modes

If you're replacing existing text, one of the simplest ways to delete the old stuff is to write over it. Normally, WordPerfect doesn't let you do that. When you type, the new text is inserted at the cursor position. This feature is called, not surprisingly, *Insert mode.*

If you want to type over your old text, however, all you have to do is press the Insert key (it's probably above the arrow keys) and you enter *Typeover mode.* Move the cursor to where you want to begin; anything you type then overwrites the old text as though it had never been there. (Old fogies can now put to rest the ghost of their typing instructors, for whom strikeovers were cardinal sins.)

A ghost of the former text does remain, however, in the form of character formatting, such as italics. If the original text included 20 characters in italics, the new text may also have 20 characters in italics. Hmm. This situation may not be what you had in mind. (See Chapter 6 to learn how to format text in italics or to get rid of this type of formatting.)

To return to Insert mode from Typeover mode, just press the Insert key again.

WordPerfect has a way to replace text without changing to Typeover mode. Just select the text you want to replace and then begin typing. WordPerfect deletes the original text and puts in your new text. For information about selecting text, refer to Chapter 4.

Just (Un)Do It

"Just doing it" is very popular nowadays, especially in sports circles. "Just undoing it" tends to be a popular topic in word processing circles. We figure that that's because we all, at some time or another, have deleted that which we should not have deleted (and probably not deleted that which we should have deleted, although that's an editorial problem).

Fortunately, WordPerfect lets you undo the deleting you just did. In fact, WordPerfect lets you undo practically anything you have done to your documents. We like that. Here's how to undo it:

1. Choose Edit➪Undo from the menu.

Poof! The last thing you did is undone.

After WordPerfect undoes your last action, it positions the cursor at the scene of the crime (at the place where the last action took place) in your document. If you change your mind and want to reverse the undo, you can choose Edit➪Redo from the menu and watch WordPerfect redo what it just undid.

If you botch things up and want to back up a few steps rather than just undo your last action, WordPerfect can help you out. Choose Edit➪Undo/Redo History from the menu bar. If you accidentally press the wrong key and you aren't sure what you did to the document, you can look in this dialog box to find out what happened and reverse the action. You get a history lesson in the form of the Undo/Redo History dialog box, as shown in Figure 5-1.

On the left, in the Undo box, you find a 1-phrase description of each of the last few things you've done. You can undo each action (starting with the action at the top of the box) by clicking on the Undo button. When you undo an action, it moves over to the Redo list on the right side of the dialog box.

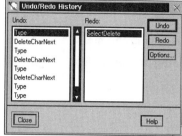

Figure 5-1:
Undoing for
those who
have over-
done it.

Note that you can undo only the top item on the Undo list. (If you have suffi-cient derring-(un)do, you can undo the top several items on the Undo list!) However, you can't select, for example, the fifth action on the Undo list and undo just that one.

Normally, WordPerfect lets you undo the last ten things you have done by using the Undo/Redo History dialog box. But heck, if you find that WordPerfect isn't remembering quite enough, you can go crazy and crank up the number of items on the Undo list all the way to 300 (the limit). To change the number of actions WordPerfect remembers, click on the Options button in the Undo/Redo History box. In the Undo/Redo Options dialog box that pops up, set the number to whatever you need. Remember, though, to keep this number as small as you can to avoid bogging down WordPerfect.

Why are we bothering to go on about all this undoing and redoing? Because it's quite useful and it beats the heck out of using correction fluid.

If you used an earlier version of WordPerfect, you're probably familiar with an Undelete command that helped you recover your overeager deletions. You're probably also used to the Undo command's being feeble. However, those industrious WordPerfect 8 programmers beefed up Undo and, as a result, got rid of Undelete.

Finding What's Lost: The Search for Sanity

If you have lost your marbles, your cool, or your sense of values, you have come to the right place. The WordPerfect Find and Replace command can help you find them. (WordPerfect can also help you replace them with something better — such as *cottage cheese* for *marbles*. You find out about replacing text later in this chapter, in the section "Finding and Replacing Text.")

In the normal scheme of things, the search for the word *sanity* requires a journey of only two, or perhaps three, steps in a WordPerfect dialog box:

1. **Choose Edit⇨Find and Replace from the menu bar or press F2.**

   The Find and Replace Text dialog box, as shown in Figure 5-2, springs to your aid.

Figure 5-2:
The Find and Replace Text dialog box.

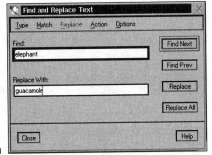

2. **Type the text you're looking for.**

   It appears in the Find box, where you can edit it (if you want) by moving the cursor around, pressing the Backspace and Delete keys, and so on.

3. **Click on Find Next (or press Enter) to search toward the end of the document.**

4. **To search toward the beginning of the document, click on Find Prev.**

If the text you're looking for exists, it appears highlighted in the document window. If the text that WordPerfect found isn't the precise instance of the text you want, just click on Find Next or Find Prev again until you get it.

If your quest is futile, WordPerfect displays a window saying that it cannot find the text. Reassure it that you're not mad by clicking on the OK button.

The Find and Replace Text dialog box stays onscreen even after you've done some finding and replacing, in case you want to do some more. The dialog box hangs around until you click its Close button.

Changing the way you search

Just when you thought that WordPerfect couldn't have any more menus, here's another one. The Find and Replace Text dialog box has its own little menu bar. If Find and Replace is working the way you want, we recommend that you pretend that the little menu bar doesn't exist. If Find and Replace is driving you crazy, look here to see whether you can get it to behave a little more to your liking.

Find and Replace has five options, which you can check out by choosing Options from the menu bar in the Find and Replace Text dialog box:

- ✔ **Begin Find at Top of Document:** Unless this option is checked, WordPerfect starts looking for what you're trying to find at the place you are in the document. Although that's usually what you want, if you want to make sure that you've found the *first* place your text appears in your document, click on Begin Find at Top of Document.

- ✔ **Wrap Text at Beg./End of Document:** It's what WordPerfect usually does: It searches starting where you are in the document and, when it gets to the end, continues searching from the beginning. That way, if what you're looking for appears *before* the place where you are in the document, you'll find it anyway. WordPerfect is even smart enough to know where it started so that after it loops around to the beginning of the document again, it stops when it finds the last occurrence of your text before the place where you started searching.

- ✔ **Limit Find Within Selection:** Often you're interested only in looking for text in a particular part of your document, such as the current paragraph. If you select the text you want to look in, you can use this option to tell WordPerfect just to look there. This option is particularly useful if you have a really long document.

- ✔ **Include Headers, Footers, etc. in Find:** Normally, WordPerfect looks through things such as headers, footers, footnotes, and other stuff that doesn't exactly appear in the body of a document when it's searching for text. (What? You don't know what headers and footers are? Take a peek at Chapter 8.) If for some reason you don't want WordPerfect to look at that stuff, you know what to do: Click on this menu item to turn off this option.

- ✔ **Limit Number of Changes:** We get back to this one when we talk about finding and replacing text, just ahead.

After you return to the document, you may want to return to where you were before you began the Find procedure. Choose the Edit⇨Go To command (or press Ctrl+G), and click on Last Position on the Position list. (This command usually works, except when WordPerfect gets a little confused.)

You can select, in your document, the text for which you want to look before you choose the Edit⇨Find and Replace command (or press F2). When you do that, the text appears automatically in the Find box as the text to search for.

Searching for sanity and finding insanity

Finding the wrong text — such as the word *insanity* when you're searching for *sanity* — is a common problem, and it's quite treatable. Your therapy is on the Find and Replace Text dialog box's menu bar; we prescribe choosing

Match⇨Whole Word. (The command otherwise assumes that you're looking for just a set of characters, even within a word.) The phrase Whole Word appears below the Find text box to remind you.

Certain things you select in the Find and Replace Text dialog box, such as Whole Word mode, are "sticky," which means that they stay "clicked" until you change them or until you close the dialog box. When you select these items from the dialog box's menu bar, you see a mark next to these commands if they're "on."

The capability to find a set of characters, even within words, is a useful feature. If you're searching a document for discussions of *reliability,* for example, you may also want to find *unreliability, reliable,* or *unreliable.* You can find any of these words by entering **reliab** (with the Whole Word option turned off) as the search text.

Getting picky about what you find

Most of the time, you don't much care what kind of *sanity* you find. Anything will do: *Sanity, SANITY, sanity, sanIty,* or *SANITY.* Obligingly, the Edit⇨Find and Replace command normally ignores the fine points, such as what's uppercase and what's lowercase.

If you're picky about which typeface, size, style, or case you want, don't give up — just put a Match to it. That is, you choose Match from the Find and Replace Text dialog box's menu bar. When you choose Match⇨Case Sensitive, Find pays attention to the uppercase or lowercase letters you type in the Find box and finds only versions of your text that have been identically typed. WordPerfect reminds you about this feature by displaying Case Sensitive below the Find text box.

When you choose Match⇨Font, WordPerfect displays the Match Font dialog box, which enables you to look for *sanity* in Helvetica, **boldly,** if you want. Check off what you want by pointing and clicking. Click on OK when you finish.

If you're among the WordPerfect secret-code cognoscenti, be aware that you can also find codes. You can look for specific codes, such as Lft Mar and Bot Mar, by choosing Match⇨Codes from the menu in the Find and Replace Text dialog box. If you would rather type a specific code, choose Type⇨ Specific Codes from the menu bar in the Find and Replace Text dialog box.

Getting fancy about what you find

Sometimes you just don't know exactly what you're looking for. For example, you may be looking for *Doctor Livingstone.* Or was it Doctor Livingstein? Livingston? Livingstern? Many programs wouldn't be much help in this kind of situation. WordPerfect goes with you into the untamed wilderness of your text, however, to find the good Doctor What's-His-Name. You must, however, arm yourself with certain weapons, called *wildcard codes,* before you venture into the wild. You can include these special codes in the text you type in the Find box.

Be warned: These codes are not for the timid. They're very useful, however, even for novices. We give you the quick rundown and then let you go exploring:

✔ **[? (One Char)]:** As its name implies, matches any single character. So, Livingst[? (One Char)]n matches Livingston and Livingsten, and Livingst[? (One Char)][? (One Char)]n finds

Livingst*ei*n and Livingst*em* but not Livingst*on* (too few characters; you told WordPerfect to look for exactly two characters between *t* and *n*).

✔ **[* (Many Char)]:** You're clever and guessed that this code matches any number of characters up to the end of a word. For example, Livingst[* (Many Char)] finds the good doctor no matter how he spells his last name.

One last detail: You can't type [? (One Char)] or [* (Many Char)] and have WordPerfect search for one or many characters. No, you have to choose Match⇨Codes from the Find and Replace Text dialog box menu bar. You're presented with a whole new dialog box full of every code you could possibly imagine. Among them are the two we talk about here. Hunt them down on the list in the dialog box and click the Insert button to put them in the Find box.

Finding and Replacing Text

If your forthcoming bestseller *The Search for Sanity* just isn't working out, don't go crazy. Just replace *sanity* with *chocolate,* for example, and see how it all hangs together. To accomplish this literary feat, use the same Edit⇨Find and Replace command (known to its friends as F2) you use to find text. Now you get to explore the further reaches of the dialog box shown back in Figure 5-2: the Replace With box and the Replace and Replace All buttons. In the normal scheme of things, replacing *sanity* with *chocolate* is simple. Follow these steps:

1. **Choose Edit⇨Find and Replace from the menu bar (or press F2).**

2. **Type in the Find box the text you want WordPerfect to find and replace (sanity, for example).**

   If you select *sanity* in your document before issuing the command, the word appears automatically in the Find text box.

3. **Click on the Replace With box and type the replacement word or phrase** (chocolate, **for example**).

4. **Click on either Find Next or Find Prev.**

   WordPerfect goes in search of your search text (*sanity,* for example). If it finds *sanity,* WordPerfect highlights it; if WordPerfect doesn't find it, the program tells you so.

5. **If your text has been found, you can click on Replace to replace it.**

   The ever-eager Replace goes in search of any additional instances of your search text.

6. **If the text hasn't been found, search in the other direction; click on Find Prev rather than Find Next.**

   As before, you can search the entire document by choosing Wrap at Beg./End of Document or Begin Find at Top of Document from the Options menu.

This list shows some general tips for replacing text:

✔ The commands on the Type, Match, and Options menus work the same way as they do for finding text.

✔ When you type something in the Replace With box, the Replace command appears on the Find and Replace dialog box's menu bar. (Until now, it has been a barely visible pale gray.) The Replace⇨Case Sensitive and Replace⇨Font commands get picky about replacement text — for example, if you want to replace *sanity* with *chocolate* in Helvetica (not to be confused with chocolate in Helvetia, which is also very good).

✔ To replace every instance of the Find text in your document, click on Replace All rather than Replace. Be careful, though: You can do a great deal of damage very quickly this way. For example, unless you turn on Whole Word mode (from the Match menu), you can end up replacing not only *sanity* with *chocolate* but also *insanity* with *inchocolate,* which isn't nearly as nice a situation as it sounds.

✔ To delete every instance of a word or phrase in an entire document, click in the Find box and type a space followed by the text you want to delete; then put nothing (not even a space) in the Replace With text box. Typing the space before the text to delete ensures that you don't end up with two spaces where the deleted word used to be.

✔ To replace only a limited number of instances of your Find text, choose Options⇨Limit Number of Changes from the dialog box's menu bar. This option is particularly useful when you're working in a long document and you expect Replace All to make only a few changes. Enter a number that's not much larger than the number of changes you're expecting to make. That way, if Replace All has decided to replace every *to* in your document with *too,* you can catch it before it destroys your document.

Fun facts about finding

The quickest way to find or replace text is to press F2.

You can leave the Find and Replace Text dialog box displayed while you work on a document, which can be helpful if you do a great deal of editing.

If you're looking for whole words, turn on the Match⇨Whole Word option. Otherwise, you find *insanity* while searching for *sanity* (and maybe replace it, too!).

WordPerfect searches in only one direction from the cursor. To search the entire document, either search both ways manually or turn on either Begin Find at Top of Document or Wrap at Beg./End of Document from the Options menu.

You can limit your search to a selected block of text in a document, although you should make the selection *after* the Find and Replace Text dialog box is onscreen. Text selected beforehand is automatically assumed to be the Find text.

Finding and Replacing Codes

If you really, really want to find and replace codes, that's okay — you don't fit *our* definition of a dummy, however! Because you're so smart, we just say that you can find the codes you want in the same way as you find the wildcard codes: by choosing Match⇨Codes from the Find and Replace dialog box's menu bar. 'Nuff said. For more information, see Chapter 9.

Typing Misspelled Words

You can't.

Well, the folks at WordPerfect haven't taken it quite that far yet — they're getting there, though. As you type along, you may notice that a couple of different things are going on, besides having words appear onscreen. Some words have a dotted red underline. Some words have a dotted blue underline. (If you see *green* underlines, you've been staring at the screen for too long; go take a chocolate break!) And, if you can type while you're looking at the screen rather than looking at your fingers, you'll find that WordPerfect even changes some words as you type. We look at each of these things in turn.

"I see red under my words"

As you do your work, WordPerfect looks over your shoulder and feels compelled to point out words it cannot find in its dictionary. It does that by underlining those words with a red dotted line. Thoughtfully, WordPerfect usually has a suggestion about what you may mean instead of what you typed.

To find out what WordPerfect thinks you should have typed, right-click on the underlined word. WordPerfect displays a list of suggested words, along with a few other options. You can add this word to your dictionary, skip it in this document, or open the full-fledged spell checker, which we talk about in a minute.

If the word you want is on the list, you're in luck: Just click on it, and WordPerfect automagically replaces what you typed with the correct word. If the word isn't on the list, you have another choice. You can tell WordPerfect that what you typed really *is* a word and should be considered to be one from now on. We use this feature for words and names (like our own names!) that we type frequently and are tired of having WordPerfect warn us about.

If the word you typed really isn't a word but you'll be using it often in this document anyway, you may want to tell WordPerfect to ignore it. For example, you may want WordPerfect to ignore product names, company names, and town names you're using in just one document. You may get tired of seeing *SoVerNet* (the Sovereign Vermont Internet provider) underlined as you write your review of rural Internet service companies. On the other hand, when you're done with this study, you'll probably never write about those companies again. If so, add *SoVerNet* to the word list for this document by clicking on the Skip in Document menu option when you right-click on *SoVerNet*.

You may see other words underlined as well, usually when two of them are in a row. Every once in a while, you're forced to write something awkward, such as "I had had a thought that that might be a good good idea." WordPerfect would really rather that you not do this, and it tells you so by underlining the repeated words. There's not much you can do about that situation, other than tell WordPerfect to stop looking over your shoulder. (See the "Stop looking over my shoulder!" sidebar, later in this chapter.)

"I see blue under my words"

Ever keeping your best interests at heart, WordPerfect is happy to point out words you *may* have typed but may not have *meant* to type. Words commonly used incorrectly (like *hear* and *here* or *their, there,* and *they're*) frequently qualify for the blue underline. Just as you do for a spelling error, right-click on the underlined word and WordPerfect tells you what kind of error it suspects you may have made and gives you a list of possible corrections.

We've never found this feature to be of much use, although if you want to explore it further, look in the section "Flying the Spell Checker Yourself," just ahead. It talks about the Grammar Checker as well because they're part of the same thing.

"I see my words change even as I type them!"

Welcome to the magic world of QuickCorrect. Actually, it's another terrific feature that *...For Dummies* readers love: You don't have to know anything about it, and it usually does just what you want. As your high-school typing teacher could tell you in an instant, most typing mistakes fall into a few general categories: reversing two letters, putting the space *after* the first letter of a word rather than before, capitalization errors, and dumb spelling errors we wouldn't make if we weren't typing so fast.

The folks at WordPerfect figured that if these are such simple common errors, why not have WordPerfect fix them for you? That's exactly what QuickCorrect does. For example, try to type *teh* as a word in a WordPerfect document. No matter how hard you try, WordPerfect changes it to *the*. WordPerfect figures (correctly, we suspect) that you meant to type *the*. If for some reason you did want to type *teh*, you have to get kind of clever.

To keep WordPerfect from QuickCorrecting something, add an extra letter to the end so that WordPerfect doesn't recognize it. In this case, how about *tehh?* Then type a space after it to tell WordPerfect that you're done with this word. Now you can go back and get rid of the extra *h*. Totally clumsy? Yes, it is; there's a better way.

If you find that you want to stop WordPerfect from correcting a misspelling or if you want to add your own common misspellings to the QuickCorrect list, you need to take a look at the QuickCorrect dialog box. Choose the Tools⇨ QuickCorrect command. You see the QuickCorrect dialog box, as shown in Figure 5-3. What's going on there is quite simple: You type the stuff in the left column, and WordPerfect replaces it with the stuff in the right column.

So you want to change, delete, or change an entry on the list of WordPerfect QuickCorrections? No problem:

1. **Scroll down until you see in the left column the word WordPerfect is correcting automatically and in the right column the word that's showing up onscreen.**

   You can do that either by using the scroll bar on the right side of the dialog box or by clicking in the Replace column and pressing the Page Down key on the keyboard.

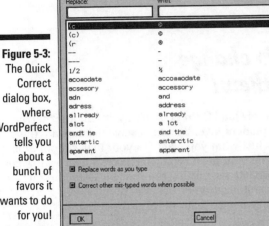

Figure 5-3:
The Quick
Correct
dialog box,
where
WordPerfect
tells you
about a
bunch of
favors it
wants to do
for you!

2. **Click on the word in the left column.**

   What happens next depends on what you want to change about
   QuickCorrect.

3. **If you don't want WordPerfect to correct this misspelling automatically, click the Delete Entry button.**

   WordPerfect asks whether you're sure that you want to delete this entry:
   Click on Yes if you're sure.

4. **If you want to add a new set of misspelled and corrected words, click
   in the Replace box and replace with another misspelled word the
   word that appears there.** For example, we have the odd habit of typing
   informatino rather than *information*. Type **informatino**, or the misspelled
   word of your choice, in the Replace box.

5. **In the With box, replace what's there with the correct spelling of the
   word.**

   In our example, type **information.**

6. **Click on the Add Entry button.**

   The pair of words (wrong and right) appears on the QuickCorrect list.

7. **When you're finished with the QuickCorrect list, click on OK.**

We particularly like a couple of useful QuickCorrect entries, like (R), which
turns into ®, (c), which turns into ©, and 1/2, which turns into ½.

Stop looking over my shoulder!

You can stop WordPerfect from looking over your shoulder and correcting your spelling and your grammar. Just choose Tools⇨Proofread from the menu bar. The menu that appears gives you four options: Off turns off spelling and grammar as you type, Spell-As-You-Go just looks at your spelling, Grammar-As-You-Go checks both your spelling and your grammar, and Prompt-As-You-Go suggests replacements for misspelled words as you type. We think that the WordPerfect Spell-As-You-Go feature is terrific because it does what it does and you don't have to worry about it much.

Beware! You may decide that your file is all ready to print just because it doesn't have any dotted red underlines in it. We wish that we could tell you that we've never cent files to the printer with there wrong words in them, but as you can probably sell from his sentence, WordPerfect can't tell whether you used the *write* word in your document — only whether the words you did use are spelled correctly. (WordPerfect does have a feature that purports to do this, in the form of the Grammatik grammar checker, although we've never found it to be very useful; it found *none* of the word errors in the preceding sentence, for example.)

Flying the Spell Checker Yourself

The WordPerfect Spell-As-You-Go feature is kind of like flying the spell checker on autopilot: It looks around your document while you're doing something else and finds misspelled words. You can, if you want, fly the spell checker by hand. Take a reality check here, however. Although one of the great joys of word processing is that you no longer really have to be able to spell, you shouldn't get too excited. WordPerfect doesn't know how to spell either. What WordPerfect *does* know how to do is check a word against a list to see whether it's there.

Spell checking your entire document

To check the spelling of words in your entire document, follow these steps:

1. **Display the Spell Checker tool.**

   Any of the following actions activates the Spell Checker dialog box:

   - Choose Tools⇨Spell Check from the main menu bar.

   - Press Ctrl+F1 (this method may not work, depending on how your keyboard is configured).

- Click on the open-book button on the toolbar.

- Click the right mouse button with the cursor located anywhere in the text area of your document; then click on Spell Check on the QuickMenu that appears.

The Spell Checker dialog box, as shown in Figure 5-4, pops up, and the spelling check begins.

Figure 5-4: The Spell Checker dialog box complains about a word in the Gettysburg Address.

It doesn't matter where you're working in the document — the spell checker checks the whole thing, from top to bottom. You can change this arrangement by changing the selection in the Check section of the Spell Checker dialog box; choose To End of Document if you want to check starting from where you are now. If (when?) the spell checker finds a word that's not in its dictionary, it assumes that the word is spelled wrong. The spell checker then highlights the word in your document and displays it in the Not found box in the Spell Checker dialog box (refer to Figure 5-4).

When the spell checker cannot find a word in its dictionary, it helpfully lists in the Suggestions box a variety of suggestions for replacement. In Figure 5-4, none of these suggestions has the same meaning as the original word. (If WordPerfect suggested *eighty* in place of *fourscore,* we'd be impressed!)

This sort of thing happens often: You use a word, person's name, or company name that WordPerfect has never heard of and WordPerfect flags it as misspelled. When that happens, just skip the word, as described in Step 2.

2. Skip or replace the highlighted word in your document.

If the highlighted word is okay, as in the example, you have two options (or three, if you count adding the word to the dictionary, which is covered in the next section):

- Click on the Skip Once button. This action means "Don't worry about it — get on with the spell checking!"

- Click on Skip Always. This action means the same thing, and it adds "And don't bother me again about this word!" (until the next time you use the spell checker).

If you believe that the highlighted word is indeed misspelled, you have three options:

- If you know the correct spelling, just double-click on the Replace With box, type the correct word, and click on the Replace button.

- If the spell checker displays the correct spelling in the Replace With box, click on Replace.

- If you're not sure of the correct spelling, scroll through the Suggestions box. If you find the correct spelling, double-click on it.

3. Repeat the preceding steps for every misspelled word.

WordPerfect continues until every word has been checked. When the spell check is complete, WordPerfect tells you so and asks whether you want to close the spell checker. Click on Yes, and the spell checker closes. If you click on No, you can leave the Spell Checker dialog box onscreen while you work on your document as usual. If it's in the way, you can drag it around just as you would any other window (refer to Chapter 2). You can always click on Close to get rid of the window.

Dealing with real words that WordPerfect doesn't know

Perhaps the WordPerfect spell checker can be forgiven for not knowing uncommon names, such as *Margy*. It's still annoying, though, to have to repeatedly skip names and other real words that are unknown to the WordPerfect dictionary. The solution is to add these words to the spell checker's dictionary so that it skips them every time you use the spell checker.

WordPerfect has many dictionaries. It checks at least the following two dictionaries whenever you run the spell checker:

✔ A main dictionary of official, genuine English (or other-language) words

✔ A supplementary dictionary of anything else you consider to be a word

The spell checker can also check additional supplementary dictionaries, such as document dictionaries and special-purpose, or *topical*, dictionaries.

Document dictionaries are specific to each individual document. A short story may have a document dictionary that contains the names of the characters in the story, for example. Perhaps a character doesn't appear in subsequent stories because of a gruesome death by editing. Therefore, you want WordPerfect to consider the name to be okay in this document; if the name appears in any other document, however, it should be flagged.

You also can create optional special dictionaries. You may write about several topics, for example, each with its own particular jargon. Although the word *e-mail,* for example, may be intentional when you're writing for programmers, it probably would be a typo if you were writing for gardeners.

Keep things simple — just add words to the basic dictionary. To add words to the dictionary, start the spell checker as you normally do. (What? You forgot how already? Refer to the preceding section for details.)

Making and unmaking mistakes in the supplemental dictionary

It's easy to go tripping merrily through your document, clicking on Add for every word the spell checker flags. Such glibness eventually causes you to add a word such as *klockwurst* to the dictionary. (The word was supposed to have been *knockwurst;* you typed it just before quitting time, however, and you were looking at the clock.) Because *klockwurst* is considered to be a genuine word, the spell checker ignores any subsequent *klockwursts.*

To correct this situation, you must go deeper into the labyrinthine depths of the spell checker than a novice normally goes. Walk this way, please:

1. **Choose Tools⇨Spell Check to display the Spell Checker tool.**

2. **In the Spell Checker dialog box, choose Dictionaries⇨Supplementary.**

   You see the Supplementary Dictionaries dialog box.

3. **In the Dictionaries in Search Order box, click on the supplementary dictionary you want to edit.**

Usually, you see Document Dictionary (the list you've been creating) and rootxus.dup (the list that comes with WordPerfect).

4. **When you have the dictionary selected, click the Edit button.**

   You see the Edit dialog box for the dictionary.

5. **In the Key Words column, scroll down the word list until you see klockwurst (or whatever your mistake was); then click on the Delete Entry button.**

   The word is gone, gone, gone.

6. **Find your way back to the Spell Checker tool by clicking on Close buttons.**

Spell checking isn't magic, although the name probably sounds promising if you're a wizard!

When the spell checker highlights a word you consider to be okay, click on the Add button in the Spell Checker tool. This step adds the word to the dictionary; as far as the spell checker is concerned, the word is a real word now. The spell checker never brings it up again and sincerely regrets having brought it up in the first place.

Spell-checking tips

To check less than an entire document, choose Check from the menu bar in the Spell Checker dialog box; then choose Word, Sentence, Paragraph, Page, To End of Document, or Selected Text. You can also check a specified number of pages from the current insertion point by choosing Number of Pages. Whatever option you check remains selected until you put the spell checker away again.

The spell checker not only checks spelling but also points out common problems, such as duplicated words, words that contain numbers, and strange capitalization. You can turn off these features if they get in your way. Just choose Options from the menu bar in the Spell Checker dialog box to see a list of what's turned on or off. Click on a feature to change its on-or-off status.

Dealing with Grammy Grammatik

If you start the spell checker from the Tools menu, you probably notice two other options: Grammatik and Thesaurus. This section talks about Grammatik a bit, and the next section discusses the Thesaurus.

As we mention in the "Stop looking over my shoulder!" sidebar, earlier in this chapter, we're not too thrilled by the Grammatik grammar checker (or any other grammar checker, for that matter). We write frequently, though, and we have opinions about what we write. Still, you may want to explore Grammatik.

The checking itself works the same way as spell checking: It starts at the beginning of a document and gives you the option to skip suggestions you don't want to see in the future. To start, choose Tools⇨Grammatik to display the Grammatik dialog box. Grammatik shows you the word it doesn't like and an explanation of what's wrong with it and then gives suggestions for improving your text.

If you really want to poke around and figure out what Grammatik thinks that it's doing, you can choose Options⇨Writing Style from the Grammatik menu bar. You see the Writing Style dialog box with a list of all the collections of rules Grammatik uses to analyze your writing. Edit one of those rules and you see the guts of Grammatik revealed.

Taming the roar of the mighty thesaurus

To see the Thesaurus, choose Tools⇨Thesaurus from the WordPerfect menu bar. The Thesaurus is actually a useful feature if you like to spice up your writing with a variety of words. The Thesaurus dialog box gives you a list of words synonymous with the word you have selected. To have the thesaurus eat your words, do the following:

1. **Double-click on the word in your document to highlight it.**

   For that matter, you can highlight it in any one of a dozen other ways — refer to Chapter 4 for the gory details.

2. **Click on Look Up in the Thesaurus dialog box.**

   A list of possible replacement words appears below the original word in the Thesaurus dialog box.

3. **To look at synonyms of any word the Thesaurus suggests, double-click the word.**

   When you double-click on the suggestion, WordPerfect looks up the word and *its* synonyms appear in the next column in the Thesaurus dialog box.

4. **To use one of the Thesaurus suggestions, click on the word and click on Replace.**

   Clicking Replace inserts that word in your document.

Part II
Prettying Up Your Text

Determined to help Wanda locate her lost WordPerfect documents, Al connects his Royco 100 Fish Finder to her hard disk.

In this part . . .

So far, so good. If you're comfortable with the techniques we discuss in Part I (or if you skipped over them), you can make documents, edit them, save them, spell-check them, and print them. More or less.

But, how do they look? Stand back a little and ask yourself, "Am I getting my money's worth from this program? Do these documents look like a million bucks (or at least as much as I paid for my computer and this book)?"

If your answer is No, this part of the book is for you. We talk about how to jazz up, tighten up, and spruce up your documents, including how to use different typefaces, control margins, set the spacing between paragraphs, and all that good stuff. After all, you don't want your carefully worded documents to come out looking as though you typed them on your old Selectric!

Chapter 6

Charming Characters

. . . .

In This Chapter

▶ Making text boldface

▶ Using italics

▶ Underlining text

▶ Making text bigger or smaller

▶ Using different fonts

▶ Getting text back to normal

▶ Copying character formatting

▶ Changing capitalization

. . . .

*W*ordPerfect enables you to control the way individual characters look —
not where they are on the page but rather their size and shape. By
"characters," we mean the letters, numbers, and punctuation that make up
your text. (We aren't talking about people like the strange guy next door who
has 47 cats and sings opera while gardening.) In addition to using underlining,
boldface, and italics to add emphasis to text, you can choose different typefaces and type sizes. In fact, the range of choices can be overwhelming.

The good news about WordPerfect is that you can see all these special effects
directly onscreen. Unlike old-fashioned word processors, newer versions of
WordPerfect draw each character and can draw them in all their formatted
splendor.

The bad news is that it's easy to get carried away with character formatting.
Nothing is more amateurish, or harder to read, than a letter or memo that
uses five typefaces on one page — readers spend all their **time** *shading* their
eyes from the ***glare*** of all that SNAZZY formatting and don't have time to
<u>absorb</u> the import of the text. Watch out when you're formatting text. Use a
little restraint, people!

Emphasizing Text with Boldface, Italics, and Underlining

We start with the easiest way to add emphasis to text. **Boldface,** *italics,* and underlining are three methods of making a word or phrase stand out and make itself known. All you have to do is follow these steps to add boldface, underlining, or italics to your text (not all three at the same time, please!):

1. **Select the text you want to emphasize.**

   Chapter 4 shows you ways to select text.

2. **Click on the Bold, Italic, or Underline button on the Property Bar.**

   If you haven't guessed, these buttons have the bold **B**, italic *I,* and underlined U on them. Alternatively, press Ctrl+B for bold, Ctrl+I for italics, or Ctrl+U for underlining. (Hey, even we can remember *these* key combinations!)

   WordPerfect displays the selected text in the font style you chose. Done!

When you use these text styles, WordPerfect inserts secret formatting codes before and after the formatted text. The first code turns the formatting on, and the second code turns it off. The names of these secret codes are `Bold`, `Italc`, and `Und`. (Like we always say, why make these code names readable when you can make them cryptic and hard to spell?) To find out how to see, move, or delete these secret formatting codes, see Chapter 9.

Formatting as you type

You can also add text styles to text as you type it. If you're about to type a word you want to emphasize, follow these steps:

1. **Click on the Bold, Italic, or Underline button on the Property Bar or press Ctrl+B, Ctrl+I, or Ctrl+U.**

   This step turns the formatting on so that whatever you type is formatted this way.

2. **Type the text you want to emphasize.**

   It appears with the formatting you choose.

3. **Turn off the formatting by clicking on the same button or pressing the same key combination you used in Step 1.**

You can tell when one of these formats is turned on by looking at the Bold, Italic, and Underline buttons on the Property Bar. If the buttons appear to be pressed in, the format is on wherever the cursor is or on whatever text is selected.

Is this part formatted?

What happens if you select a bunch of text and some of the text is already formatted? Suppose that you select a sentence that contains one italicized word. When you select the sentence, the Italic button does *not* appear to be pressed in because the whole selection (sentence) isn't in italics. If you click on the Italic button while the sentence is selected, WordPerfect italicizes the entire sentence; if you click on the button again, WordPerfect unitalicizes the entire sentence.

Yikes! Getting rid of formatting

If you have gone a little overboard with formatting, WordPerfect can turn it off again. Follow these steps:

1. **Select the text you want to unformat.**

2. **Look at the Property Bar.**

   If all the text you selected is formatted, the relevant text-style button looks as though it's pressed in. For example, if all the text you selected is bold, the Bold button looks as though it's pressed in.

3. **Click on the pressed button.**

   This step releases the button so that it isn't pressed in anymore, and the formatting should disappear. If one click doesn't do the trick, click on the button again.

Here's an alternative to Step 3: Press the equivalent key combination (Ctrl+B, Ctrl+I, or Ctrl+U) to remove the formatting for the selected text.

You can use more than one type of formatting at the same time. You can make text both **bold and italic,** for example. Just click on both the Bold and Italics buttons (one at a time, please) on the Property Bar or press Ctrl+B and then Ctrl+I; ditto to turn the formatting off.

When you format characters, WordPerfect inserts secret codes into your document to tell it where to turn the formatting on and off. If you have trouble removing formatting or getting WordPerfect to format the right text, see Chapter 9 to find out how to see and delete these secret codes.

Making Text Larger or Smaller

Sometimes, you want to make your text big, big, big. For a headline or the title of a report, you may want to make a nice, big, centered title. We discuss centering in Chapter 7; for now, these steps show you how to make text big:

1. **Select the text for which you want to change the size.**

   You usually select an entire line when you change font size because a line with letters of different sizes usually looks strange.

2. **Click on the Font Size button on the Property Bar.**

   It's the button that says something like 12, for 12-point type. A little menu of font sizes drops down from the button, showing the available sizes. (We talk about fonts in the next section.)

3. **Pick a size by clicking on it.**

You can also set text back to its original size. Select it again, click on the Font Size button again, and select the same size you used for the surrounding text.

What size is the text you're already using? The leftmost items on the Property Bar show the font and font size.

Depending on which font you're using, text looks larger or smaller. For example, 10-point Helve-WP (Helvetica) looks much larger than 10-point Roman-WP looks. Luckily, you can see how things look onscreen and make adjustments as necessary.

Only rare situations call for type that's smaller than 7 points high. The size of onscreen type doesn't necessarily reflect the size it will be on paper, so try printing your document before settling on type sizes. Have pity on us aging readers and don't make your type too small.

If you plan to fax your document, make the text a little larger than usual — maybe 12 points. Faxes always look grainy, so they're much more readable if the type is large.

What are these sizes measured in?

Text sizes are measured in *points,* which is an old-fashioned term that predates not only word processors and computers but also typewriters. Most normal text is either 10 or 12 points high. There are 72 points to an inch, so 12-point text is ⅙-inch high (¹²⁄₇₂). If you're formatting a title, make it 14 or 18 points.

Don't ask us why they're called points; *Encyclopedia Britannica* probably knows.

When you change the font size of some text, WordPerfect inserts secret codes, named (amazingly enough) Font Size.

Fonts of Wisdom

Okay, okay — bad pun. We won't let it happen again. Anyway, it's time to talk about the heart of character formatting: the font, which is a fancy word that means something like *typeface*. (Or is it the other way around?) A *typeface* is a set of shapes for letters, numbers, and punctuation. A *font* is a typeface in a particular size and may also be in boldface and italics. The text you're reading now, for example, is printed in the Cheltenham typeface. The section headings are printed in the Cascade typeface.

When WordPerfect starts up, it usually displays and prints everything in a fairly nice-looking 12-point size typeface named something like Courier-WP.

Changing the font for some text

To change the font in which some text appears, follow these steps:

1. **Select the text for which you want to change the font.**

2. **Click on the little downward-pointing triangle beside the current font name (usually Courier-WP) on the Property Bar.**

   WordPerfect refers to this thing as the Font Face button because it shows the typeface of the font you're using. A list of available fonts appears to the left of the button. As you move the cursor over this list of font names, a sample of the font appears just to the right of the list.

3. **Choose a font from the list.**

   Poof — the selected text changes to the new font. Although the Property Bar may not show it immediately, if you move the cursor to the section of text you just formatted, the Property Bar shows the font and font size in which that text is displayed.

When you change the font for some text, WordPerfect inserts two secret formatting codes, one at the beginning and the other at the end of the text you formatted. The first code changes the font; the second one changes it back. It's all very logical. Even the name of the code is logical: Font.

Not just another pretty face

You can use lots of fonts with WordPerfect. Some fonts have little doohickeys *(serifs)* at the ends of the lines that make up the letters; look at the tops of the capital letters. These fonts are named, not surprisingly, *serif* fonts. Other fonts don't have these little lines and are *sans serif* fonts. (It makes perfect sense in French.) In some fonts, all letters are the same width *(fixed-space* fonts); in others, such as the one you're reading, some letters are wider than others (they're *proportionally spaced* fonts).

The fonts that come with X and the Linux version of WordPerfect aren't the same as the fonts you usually see on Windows and Macs, although many are similar. The most popular fonts for PCs are Times Roman, a serif font that looks like an uglier version of the body text in this book; Helvetica, a modern-looking sans serif font; and Courier, which looks like the type on an old-fashioned typewriter. Because some font names are trademarks, however, your versions of these fonts may have other names. Times Roman may be named Roman-WP, for example, and Helvetica may be named Helve-WP or Arial.

If you repeatedly use a small number of font and size combinations, you can try the QuickFonts button on the Property Bar. The button has a fancy-looking (almost unrecognizable) blue *F* with a yellow lightning bolt beside it. This feature lists the last ten or so fonts you've picked from the Font Face list on the Property Bar. On the other hand, if you often use the same font and size combinations, you should consider using styles too; read Chapter 10.

Changing the font for the rest of the document

If you want to change fonts part of the way through a document, you can tell WordPerfect that from this point forward another font should appear. Follow these steps:

1. **Move the cursor to the location at which you want to use a new font.**

   If you want all the pages starting with page 2 to use a different font, for example, move the cursor to the top of page 2.

2. **Click on the Font Face button on the Property Bar.**

   A list of available fonts drops down from the button.

3. **Choose a font from the list.**

   The font name on the Property Bar changes to the new font, and the text that comes after the cursor changes to the new font. You can do the same trick with the Font Size button. It's just beside the Font Face button and usually shows the number 12.

Choosing a font from the Font Face list may not change the font for the entire remaining part of the document. Your action inserts a secret code that tells WordPerfect to change the font at this point, and this change stays in effect until the next secret font-change code, if another one is in the document. (See Chapter 9 to discover how to find and eliminate any secret formatting codes you don't want.)

You can use the same method to select a font at the beginning of the document by moving the cursor to the top of the document and then clicking on the Font Face button. A better way exists, however, as described in the next section.

The Master Control Panel for Character Formats

The first half of this chapter describes three facets of character formatting: text styles (boldface, italics, and underlining), font sizes, and fonts. Wouldn't it be nice to see and change them in one unified display — a place in which you can set all three types of formatting at one time?

Done. We have said the magic word. Such a thing exists: the Font dialog box, as shown in Figure 6-1. To display it, choose Format⇨Font from the menu bar or press F9.

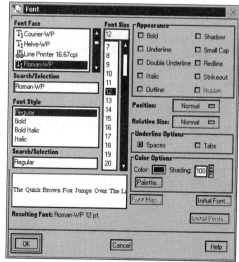

Figure 6-1: One simple dialog box shows all your character formatting.

Another way to display this dialog box is to position the mouse pointer anywhere in your text, click the right mouse button to display a QuickMenu, and then choose _F_ont from it.

Using the options in the Font dialog box

This big, scary-looking dialog box contains all the character formatting you could want. You can use the Font dialog box to format text you've already typed or to instruct WordPerfect to format the text you're about to type.

To select character formatting for text you haven't yet typed, position the cursor wherever in your document you want to start typing, display the Font dialog box and choose the formatting you want, and then click on OK. WordPerfect inserts at the cursor position some secret formatting codes that affect the text following the codes. When you start typing, the text appears in the format you selected.

If you want to format text you've already typed in your document, choose one of these methods to select what you want to format:

- ✔ To format a block of text, first select the text and then use the Font dialog box to format the selected text. WordPerfect inserts two secret formatting codes: one at the beginning of the block of text, to turn formatting on; and the other at the end of the block of text, to return formatting to normal.

- ✔ To format the rest of the text in the document, position the cursor at the point where you want the font to change and then use the Font dialog box. WordPerfect inserts just one secret code to turn the formatting on at the cursor location.

In the lower-left part of the Font dialog box, a box contains some text, usually the name and size of the font you're using. As you choose character formats in the dialog box, WordPerfect formats this text accordingly so that you can see how your text will look.

To change the typeface, choose one from the Font Face list, which is the same list of typefaces you see when you click on the Font Face button on the Property Bar.

To set the font size (in points), choose a size from the Font Size list, which is the same list of sizes you see when you click on the Font Size button on the Property Bar.

If you want boldfaced, italicized, or underlined characters, look in the Appearance section of the dialog box and click on the Bold, Underline, or Italic options there so that the boxes are filled in for the options you want.

The Appearance section of the dialog box lists some other groovy formatting, too, including Double Underline, Outline, Shadow, Small Cap, Redline, Strikeout, and Hidden; see Table 6-1 for samples of all these styles. (The table doesn't show hidden text because hidden text is invisible when it's printed.)

Table 6-1	Font Styles and Examples
Character Format	*Sample Text*
Bold	This **coffee** tastes like sludge!
Underline	This <u>coffee</u> tastes like sludge!
Double Underline	This <u>coffee</u> tastes like sludge!
Italic	This *coffee* tastes like sludge!
Outline	This coffee tastes like sludge!
Shadow	This coffee tastes like sludge!
Small Cap	This COFFEE tastes like sludge!
Redline	This coffee tastes like sludge!
Strikeout	This ~~coffee~~ tastes like sludge!

Scientific types who want to create a subscript or superscript should click in the Position box, which usually says Normal. WordPerfect displays a small pop-up list of choices: Superscript, Normal, and Subscript. Click on your choice.

If you're underlining words and you have strong opinions about underlining spaces and tabs, you can tell WordPerfect about them by clicking in the Underline Options box.

After you select just the right formatting, click on OK or press Enter to close the Font dialog box. If you selected text before opening the Font dialog box, the selected text is formatted; otherwise, the formatting starts at the current cursor position.

If you want to forget the whole thing, click on Cancel or press Esc to escape from the Font dialog box with your text unscathed.

When you use the Font dialog box, WordPerfect sticks the appropriate secret formatting codes into your document. To get rid of them, you may have to read Chapter 9.

Formatting an entire document

What if you want to tell WordPerfect which font to use for an entire document, from soup to nuts? Every document has a *document default font,* which is the font WordPerfect uses for all text except where you specifically tell it otherwise. WordPerfect uses this font for not only the regular text in the document but also page headers and footers (described in Chapter 8) and footnotes.

To set the document default font, you use the Document Default Font dialog box. It doesn't matter where the cursor is when you perform this little operation; make sure, however, that no text is selected. Then follow these steps:

1. **Choose Format➪Font from the menu bar or press F9 to display the Font dialog box, as shown in Figure 6-1.**

2. **Click on the Initial Font button.**

   WordPerfect displays the Document Default Font dialog box, as shown in Figure 6-2. In case you're wondering, you can also display this dialog box by choosing File➪Document➪Default Font from the menu bar.

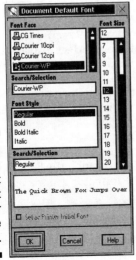

Figure 6-2: Telling WordPerfect which font to use for an entire document.

3. **Select the Font Face, Font Size, and Font Style.**

   The settings in this dialog box look and act like the ones in the Font dialog box.

4. **Click on OK or press Enter to close the dialog box.**

   WordPerfect changes the font for all the text in the document, except where you formatted a section of text by using the Font dialog box or the Font Face, Font Size, Bold, Italic, or Underline buttons on the Property Bar.

Copying Character Formatting

After you have formatted some text the way you want it, you can tell WordPerfect to format some other text the same way. (Very useful!) WordPerfect calls this feature *QuickFormat.* These steps show how to use it:

1. **Move the cursor into the middle of some text that's nicely formatted.**

2. **To turn QuickFormat on, choose the Format➪QuickFormat command.**

   Alternatively, your toolbar may include a button named QuickFormat (with a picture of a paint roller and a lightning bolt). If so, click on it. Another way to turn QuickFormat on is to use a QuickMenu. (This discussion is getting a little too Quick for us.) With the mouse pointer pointing to your text, click the right mouse button to display a QuickMenu; then choose QuickFormat from it.

   You see the QuickFormat dialog box, as shown in Figure 6-3.

Figure 6-3:
How do
you want
WordPerfect
to copy your
formatting?

3. **Choose which types of formatting you want to copy: Fonts and Attributes, Paragraph Styles, or Both; then click on OK.**

   The mouse pointer turns into the strangest-looking gizmo we have ever seen: a little paint roller with an I-beam insertion point next to it. We guess that WordPerfect wants to suggest that it will "paint over" any text with the new format.

4. **Select the text to which you want to copy the formatting.**

   As soon as you select the text, WordPerfect QuickFormats it instantly. Very speedy!

   The mouse pointer still has that strange shape. How the heck do you turn this thing off?

5. **To turn QuickFormat off, choose For̲mat⇨Q̲uickFormat again.**

   Or, click on the QuickFormat button on the toolbar or use the QuickMenu gambit described in Step 2. In any event, the cursor returns to its normal pointy self.

Congratulations! — you've just created and used your first styles. "Styles?" you ask. WordPerfect styles (the subject of Chapter 10) are just like QuickFormat, only better. WordPerfect uses QuickFormat to get you used to them.

Changing Capitalization

dON'T yOU hATE iT wHEN yOU pRESS tHE cAPS lOCK kEY bY mISTAKE? We do. It's easy to type merrily along, hardly looking at the screen, until you see what you have done. Oops! In this situation, WordPerfect is your kind, thoughtful friend; it can fix the capitalization of text you have already typed. It's technology to the rescue!

To change some text into all CAPITAL LETTERS, all small letters, or even All Small Letters Except For The First Letter Of Each Word, follow these steps:

1. **Select the text you want to fool with.**

2. **Choose the E̲dit⇨Con̲vert Case command.**

   WordPerfect gives you three choices: Lowercase, Uppercase, and Initial Capitals. Cool!

3. **Choose one.**

   WordPerfect changes the text as requested. The text remains selected, in case you want to do anything else with it.

You can use these commands only if you have selected some text; otherwise, they're unavailable and appear in gray on the menu.

The Initial Capitals option isn't smart enough to know exactly which words to capitalize in a title or a name. After you use this option, you probably have to go back and make a few changes, to uncapitalize (smallize?) the first letters of prepositions, articles, and all those other types of little words you learned about in third grade.

Chapter 7

Sensational Sentences and Poignant Paragraphs

· ·

In This Chapter

▶ Using the ruler

▶ Setting margins

▶ Centering text

▶ Pushing text over to the right margin

▶ Justifying your text

▶ Hyphenating or not hyphenating

▶ Playing with tabs

▶ Indenting text

▶ Changing the line spacing and the spacing between paragraphs

· ·

*C*hapter 6 tells you how to use all kinds of spiffy-looking character formatting so that your documents look much more professional. Wait — what about fooling around with margins, centering, indenting, and line spacing? That's what this chapter is all about.

Margins and spacing are extremely important because they can make documents look much longer or shorter than they really are. Suppose that you're a student who has an assignment to write a 10-page paper. With schedules and priorities being what they are, however, not to mention movies and pizza bashes, you have had time to write only 7 pages.

Not a problem. Widen those margins. Pad that line spacing. Add a little white space to your prose. You can inflate it like a hot-air balloon. (We aren't suggesting any similarity to your prose, of course.)

We can also address the opposite problem: packing it in. What if your boss reads only one-page memos but you have a great deal of detail to include? WordPerfect to the rescue! Shave those margins, tighten that spacing, and maybe even shrink the font size a tad. You can squash everything in. If the whole thing still doesn't fit, just remove all adjectives and adverbs; that's what we do.

This chapter shows you how to mess around with margins, tabs, and justification, which WordPerfect calls the *line formatting* of your text. We also explain how to control the space between lines and paragraphs and how to indent the beginning of paragraphs — the *paragraph formatting.*

Using the Ruler

The first thing you have to do is display the WordPerfect ruler, if it's not already onscreen. If you don't see a horizontal strip just below the Property Bar, marked off in inches (or centimeters, for you jet-setters), click the View menu from the menu bar. On the menu that drops down, you should see the word *Ruler.* (If you don't, someone's been messing with your copy of WordPerfect. Assume that this person was trying to do you a favor and go find him.) In front of the word *Ruler,* a small square means that the ruler is visible and no small square means that it's not. ***Note:*** If you see a small square but not the ruler onscreen, get new glasses, squint harder at Figure 7-1, stop drinking so much coffee, clean the lint off the screen, or go find your local WordPerfect wizard.

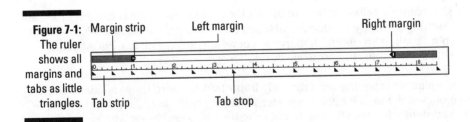

Figure 7-1: The ruler shows all margins and tabs as little triangles.

Margin strip   Left margin   Right margin

Tab strip   Tab stop

If no small square appears in front of the word *Ruler* on the View menu, click on the word *Ruler.* Two things happen: The menu goes away, and the ruler appears, as shown in the figure.

The ruler shows you the margins and tabs that are in effect in your document at the point where the cursor is located. When you change settings on the ruler, WordPerfect inserts the appropriate codes in your document. No information is really *stored* in, on, or around the ruler; it's just a nice graphical display of the state of your document. When you open another document, the stuff on the ruler changes to reflect the settings in the new document.

You can use the same View⇨Ruler command to get rid of the ruler later, when you finish with it.

What are all those little triangles?

The ruler packs a great deal of information about margins and tabs into a small space. It's made up of the following two horizontal strips with accompanying little black gizmos:

- ✔ **Margin strip:** A thin, horizontal strip above the numbered-inches part of the ruler that shows you the margins. The black gizmos at the left and right ends of the white part of this strip show the positions of the left and right margins. The gray parts at the left and right ends of the ruler are outside the margins. If you look carefully at the little black gizmos, the outer part of each gizmo shows the margins for the document and the little inner triangles show the position of paragraph format margins, which are separate margins you can set for each paragraph. (You proba-bly won't need them, so don't worry if you can't tell one part of the gizmos from another; instead, see the section "Changing margins for a paragraph or two," later in this chapter.)

- ✔ **Tab strip:** A thin, horizontal strip below the numbered part of the ruler that contains little triangles. The triangles show the positions of the tab stops. A *tab stop* is the position across the line where the cursor moves when you press the Tab key.

What's the ruler for?

The ruler shows you the margin and tab settings that are in effect wherever the cursor is right now (not the mouse pointer, which is the pointy arrow thing, but rather the cursor, which is the blinking vertical line). You can set the margins, tabs, and other line formats at the beginning of your document, and you can change them partway through the document. If you want to include a long quotation in an article you're writing, for example, you can choose to indent only the paragraphs that make up the quotation.

In addition to showing you the current positions of margins and tabs, the ruler can help you change them — you can use the mouse to drag the little margin gizmos and tab triangles around onscreen. In the rest of this chapter, we usu-ally tell you (at least) two ways to perform each formatting task: one by using a menu or pressing a key and the other by using the ruler. You can decide which method you prefer; WordPerfect doesn't care which one you use.

Setting Margins

Setting Margins

As you may recall from high school typing class, the left, right, top, and bottom margins control how much blank space to leave along the edges of the paper. Normally, everything you type appears within these margins. The purpose of margins, of course, is to provide white space in which a reader can doodle while staring off into space. WordPerfect usually sets the left, right, top, and bottom margins to 1 inch, which is quite generous. You may want to make the margins smaller, to discourage excessive doodling.

Dragging the margin lines

WordPerfect 8 can show you where the left, right, top, and bottom margins are by using gray dotted lines, called *guidelines*. We like these, although they've had a checkered history in WordPerfect. In some versions, after you installed WordPerfect, the guidelines were on the screen. In other versions, you had to ask WordPerfect to turn the guidelines on. Anyway, here's how to turn them on or off: Choose View➪Guidelines. You see the Guidelines dialog box, as shown in Figure 7-2.

Figure 7-2:
WordPerfect is willing to guide you anywhere.

This dialog box enables you to choose which guidelines you want to see in the WordPerfect window. Not that we're gluttons for punishment or anything, but we find all the guidelines pretty useful and usually keep all check boxes in this dialog box checked.

There; now that you have guidelines on the screen, you can change the margins by dragging them around. Follow these steps:

1. **Move the cursor to the tippy-top of the document.**

   The quickest way is to press Ctrl+Home. If you want to change the margins for the whole document, you have to start at the top, at the beginning of the first line of your document. To change the bottom margin, move to the bottom of the first page of the document.

2. Move the mouse pointer to the guideline for the margin you want to move.

When the pointer is on the guideline, it turns into a line with arrows pointing in the two directions in which you can drag the guideline. To move the left or right margin for the whole document, the easiest way is to point to the left or right margin *above* the top margin line.

3. Drag the guideline where you want it.

Not to belabor the point, but you can drag the left or right margin guidelines left or right, and you can drag the top or bottom margin guidelines up or down. When you release the mouse button, the guideline stays where you put it and the text in your document moves to stay within the margins. If you move the left or right margin, the margin gizmos in the margin strip of the ruler move, too.

When you change the left margin, the top end of the guideline may refuse to move. Don't worry; WordPerfect is just being obstinate. The margin will look fine.

If you would rather just use a nice, safe dialog box, read the next section. We prefer the guidelines; only you can decide which method you prefer.

Using the Margins dialog box

These steps show you how to set the margins in your document by using a dialog box, if you don't like dragging things with the mouse:

1. Move the cursor to the tippy-top of the document.

The quickest way is to press Ctrl+Home.

2. Choose Format⇨Margins.

This step displays the Margins dialog box, as shown in Figure 7-3.

Figure 7-3:
Setting margins for your document.

3. Enter measurements in the Left, Right, Top, and Bottom boxes.

You can type numbers or click on the little up or down triangle buttons to the right of each box to increase or decrease the numbers by ⅒-inch per click. As you change the measurements, WordPerfect changes the margins on the little page diagram in the dialog box so that you can see the effect you will achieve.

4. **To change the margins to the measurements you entered, press Enter or click on OK.**

   If you would rather forget the whole thing, press Esc or click on Cancel.

Another way to see the Margins dialog box is to move the mouse pointer to the margin strip on the ruler, click the right mouse button to display the ruler QuickMenu, and choose Margins from it.

When you set the margins, WordPerfect inserts invisible, secret formatting codes (named `Lft Mar` and `Rgt Mar`) that contain the new margin information. (WordPerfect code names are always cryptic and strange; otherwise, they wouldn't be exciting and secret.) See Chapter 9 to find out how to see these secret codes and delete them, if necessary.

Changing the margins for the rest of the document

You can change the margins partway through your document, which is useful if it contains more than one distinct part, such as an executive summary followed by a detailed proposal. You can use different margins for the different parts of the document. (Okay, we're reaching for an example here.)

To change the margins for the rest of the document, follow these steps:

1. **Move the cursor to the position where you want the margins to change.**

   This position is usually at the top of a page, although it doesn't have to be.

2. **Display the Page Setup dialog box with the Page Margins tab selected.**

   Choose Format➪Margins or double-click on the margins strip of the ruler — you get the idea.

3. **Fill in the margin measurements you want to use.**

4. **Click on OK or press Enter.**

   The dialog box goes away. The text following the cursor position moves to fit in the new margins.

These steps show you how to do the same thing with the mouse and the guidelines:

1. **Move the mouse pointer to the point in the document where you want the margins to change.**

   To change the top or bottom margin, go to the first page on which you want to set the new margin and use the top or bottom margin guideline on that page.

2. **Use the mouse to drag the guideline to the position where you want the new margin.**

   When you release the mouse button, WordPerfect sets the margin for the rest of the document to the position you chose. If you change the left or right margin, the guideline gets a kink in it, showing where it changes to the new position, as shown in Figure 7-4.

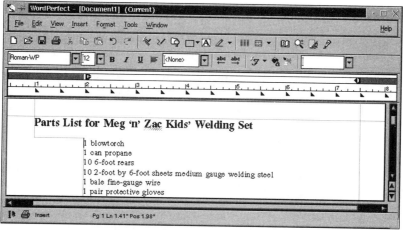

Figure 7-4: The margin guideline acquires a kink when you change the margin in the middle of the document.

If you changed the left or right margin, WordPerfect changes that margin beginning with the line the cursor is on. See Chapter 8 for more information about page formatting, including top and bottom margins.

Changing margins for a paragraph or two

Indent

When you use paragraph formatting, you can specify special margins for one or two paragraphs. If you include long quotations in your text to impress people with your erudition, you may want the quotations to be indented more than the rest of your prose. Although WordPerfect provides three separate features for accomplishing this task, we figure that you probably have more urgent things to do than read about all of them.

Our favorite way to change the margins for one or more paragraphs is to indent them, as shown in these steps:

1. **Move the cursor to the beginning of the paragraph you want to indent.**

2. **Choose Format⇨Paragraph⇨Indent or press F7.**

   WordPerfect inserts an invisible secret indent code, and the left margin of the paragraph moves to the right by one tab stop. (You can read more about tab stops later in this chapter.)

WordPerfect also provides the following useful variations:

✔ To indent both the left and right margins for a paragraph, choose Format⇨Paragraph⇨Double Indent.

✔ If you want to create a hanging indent, WordPerfect can do that, too. In a *hanging indent,* the first line of the paragraph is not indented and the rest of the lines are. Choose Format⇨Paragraph⇨Hanging Indent at the beginning of the paragraph.

✔ To indent several paragraphs, you can select the paragraphs and press F7. WordPerfect inserts a secret indent code for each one.

✔ An indent code indents the paragraph one tab stop. To control how far your paragraph is indented, you can move the tab stops; see the section "Playing with Tab Stops," later in this chapter.

WordPerfect inserts, as usual, a secret format code to record your request to indent the paragraph. The name of the regular code is (believe it or not) Hd Left Ind. The double-indent code is Hd Left\/Right Ind (which has a certain logic to it). To set a hanging indent, WordPerfect inserts two codes: Hd Left Ind and Hd Back Tab. See Chapter 9 to find out how to see and delete these secret codes.

Changing the Justification

Justification is a serious-sounding word — one that makes us think about moral imperatives, rationales for our actions, and other philosophical stuff. What a disappointment when we learn that it has to do with sticking spaces into lines of text. Such is life.

In word processing and typesetting, as you may already know, justification deals with the moral problem of different lines of text being different lengths. If we could just write so that every line in a document had the same number of characters, we wouldn't have this problem. But, no — we insist on making sense (with the possible exception of the contents of this book).

Kinds of justification

Although most people think that WordPerfect has four ways to justify text, it has these five:

Left Justification

Right Justification

Center Justification

Full Justification

All Justification

- ✓ **Left justification:** Text begins at the left margin and fills as much space as it takes up. Because different lines contain different text, the right edge of the text is uneven, or ragged. That's why this method is also called *ragged right*. Most of the text in this book uses left justification.

- ✓ **Right justification:** This method works the same way as left justification, except that the lines are shoved over to the right margin. The left edge of the text is ragged, and the right edge is straight. (Wonder why nobody calls it ragged left or straight right?)

- ✓ **Center justification:** This type of justification is usually used only for titles. It centers each line on the page so that both the left and right edges of the text are uneven.

- ✓ **Full justification:** The trickiest type; both the left and right edges of the text are nice and straight. How do you manage this type if different amounts of text are on each line? The extra space is broken into little pieces and stuck in among the words on the line so that all the lines are padded to fill the space between the left and right margins. Magazines, newspapers, and books usually use full justification, which is also called *justified text*.

- ✓ **"All" justification (as WordPerfect calls it):** This method is similar to full justification, only more so. In full justification, the lines at the end of paragraphs are exempt. If the last line of a paragraph contains only a few words, for example, the text begins at the left margin and stops where it stops. With "all" justification, however, WordPerfect justifies *all* lines. No line is safe. If the last line of a paragraph contains only a word or two, WordPerfect sticks inches of white space between each letter, if that's what it takes to stretch the line out to the right margin. We don't imagine that you will use this type of justification often; it looks downright weird.

Centering, right-aligning, and justifying text

To tell WordPerfect how to justify your text, follow these steps:

1. **Decide how much of your document you want to justify.**

   Using the same procedure, WordPerfect can justify a whole document, a single paragraph, or a group of paragraphs.

2. **Move the cursor into position.**

To select the type of justification to use for the entire document, move the cursor to the beginning of the document. To set justification for the rest of the document, move the cursor to the point at which you want the justification to change. To justify only a paragraph or two, select the text you want to justify.

3. **Choose Format⇨Justification.**

   WordPerfect comes back at you with another menu of options: the five types of justification.

4. **Choose one type of justification.**

   Alternatively, you can press one of these key combinations:

   - Ctrl+L for left justification

   - Ctrl+R for right justification

   - Ctrl+E for center justification

   - Ctrl+J for full justification

"All" justification has no key combination, which makes sense because it's hard to imagine that many people use it.

 A much easier way to justify a paragraph is to use the Property Bar. Just as bold, italic, and underlining are properties of your charming characters (refer to Chapter 6 if you don't know what we're talking about), the right-, left-, full-, and center-justification are properties of your pretty paragraphs. On the Property Bar, just to the right of the Underline button, is the Justification button. Click it and a menu drops down with the five kinds of justification, including a little picture, in case you forget which is which.

Dissecting your lines

If you're a particularly inquisitive reader, you may have noticed another place in the maze of WordPerfect menus with commands such as Center and Flush Right. You can find them by choosing the Format⇨Line command. What's the difference between centering text with Format⇨Line and with Format⇨Justification? Format⇨Line applies to only the line you're on or only the lines you have highlighted. Format⇨Justification applies to the paragraph you're in or the paragraphs you have highlighted.

Most of the time, you're better off using Justification. The only two times we can think of to use Format⇨Line are if you want to break a single line into several pieces or if you know that you want to center (or flush right) just the one line you're typing. Breaking a line into several pieces may be useful in a header or a footer; we talk about them in Chapter 8. Making a line flush right is useful for putting the date at the top of a letter. Take a look at the sidebar "Printing today's date," later in this chapter, for an example.

As usual, WordPerfect inserts secret codes to indicate the type of justification to use. If you selected some text, codes are stuck in at the beginning and end of the selection — one to change the justification and the other to change it back. If no text was selected when you selected the type of justification, WordPerfect adds one code.

 If you really want to fool around with the way WordPerfect spaces the letters across the line, try the Format⇨Typesetting⇨Word/Letter Spacing command, which displays the Word/Letter Spacing dialog box. This technique is overkill if we ever saw it. You can control just how much white space WordPerfect can stick in among the letters to justify text, suggest that WordPerfect crowd the letters together just a tad, or fiddle with the average amount of space between the words. If this is your cup of tea, go for it; we wouldn't dream of standing in your way.

To Hyphenate or Not to Hyphenate

WordPerfect can hyphenate automatically, by deciding (sometimes rightly, occasionally wrongly) where to hyphenate words that are too long to fit on a line. Hyphenation is usually a good idea when you use full justification; otherwise, hyphenation usually looks dumb. (That's just our opinion!)

To tell WordPerfect to hyphenate words as necessary, follow these steps:

1. **Move the cursor to the beginning of the document.**

   Usually, you should use hyphenation on an entire document or not at all. Life is confusing enough as it is. You can't select a portion of your document and tell WordPerfect to hyphenate it, either. If you just want to hyphenate a portion of a document, go to the place where you want hyphenation to start and turn it on; then go to the place you want it to stop and turn it off.

2. **Choose Tools⇨Language⇨Hyphenation.**

   WordPerfect displays the Line Hyphenation dialog box. Ignore the cute little diagram, the percentages, and everything. No one we have ever met ever wanted to change the parameters a program uses when it does hyphenation. In fact, you can forget that you ever saw this box.

3. **Click on the little Hyphenation On box so that it's filled in.**

4. **Click on OK or press Enter.**

   The dialog box vanishes.

Printing today's date

Everyone's favorite thing to print flush right is today's date at the beginning of a letter. WordPerfect can not only print the date at the right margin but also provide the date. Follow these steps:

1. **Move the cursor to the beginning of the letter in which you want the date to appear.**

   The location should be after your letterhead and before the address to which you're sending the letter.

2. **Choose Format⇨Line and select Flush Right from the choices that appear.**

   Alternatively, press Alt+F7 to make the line flush right.

3. **Press Ctrl+D to insert today's date.**

   Wow! Betcha didn't know that it would be that easy.

At some point as you work on the document, WordPerfect decides that a word should be hyphenated because it doesn't fit at the end of one line and is too long to move to the beginning of the next line. If that word is in the WordPerfect hyphenation dictionary, no problem! WordPerfect sticks in the hyphen and away it goes. If that word isn't in the WordPerfect dictionary, however, you see — with no warning — the small Position Hyphen dialog box. It's the WordPerfect way of asking how to hyphenate a word it doesn't recognize; the dialog box displays the word to hyphenate, with the suggested location of the hyphen.

You have several options:

- ✔ Click on the Insert Hyphen button to insert the hyphen where WordPerfect suggests.

- ✔ Press the left- and right-arrow keys on the keyboard to move the hyphen to a better place to split the word and then click on Insert Hyphen.

- ✔ Decide that this long word should really be two separate words. Choose this option if you left out a space accidentally (which is our top-rated typo). Click on the Insert Space button.

- ✔ Decide that you have no good way to split the word in two and that the whole thing should be moved to the beginning of the next line. A classic example is the word *strength,* a long word that cannot be hyphenated. (Isn't it amazing how much trivia we authors can dredge up?) In this case, click on Ignore Word.

When WordPerfect hyphenates a word, it doesn't insert a plain old ordinary hyphen. No, indeed. If it did, and if you edited the paragraph some more so that the word were no longer at the right margin, WordPerfect would glue the word back together, and the hyphen would still show up. Every once in awhile, you see this situation in a newspaper or magazine: a hyphen in the middle of a word where it doesn't belong. Now, whenever you see it happen, you can sneer, "That word processor should have inserted a *soft hyphen!*"

WordPerfect *does* insert a soft hyphen, which looks just like a regular hyphen when the word is split in half at the margin but which disappears into the World of Secret Codes if the word is glued back together again. Totally cool.

Playing with Tab Stops

In word processing, you use tabs and spaces a little differently than you do when you type on a typewriter. One reason is that WordPerfect is smarter than a typewriter; you can tell it to do such things as center text and flush it to the right without using a bunch of spaces or tabs. Another reason is that because most computer fonts are *proportionally spaced* (different letters are different widths; refer to Chapter 6), using spaces to line things up doesn't work very well. If you don't know what we mean, read on. What follows is a discussion of spaces, tabs, and tab stops.

Stop! Tab!

A *tab stop* (did we say this already?) is a position across the line where tabs stop. Logical enough. When you press the Tab key, WordPerfect moves toward the right across the line until it gets to the next tab stop; then it stops. WordPerfect allows you to define a more-or-less-unlimited number of them across the line.

Setting tab stops

As WordPerfect was delivered from the factory, your document probably contains tab stops every half-inch. How can you tell? Display the ruler, that's how! (Remember that if you don't see it, choose View⇨Ruler from the WordPerfect menu.)

On the ruler's tab strip (just below the inch markings), little black triangles mark the positions of the tab stops. The ones WordPerfect provides are, by default, left tab stops (the most commonly used type) and are symbolized by triangles that point down and to the left.

Types of tab stops and other boring information

WordPerfect has a bunch of different kinds of tab stops. This subject is the kind of boring, petty stuff you probably haven't thought about since high school, and we urge you to skip this sidebar if you possibly can.

Still with us? Okay, here goes. This sidebar describes the different types of WordPerfect tab stops, along with what happens when you press the Tab key to move to each type. The table at the end of this sidebar shows a live demonstration.

✔ **Left, or L:**

What you type appears to the right of the tab-stop position. On the ruler, left tab stops are indicated by little black triangles that point down and to the left.

✔ **Right, or R:**

What you type appears to the left of the tab-stop position. This tab stop doesn't sound aptly named, does it? It's a right tab stop because the text is flush right, or right-aligned, at the stop. On the ruler, the triangles for right tab stops point down and to the right.

✔ **Center, or C:**

What you type appears centered on the tab-stop position. On the ruler, center tab stops are shown by little upward-pointing triangles.

✔ **Decimal, or D:**

This type of tab stop is designed for numbers that have decimal points, such as columns of dollar amounts. WordPerfect positions the text with the decimal point at the tab-stop position; columns of numbers look much tidier if their decimal points line up vertically. If you type something that has no decimal point, WordPerfect right-aligns it. On the ruler, a decimal tab stop is indicated by an upward-pointing triangle with a little dot in the middle.

✔ **Dotted versions of the preceding four types:**
You can tell WordPerfect to display a line of dots (a *dot leader*) that leads up to the entry. You see this kind of thing in the tables of contents in books such as this one. On the ruler, dotted tab stops are shown by triangles with dots above them.

Left	Center	Right	Decimal	Dotted Right
Tom	Jones	Blue	$150.00	.....Page 1
Jo	Bloggswirth	Greenish	75.00	2
Sue	Fish-Frei	Purple	235.50	3
Mary	Green	Red	100.00	4

You may not want a tab stop every half-inch, and you may want to create tab stops of types other than left tab stops. If you're typing a list of names and phone numbers, for example, you may want just one tab stop at the position where you want the phone numbers to appear. Luckily, WordPerfect enables you to fool around with the tab stops at will.

Put your tab codes in the right place!

Before setting your tab stops, you must move the cursor to the right place. We even tell you where the right place is!

To set the tab stops for an entire document, move the cursor to the beginning of the document by pressing Ctrl+Home.

To change the tab-stop positions partway through a document, you can do that, too. If your report contains two different tables, for example, you may want to set the tab stops once at the beginning of the first table and again at the beginning of the second. Move the cursor to the place where you want the new tab-stop positions to take effect (at the beginning of a table, for example).

To set the tab stops for a table, don't even use tab stops! Instead, use the WordPerfect table feature, which is described in Chapter 14, in the section about working with tables.

When you change or create tab stops, WordPerfect inserts a secret code that contains the positions of *all* tab stops that are in effect. The tab-stop changes you make take effect at that point and continue for the rest of the document or until they encounter the next secret tab-stop code. If you change the tab stops several times with the cursor in different places, you can end up with a document littered with tab-stop codes, and the tab stops may change when you don't expect them to. Luckily, WordPerfect 8 lets you easily see where you've changed the tab stops; a little *tab set icon* appears in the left margin of your document, with an arrow pointing to an indentation in a paragraph. If you end up with unwanted tab-stop codes in your document, see Chapter 9 to find out how to see them and get rid of them.

The secret code that WordPerfect inserts when you change tab stops is named Tab Set and is followed by the positions of all the tab stops.

You have (as always) two ways to position tab stops: Use commands or use the ruler. The command for setting tab stops, Format⇨Line⇨Tab Set, displays the Tab Set dialog box. This dialog box is horrific, terrifying, and downright scary-looking, and we refrain from reproducing it here for fear of chasing you away from word processing forever. We prefer that you stick to the ruler method, which is a snap.

Moving tab stops around

To move an existing tab stop, follow these steps:

1. **Move to the place in your document where you want the modified tab stops to take effect.**

This spot is usually at the beginning of the document or the beginning of a table.

2. **Click on the little triangle on the ruler for the tab stop you want to move.**

3. **Hold down the mouse button and drag the triangle left or right along the ruler to its new position.**

When you release the mouse button, WordPerfect moves the tab stop to the position where you left the triangle. A tab set icon (an arrow pointing to an indentation in a paragraph) appears in the left margin of your document to show that you've created a secret tab-stop code there.

Blowing away tab stops

To get rid of a tab stop, follow these steps:

1. **Move to the place in your document where you want the change to take place.**

2. **Click on the triangle for the tab stop and drag the triangle down off the ruler.**

Off the ruler, tab stops die from lack of oxygen. You never see the tab stop again.

If you move or delete a tab stop by mistake, choose Edit➪Undo or press Ctrl+Z to undo your change. You can also click on the Undo button (the button with the U-turn arrow pointing to the left) on the toolbar.

To get rid of all existing tab stops, follow these steps:

1. **Right-click on the tab strip on the ruler.**

It doesn't matter whether you click on a tab stop or between tab stops. A QuickMenu appears.

2. **Choose Clear All Tabs from the QuickMenu.**

Blammo — no more tab stops.

Making a brand-new tab stop

To create a new tab stop, follow these steps:

1. **Tell WordPerfect which kind of tab stop you want to make, by right-clicking on a white area (between two tab stops) on the tab strip.**

You see a QuickMenu that includes the Eight Types of WordPerfect Tab Stops. To find out about the available types, refer to the sidebar "Types of tab stops and other boring information," earlier in this chapter.

2. Choose the type of tab stop you want from the QuickMenu.

You're ready to create the tab stop. Get ready; this process is complex and painstaking.

3. On the tab strip on the ruler (the part where the triangles appear), point to the position where you want the tab stop and click.

That's all there is to it! WordPerfect creates the tab stop and the little triangle to go with it. A tab set icon appears in the left margin of your document to alert you to a change in tab stops.

After you have the tab stops where you want them, you're ready to use them. Just press Tab when you want to leave white space in the area from the cursor location over to the next tab stop.

Indenting the First Line of Each Paragraph

Indenting the first line of each paragraph is one of the all-time-favorite uses of tabs. If you want the first line of a paragraph to be indented, you can press the Tab key as you begin typing the paragraph. Or, you can insert the tab later, after you type the paragraph. No big news here.

If you want to indent the first lines of a *bunch* of paragraphs, however, you can tell WordPerfect to do it automatically, without your having to stick a tab at the beginning of each one. These steps show you how:

1. Select all the paragraphs for which you want to indent just the first line.

The paragraphs must be together, with no other paragraphs, titles, or whatever mixed in. (You can always select one group of paragraphs at a time and repeat these steps for each one.) If you want to indent the first line of every single paragraph in the document, don't select any text; instead, move the cursor to the beginning of the document. If you want to indent all paragraphs starting partway through the document, move the cursor to the point where you want this formatting to begin. Whew!

2. Choose Format▷Paragraph▷Format.

WordPerfect displays the Paragraph Format dialog box, as shown in Figure 7-5.

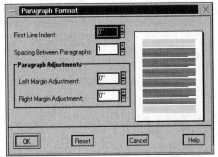

Figure 7-5:
Formatting a
bunch of
paragraphs
so that their
first lines
are
indented.

3. **In the First Line Indent box, enter the amount (usually about half an inch) by which you want to indent each first line.**

4. **Click on OK or press Enter.**

   Voilà! WordPerfect adds that little bit of white space at the beginning of each paragraph, just the way your typing teacher taught you. Look, Ma — no tabs!

Another way to display the Paragraph Format dialog box is to right-click on the margin strip on the ruler and then choose Paragraph Format from the QuickMenu that appears.

Whether you choose to use tabs or paragraph formatting, don't use spaces to indent paragraphs. In word processing circles, this method is considered tacky. The problem with spaces is that they're different widths, depending on which font you use (refer to Chapter 6 for information about fonts). Tab stops are always exactly the width you see on the ruler.

The advantage of using tabs is that if you decide to indent paragraphs by a different amount, all you have to do is slide that first tab stop over by a hair. Then all the tabs that depend on that tab stop move, too. When you perform this procedure, be sure that the cursor is in the right place: at the beginning of your document (assuming that you want to change the look of all the paragraphs in it).

Whenever you use a tab to indent a line, you should have pressed Enter to end the preceding line. In other words, the line you're indenting shouldn't begin as a result of WordPerfect's use of word wrap to fill the lines of a paragraph.

To indent *all* lines in the paragraph or all *except* the first line, refer to the section "Changing margins for a paragraph or two," earlier in this chapter. Never stick a tab at the beginning of each line of a paragraph. Yuck! Ptooey! If you do, when you edit the paragraph later, the tabs will be all over the place, and your paragraph will have unsightly gaps in all the wrong places. *Please* indent.

When you press the Tab key, WordPerfect inserts various secret codes, depending on the type of tab stop to which the tab moves. The codes are named `Left Tab`, `Right Tab`, `Center Tab`, `Dec Tab`, `...Left Tab`, `...Right Tab`, and so on.

Changing the Line Spacing

Line Spacing

If the stuff you write is sent to an editor (as ours is — pity the poor woman!), you probably have to double-space your text to leave lots of room for making corrections, expressing confusion, and doing some general doodling. Fortunately, WordPerfect can accommodate you:

1. **Move the cursor to the point at which you want the line spacing to change.**

    To change the line spacing for the entire document, move to the beginning of the document by pressing Ctrl+Home. To change the line spacing for a paragraph or two (for a long quotation, for example), select the paragraphs you want to change.

2. **Choose Format⇨Line⇨Spacing.**

    WordPerfect displays the Line Spacing dialog box, as shown in Figure 7-6.

Figure 7-6:
Double-spacing your document to make it look longer.

3. **Enter a number in the Spacing box.**

    Enter **2** to get double-spaced text, for example. You can also enter fractions or decimals. To add just a little space between the lines, you can enter **1.1** or **1.2**. Click on the little arrows at the right end of the Spacing box to increase or decrease the number in the box a tad.

4. **Click on OK or press Enter to dismiss the dialog box. (Shoo!)**

    WordPerfect does your bidding and adds the vertical space you requested between each line of text.

When you change the line spacing, WordPerfect inserts a `Ln Spacing` secret code.

Changing the Spacing Between Paragraphs

You can tell WordPerfect to leave extra space between paragraphs in a document and not add any space between the lines of the paragraph. This capability results in text that looks sort of like this book does — an effect we prefer over first-line indenting. Take that, Miss Perpetua! (She was Margy's high school typing teacher.)

This procedure involves paragraph formatting and the use of the Paragraph Format dialog box (refer to Figure 7-5). Follow these steps:

1. **Move the cursor to the beginning of the document by pressing Ctrl+Home (assuming that you want to use this kind of thing for the entire document).**

2. **Choose Format⇨Paragraph⇨Format.**

   WordPerfect displays the Paragraph Format dialog box (refer to Figure 7-5).

3. **In the Spacing Between Paragraphs box, enter the number of lines you want between paragraphs.**

   Entering **1** means that you want no extra space. We recommend entering **1.5**, which adds a blank half-line between each paragraph — enough to separate the paragraphs visually. (Don't we sound like we know what we're talking about?)

4. **Click on OK or press Enter to leave the dialog box.**

Changing the paragraph spacing inserts a secret `Para Spacing` code into your document.

Chapter 8

Perfect Pages
and Dashing Documents

● ●

In This Chapter

▶ Setting the page size

▶ Adjusting the top and bottom margins

▶ Starting a new page

▶ Keeping text together

▶ Centering a page from top to bottom

▶ Looking at different views of your document

▶ Numbering pages

▶ Adding heads and feets

● ●

*I*n earlier chapters, we talk about making your characters look just right, fooling with margins and indentation, and other heady stuff. Now, for The Larger Picture: formatting your document as a whole. This chapter explains how to tell WordPerfect on what size of paper you plan to print your masterpiece; where to begin new pages; and what (if anything) to print at the top and bottom of each page, such as page numbers. This kind of formatting separates the — men from the boys? women from the girls? toads from the water buffaloes? — pros from the amateurs in the world of word processing.

Setting the Page Size

Page Size

WordPerfect wants to know everything about your document — in particular, which kind of paper you plan to print it on. (Letterhead? Envelopes? Labels?) WordPerfect doesn't care what the paper looks like; the program can't tell embossed rag stationery with gold-leaf edges from cheapo copying paper; it just wants to know the paper's size.

An art lesson: Portraits and landscapes

We interrupt this book for a brief lesson on art — specifically, on the shapes of paintings.

As you have noticed from your extensive experience in art galleries, pictures of people tend to be taller than they are wide, to make room to include a complete hat-to-collar portrait. Pictures of places tend to be wider than they are tall so that they can include more landscape and less sky.

The many art lovers among the computer scientists of the world decided to use this situation as the basis for naming the way text is printed on paper. If you hold the paper so that it's taller than it is wide and then print lines of text that run across the short way, it's called *portrait orientation.* This orientation is the normal, everyday way to use paper. If, on the other hand, you turn the paper sideways so that it's wider than it is tall and then print on it accordingly, you have *landscape orientation.* Toddlers usually use paper this way, in our experience.

If you don't mention anything about paper, WordPerfect probably assumes that you'll use the usual: letter-size paper you stick in the printer in the usual way. If you plan to print on the paper sideways (*landscape* orientation), however, or if you plan to use legal-size paper, envelopes, or whatever, you had better tell WordPerfect about it. Otherwise, you may run into trouble with your margins.

To tell WordPerfect about the size of the paper on which you plan to print your document, follow these steps:

1. **Move the cursor to the beginning of the document by pressing Ctrl+Home.**

   Because paper size is something that usually applies to an entire document, set the cursor right at the beginning.

2. **Choose File➪Page Setup➪Page Size.**

   WordPerfect displays the Paper Size dialog box, as shown in Figure 8-1.

   Most of the dialog box consists of the Available Paper Definitions box, which contains, not surprisingly, paper definitions. One of them is highlighted, probably Letter (Portrait). The exact list you see depends on the kind of printer you use, because different printers can accept different paper sizes. Our list consists of standard American and European sizes for paper and envelopes, including the ones shown here:

   - A4 (European paper, a tad bigger than American letter size)

   - Envelope COM10 (a regular business envelope)

- Envelope DL (another envelope size)
- Legal (legal-size paper, which is longer than letter-size)
- Letter (our favorite)

Wherever the paper definition includes the notation (Portrait) or (Landscape), WordPerfect is telling you how the paper is positioned in the printer (see the sidebar "An art lesson: Portraits and landscapes," earlier in this chapter).

3. **To use a different paper size, click on the paper definition you want to use.**

   The paper size that appears highlighted in the Available Paper Definitions box is the one you're using for this document.

4. **Click on the OK button.**

Figure 8-1:
Choosing
the kind
of paper
on which
to print.

If the list of available paper sizes looks odd, make sure that the correct printer is selected.

Use landscape printing for documents that are too wide to fit on the paper the regular way, especially for tables that have numerous columns. Also, people always "ooh" and "ahh" when you produce a document printed sideways on the page, which is another good reason to use it.

When you set the paper size, WordPerfect inserts a secret Paper Sz/Typ code (yes, another inspired code name!) in your document. To find out more about these codes, including how to delete them, see Chapter 9.

Adjusting the Top and Bottom Margins

Top and Bottom Margins

After WordPerfect knows the size of your paper, it has opinions about your margins. Unless you tell WordPerfect otherwise, it assumes that you want 1-inch margins all the way around the page, measuring from the edge of the paper. We generally find this measurement to be a little too airy and spacious for our tastes, and we usually change it — unless we're getting paid to write by the page, of course.

To change the left or right margin, refer to Chapter 7, which explains how to use the ruler, guidelines, or Margins dialog box for this task.

To change the top or bottom margin, follow these steps:

1. **Move the cursor to the point at which you want the new margins to take effect.**

   To change the top or bottom margin for the entire document, move to the beginning of the document by pressing Ctrl+Home. To change the margin beginning at a page other than page 1, move to the top of that page.

2. **Display the Margins dialog box by choosing Format⇨Margins.**

   If you want to see a picture of the Margins dialog box, turn to Chapter 7 and check out Figure 7-3. You don't have to, though; it's just a small dialog box with entries for Left, Right, Top, and Bottom margins.

3. **Fill in the measurements for the top and bottom margins and then click on OK.**

   The little page diagram changes to show you how the page will look, more or less. If you're using draft view (described later in this chapter, in the section "Looking at Different Views of Your Document"), you don't notice a difference, except that the page breaks move.

   As an alternative, you can put the cursor where the changes should take effect and then change the top and bottom margins by clicking on and dragging the guidelines.

When you change the top or bottom margin, WordPerfect inserts a secret `Top Mar` or `Bot Mar` code in the text at the top of the current page. See Chapter 9 to find out how to fool with these codes.

Starting a New Page

Blank Page

If you have typed any significant amount of text in WordPerfect, you probably have noticed that every so often it suddenly introduces a huge gap between one line and the next. This gap is the WordPerfect way of telling you that you just filled one page and are starting at the top of the next page — a sort of digital equivalent of ripping the paper from your typewriter and sticking a new sheet under the platen.

WordPerfect keeps track of where on the page each line appears. You can see your position on the page by looking at the Application Bar, where it says Ln (short, we guess, for Line), followed by a measurement in inches (or maybe centimeters). This spot is your position from the top edge of the paper.

What if you don't want to fill a page before starting the next one? You can insert a secret code (not another one!) that tells WordPerfect to skip to the top of the next page, regardless of whether this one is full. This feature is called a *page break*. The page breaks that WordPerfect sticks in when pages are full are *soft* page breaks. If you want to put in a break yourself, it's a *hard* page break. (See Chapter 9 to find out about the difference between hard and soft codes.)

To insert a hard page break, just press Ctrl+Enter. Poof! The cursor dashes down to the top of a new page. If you were in the middle of the line, the part of the line after the cursor moves with you down to the new page.

To get rid of a hard page break, move the cursor to the beginning of the page *after* the page break and press the Backspace key (assuming that Linux is configured for the Backspace key to delete the preceding character). This step backs you up, and, with luck, deletes the page-break code in the process. Alternatively, you can move the cursor to the last character *before* the page break and press the Delete key — same idea. If this step doesn't work, see Chapter 9.

You may be tempted to begin a new page by pressing Enter over and over until the page is full of carriage returns and you arrive at the top of the next page. We hate to be judgmental — in our humble opinion, however, this action is *wrong, wrong, wrong*. Here's why: If you edit the earlier part of your document so that it gets just a teeny bit shorter, everything shifts up a tad. Now you have too few carriage returns to fill the page, and the text begins at the bottom of the preceding page rather than on a new page — not the effect you want. Take our advice: Insert a hard page break instead. It's so much less work!

The name of the secret hard-page-break code is HPg, in case you were wondering. The soft page breaks that WordPerfect adds are HRt-SPg or SRt-SPg, depending on whether the page break occurs between paragraphs or in the middle of a paragraph.

Keeping Text Together

You have complete control over where hard page breaks occur because you put them in yourself. WordPerfect sticks in soft page breaks, however, whenever it decides that no more lines can fit on a page. Sometimes, it chooses singularly bad spots to begin a new page — in fact, we suspect malice at those times. A technical term was created for lousy positioning of page breaks: *bad breaks*. (We always thought that it was a skiing term.)

Avoiding broken homes (widows and orphans)

A page looks lousy when a paragraph begins on the last line of the page so that only one line of the paragraph appears before the page break. This traditional typesetting no-no has a traditional name: widow (or is it orphan?). Our dictionary informs us that this line is an *orphan*. A *widow* occurs when the last line of a paragraph appears at the top of a page all by itself. (At your next backyard picnic, amaze your friends by conducting a pop quiz to see who knows the difference.)

Luckily, you don't have to know about this stuff or even think about it because WordPerfect does your worrying for you. Follow these steps to avoid the dreaded social disease of bad breaks:

1. **Move the cursor to the beginning of the document by pressing Ctrl+Home.**

   The following command and the resulting secret code apply to the entire document.

2. **Choose Format⇨Keep Text Together.**

   WordPerfect displays the Keep Text Together dialog box, as shown in Figure 8-2.

   The dialog box contains three settings that have to do with positioning page breaks, and we discuss all three in this chapter. Your immediate concern, however, is those widows and orphans.

Figure 8-2:
Preventing
widows and
orphans.

3. **Click on the box labeled Prevent the first and last lines of paragraphs from being separated across pages; the box should be filled in when it's selected.**

   This box is in the Widow/Orphan section of the dialog box.

4. **Click on OK or press Enter to leave the dialog box.**

WordPerfect now avoids leaving widows and orphans alone at the top and bottom of pages. Instead, it moves page breaks up or down a line as necessary. Although the pages won't be completely full, that's the price you pay for family cohesion.

When you follow the preceding steps, WordPerfect creates a `Wid/Orph:On` code in your document. Chapter 9 describes how to see and delete this code if necessary.

Keeping your act together

A document may contain information that should not be split over a page break. A columnar table looks crummy if it's split up, for example, unless it's longer than one page. You can select part of your document and tell WordPerfect, "Let no page break enter here!" Follow these steps:

1. **Select the text you want to keep together.**

   Refer to Chapter 5 to find out how to select text, if you don't already know. For tables, be sure to include any headings or titles.

2. **Choose Format➪Keep Text Together.**

   WordPerfect displays the Keep Text Together dialog box (refer to Figure 8-2).

3. **Click on the box labeled Keep selected text together on same page so that the box is filled in.**

   This box is in the Block Protect section of the dialog box.

4. **Click on OK or press Enter.**

Block protect sounds like the maneuver a two-year-old uses when another kid comes to visit, although WordPerfect isn't talking about that kind of block. In earlier versions of WordPerfect, selecting text was always called *marking blocks,* and doing anything with a bunch of text was a *block operation.* WordPerfect has now adopted Windows-speak, which requires that you refer to a bunch of text as a *selection.* It's another example of the Great March of Progress.

When you follow these steps, WordPerfect inserts two `Block Pro` codes in your document: one at the beginning of the selected text and one at the end.

Keeping your head together

Specifically, this heading means keeping headings with the text that follows them. (You were thinking of the great Carole King hits of yesteryear, weren't you? — unless you're too young to remember them.) Leaving a heading stranded all alone at the bottom of a page while the text that follows the heading begins on the following page is considered tacky and gauche.

Unlike preventing widows and orphans, which you can do by issuing one command at the beginning of your document, you must issue a separate command for each heading you want to keep with the text that follows it. (The solution to this annoying situation is to use styles to format headings; jump to Chapter 10 if this subject interests you.)

To prevent WordPerfect from separating a head(ing) from its body, follow these steps:

1. **Move the cursor to the beginning of the line that contains the heading.**

2. **Choose Format⇨Keep Text Together.**

   WordPerfect displays the Keep Text Together dialog box (refer to Figure 8-2). Look at the Conditional end of page section of the dialog box.

3. **Click on the box labeled Number of lines to keep together so that it's filled in.**

   It's in the Conditional End of Page section of the dialog box.

4. **Type a number in the text box.**

   To keep together the heading line and the first two lines of the text that follow it, enter **3**. If you use a blank line to separate the heading from the text, you may want to enter **4**.

5. **Click on OK or press Enter to leave the dialog box.**

If the heading and the first few lines that follow cannot fit at the bottom of the page, WordPerfect now moves the whole kit and kaboodle to the top of the next page.

When you follow these steps, WordPerfect inserts a `Cond1 EOP` (Conditional End of Page) code into your document. If you use styles to format headings, you can insert a `Cond1 EOP` code into the heading style to avoid headless-ness throughout your document. (See Chapter 10 to find out more about styles.)

Don't use too many Block Protect and Conditional End of Page codes in your document or else WordPerfect will have a heck of a time finding anywhere to put page breaks. Cut it some slack!

Centering a Page, from Top to Bottom

Center Page

When you create a title page for a document, the titles look nice if they appear in the middle of the page, both up and down and left to right. Chapter 7 talks about how to center text between the left and right margins. (Oh, all right: Select the text to center and press Ctrl+E.) The following steps show you how to center the titles top to bottom. Although you can just press Enter a bunch of times above the titles, it's a ba-a-a-ad idea. Let WordPerfect put your titles in exactly the right place.

1. **Move the cursor to the top of the page that contains the text to be centered top to bottom (in most cases, it's the first page of your document).**

2. **Choose Format⇨Page⇨Center.**

   WordPerfect displays the Center Page(s) dialog box, as shown in Figure 8-3.

3. **To center this page, choose Current Page.**

4. **Click on OK or press Enter.**

   WordPerfect moves the text on the page up or down to its center.

You can tell the vertical position of the text on the page by looking at the `Ln` measurement on the Application Bar.

To revoke centering on a page, move the cursor to the top of the page, choose Format⇨Page⇨Center to display the Center Page(s) dialog box, and choose No Centering.

When you center the current page, WordPerfect quite sensibly inserts the secret `Cntr Cur Pg` code. Centering the current and subsequent pages produces a `Cntr Pgs` code. Chapter 9 tells you how to see these magical codes for yourself. (If you can deal with codes, double-click on the `Cntr Cur Pg` or `Cntr Pgs` code to display the Center Page(s) dialog box so that you can change the setting.)

Looking at Different Views of Your Document

WordPerfect can show your document from several angles, depending on how closely you want the view to resemble the printed page. This list shows the different views you can choose:

- ✔ **Draft:** Page breaks appear as horizontal lines across your document, and you cannot see top or bottom margins, extra space on a partially full page, headers, footers, or page numbers.

- ✔ **Page:** WordPerfect shows how the page will look, including all margins, headers, and footers. Page breaks look like blank gaps between one page and the next. How big your text looks depends on what the Zoom setting is. We talk all about that topic in Chapter 19.

- ✔ **Web Page:** You can see your page roughly as it would be displayed in a *Web browser* (the program you use to look at World Wide Web pages on the Internet). Be cautious when you're using this view; WordPerfect warns you that some of your formatting may be lost.

To switch between these three views, choose Y̲iew from the menu bar and then choose D̲raft, P̲age, or We̲b Page.

We bring up the subject of views because we're about to talk about page formatting you can see only in page view: page numbers, headers, and footers.

If your Alt and Ctrl keys are configured to work with WordPerfect, a faster way to switch to Draft view is to press Ctrl+F5. A quicker way to jump to Page view is to swat Alt+F5. WordPerfect has no fast way to let you see Web Page view. For the most part, you can probably just work in Page view. We always do. Why not see everything, after all?

Numbering Pages

After you have a document with more than one page, you probably will want to number the pages. Few things are more annoying than a sheaf of pages with no page numbers that have gotten (or may have gotten) out of order. Don't look like a schnook; number your pages.

For some strange reason — probably some quirk of software history — WordPerfect has not one but two ways to number pages. (Why do we say this with surprise? WordPerfect always seems to have two ways to do everything.) The following list shows the two ways:

✔ Use the Format⇨Page⇨Page Numbering⇨Numbering command to tell WordPerfect to begin numbering the pages. You can tell WordPerfect where the numbers should appear and also enter other text, such as today's date or the document title, to include with the page number.

✔ Use the Insert⇨Header/Footer command to define headers or footers, which can include page numbers.

These two approaches are similar, and we talk about headers and footers in a minute. These steps show how to use the first method to number your pages:

1. Move the cursor to the top of the page on which you want page numbers to begin.

If your classy-looking document has a cover page, for example, you can begin numbering on the next page.

2. Choose Format⇨Page⇨Page Numbering⇨Numbering.

WordPerfect displays the Page Numbering dialog box, as shown in Figure 8-4.

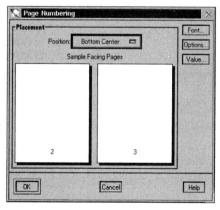

Figure 8-4:
Your pages
are
numbered!

3. **Tell WordPerfect where to print the page numbers.**

   Click in the Position box. You see a long list of choices that fall into three groups: No Page Numbering, Top, and Bottom. Within the Top and Bottom groups, you can select Left, Center, Right, or Alternating. The Alternating option does not mean that you and a friend have gotten your bikinis mixed up — it indicates that the page number appears on the right side of odd-numbered pages and on the left side of even-numbered pages, and vice versa for inside alternating. Alternating is just right for documents printed on both sides of the paper (this book, for example) because the page numbers appear on the outside edge of each page.

   Fortunately, you don't have to remember which numbering format is which. After you select a format, just check out the example of the page-numbering format at the bottom of the dialog box. Is this cute or what?

4. **If you want your pages to show Page or other text along with the page number, click on the Options button to display the Page Numbering Options dialog box.**

   If a plain, unadorned page number works for you, skip down to Step 7 instead.

5. **In the Format and Accompanying Text box, type what text you want to appear beside your page number.**

   The simplest thing to do is to type the word *Page* and a space in front of the [Pg #] code.

6. **Click on OK to get back to the Page Numbering dialog box.**

   WordPerfect shows how the page numbers will look on the sample facing pages.

   If you want the page number to appear in a different font, click on the Font button and then choose the font and font size from the dialog box that appears (which looks an awful lot like the Font dialog box we describe in Chapter 6). Then click on OK to return to the Page Numbering dialog box.

7. **Click on OK to bug out of this dialog box.**

WordPerfect now prints page numbers on this page and on all following pages in the document — even pages you add later.

When you tell WordPerfect to number pages, it adds a secret Pg Num Pos code at the top of the page. (See Chapter 9 for information about secret codes.)

For all you Roman-numeral fans

You don't have to use boring, pedestrian Arabic numbers for page numbers. You can use small Roman numerals to number the pages in the introduction of a report, for example. To tell WordPerfect which type of numbers to use (Roman or Arabic), follow these steps:

1. **Move the cursor to the top of the page on which you want the numbering to begin.**

2. **Choose Format⇨Page⇨Page Numbering⇨Numbering.**

   You see the Page Numbering dialog box, as shown in Figure 8-4.

3. **Click the Options button to display the Page Numbering Options dialog box.**

4. **Find the Page label and click on the button to its right.**

   A list of numbering options appears, including regular (Arabic) numbers, Roman numerals, and letters.

5. **Choose a number style.**

   When you make your choice, it appears in the Page box.

6. **Click on OK to leave the Page Numbering Options dialog box, and click on OK again to leave the Page Numbering dialog box.**

Stop! Don't type that page number!

Untutored word processing novices have been known to enter page numbers at the bottom of every page. A moment's thought tells you why that's a terrible, awful, yucky idea. If you insert a line at the bottom of each page and type the page number, what are you gonna do when an important update requires you to insert a few additional lines on page 1? Suddenly, all the page numbers that used to appear at the bottom of the pages slide down to print a few lines down from the top of the following pages. What a mess!

Maybe you think that you got clever and have read ahead to find out how to put your own numbers in footers. Although this technique may look right at the beginning, it would require a new footer for each page. As soon as one of those footers moves on to another page, your page numbers will be wrong.

The moral of the story is "Never type page numbers as text." Always use either page numbering or headers or footers (described later in this chapter) to do it for you.

You can even switch page-number styles partway through the document: Just move the cursor to the top of the page on which you want the style to change and follow the preceding steps.

Starting over again at 1

If you want to change your page numbering partway through a document, you can. If your report titled "Ten Thousand Uses for Chocolate" begins with an Introduction, for example, you can restart the page numbering at 1 on the first page that follows the introduction. Follow these steps:

1. **Move the cursor to the top of the page on which you want to restart page numbering at 1.**

2. **Choose Format⇨Page⇨Page Numbering⇨Numbering.**

   WordPerfect displays your friend the Page Numbering dialog box.

3. **Click on the Value button.**

   The Numbering Value dialog box appears. This dialog box includes much more than just the settings for page numbers; it also enables you to control the numbering of other items we don't describe in this book. Our advice is to ignore all except the Page Settings part of the dialog box.

4. **In the New Page Number box (in the Page Settings part of the dialog box), type the number you want this page to be.**

   In this case, you want the page to be page 1, no matter how many pages of Introduction you write.

5. **Click on OK to leave the Numbering Value dialog box.**

Adding Heads and Feets

Throughout the first part of this chapter, we give you all the gory details of page numbering, and now we have to admit that we usually don't use the Page Numbering dialog box to number our pages. We usually have lots of other things we want to include at the top or bottom of each page, such as the title of the document, today's date, and notes that say *Draft* or *Confidential! Destroy Before Reading!* The easiest way to print all this stuff at the top or bottom of each page is to use headers and footers.

The cool thing about headers and footers is that they can contain almost anything — one line of text, an entire paragraph, or even a picture. Also, because your document can contain two different headers (Header A and Header B) and two different footers (Footer A and Footer B, believe it or not), you can print different headers and footers on the facing pages of documents printed on both sides of the page.

Some grammar maniacs insist that headers and footers are more properly named *headings* and *footings*. Ignore them.

Making a header or footer

These steps show how to make a header or footer:

Header

1. **Choose <u>V</u>iew⇨<u>P</u>age to switch to page view so that you can see the headers and footers you create.**

   Headers and footers are invisible in Draft view. You're probably already in Page view, but we want to make sure.

Footer

2. **Move to the beginning of your document by pressing Ctrl+Home.**

   If you want headers and footers to begin partway through your document, move to the top of the first page on which you want the header or footer to appear.

3. **Choose <u>I</u>nsert⇨<u>H</u>eader/Footer.**

   You see the Headers/Footers dialog box, as shown in Figure 8-5.

Figure 8-5: Defining heads and feets.

4. **Choose the header or footer you want to create.**

   If you plan to use one header or footer for the entire document, choose Header A or Footer A. If you plan to use two headers or two footers (to number facing pages, for example), choose either A or B. This book, for example, has different headers and footers for the even- and odd-numbered pages.

5. **Click on the Create button.**

   This step tells WordPerfect to insert a new secret header or footer code in your document. WordPerfect adds a blank section, outlined by gray guidelines, as shown in Figure 8-6, at the top (for headers) or bottom (for footers) of the page; you can begin typing your header or footer on this line. Notice that headers and footers get their own guidelines. You can drag all margins except the top margin of a header (you have to change the page's top margin) or the bottom margin of a footer (you have to change the page's bottom margin).

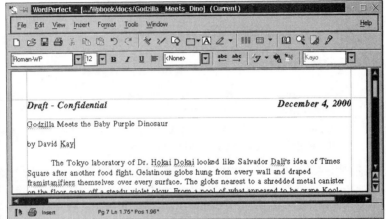

Figure 8-6:
Typing a header to appear on every page of a document.

To skip printing the header or footer on the first page of the document (a common technique), move to the beginning of the document anyway. You can tell WordPerfect to suppress printing the header and footer on the first page; this procedure is described later in this chapter.

You can have several Header A's, Header B's, Footer A's, or Footer B's in your document. If you think that this arrangement would be confusing, you're right; don't use it.

You can create Header or Footer B before you create Header or Footer A; WordPerfect doesn't care. On the other hand, you may get confused. We stick with A if we're using only one header or footer. If you use two at a time (both Header A *and* Header B), one prints over the other. Avoid this problem by defining one header or footer for odd pages and the other for even, as explained later in this chapter.

When you create a header or footer, WordPerfect inserts a secret code named Header A (or whichever header or footer you choose). The code also contains all the text that appears in the header or footer, including formatting. To see or delete this code, refer to Chapter 9.

Typing the text in a header or footer

After you create a header or footer, your job is to type the text you want to appear in it. To help you, WordPerfect adds a few items to the Property Bar. Check out the changes shown in Figure 8-7.

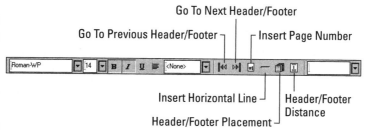

Figure 8-7:
Header and footer buttons on the Property Bar.

Go To Next Header/Footer

Go To Previous Header/Footer ⌐   ⌐ Insert Page Number

Insert Horizontal Line ⌐   Header/Footer Distance

Header/Footer Placement ⌐

The new line that WordPerfect adds to your document (see Step 5 in the preceding section) is no ordinary new line — it's in a special zone that contains the text for your header or footer. You cannot use the cursor-control keys to move between the header or footer zone and the rest of the document. You can use the mouse to click where you want to edit; this action enables you to switch between editing the regular document and your header or footer.

The standard three-part header

If you want some text at the left margin, some text centered, and some text at the right margin, you can tell WordPerfect to center and right-align parts of your header. You can print the document title at the left margin, for example, the page number in the center of the header, and today's date at the right margin.

To make a header such as this one, start typing the stuff that goes at the left margin; **The Complete History of Chocolate**, for example. When you get to the part you want to have centered (**Page 536**, for example), choose the Format⇨Line⇨Center command and start typing at the center of the line. When you get to the part you want to have flush against the right margin, (**Printed 12/25/2000**, for example), choose Format⇨Line⇨Flush Right and keep typing.

You may find that the text that's flush to the left margin gets typed over by the text that's centered and that the text that's centered gets typed over by the text that's flush right. That situation happens because you told WordPerfect where to put that text, and, by golly, it's going to do just what you said. If not enough space is available to put each thing in its place, that's not a WordPerfect problem. Your only choice is to make the left-hand text, or the center text, or the right-hand text a little shorter.

While you're editing a header or footer, WordPerfect would really rather that you stay focused on what you're doing. Some buttons on the toolbar and some menu commands get fuzzy and unusable, therefore, when you're editing a header or footer. For example, you cannot use the New, Open, Save, and Print buttons on the toolbar or their equivalent menu commands while you're editing a header or footer. *C'est la vie.*

To enter some text in your header or footer, follow these steps:

1. **Move the cursor to the header or footer zone, if it's not already there.**

   You can tell when you're editing a header or footer because the Property Bar acquires the header/footer buttons shown in Figure 8-7. You can also tell by looking at the title bar of the WordPerfect window. The title bar displays not only the name of the document you're editing but also the name of the header or footer you're working on (`Zuke_soup.wpd - [Header A]`, for example).

2. **Type the text.**

   You can control the font, font size, and text style in the usual ways (refer to Chapter 6). If you want the header or footer to be more than one line long, be our guest; just keep typing. Go ahead and press Enter at the end of the line if you want to include more than one paragraph.

   What about page numbers, you ask? Aha! It's time to use those cute buttons on the Property Bar that magically appeared when you entered Header/Footer Land.

 3. **To include the current page number in the header or footer, move the cursor to the place where you want the page number to appear and click the Insert Number button on the Property Bar.**

   This button has a little #1 on it. When you click on it, a little menu appears.

4. **Choose Page Number (as you probably have guessed).**

5. **Click anywhere in the document *except* in the header or footer to get back to the real world.**

When you type the text of your document, you don't have to leave room for the headers or footers. WordPerfect sticks them in at the top and bottom margins of the page and shoves the other text out of the way.

If you want to print the current date in the header or footer, see the section in Chapter 22 about inserting the date or just press Ctrl+Shift+D.

If you want your header or footer to contain lines, boxes, or even pictures, see Chapter 15.

You can format text in your headers and footers by using the same commands you can use for text in the rest of your document. Commands you cannot use appear grayed out on the WordPerfect menus, which is the subtle WordPerfect way of telling you that you cannot choose these commands.

If you cannot see your headers or footers, you're probably using Draft view, in which they're invisible. Choose View➪Page to switch to page view.

Controlling where headers and footers are printed

After you create a header or footer and type its text, you can tell WordPerfect which pages to print it on. While editing a header or footer, click on the Header/Footer Placement button on the Property Bar, the button with a stack of three pages on it. WordPerfect displays the Placement dialog box, as shown in Figure 8-8. Choose Odd Pages, Even Pages, or Every Page, and then click on OK.

Figure 8-8:
Telling
WordPerfect
where
to print
headers and
footers.

"Don't print it here!"

You can tell WordPerfect not to print the header or footer you just went to so much trouble to create. Why would you want to? We can think of these two good reasons:

- ✔ You don't want the header to print on the first page of your document. When you write a letter, for example, you may want all the pages except the first one to have a header that says *Joe Jones, Sept. 8, 2000, Page 2* (with the correct page number, naturally). Therefore, you want to suppress the header or footer for one page.

- ✔ Your document may have two or more sections, and you may want to use a header or footer for only the first section. You can discontinue the header or footer for the rest of the pages in the document.

To suppress the printing of a header or footer, you tell WordPerfect to skip printing it on a particular page. To suppress a header or footer for one page, follow these steps:

1. **Move the cursor to the page on which you don't want to print the header or footer.**

   Make sure that the cursor isn't in the header/footer area.

2. **Choose Format⇨Page⇨Suppress.**

   WordPerfect displays the Suppress dialog box, as shown in Figure 8-9.

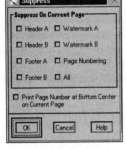

Figure 8-9:
Skipping printing a header or footer on one page.

3. **Choose the headers or footers you don't want to print.**

   You can select as many items as you want. If you don't want any headers or footers or watermarks or anything on this page, select the All check box.

4. **Click on OK.**

   The headers or footers disappear from the page, only to reappear on the next page.

When you suppress the printing of a header or footer on a page, WordPerfect creates a secret code named Suppress at the top of the page.

Discontinuing headers and footers

To discontinue printing a header or footer, you tell WordPerfect to stop printing this header or footer for good. Follow these steps:

1. **Move to the first page on which you don't want the header or footer to print.**

2. **Choose Insert⇨Header/Footer to display the Headers/Footers dialog box.**

3. **Choose the header or footer you want to discontinue.**

   You can select only one. If you want to discontinue all of them, you have to repeat these steps for each one. (Sigh.)

4. **Click on the Discontinue button.**

   The dialog box disappears in a puff of bytes, and so does your header or footer from this page and all subsequent pages in the document.

When you discontinue a header or footer, WordPerfect inserts a secret code named End Header A (or whichever header or footer you chose). To see or delete this code, see Chapter 9.

After you discontinue a header or footer, you cannot turn it back on. To cancel discontinuing it (that is, to undo the preceding steps), you must delete the secret end code. If you just want to skip printing the header or footer for a page or three, suppress the header or footer on each page rather than discontinue it.

Getting rid of a header or footer

If you change your mind about a header or footer and you want to get rid of it for good, you can delete the contents. (You know that you've succeeded when the special guidelines go away.) You can also delete the secret code that defines the header or footer. Chapter 9 tells you how to find and exterminate codes you no longer want.

Chapter 9

The WordPerfect Secret Decoder Ring

● ●

In This Chapter

▶ Knowing what secret formatting codes are

▶ Using character codes

▶ Dealing with character-formatting codes

▶ Undoing sentence and paragraph formatting

▶ Undoing page and document formatting

▶ Finding codes

▶ Replacing codes automagically

▶ Putting codes in their places

▶ Using mysterious codes

● ●

*A*fter you have worked on a WordPerfect document for a while, it may develop strange quirks and annoying tics. You may even suspect that your document is haunted and consider calling the local Byte Exorcist. WordPerfect has a simple reason for its mysterious behavior: So far, you haven't been able to see The Whole Picture.

As we allude to in preceding chapters, there's more to a WordPerfect document than meets the eye. To perform all its impressive formatting tricks, WordPerfect scatters hidden and powerful *codes,* or *formatting codes,* in your document. If these codes get discombobulated, your document can go haywire, too.

Ideally, you should never have to see these codes. After all, you don't care how WordPerfect does things — you just want them done. This is real life, however, and in real life, things go awry — horribly awry, at times. At these times, you must know how to roll up your sleeves, face those WordPerfect codes, and fix them. The solution isn't really that bad; you don't even get your hands greasy.

What Are Secret Formatting Codes?

WordPerfect codes are special objects that WordPerfect inserts in your document to turn special features on or off. The usual way to insert a code in your document is to choose a formatting command or click on a formatting button. WordPerfect saves the codes with your document.

WordPerfect has three types of codes: character codes, single codes, and paired codes. (We just made up these terms.) We describe each type of code in gory detail later in this chapter and tell you how to spot them and what they do. This list briefly describes the types of codes:

- **Character:** Represents special characters, such as Tab. Some codes represent keys on the keyboard, and others (such as Indent) don't.

- **Single:** Turns on a formatting feature. The Lft Marg and Rgt Marg codes, for example, set the left and right margins, beginning at the position of the code. The formatting the code applies remains in effect for the rest of the document or until WordPerfect runs across another occurrence of the same code.

- **Paired:** Comes in pairs (you guessed that, we know). WordPerfect also calls these codes *revertible* codes — who knows where that little piece of jargon comes from? The first code in the pair turns a feature on, and the second one turns it off. Bold codes, for example, come in pairs: one to turn on boldface and the other to turn it off. The text between the two codes is in boldface.

Seeing the Codes

"This code business is all very exciting," you say. "So where are all these codes that have been running around in my documents like cockroaches in the dark?"

It's a good question with a simple answer: You can use the View➪Reveal Codes command to see the codes in your document. (Another method is to right-click on the text of your document and choose Reveal Codes from the QuickMenu that appears. Shift+Ctrl+F3 might work, too, or Alt+F3.) Figure 9-1 shows the WordPerfect window with the Reveal Codes window at the bottom.

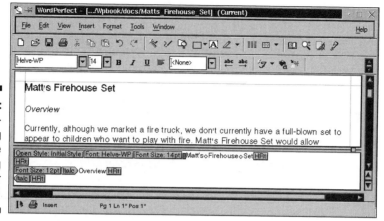

Figure 9-1:
Strange-
looking
codes are
lurking
in your
document!

Understanding the Reveal Codes window

The Reveal Codes window shows the same text you see in the regular window. Because the Reveal Codes window usually cannot hold as much text as the regular window can, the Reveal Codes window shows the part that's right around the cursor position. The cursor appears as a red box; its location in the Reveal Codes window corresponds to its position in the regular window. If you click on a spot in the Reveal Codes window, the red cursor-box moves there and the regular cursor moves to the corresponding point in the regular window. If you click on a spot in the regular window, the cursor moves there and the red cursor-box moves to the corresponding place in the Reveal Codes window.

Scrolling up or down in the Reveal Codes window can be tricky. When you press the navigation keys on your keyboard, such as PgUp and PgDn, the cursor moves in the regular window and the red cursor-box moves in the Reveal Codes window.

Text in Reveal Codes is completely unformatted. Spaces appear as little diamonds, and codes look like little buttons. Character and single codes look like little rectangular buttons, and paired codes (such as the two Italc codes) have pointed ends, with the points of each pair pointing toward each other.

You can type, edit, and perform all your normal WordPerfect activities while the Reveal Codes window is visible; some people like to leave it open all the time. (Of course, some people consider going to the dentist to be a recreational activity.)

You can control the colors that WordPerfect uses for the text and background of the Reveal Codes window, how much information is shown for each code, and some other arcane facets of the Reveal Codes window. Chapter 19 shows you how to customize this stuff. Watch out, though: This subject is getting into seriously nerdy activities, don't you think?

What the heck do all those codes do? The rest of this chapter discusses the codes you usually encounter and how to get rid of ones you no longer want.

Adjusting the size of windows

A dividing line separates the regular window from the Reveal Codes window, and a small box appears near the right end of the dividing line. Using the mouse, you can click on the box and drag the line up or down.

Getting rid of the Reveal Codes window

When you finish looking at your codes, you can make the Reveal Codes window go away. Seeing codes leap around at the bottom of the screen is, after all, a little distracting. Use one of these methods to send the Reveal Codes window back into byte oblivion:

- ✔ Choose View⇨Reveal Codes again.
- ✔ Click on the box near the right end of the dividing line and drag it down to the Application Bar.
- ✔ Right-click anywhere in the Reveal Codes window and choose Hide Reveal Codes from the QuickMenu that pops up.

Cracking the Codes

Now that you know how to bring the secret WordPerfect formatting codes into the light of day, what can you do with them? Unlike cockroaches (which they otherwise resemble closely), WordPerfect codes don't scurry away when they're brought to light. In the Reveal Codes window, you can examine them, modify them, and even delete them.

If you don't want to know about codes, skip the rest of this chapter. If you run into trouble with your document and it starts acting as though it has fleas, come back here to find out what's going on.

A note to Microsoft Word users

If you have used Microsoft Word, you may wonder whether the WordPerfect View⇨ Reveal Codes command has anything to do with the Field Codes command in Word. In a couple of words: not really.

Because Word doesn't use codes for formatting, its Field Codes feature doesn't show you anything about fonts, margins, page layout, and the like. Instead, the Word codes provide a way to include text that is under the control of the

Word program — today's date, for example, which Word can update automatically. Some WordPerfect codes do this, too (see Chapter 22 to find out how to create a code that prints today's date), although most don't. As a result, viewing codes in Word (by checking the Field Codes check box on the Word View tab in the Tools⇨Options dialog box) shows you many fewer codes; many Word documents contain *no* codes.

Looking at codes

Some codes contain much more information than you might think. You may see a Header A code at the beginning of your document, for example; this code indicates that you have defined a header. To see more details about this code, place the cursor directly before the code. (Remember that the cursor appears as a little red box.) Suddenly, the code expands until it says Header A: Every Page, Chocolate in the Workplace. Many codes contain more information than meets the eye; place the cursor in front of a code to see just what it says.

Modifying codes

To change a code, try double-clicking on it in the Reveal Codes window. This action tells WordPerfect that you want to do something to the code, and WordPerfect tries to guess what that something is. If you used a dialog box to insert the code in the first place, WordPerfect displays the same dialog box again. If you double-click on a Para Spacing code, for example, WordPerfect pops up the Paragraph Format dialog box, which displays the values you specified when you created the code. (This feature is rather useful.) If you change the information in the dialog box and then click on OK, WordPerfect updates the code to match.

Hard- and soft-core codes

WordPerfect has two versions of many codes: one hard and one soft. This terminology has nothing to do with ripeness, materials used, or anything we can't mention in a G-rated book such as this one. No, it has to do with how seriously WordPerfect takes them.

WordPerfect inserts a soft code and could just as well take it right back out. The program continually shuffles the codes around. When you edit the text in a paragraph, for example, WordPerfect changes SRt codes into spaces (and vice versa) as necessary so that the margins are correct. It never deletes a HRt code, however. (See the section "Using Character Codes," later in this chapter, to find out what the HRt and SRt do.)

Deleting codes

The position of each code is important, and codes that are in the wrong place can be a headache. If you see a code that seems to have wandered off into the woods, you can trash it. Move the cursor in front of the code and press Delete, or move the cursor just after the code and press Backspace. Or, simply drag the code aboveground — into the top window, where it evaporates in the warm light of day.

When the Reveal Codes window isn't displayed, WordPerfect skips most codes when you press the Delete or Backspace keys so that you don't delete codes accidentally. When the codes are revealed, however, WordPerfect figures that you can see what you're doing, and when you press Delete, it deletes the code to the right of the red cursor.

Save your document (press Ctrl+S) before you make any changes in codes, because it's easy to make a horrendous mess with this code stuff. If you save your document before you goof up, you can just close the messy one (click the Close button or choose File⇨Close from the menu bar and click No to throw away your ill-advised changes) and reopen the original (choose Program from the program window's menu bar, and then select the filename from the list of recently used documents at the bottom of the Program menu).

Now that you know how to see and dispose of the WordPerfect secret codes, it's time to look at the different types of codes and what they do.

Using the Open Style Code

At the beginning of every document, you may notice a mysterious `Open Style` code. WordPerfect doesn't allow you to delete this code. It tells WordPerfect that unless you insert codes to tell it otherwise, WordPerfect should format the document by using the Initial Codes Style settings. What are the Initial Codes Style settings? We were wondering that ourselves. For the full story, see the section in Chapter 10 about the InitialStyle style.

Using Character Codes

The most common codes in every document are carriage-return (line-ending) codes, including the two in this list:

- ✔ `SRt`: A carriage-return character that WordPerfect inserts automatically whenever you reach the right margin; usually called a *soft return*. The *S* stands for "soft." (Refer to the preceding sidebar, "Hard- and soft-core codes," to find out why,).

- ✔ `HRt`: A character that WordPerfect inserts automatically whenever you press the Enter key to signal the end of a paragraph; also known as a *hard return*.

WordPerfect includes dozens and dozens of other codes. This list shows some other popular character codes:

- ✔ `Left Tab`: You see this code when you press the Tab key to move to a left tab stop. (Chapter 7 discusses types of tab stops.) When you press the Tab key to move to another type of tab stop, you get a `Right Tab`, `Center Tab`, `Dec Tab`, `...Left Tab`, `...Right Tab`, `... Center Tab`, or `...Dec Tab` code.

- ✔ `Hd Back Tab`: The "back-tab" code you see when you press Shift+Tab, used mainly in hanging indents. (Refer to the section in Chapter 7 about changing margins for a paragraph or two.)

- ✔ `HPg`: The hard page break you produce by pressing Ctrl+Enter (or choosing Insert⇨New Page).

- ✔ `SRt-SPg` **and** `HRt-SPg`: When WordPerfect inserts a soft page break because a page has become full, it may also stick in one of these codes. (Don't worry about the difference between the two.)

✔ Auto Hyphen EOL **and** TSRt: If you use the WordPerfect automatic-hyphenation feature (refer to Chapter 7), WordPerfect sticks in these two codes whenever it decides to hyphenate a word at the right margin. First, you see Auto Hyphen EOL (EOL is computerese for *end of line*); then you see TSRt (*temporary soft return*, maybe?).

You can delete any of these codes to get rid of the characters they represent.

Dealing with Character-Formatting Codes

Chapter 6 shows how to format the characters in your documents seven ways from Sunday. Whenever you use character formatting, WordPerfect creates a flurry of secret codes. Most codes are paired and mark the beginning and end of the text to be formatted. This list shows some character-formatting codes you may see:

✔ Bold: A pair of these codes encloses text in boldface.

✔ Italc: Likewise, these codes surround text in italics. (Can't those WordPerfect folks spell?)

✔ Und: These codes appear around underlined text.

✔ Font Size: A lone code changes the font size from its location to the end of the document or until you get to another Font Size code. A pair of Font Size codes can also enclose text that appears in a different size.

✔ Font: Likewise, one Font code (or a pair of Font codes) changes the font (typeface).

Undoing character formatting

To undo character formatting, just blow away the formatting codes in the Reveal Codes window. For paired codes, you have to delete only one of them. When one of a pair of paired codes disappears, the other dies, too (from grief, we assume).

Editing formatted text

After you format your text with character-formatting codes, editing can be a little tricky. If you format a heading in boldface, for example, a word you add to the end of the heading may not be in boldface.

Why not? Because the new text was typed after the closing `Bold` code. Without using the Reveal Codes window, it's difficult to see whether the cursor is inside or outside a pair of formatting codes.

Some types of formatting are shown on the toolbar and Property Bar. If the cursor is in bold text, for example, the Bold button appears to be pushed in. Likewise, the Font Face and Font Size buttons on the Property Bar tell you the font and size of the text where the cursor is. To be sure, however, you have to use the Reveal Codes window.

If you end up with your formatting codes in the wrong place, you can delete them and create them again. Alternatively, you can use cut-and-paste commands (refer to Chapter 5) to move the text around so that the codes are in the right places. Because this procedure looks weird when you do it and can be tricky, be sure to save your document before trying this type of code acrobatics.

Undoing Sentence and Paragraph Formatting

In Chapter 7, you fool around with the margins and tab stops in your document as well as with some other things that affect entire paragraphs of text at a time. As you can imagine, WordPerfect inserts a secret code every time you use one of these formatting commands. This list shows some codes you may encounter:

- ✔ `Tab Set`: Contains the settings for all the tabs you can see on the ruler. Even if you change just one stop, the `Tab Set` code stores the positions of all of them. This code belongs at the beginning of a paragraph — never in the middle of a line.

- ✔ `Hd Left Ind`: The indent character you get when you press the F7 key or choose Format➪Paragraph➪Indent.

- ✔ `Hd Left Ind` **and** `Hd Back Tab`: Used for hanging indents. When you create a hanging indent, WordPerfect inserts two — count 'em, two — codes. First, it inserts a `Hd Left Ind` code so that all the lines of the paragraph are indented; then it inserts a `Hd Back Tab` code so that the first line of the paragraph is unindented. It's not elegant, but it works.

- ✔ `Hd Center on Marg`: Centers a line between the left and right margins.

- ✔ `Hd Flush Right`: Pushes text to the right margin.

- ✔ `Hyph`: Indicates that you have turned on the hyphenation feature.

You may see the following codes by themselves or in pairs. If you see just one, it sets the formatting for the rest of the document or until you get to another of the same kind of code. If you see a pair of these codes, they set the formatting for the text enclosed by the pair. This list briefly describes the codes:

- Lft Marg **and** Rgt Marg: Set the left and right margins in your document, beginning at the position of the code, and belong at the beginning of a paragraph

- **The** Just **family of codes:** Tells WordPerfect how to justify the text between the left and right margins

- Ln Spacing: Sets the spacing between lines

You can delete any of these codes to remove unwanted formatting from your document. When formatting codes come in pairs, you can delete just one of the pair; then they both disappear.

Undoing Page and Document Formatting

Most codes that affect entire pages or an entire document appear at the beginning of a document, or at least at the top of the page. That arrangement makes them a little easier to find in the Reveal Codes window. To cancel the formatting controlled by these codes, just delete the code.

Chapter 8 describes commands that format pages and entire documents. This list shows the codes created by the commands we describe there:

- Paper Sz/Typ: Sets the paper size and paper type for the document.

- Top Mar **and** Bot Mar: Set the top and bottom margins.

- Cntr Cur Pg: Centers the current page between the top and bottom margins.

- Wid/Orph: Tells WordPerfect how to deal with widows and orphans (the ones we describe in Chapter 8, in the section about keeping text together).

- Condl EOP **(conditional end of page):** Tells WordPerfect to keep the next few lines together and not to split them with a page break.

- Block Pro: Encloses text that should not be split by a page break. This code should always appear in pairs.

- Pg Num Pos: Tells WordPerfect where to print page numbers.

- Header A, Header B, Footer A, **and** Footer B: Defines what WordPerfect prints at the top and bottom of each page. When you discontinue headers, you get codes named Header A End, Header B End,

`Footer A End`, and `Footer B End`. When you suppress the printing of headers or footers on a page, WordPerfect sticks a `Suppress` code at the top of the page.

Finding Codes

The Reveal Codes window is not a model of readability; user-friendliness is not its middle name. (Heaven knows that it's a vast improvement over the Reveal Codes window in earlier versions of WordPerfect. The window looked like a strange form of algebra crossed with some kind of circuit diagram.)

The main difficulty in using the Reveal Codes window is finding the code you want. Because the line endings don't correspond with those in the regular window, you may get confused about where you are.

Bring on the WordPerfect Edit⇨Find and Replace command! (We describe it in Chapter 5.) In addition to using the Find and Replace Text dialog box to find text, you can use it to find codes.

You can tell WordPerfect to look for codes in two ways. Both these methods can be useful:

- ✔ **Codes:** Tell WordPerfect the type of code to look for — a `Lft Mar` (left margin) code, for example. This method is useful when you want to know what the heck is going on with the margins in your document.

- ✔ **Specific codes:** Tell WordPerfect the exact code to look for (a `Lft Mar` code that sets the left margin to 0.5 inch, for example). This method is useful if you have decided to change all ½-inch margins to ¾-inch margins and aren't interested in any other margin settings. You can also automatically replace all ½-inch margin codes with ¾-inch margin codes; see the section "Finding specific codes," later in this chapter.

Because both methods call for using two dialog boxes at the same time, your screen may begin to look like a Dadaist painting. Give them a try, though, if you have the courage.

Finding all codes of one type

To find all codes of one type in your document (all the `Tab Set` codes, for example, regardless of the tab-stop positions they contain), follow these steps:

1. **Move the cursor to the beginning of the document or to the beginning of the part of the document you want to search.**

2. **Choose Edit➪Find and Replace or press F2.**

   You see the Find and Replace Text dialog box, as shown in Figure 9-2. This dialog box has its own little menu bar (which we describe in more detail in Chapter 5).

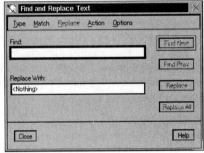

Figure 9-2:
Finding
codes
wherever
they may
lurk.

3. **Choose Match➪Codes from this menu bar.**

   WordPerfect displays the Find Codes dialog box, as shown in Figure 9-3. The Find Codes box lists all the secret codes you can search for.

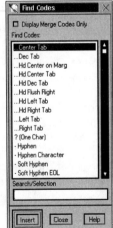

Figure 9-3:
Choosing
the code for
which to
search.

4. **Choose the code you want to search for.**

   Choose the Tab Set code, for example.

5. **Click on the Insert button in the Find Codes dialog box.**

   The code name appears in the Find box in the Find and Replace Text dialog box.

6. **Click on the Close button in the Find Codes dialog box.**

   You have finished telling WordPerfect which code you want to look for.

7. **Click on the Find Next button in the Find and Replace Text dialog box.**

   WordPerfect looks for the code or codes you specified and moves the red cursor-box just to the right of the code in the Reveal Codes window.

When you display the Find and Replace Text dialog box, its Find box contains text or codes — the last information you searched for. Because the content of the Find box is selected, though, any content you insert replaces the former content. You can also just delete the information if you don't want to search for it again.

If WordPerfect cannot find your code, it displays a small dialog box that tells you so. Click on the OK button to make this dialog box go away.

For more information about using the Find and Replace Text dialog box, refer to Chapter 5.

Here are some useful tips for searching for codes:

✔ To search backward through your document, click on the Find Prev button in the Find and Replace Text dialog box.

✔ On the Find Codes list in the Find Codes dialog box, the first 16 codes have names that begin with punctuation, such as . . . Left Tab (a tab that moves to a left tab stop with dot leaders). After these codes, the other codes are listed in alphabetical order. To locate in the Find Codes dialog box a code whose name begins with *T,* use the scroll bar to zoom down to the *T*s.

✔ If you plan to continue looking for codes (or text) in your document, you can leave the Find and Replace Text dialog box open while you edit the document. This practice is faster than opening and closing the dialog box for each search, although it does clutter the screen. You can move the Find and Replace Text dialog box to an out-of-the-way part of the screen by clicking and dragging its title bar.

   You can also leave the Find Codes dialog box open if you plan to look for different codes. Just skip clicking on its Close button until you finish with it.

✔ You can search for a sequence of codes, too. WordPerfect uses the two codes Hd Left Ind and Hd Back Tab, for example, to create a hanging indent. To search for this combination of codes in this order, select Hd Left Ind in the Codes dialog box, click on Insert, and then select Hd Back Tab from the list and click on the Insert button again. The two codes appear in the Find box. When you click on the Find Next button in the Find and Replace Text dialog box, WordPerfect looks for the sequence of codes.

✔ You can also search for a mixture of codes and regular characters. To search for a tab followed by an asterisk, for example, you can use the Find Codes dialog box to make [Tab (all)] appear in the Find Codes box and then type an asterisk.

Finding specific codes

WordPerfect has another way to look for codes that contain additional information. A *margin code* contains extra information, such as the size of the margin you want. A Bold code, on the other hand, contains no other information. For codes that contain additional information, you can search for all codes that have a particular setting (all Font codes that set the font to 12-point Helve-WP, for example). Follow these steps:

1. **Move the cursor to the beginning of the document or to the beginning of the part of the document you want to search.**

2. **Choose Edit➪Find and Replace or press F2.**

   WordPerfect displays the Find and Replace Text dialog box (refer to Figure 9-2).

3. **Choose Type➪Specific Codes from the menu bar in the Find and Replace Text dialog box.**

   You see the Specific Codes dialog box, as shown in Figure 9-4.

Figure 9-4:
Choosing
the type
of code to
look for.

4. **In the Specific Codes dialog box, choose the type of code for which you want to search.**

   WordPerfect lists only the types of codes that contain additional information. (To search for a code that isn't on this list, use the Match➪ Codes command, described in the preceding section.)

5. Click on the OK button in the Specific Codes dialog box.

The Specific Codes dialog box goes away, and WordPerfect changes the Find and Replace Text dialog box to match the type of code you're looking for. If you choose Font as the type of code for which to search, WordPerfect transforms the Find and Replace Text dialog box into a Find and Replace Font dialog box. The menu bar and buttons are unchanged, but rather than have to choose the text for which to search, you can just enter the information the code contains. The Find and Replace Font dialog box, for example, lets you enter the font name and font style.

6. Go ahead and do it: Enter the settings of the code for which you want to search.

Choose Helve-WP for the font name, for example, and Italics for the style.

7. Click on the Find Next button to search for the next occurrence of the code.

When you search for a specific code, you cannot search for a combination of codes and text or for a sequence of more than one code. (Bummer.)

If WordPerfect cannot find the code, it displays a dialog box that tells you so. Click on OK to make this dialog box go away. If you're sure that the code is in there somewhere, try using the Match⇨Codes method described in the preceding section.

Knowing what to do after you find your code

After you find the code you're looking for, you can delete it by pressing the Delete key. If the code was created by means of a dialog box, you can modify the code by double-clicking on it in the Reveal Codes window.

Display the Reveal Codes window when you're finding codes so that you can see whether WordPerfect found the one you want.

Replacing Codes Automagically

Here's a fairly common scenario: You formatted your document tastefully with several fonts, including CG Times (a version of Times Roman). You find out, though, that the Roman-WP font looks much nicer when you print. What's the best way to change all those Font codes from CG Times to Roman-WP without going nuts?

Like all decent word processors, WordPerfect has a find-and-replace command (which we describe in Chapter 5). It swoops through your document, looking for the offending text and changing it to the proper text. The good news is that you can use the command to look for and change the WordPerfect secret codes, too.

The bad news is that you cannot use the find-and-replace command to replace paired codes. You may have used pairs of Bold codes, for example, to make section headings in a report boldfaced and later decide to use italics instead. If you use the find-and-replace procedures described in the following section to replace all the Bold On codes (the ones at the beginning of the boldfaced heading) with Italc On codes, it just doesn't work.

Probably the best way to get around this whole business of finding and replacing codes is to use *styles*, which enable you to standardize the codes you use for various parts of your document. Chapter 10 describes how to use styles.

Be sure to save your document before you use the find-and-replace feature. You never know what may go wrong. We guarantee enormous amounts of smugness if something goes wrong after you just saved your document.

Replacing specific codes with other codes

Although the WordPerfect find-and-replace feature can be confusing and shouldn't be used with paired codes, it's great for replacing character codes and single codes. You can replace all the specific codes with other codes of the same type, such as changing all the Font:Helve-WP codes to Font:Roman-WP Regular. Follow these steps:

1. **Move to the beginning of your document by pressing Ctrl+Home.**

   If you want to replace the codes in only part of your document, move to the beginning of that part.

2. **Choose Edit⇨Find and Replace or press F2.**

   WordPerfect displays the Find and Replace Text dialog box (refer to Figure 9-2). This dialog box has its own little menu bar (described in more detail in Chapter 5).

3. **With the cursor in the Find part of the Find and Replace Text dialog box, choose Type⇨Specific Codes to display the Specific Codes dialog box (refer to Figure 9-4).**

4. **Choose the type of code (Font, for example) you want to replace.**

5. **Click on the OK button to dismiss the dialog box.**

   WordPerfect transforms the Find and Replace Text dialog box into a dialog box that's more appropriate for the type of code you're replacing (the Find and Replace Font dialog box, for example).

Both the Find and Replace with text boxes are transformed into boxes that are appropriate for the type of code with which you're working. If you're replacing Font codes, for example, WordPerfect displays settings for fonts and font styles.

6. Choose the settings for the existing codes you want to get rid of and for the new codes with which you want to replace them.

Choose Arial for the Find font setting, for example, and Times New Roman for the Replace with setting.

7. To find the first instance of the code you're looking for, click on Find Next.

Just tell WordPerfect to start looking; you don't have to tell it again.

8. To replace the codes one by one so that you can eyeball each occurrence before making the replacement, click on the Replace button in the dialog box.

When you click on Replace, WordPerfect replaces the code in the Find box with the code in the Replace with box. To skip the code, click on Find Next. To replace this code and all the rest of the codes of this type in your document, go wild and click on Replace All.

9. When you finish, click on Close to make the Find and Replace dialog box go away.

If you cannot see your codes, choose View➪Reveal Codes in the WordPerfect window to open the Reveal Codes window.

Replacing codes with other codes

The preceding section tells you how to replace WordPerfect codes with codes that are of the same type but contain other settings. You can also replace one type of code with another — Hd Left Ind codes (indents) with Hd Left Tab codes (regular ol' tabs), for example. (Remember that you can't replace codes such as Bold On/Bold Off with other paired codes such as Italic On/Italic Off.) The following steps show you how:

1. Move to the beginning of your document by pressing Ctrl+Home.

To replace the codes in only part of your document, move to the beginning of that part.

2. Choose Edit➪Find and Replace or press F2.

WordPerfect displays the Find and Replace Text dialog box (refer to Figure 9-2).

3. **Click in the Find part of the dialog box and choose <u>M</u>atch⇨C<u>o</u>des from the dialog box's menu.**

   You see the Find Codes dialog box (refer to Figure 9-3).

4. **Choose the type of code you want to replace (Hd Left Ind, for example).**

5. **Click on Insert to stick the code into the Find box in the Find and Replace Text dialog box.**

6. **Click the Close button to shut the Find Codes dialog box.**

   You return to the Find and Replace Text dialog box, already in progress.

7. **Click in the Replace With box, choose Replace⇨Codes from the menu, and select the new code you want added (Hd Left Tab, for example).**

8. **Click on Insert to stick the code into the Replace with box of the Find and Replace Text dialog box.**

   You have told WordPerfect what to look for and what to replace it with.

9. **Click on the Close button in the Find Codes dialog box.**

   You're finished inserting codes, and you probably want some of your screen back. The Find box contains the code or codes you want to replace, and the Replace With box contains the code or codes you want to replace them with.

10. **Click on the Replace button in the Find and Replace Text dialog box to replace codes one at a time, or click on Replace All to go for the gold.**

11. **Click on the Close button when you finish replacing codes.**

    Take a look around your document to see what havoc you have wrought.

You cannot use this method to insert codes that require additional information. You cannot replace all your Bold codes with Font codes, for example, because Font codes require additional information (the font name and style). It's just a WordPerfect limitation. Not that we can blame WordPerfect — this find-and-replace business is complicated enough as it is.

Using this method, you can replace combinations of codes and text with other combinations of code and text.

Deleting all codes

You can use the Find and Replace Text dialog box to get rid of all codes of one type in your document (all Font codes, for example). Use the preceding steps to tell WordPerfect which codes you want to find, but don't enter anything in the Replace With box. When you click Replace or Replace All, WordPerfect replaces these codes with nothing.

A Summary of Mysterious Codes

"What the heck is the !@#$% code? And who the #$%^&* put it in my document?" This cry has been heard throughout the land since WordPerfect first shipped back in the early 1980s.

If you encounter a code you have never seen and that isn't described in this chapter, stay calm; you can always delete the code, after all. To find out what it is, place the cursor on top of it. A little yellow box pops up and gives you a hint. If the hint isn't enough, double-click on the code. Depending on the code, you probably see the same dialog box that inserts the code. You can click on the Help button in the dialog box or press the F1 key to get help about this feature.

Chapter 10

Documents with Style

. . . .

In This Chapter

▶ Creating and applying styles

▶ Using headings and other built-in styles

▶ Using more built-in styles

▶ Changing styles with the Styles Editor

▶ Turning styles off and chaining styles

▶ Reusing styles and getting rid of them

. . . .

*W*hen Og, the popular and celebrated mammoth hunter, trimmed his body with the colorful viscera of a woolly mammoth, the Og style caught the popular imagination. Anyone could simply walk into the local haberdashery, request an Og, and come out with all the necessary fine points taken care of. No need to specify all the details, such as the woven-tripe neck-lace, the bone in the hair, the brain-tanned bladder sporran — the word *Og* said it all. In the following year, when Og decided that the necklace should be sinew and not tripe, folks could still order an Og and be in style.

A more contemporary application of these named styles is text formatting. Text-formatting styles take advantage of the fact that most text formatting is repetitive. In this book, for example, all the level-1 headings have the same format, as do all the level-2 headings, the normal text, the captions, and other elements. Rather than continually respecify for each block of text all the details of typeface, point size, indentation, justification, and the rest, why not call one collection of formats Heading 1, another Heading 2, and another Caption, for example? That way, the only formatting a block of text needs is a style name. Applying a named style is much simpler than accurately repeat-ing the same half-dozen formatting commands over and over.

Another advantage is that after text is formatted by styles, any change in style definitions immediately takes effect throughout the document. An Og remains an Og; it just looks different. In our opinion, styles are the most useful, least-used feature of WordPerfect. The first time you have to whip out a document really quickly and still have it look good, you'll feel smug about the time you took to find out about styles and the time you spent setting them up (and, especially with QuickStyle, it doesn't take long).

What Is a Style?

A WordPerfect *style* is a combination of various types of formatting, such as fonts and indentation — the kind of stuff you typically do with the Format commands — assigned to a name. Then you can apply the style by name to text in your document that you want formatted that way.

Usually, you use a style for some simple combination of paragraph layout and font or font style, such as centered and bold. You can also use line, page, and document formatting, however. You can use anything, in fact, that changes the appearance of your document, from margins to page breaks.

After you use a style, any change in the definition of the style ripples through your document, changing appearances wherever you applied that style. This capability is way cool.

When you format text by using styles, however, a bit of a conflict occurs in places where you formatted the text directly by using the Format command or the function keys. WordPerfect resolves this conflict in favor of the directly formatted text. If you have indented a paragraph by choosing Format⇨Paragraph⇨Indent or pressing F7, for example, and then you apply a paragraph style that isn't indented, the indentation remains. Directly applied formatting can be tricky to remove, too, and often requires you to delete the secret codes we discuss in Chapter 9. If you use styles, be diligent about them. As much as possible, don't revert to your old, unprincipled ways of formatting your text directly by using the Format menu's commands.

A Style By Any Other Name Would Smell As Sweet

WordPerfect has two kinds of styles: character and paragraph. (Okay, it has document styles too, but forget about them for now.) *Character* styles, as the name would lead you to believe, affect the format of characters: what font they appear in, whether they're bold or italic or underlined, and what color they are, for example. In fact, pretty much anything you can find under the Format⇨Font command can be part of a character style.

Paragraph styles include all the things in character styles (that's all the Format⇨Font stuff) along with paragraphy things like center or right justification (you can read about them in Chapter 7), tab settings, and borders around paragraphs (which we talk about in Chapter 14).

Creating and Applying a Style

The key to everything about styles lurks at the bottom of the Format menu: the Format⇨Styles command. If you think that you already understand styles, the brave, foolish, or knowledgeable can launch into the Format⇨Styles command. Good luck.

The rest of us will sneak up on styles a little more slowly. Rather than start with the Format⇨Styles command, we begin by formatting a bunch of text the way you want it, as an example. Then we record that formatting as a style. Because this method is straightforward and fast, WordPerfect calls it *QuickStyle*. This section explains how to do it.

Creating a style by using QuickStyle

Remember that WordPerfect has two kinds of styles: character and paragraph. We start by using QuickStyle to create a character style. Suppose that you want foreign words in your document to be in bold and italic. You can do it the easy way by creating a style named Foreign and applying it to all the foreign words in your document. These steps guide you through this process:

1. **Format some text in bold and italics as an example for WordPerfect. Position the cursor anywhere in the formatted text.**

   Preferably, format some text to which you want to apply the style anyway. To format in bold and italic, select the text and then press Ctrl+B and Ctrl+I.

2. **Click on the Select Styles list on the Property Bar (click the downward-pointing triangle button to the right of the Select Styles box) and select QuickStyle at the bottom of the list.**

   The Select Style list on the Property Bar is the drop-down list just to the left of the "abc" button; it usually says <None> until you've started creating styles.

   WordPerfect has a bunch of predefined styles; we talk about those in a minute. For now, concentrate on QuickStyles. The Styles QuickCreate dialog box appears, as shown in Figure 10-1.

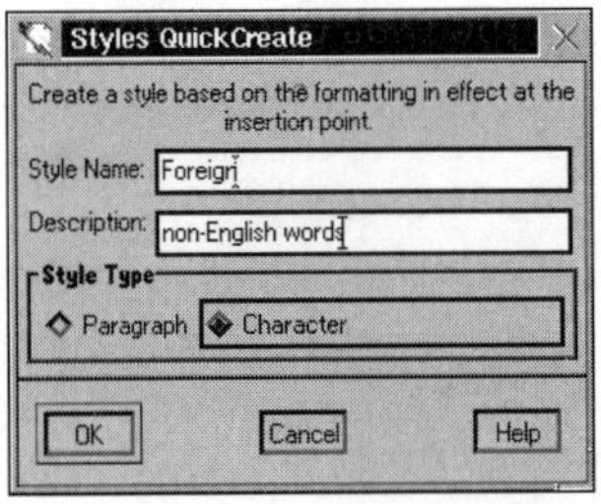

Figure 10-1:
The Styles
QuickCreate
dialog box.

Another way to display the Styles QuickCreate dialog box is to choose Format⇨Styles and then click on the QuickStyle button.

3. **Make up a name for your style (such as** Foreign) **and type it in the Style Name box, where the cursor awaits you.**

   Don't exceed 12 characters; WordPerfect doesn't allow more than that limit.

4. **If you want, type something in the Description box that describes the style's purpose.**

   You could type something such as **character formatting for foreign text**.

5. **In the Style Type section at the bottom of the dialog box, click on Character.**

   This step tells WordPerfect to create a character style. Remember that WordPerfect has two kinds of styles: character and paragraph. Although you get to choose one for your QuickStyle, we're talking about character styles here.

6. **Click on the OK button.**

   The Styles QuickCreate dialog box goes away and WordPerfect creates the style.

   If you click the Select Styles arrow again, you see your new style on the available styles list.

That's it — you did it. You have created a style named Foreign, which you now can apply by name to any selected text in your document.

Applying a character style

To apply your character style, select some text and click on the arrow button next to the Select Styles box on the Property Bar. This time, the style list contains your very own style. Click on it to apply your new style to the selected text.

"The Enter key is broken"

The Enter key behaves *very strangely* if you're using a character style while you type. Suppose that you create a character style (like Foreign), and choose it from the Select Styles list on the Property Bar. With the style on, you type along, and the text you type is nicely formatted according to the style. Everything behaves normally until you get to the end of a paragraph. Then you press the Enter key and expect a new paragraph to begin. Instead, *nothing happens!* Your problem is that you're typing and applying a character style at the same time. Why that's a problem is beyond us — in WordPerfect, though, it's definitely a problem.

If you select a character style (either from the Select Styles list on the Property Bar or from the Style List dialog box) and continue to type merrily along, the behavior of the Enter key changes. Rather than start a new paragraph, pressing

Enter inserts a code to turn the character style off and then on again. It does *not* start a new paragraph. Instead, pressing Enter inserts a closing character style code and an opening character style code. We have to admit that it's one of the more mysterious behaviors in WordPerfect; you have been warned.

To solve this problem, press the right-arrow cursor key to move your typing cursor *past* the closing character style code. This code is invisible unless you open the Reveal Codes window (which you don't have to do to use this trick). If you do open the Reveal Codes window, however, what's going on should become clear.

We don't use character styles often (paragraph styles are far more useful); when we do, however, we apply them *after* we type our text.

Creating a paragraph style by using QuickStyle

Certain types of formatting do not belong in a character style. Paragraphy-type things, such as indentation, belong in a paragraph style. These things include stuff you normally do with the Format⇨Paragraph command. Paragraph styles can include both paragraph-type things and character-type formatting, such as boldface and font styles.

To define a style for a heading, a caption, or something else that makes up an entire paragraph of its own, use a paragraph style.

Paragraph styles are a little picky about what formatting they do pick up. Remember that WordPerfect gives you at least two ways to do anything, including indent a paragraph. Paragraph styles pick up paragraph formatting applied only from the Format⇨Paragraph⇨Format, Format⇨Paragraph⇨Drop Cap, and Format⇨Paragraph⇨Border/Fill commands. A handy line on the Format⇨Paragraph menu reminds you that anything below the line doesn't get picked up by paragraph styles. Besides, you can do all that stuff below the line by using the Format⇨Paragraph⇨Format command anyway.

To create a paragraph style, you perform the same steps as you do to create a character style; when you get to the QuickStyle dialog box, however, make sure that the Style type is Paragraph.

Applying a paragraph style

Applying paragraph styles is much like applying character styles. Put the cursor in the paragraph you want to style. (Because paragraph styles can apply only to whole paragraphs, you don't have to select text when you want to format just one paragraph.) If you want to format multiple paragraphs, select them. Then click on the downward-pointing triangle button next to the Select Styles box on the Property Bar. When the style list appears, click on the style name to apply it to the selected paragraphs.

WordPerfect tells you which style is applied to the paragraph where the cursor is. Just look in the Select Styles box on the Property Bar. Click on the arrow next to the Select Styles box to select another style for the paragraph. If you select a style and nothing happens, you've selected a character style. Generally, this idea is a bad one; see the sidebar "The Enter key is broken," earlier in this chapter.

Built-In Styles

Before you go on to changing styles, we should introduce the built-in styles, labeled Heading 1 through Heading 5 and InitialStyle. Not surprisingly, *headings* are styles for your headings and subheadings. Their definitions are preset, for convenience, because headings are what most people use styles for most of the time. To see them, click on the Select Styles button on the Property Bar.

Heading styles

Heading styles (Heading 1 through Heading 5) do nice things, such as make your headings all bold and enter them in the table of contents (if you ask WordPerfect to create one). They're nicely specified styles, fortunately, because changing them often requires you to understand (ugh!) secret codes.

Apply heading styles as you would apply any other paragraph style: With the cursor in the paragraph to be formatted, click on the downward-pointing triangle button next to the Select Styles box on the Property Bar and choose the heading style you want. After you apply these styles, you may want to use them to create a table of contents. If you do, take a look at Chapter 17; hidden in the section about reports, books, and other big documents is a subsection on creating a table of contents!

The InitialStyle style

The other built-in style, InitialStyle, specifies the way your text looks when you create a new document, before you do anything to change its appearance. You don't have to apply InitialStyle; it happens automatically at the beginning of your document. Unless you apply other styles, all the text in your document is formatted according to InitialStyle.

InitialStyle is, in fact, the central place where your choices are recorded when you click on the Initial Font button in the Font dialog box (described in Chapter 6, in the section about formatting an entire document) or the File⇨Document⇨Default Font command (described in Chapter 19, in the section about setting your favorite font).

To add or change something in InitialStyle or a heading style, check out the Styles Editor, described in the section "Creating Styles from Scratch, or Modifying Existing Styles," later in this chapter.

If you want to remove something, you have to deal with secret codes (refer to Chapter 9). If you're not up to reading Chapter 9 in its entirety, you can also try a little guesswork while you're using the Styles Editor.

More built-in styles

WordPerfect comes with a grab bag of predefined styles you can use. Although they're not normally on the style list, you can bring them in by following these steps:

1. **Choose Format⇨Styles from the menu bar.**

   You see the Style List dialog box. We talk about this dialog box in gory detail in just a moment; because you've decided that you're a glutton for styles, however, you get a sneak preview.

2. **Click on the Options button and choose Setup from the list that drops down.**

   The Style Setup dialog box appears.

3. **Click on the System Styles box.**

4. **Click on OK.**

A zillion more styles now appear on the Name list in the Style List dialog box. These styles include those that WordPerfect uses when it generates tables of contents, indexes, footnotes, and other cool things. You can then choose from among a few dozen useful styles in the Name box.

The Master Control Panel for Styles: The Style List

If you've read everything to this point in the chapter, you've managed to create and apply styles without resorting to the Format⇨Styles command. This command displays the Style List dialog box, as shown in Figure 10-2. The Name box lists all styles defined in the current document.

Figure 10-2:
The Style List dialog box.

To use a style in a document, click on the style name and then click the Apply button to apply it to the selected text (for character styles) or to the place where the cursor is (for paragraph or document styles). Table 10-1 gives you the lowdown on what you can do with the style list. We talk in detail in the next section about modifying styles.

Table 10-1	Style List Buttons
Option	*What It Does*
Apply	Applies the highlighted style to the highlighted text if the style is a character style; to the highlighted paragraphs or the paragraph the cursor is in if the style is a paragraph style; or to the rest of the document if the style is a document style
QuickStyle	Displays the Styles QuickCreate dialog box, which enables you to create a style with the same format as the text at the cursor location
Create	Displays the Styles Editor dialog box to enable you to create a new style
Edit	Displays the Styles Editor dialog box so that you can change the codes for the style highlighted in the Name box
Options	Provides more options for styles: Setup, Copy, Delete, Reset, Retrieve, and Save As

Creating Styles from Scratch and Modifying Existing Styles

The Style List dialog box is your gateway to creating styles yourself from scratch or modifying styles that came with WordPerfect or that you created with QuickStyle. Modifying styles requires that you know something about secret codes. Fortunately, the task is worthwhile. Few things are as satisfying as having every paragraph in your document hooked up to a style so that you can use the Styles Editor to change the formatting of whole swathes of documents at will. (Although we can think of one or two things that are more satisfying, you can't do them with your computer.)

When you click on the Create or Edit buttons in the Style List dialog box, you get to the heart of styles: the Styles Editor. (If you're a frequent flier in the Reveal Codes window, you can also double-click on a style code in there to see the Styles Editor.) Check out Figure 10-3 and the descriptions in Table 10-2.

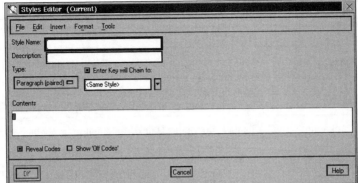

Figure 10-3:
The Styles
Editor dialog
box.

Table 10-2	Styles Editor Options
Option	*What It Does*
Styles Editor menu bar	Provides formatting options for the style. (They enable you to insert codes to format your text. The most-often-used formatting commands are on the Format menu. To apply character formatting from this dialog box, for example, choose Format⇨Font from its menu bar to display the Font dialog box.
Style Name	Displays the name of the style. For styles you created, you can change the name. You can't change the names of the WordPerfect built-in styles.
Type	Lets you control what type of style is applied: character, paragraph, or document. For details, see the section "A Style By Any Other Name Would Smell As Sweet," near the beginning of this chapter.
Enter Key will Chain to	Tells WordPerfect what the style of the next paragraph should be. (For example, a Heading 1 paragraph may usually be followed by an Indented Text paragraph.)
Contents	Shows you all the secret codes WordPerfect uses to make the style happen. (Refer to Chapter 9 if you haven't already.) If the style has in it any regular text (such as "Figure No." or "Question:"), this text appears here as well.
Reveal Codes	When it's selected, displays formatting codes in the Contents box. You can turn this option off; the Contents box then shows only the regular text that's part of the style, however, and we just told you how useful we think that is.
Show 'Off Codes'	Lets you insert codes that take effect when the style ends. Do yourself a favor: Just don't.

Creating a style from scratch

Fire up the Styles Editor (refer to Figure 10-3) by using the Format⇨Styles command and clicking on Create. Using the descriptions in Table 10-2, here's how you go about creating a style from scratch:

1. **Enter a name for your style in the Style Name box.**

   A style name can be as many as 12 characters long. Because the style list on the Property Bar shows you only the beginning of the style name unless you click on it, you may want to make your style names begin with different words.

2. **Select a type for your style.**

   Create a *character* style if you don't want your style to apply to the whole paragraph. Create a *paragraph* style if you want to control margins and indenting or you want the whole paragraph to have a single "look." Create a *document* style if you want that style to be applied to all text, starting where you insert the style code and continuing to the end of the document. (We use paragraph styles most of the time, for formatting headings, captions, and other elements that appear in a paragraph by themselves.)

3. **Format!**

   Go wild. At the top of the Styles Editor, you see a miniature version of the WordPerfect menu bar. The menu commands are there for two reasons: to format your text and to help you correct it. For example, if you include any regular text in the Contents box, you can spell-check it. Forget about such frivolity; you're here to format text, so just stick to that. Unfortunately, you don't see a sample of what your text will look like, so you just have to envision it from looking at the codes. Don't forget — you can always format first and then create the style by using QuickStyle.

4. **Click on the little box labeled Enter Key will Chain to, if you care.**

   This feature really asks, "What do you want to happen when you're typing along in this style and you spawn a new paragraph by pressing Enter? Do you want the new text to continue in this style or what?" When you click the down-arrow button to the right of the associated box, you see that you have three possible answers to this nitpicking question:

   • **<None>:** Means "Turn off styles altogether."

   • **<Same Style>:** Means "Begin a new paragraph in this same style."

   • **Any of your own homegrown styles on the style list (not the system stuff, such as Heading 1):** Means "Begin a new paragraph with this style." These *chaining styles* are useful when styles normally follow each other, such as introductory text after a heading.

For character styles, you have one more option. Click on the little box labeled Enter Key will Chain to and unselect it. This way, pressing the Enter key means "Keep going in this same style." If you don't unselect this option, pressing the Enter key will do, essentially, nothing. (Refer to the sidebar "The Enter key is broken," earlier in this chapter.)

5. **After you've completed all your formatting, click on OK.**

   You're back at the style list.

6. **Click on Apply to apply the style you just made to the selected characters or paragraph.**

   Alternatively, you can just click Close to get rid of the style list. Although your style is defined, it's not in use yet. Or, you can keep defining styles and pick one to apply when you're finally ready to leave Style Land.

To change something, such as changing boldface to underline, you probably have to use the secret codes. Look in the Contents box at the bottom of the Styles Editor dialog box for a box that contains a suggestive word, such as Bold. Try double-clicking on it. Something should happen, such as the appearance of a Font dialog box. When it does, you can make your change. Close this dialog box, whatever it is, and you change the secret code.

To delete something in the Contents box, such as the Very Large font style, click on it and then drag it from the Contents box and into the Real World (anywhere outside the Contents box), where scummy secret codes cannot survive.

If you make a mistake while you're modifying styles in the Styles Editor dialog box, the Undo command on the Styles Editor menu bar can help you. Just choose Edit⇨Undo or press Ctrl+Z.

Modifying existing styles

The Styles Editor (refer to Figure 10-3) is also the place to change the format of existing styles. To edit a style, choose the Format⇨Styles command, select the style to edit, and click on the Edit button. The only difference between changing a style and creating a new one, in fact, is that you don't get to type a name for the style. WordPerfect doesn't let you change the type (character, paragraph, or document) of an existing style, and it prevents you from renaming its built-in styles (like Heading 1).

Revealing your secret style codes

If you understand the secret codes in WordPerfect (refer to Chapter 9), you probably understand the bottom window in the Styles Editor dialog box. The window shows which codes are being encapsulated into the style, just as a Reveal Codes window does.

Moreover, you probably understand why character and paragraph styles are denoted as (paired) and document styles as (open) in the Type box in the Styles Editor. *Paired* styles contain paired style codes; *open* styles contain single, unpaired style codes.

When WordPerfect applies a paired (character or paragraph) style to your document, it uses pairs of codes to bracket the affected text. These codes use only the style name, which gives you complete freedom to edit the style definition without putting a bunch of screwy codes in your text. When WordPerfect applies an open (document) style, it uses single codes — again, using only the style name. Magically, these (unpaired) style codes can apply character formats, such as bold text — bold text requires a paired code (refer to Chapter 9). Works anyway — go figure.

Creating a document style

A few sections earlier, we say that WordPerfect has two (really three) kinds of styles. Well, it's time to talk about that third kind: document styles. Sometimes, you want to create a style that applies beginning at a certain point and to perhaps everything past that point. This type of style, a *document style,* is a little weird. Unlike character and paragraph styles, a document style has no predetermined point at which it ends. As a result, it generally continues until another style begins.

Document styles can include not only the formatting codes you normally apply with the Format⇨Page command but also the codes for anything else you choose from the Format menu, including Font, Line, Paragraph, and Column commands. For that matter, document styles can include the codes for darn near any command you choose from the Insert, Tools, Graphics, and Table menus, including insert page breaks, change headers and footers, insert dates, insert graphics, or make quacking noises (if you go for that sort of thing and your computer has speakers).

Using a document style is a good way to set up the overall layout of a document, including its margins, the paragraph formatting for most paragraphs, and the font for most text.

You cannot create a document style by using the QuickStyle method; you must use the Styles Editor method we just described. For Type, select Document. Aside from that, the style behaves pretty much like a regular style.

Applying a document style

To apply a document style, first position the cursor where you want the style to begin (probably at the beginning of a paragraph, and possibly at the beginning of a page). If your document style inserts anything, such as page breaks, they appear wherever the cursor is when you turn on the style.

Turning Off Styles and Chaining Styles

Suppose that you have applied a style and you're merrily typing along, updating your résumé to include the phrase "Mastery of WordPerfect styles." You finish a delightfully styled paragraph, press Enter, and bingo! — you start another similarly styled paragraph. Although this automatic spawning of a similarly styled paragraph is a lovely feature, what if you don't want another similarly styled paragraph?

Or, suppose that you're typing a letter to Aunt May in a character style that uses the lovely ShelleyVolante font and you want to turn it off to write a more legible note to nearsighted Uncle George. Do one of these two things:

✔ To turn off a paragraph style in the paragraph in which the cursor is located, click on the arrow next to the Select Styles button on the Property Bar and then click on ⟨None⟩ on the list.

✔ If you have been typing along in a character style and now want to turn it off for the following text, press the right-arrow key on your keyboard. This step moves the cursor past the secret style-end code. When you type again, the style is no longer in effect.

Recycling Styles

Reusing work you have already finished is always a smart idea, and styles help you reuse your formatting efforts. You can reuse styles in either of two ways:

✔ Retrieve them from an existing document into a new document.

✔ Save them in another file.

Dragging in styles from another document

Retrieving styles from another document is the lazy way to use a style you've already created and, therefore, our favorite. Follow these steps:

1. **Choose Format⇨Styles.**

   You see the Style List dialog box (refer to Figure 10-2).

2. **Click on the Options button.**

   You see the Options drop-down menu.

3. **Choose Retrieve.**

   The Retrieve Styles From dialog box appears.

4. **Type the name of the document from which you want to retrieve styles, or click on the file-folder icon to select the file from a list. (See Chapter 14 to find out how this method works.)**

5. **If you want just the user styles (the ones you or the document's author made) or the system styles (the built-in WordPerfect styles), click on the appropriate box in the Style Type part of the Retrieve Styles From dialog box.**

   Normally, you get both types of styles. WordPerfect asks whether you want to override the current styles.

6. **Click on the OK button.**

   In all likelihood, you want to override the current styles.

7. **Click on Yes.**

Creating the Martha Stewart library of styles

To be Really Systematic and Organized, you should save your styles in a central location. This procedure enables you to control styles from a single point.

In one of two possible approaches, you copy your styles to a document template that automatically brings in styles when you create a new document using that template. (Chapter 17 describes templates and all the wonderful things you can do with them.) The other method, in which you save your styles in a separate file, requires you to retrieve the styles from that file manually. This method has the advantage, however, of allowing you to save all your styles — styles for memos, for example — under one name.

If most of what you create will use the same styles, copy your styles to the standard template, on which all documents are based. (This approach is also great for pack rats, who don't mind if every style they ever create is stored in one place.) To copy styles to the standard template, follow these steps:

1. **Choose Format⇨Styles.**

   You see the Style List dialog box.

2. **Click on a style you want to copy.**

3. **Click on the Options button in the Style List dialog box.**

   The little Options menu pops up (or down).

4. **Click on Copy on the Options menu.**

   The Styles Copy dialog box appears.

5. **Click on Personal Library in the Copy To area.**

6. **Repeat Steps 1–5 for each style you want to copy.**

From now on, whenever you create a new document, these styles are available.

In the other method — saving your styles to a file — click on Options, click on Save As, and then type a directory and filename. (Or, you can click the file-folder icon to use a dialog box for this procedure.) Give the file an extension that will remind you that styles are in the file, such as `.sty`.

To use these styles, just open your new document, choose Format⇨Styles, click on the Options button, and then choose Retrieve.

Getting Rid of Styles

After awhile, particularly if you're of the pack rat persuasion and keep all your styles in the same place, you will want to delete a few of them. You cannot delete built-in styles, however — only your own. These steps show you how:

1. **Choose Format⇨Styles to display the Style List dialog box.**

2. **Click on a style you want to delete.**

3. **Click on the Options button in the Style List dialog box.**

   If the Delete option is grayed out, you're trying to delete a built-in style. Stop that.

4. **Choose Delete from the menu that drops down.**

   The Delete Style dialog box appears, asking whether you want to delete the style definition and take out all the codes for that style in your document (the Include Codes option) or remove the definition and leave the formatting in place (the Leave Codes option).

5. **Choose either Include Codes or Leave Codes.**

6. **Click on OK, and you're finished.**

Part III

Things You Can Do with Documents

The 5th Wave By Rich Tennant

"YES, WE STILL HAVE A FEW BUGS IN THE WORD PROCESSING SOFTWARE. BY THE WAY, HERE'S A MEMO FROM MARKETING."

In this part . . .

*I*t is a little-known fact that when humans lived in the trees, they didn't have a word for *forest*. (Okay, so they didn't have a word for anything else, either. Be that way.) The reason was that they couldn't (everyone say it together now) "see the forest for the trees." They couldn't, that is, until they had mastered the trees, climbed the mountains, and attained the perspective that enabled them to say, "Whoa — look at them forests!"

Likewise, all who master the world of mere words and ascend the heights of word processing eventually find themselves saying, "Whoa — look at them *documents!*" (Grammar hasn't progressed much over the millennia.) Accordingly, this part of the book explores the printing, moving around, and overall wrangling of your documents. Head 'em up and move 'em out!

Chapter 11

On Paper at Last: Printing Stuff

In This Chapter

▶ Getting the printer ready

▶ Printing parts of a document, an entire document, or several documents

▶ Printing a document on disk

▶ Canceling a print job

*E*veryone has heard about the Paperless Office of the Future. Remember when computers were new and everyone claimed that after we all started using them, we could stop using paper? Lo and behold, look around your office. Do you see paper? Everyone seems to have twice as much paper as before — *that's* how much paper you see.

In real life, you usually want to print your documents, and this chapter talks about how to do it. For details about creating and printing some popular documents, including mailing labels and envelopes, see Chapter 17.

Ready to Print?

You have written and formatted your document, and it looks *m-a-ahvelous*. Now you're ready to see how it looks on paper. Before you can do so, however, you had better be sure that your printer is ready to help.

The basics

Make sure that your printer is plugged in to both the wall and your computer. The connection to the wall provides power, and the cable to your computer provides a way for the information in your document to get from the computer into your printer.

Be sure that your printer has the appropriate ribbon, ink cartridge, or toner cartridge, depending on your printer — unless you're interested in printing your document in white on white.

You need paper, as you may have guessed. Your printer may use individual sheets of typing paper or continuous-feed perforated paper. Whatever your printer likes to eat, make sure that it has paper.

You should also make sure that your printer is paying attention to what your computer has to say. Most printers can be either *online* or *offline* (either listening to the computer or not listening, respectively). These printers have an online light that tells you whether the printer is online and an online button you can press to switch between online and offline. If your printer is offline, it ignores any information your computer sends to it; it's like being turned off.

If your printer uses sheets of paper, you may want to print drafts of documents on the other side of used paper. We keep a stack of paper with stuff on just one side and use it for everything except the final drafts of our documents.

Do Linux and WordPerfect know that you have a printer?

Before WordPerfect 8 can print anything, Linux must know all about your printer. When you (or someone) installed Linux on your computer, you should have told Linux which printer (or printers) you have. To tell Linux about your printers, ask the person who set up your Linux system whether a printer is installed or consult *Linux For Dummies*, 2nd Edition, by Jon Hall, Craig Witherspoon, and Coletta Witherspoon (IDG Books Worldwide).

WordPerfect also needs to know which printer you have. To find out what printer WordPerfect thinks you have, you can display the Select Printer dialog box by choosing File⇨Print (or pressing F5 or clicking the Print button on the toolbar) to display the Print dialog box and then clicking the Select button. The Select Printer dialog box, as shown in Figure 11-1, shows the printers WordPerfect knows about (if your computer is connected to a Local Area Network, or LAN, this list may include printers connected to other computers). If your printer doesn't appear on the list, your Linux expert may be able to help.

Where's the print preview feature?

Some other word processors have a print preview feature to show you exactly what things will look like on the page. WordPerfect doesn't have this feature because it does a good job of showing you what your document will look like while you're editing it. Isn't that what WYSIWYG (What You See Is What You Get) is all about?

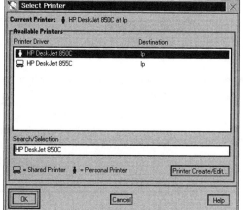

Figure 11-1:
WordPerfect
needs to
know about
the printers
on your
system.

If your printer is connected to your computer and Linux is configured to print to it but the printer doesn't appear on the Available Printers list in the Select Printer dialog box, follow these steps:

1. **In the Select Printer dialog box (which you display by pressing F5 or clicking the Print button on the toolbar), click on the Printer Create/Edit button to display the Printer Create/Edit dialog box.**

   This dialog box lets you add new *printer drivers* — descriptions of printers.

2. **Click on the Add button, select your printer on the Available Printer Drivers list, and click on OK.**

   WordPerfect asks whether you really want to create the new printer driver.

3. **Click on OK again to create the printer.**

4. **With the new printer still selected, click on the Setup button.**

   You see the Printer Setup dialog box, where you can tell WordPerfect all kinds of things about your printer, like which cartridges or fonts you're using, what you want to use for the initial font — that kind of stuff. For now, leave those settings alone, except for telling WordPerfect how to send print jobs to this printer.

5. **Click on the Destination button, choose Linux's name for the printer (usually `lp` unless you have more than one printer) from the list that appears, and click on OK.**

6. **Click on OK again to dismiss the Printer Create/Edit dialog box.**

7. **Back in the Select Printer dialog box, make sure that the printer you want to use is selected and click on OK. Click on Cancel to dismiss the Print dialog box.**

Where's the printer?

If your computer is connected to a network and you use a network printer, someone else is probably in charge of making sure that the printer is connected to all the right cables. You should still check to make sure that the printer has paper, however, because the guy in the next cubicle may have the annoying habit of printing 200-page reports without refilling the paper tray.

You may also want to talk to your network administrator to find out which types of printers you can use and whether Linux on your computer knows how to print on them.

WordPerfect now knows which kind of printer you have.

Even after telling WordPerfect about your printer, you may have trouble printing. Linux might not be able to figure out how to send information to your printer, or the printed results may be strangely formatted. If so, you need to talk to a Linux wizard for help — be armed with as much information about your printer as you can, along with a warm batch of chocolate chip cookies.

Printing the Entire Document

WordPerfect gives you a good idea of what your document will look like when it's printed. If you use Page view (by choosing View⇨Page), you can even see where your headers and footers appear, as well as the top and bottom margins of the pages. (Chapter 8 describes Page view and the other views WordPerfect provides.) You cannot get the total effect, however, until you see your document on paper.

These steps show you how to print your document:

1. **Make sure that your printer is turned on, online, and ready to print.**

   Make sure that the right kind of paper is loaded — recycled paper for drafts and nice, new, blank paper for final versions, letterhead, or whatever. We always keep a stack of paper near our printer with embarrassing first drafts printed on one side, ready for less embarrassing second drafts to be printed on the other side.

2. **Save your document, just in case something dire happens while you're printing it.**

   Practice safe printing!

3. Click on the Print button on the toolbar.

This button looks like a sideways view of a pasta maker. Alternatively, you can choose File⇨Print or press F5. WordPerfect displays the large and imposing Print dialog box, as shown in Figure 11-2. If your dialog box looks a little different, don't be concerned. Some settings may come and go depending on what kind of printer you have. If your dialog box looks *really* different, you may have some strange printer connected to your computer. Go find the computer wizard who connected it and ask her what's going on.

Figure 11-2:
Telling
WordPerfect
the who,
what,
where,
when, and
why of
printing your
document.

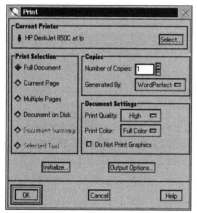

If you have some text selected when you click on the Print button, the Print dialog box assumes that you just want to print what is selected. If that's not true, no problem. Just click on Full Document or Current Page or whatever you want in the Print Selection section of the dialog box.

4. Ignore all those interesting-looking settings, and just click on OK.

WordPerfect informs you that it's preparing the document for printing. Other dialog boxes may flit across the screen as WordPerfect formats the document for printing. At long last, the printer starts to hum and begins to print.

You can continue to use WordPerfect while your printer prints. You can open another document, edit the current document, or do whatever you want. You probably shouldn't close either your document or WordPerfect, however, because the chances of printing a document correctly on the first try are zero. We would bet dollars to doughnuts that you will see a large typo that was staring you in the face from the screen for the past half-hour but that became truly visible only on paper.

If the printer doesn't print anything, don't just print it again. Your document may still be wending its way through WordPerfect, Linux, the printer daemon (we're not making this up), and the spooler on its way to the printer. The document may have gotten stuck on its way. (Intestinal distress happens even to computers.) Make sure that the printer is turned on and online. If nothing happens after a minute or two, see the section "Canceling a Print Job," near the end of this chapter.

If you're looking at the Print dialog box and decide not to print the document after all, just press the Esc key or click on the Cancel button in the dialog box (clicking on the Close button in the upper-right corner of the dialog box works, too). No harm done, and no paper wasted.

Before printing the final draft of a document, you may want to consider checking its spelling. See Chapter 5 for complete instructions.

Printing Part of a Document

When a document gets long (like some chapters in this book), you may not want to print the whole thing. What if you just printed a 30-page report, for example, and then find and correct a typo on page 17? Not to worry — you can print a single page — or any selection of text, for that matter.

Printing selected text

To print a selection of text, follow these steps:

1. **Get the printer ready (turn it on and all that).**

2. **Select the text you want to print. (Refer to Chapter 4 to find out how.)**

3. **Click on the Print button on the toolbar.**

    Alternatively, press F5 or choose File⇨Print from the WordPerfect menu bar.

    The Print dialog box appears (refer to Figure 11-1). Notice that toward the bottom of the Print Selection section is a button labeled Selected Text. If you don't have text selected, WordPerfect automatically selects the Full Document option.

4. **Click on OK.**

    WordPerfect prints the selected text.

When your printer prints backward

Some printers print in such a way that you're always reordering multiple-page documents. What you really need to be able to do is print the last page first. Then, when the printer finished printing, everything would be in the right order. Fortunately, you can tell WordPerfect to do just that. Before you click on the Print button, click on the Output Options button near the bottom of the Print dialog box. You see the Output Options dialog box. Click on the Print in Reverse Order (Back to Front) box. You're ready to print!

Printing a specific page

Follow these steps to print one page:

1. **Make sure that your printer is ready to print.**
2. **Place your cursor anywhere on the page you want to print.**
3. **Click on the Print button on the toolbar.**

    Alternatively, press F5 or choose File⇨Print to display the Print dialog box.

4. **Choose Current Page in the Print Selection section and click on OK.**

Printing a bunch of pages, but not all of them

To print a few pages, do the following:

1. **Make sure that your printer is all set to print.**
2. **Make a note of the page numbers you want to print.**

    It doesn't matter where the heck your cursor is.

3. **Click on the Print button on the toolbar.**

    Or press F5 or choose File⇨Print from the menu bar. Just get that Print dialog box onscreen.

4. **Select Multiple Pages in the Print Selection section of the dialog box, and then click on OK.**

The Multiple Pages dialog box appears, waiting for you to type a page number or a range of pages. If you want to print page 10 only, type **10** in the Page(s) box. To print pages 10 through 20, type **10-20** in the Page(s) box. See Table 11-1 for more info about page ranges.

5. **Click on OK until you're out of all the dialog boxes.**

   WordPerfect prints the pages you specified and skips all the other pages.

Printing random pages

The Multiple Pages setting allows you to print contiguous and noncontiguous pages in your document easily. Use the options in Table 11-1 to find out how to specify different groups of pages. Click OK to print the pages you need.

If you have a fancy document with chapters or sections (or both), you can mix and match various combinations of pages. This feature is most useful, though, for printing just parts of your document that make sense to you, like a particular chapter or section. For example, you could print Chapter 2 by specifying **2** in the Chapters box and all in the Page(s)/label(s) box. See Chapter 17 for more information about complicated documents.

Table 11-1	Print-Range Page Numbers
Entry	*Meaning*
all	Print all the pages in the document.
x	Print page *x*.
x,y,z	Print pages *x, y,* and *z* (separate page numbers with commas or spaces).
x-y	Print pages *x* through *y*, inclusive.
x-	Print page *x* through the end of the document.
-x	Starting at the beginning of the document, print through page *x*.
x,y-z	Print page *x* and then pages *y* through *z* (you can include as many page ranges as you want, separated by commas or spaces).
	If you specify a list of pages *(x,y,z)* or a list of page ranges *(x–y, w–z)* the list must go from lowest to highest. For example, 5,1,3 prints only page 5; 10-15, 1-5 prints only pages 10–15.

Printing on Both Sides of the Paper

Printing documents on both sides of the paper, such as in a book, is cool. This method not only makes your document look terribly official but also marks you as an Ecologically Sound Person, which is important in this day and age. If you want to print your document on both sides of the paper (*duplex printing*) but your printer doesn't do that automatically, don't worry — you're not out of luck. Your green reputation doesn't have to suffer.

If your printer can do two-sided printing

If your printer knows how to do two-sided printing (some laser printers do), you need to tell WordPerfect that you want to print on both sides of the page. To set up two-sided printing on your printer:

1. **Choose Format⇨Page⇨Page Setup⇨Two-Sided Printing.**

   You see the Two-Sided Printing dialog box, as shown in Figure 11-3.

2. **Select the side of the paper that will be bound (usually the left side) and the amount of space to allow for binding. Click the Duplexing button and select one of the Edge options from the drop-down list.**

   The From Long Edge option sets the binding for the long edge of your paper, and it's the option that's used most often. Don't worry if you're not going to bind your document; WordPerfect just needs to know where the edge would be if you were going to bind it.

Figure 11-3:
Printing on
both sides
of the paper.

3. **Click on OK to leave the Two-Sided Printing dialog box.**

Now, when you print, your printer prints on both sides of the paper automagically!

If your printer doesn't know how to print on both sides

If your printer knows only how to print on one side of the paper, WordPerfect can still help you use both sides. Although you have to take more steps, it's doable: First, you print all the odd pages, and then you turn the paper over, stick it back in the printer, and print all the even pages on the backs of the odd pages. With luck, the right pages are back-to-front! Voilà — two-sided printing. Try this system with a small document first.

Here are the steps for manual, two-sided printing:

1. **Make sure that your printer is eager to print.**

   Also make sure that the paper you plan to use is blank on both sides.

2. **Click on the Print button on the toolbar.**

   Alternatively, press F5 or choose File⇨Print. You see the Print dialog box.

3. **Click on the Output Options button.**

   WordPerfect displays the Output Options dialog box, as shown in Figure 11-4.

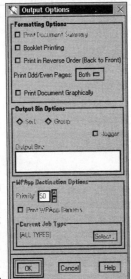

Figure 11-4: WordPerfect has some fancy printing options.

4. **Change the Print Odd/Even Pages setting to print, well, either all the odd pages or all the even pages. To keep things simple, start with the odd pages. Click on OK to leave the Output Options dialog box, and click on OK again to print the odd pages.**

   Remember that if your printer knows how to print on both sides of the page, you don't have to go through these manual printing steps — see the preceding section instead. If you're like us and your printer wouldn't know duplex printing from duplex painting (as in painting a dwelling that contains two separate residences), press on with the rest of these steps.

5. **Flip the paper over so that you're ready to print the pages you didn't print the first time.**

   After all the odd-numbered pages have been printed, put them back in the paper tray so that WordPerfect can print on the other side of the paper. Make sure that page 1 is printed-side-down and on top so that WordPerfect prints page 2 on its back side. (You may have to turn each page over individually, not just flop the stack over.)

   Also make sure that the paper is facing the right way so that page 2 isn't upside-down and doesn't print on the same side of the paper as page 1. Because the exact orientation you need depends on your printer, you may want to experiment with a short document and make notes so that you know how to handle the pages next time.

6. **Repeat Steps 2–4.**

   This time, choose the Even pages option in Step 4.

Printing several copies

After you begin printing a document, you may want several copies. Hey, why not save yourself a trip to the copying machine? Of course, if you're printing 10 copies of a 25-page document on the only printer in the office, you may not make yourself popular with your coworkers, but that's your decision.

To tell WordPerfect how many copies to print, follow these steps:

1. **Make sure that your printer is hot to print.**

2. **As usual, click on the Print button on the toolbar.**

   Also, you can press F5 or choose File⇨Print to display the Print dialog box.

3. **In the Number of Copies box, enter the number you want.**

   You can click on the little up- and down-arrow buttons to increase and decrease the numbers.

You can also tell WordPerfect whether your printer knows how to print multiple copies itself. Some printers are smart enough that you can send them a document once, along with instructions to print it a certain number of times. Because most printers are not this smart, though, WordPerfect has to send the same document to the printer over and over. If your printer is among the high-IQ printers of the world, set the Generated By setting to Printer rather than to WordPerfect.

4. Click on OK.

Printing a Document on Disk

What if you want to print a document that isn't open? What if you wrote, saved, and printed a magnificent letter this morning, for example, and now you want to print an extra copy to show to your mother? You can open it first, admire it onscreen for a while, and then print it. There's a faster way, though, as shown in these steps:

1. Set your printer so that it's rarin' to print.

It doesn't matter where your cursor is or even which document is open.

2. Click on the Print button on the toolbar.

If you prefer, press F5 or choose File⇨Print. Either way, WordPerfect displays the Print dialog box.

3. In the Print Selection section of the Print dialog box, click on Document on Disk and then click on OK.

Poof! The Document on Disk dialog box appears, in which you can type the name of the document you want to print. What? — you don't want to type the whole name of the document? No problem, click on the little file-folder icon all the way at the right end of the Filename box.

If the document isn't in the current directory, you must enter the document's full pathname. If you don't know what the heck we're talking about or if you want to know how to use that cute little file-folder icon next to the Document on Disk box, see Chapter 13.

4. Click on OK in all the dialog boxes.

WordPerfect prints the document without displaying it onscreen.

You can also print only selected pages from the document on disk by entering page numbers in the Page(s) box.

If the file doesn't exist or you type its name wrong (it can happen to anyone), WordPerfect displays the message that the file was not found. Click on the OK button to get rid of the message and try again. For help in finding files, see Chapter 13.

Canceling a Print Job

So far, printing has been pretty smooth sailing. Display a dialog box or two, click on the buttons, and presto — your document is on paper. Then one day, disaster strikes: You send your 150-page report to print while you're in the middle of reorganizing it. It's time to tell WordPerfect, "Stop printing! Never mind! I didn't mean it!"

Who ya gonna call?

When you print, WordPerfect (like all Linux programs) prints by committee. When WordPerfect prints, it sends the information in your document to the Linux *printer daemon* (also called *lpd*), a program in charge of sending print jobs to printers. The printer daemon takes it from there. WordPerfect keeps track of what is going on, though, and lists your print jobs in a job queue.

If your computer and printer are connected to a network rather than directly to each other, your document gets passed to the network print manager, which then sends it to the printer. A talk with your network administrator may be in order (accompanied by a few chocolate chip cookies) so that you can find out how to cancel a print job after it has been sent to the network print manager.

WordPerfect, stop printing!

While your document is printing, you can tell Linux and WordPerfect to forget the whole thing by following these steps:

1. **Switch to the WordPerfect program window.**

   Remember that the *program window* is the small window that hangs around displaying the WordPerfect logo. To display the program window, click on its button on the taskbar (if you use KDE, GNOME, or another window manager that displays a taskbar containing buttons for all your open windows).

2. **In the program window, choose <u>P</u>rogram⇨Printer <u>C</u>ontrol.**

   All pending print jobs are displayed in the Printer Control dialog box, as shown in Figure 11-5, in the Queued Jobs section. If you don't see your print job, select a different destination from the Available Destinations list. If you don't know your printer destination (usually *lp* for your local printer), just keep clicking on entries on the Available Destinations list until the name of your print job shows up in the Queued Jobs area.

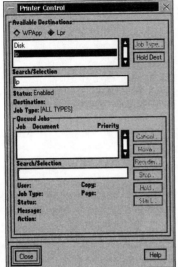

Figure 11-5:
The Printer
Control
dialog box.

3. **Select your print job on the Queued Jobs list and click the Stop button.**

When WordPerfect asks you to confirm that you want to stop the job, click on OK. Your print job is stopped.

If you change your mind and decide that you don't want to cancel the print job, click on the Close button to make the Printer Control dialog box go away. You can also leave this window open, if you want to check often on the status of a print job.

Chapter 12

Juggling Documents on Your Screen

· ·

In This Chapter

▶ Working on more than one document at the same time

▶ Closing documents

▶ Sizing windows

▶ Maximizing and minimizing documents

▶ Combining documents

▶ Knowing what to do if a file already exists

▶ Using foreign files

· ·

*I*magine living in New York City, in an apartment that has a powerful telescope. Using your telescope, you can look into the windows of your various neighbors. In one window, you see an office worker typing away. In another, you see a warehouse. In a third, someone is washing the dishes. In the fourth — oops! Close the curtains!

In the same way, WordPerfect for Linux enables you to work on more than one document at the same time. As you open each document, WordPerfect creates a window to display it. You can open several documents at one time and view several windows simultaneously. Hey, that's what X Windows is all about!

This chapter explains this multiwindowing stuff to you. You don't even need a telescope to do it. Using these techniques, you can improve your productivity by viewing and editing related documents at the same time, or you can turn your Linux desktop into a big mess, as shown in Figure 12-1. The choice is yours.

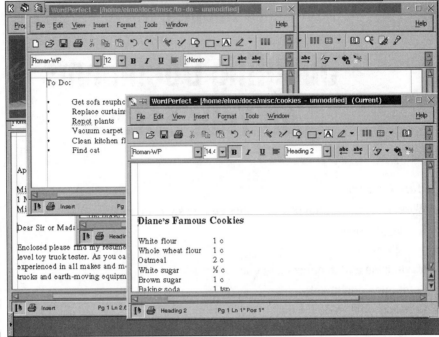

Figure 12-1:
Using
multiple
documents
can get out
of hand.

While we're on the subject of opening documents, toward the end of this chapter we talk about how to open files that *don't* contain WordPerfect documents, such as documents created by other word processing programs.

How Can You Work on Two Documents at a Time?

To work on a document, you open it in a new document window by choosing the Program⇨Open Window command in the program window. WordPerfect creates a new window for the document on your desktop.

After you open a document, you can open *another* document. WordPerfect keeps the first document open but partly covers its document window with a second window that contains the second document.

Switching between open documents

How do you get back to the document you opened first? If it's still visible, you can just click in its window with your mouse. What if your desktop looks like Figure 12-1, though, and you can't find the window? Aha! — the Window command on the menu bar is the solution. When you choose Window, you see a menu that contains five commands (Cascade, Tile Top to Bottom, Tile Side by Side, Minimize All, and Close All), followed by a numbered list of documents you have open. To switch to another open document, just choose its name from the menu.

To switch documents without using the mouse, press Alt+W to open the Window menu. Press the cursor keys to scroll down to the name of the document you want and press Enter.

Making baby documents

When you want to begin writing something new, you need a brand-spanking-new document with no text in it. No one ever told you how baby documents are made? It's about time you learned the Facts of Life. You can create a new document from either the program window or a document window.

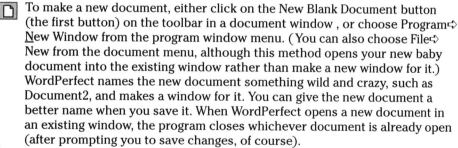

To make a new document, either click on the New Blank Document button (the first button) on the toolbar in a document window , or choose Program⇨ New Window from the program window menu. (You can also choose File⇨ New from the document menu, although this method opens your new baby document into the existing window rather than make a new window for it.) WordPerfect names the new document something wild and crazy, such as Document2, and makes a window for it. You can give the new document a better name when you save it. When WordPerfect opens a new document in an existing window, the program closes whichever document is already open (after prompting you to save changes, of course).

You can also create a new document in a new window by pressing Ctrl+N — this keystroke works in either the program window or a document window.

Closing the curtains

When you finish working on a document, don't leave it lying around open. Each open document slows WordPerfect just a little. To close the window that contains a document, click on the window's Close button (usually an X in the upper-right corner of the document window, although it varies depending on which window manager you're using) or choose File⇨Close.

According to the WordPerfect File menu, Ctrl+F4 is also supposed to close the file. If you happen to be running KDE on your Linux computer, though, KDE grabs that Ctrl+F4 command before WordPerfect ever has a chance to see it. KDE has its own ideas about what Ctrl+F4 means; it switches your display to Desktop 4, and WordPerfect never closes the window. No harm done — just switch back to the KDE desktop that displays WordPerfect, by clicking on the desktop icon on the KDE taskbar.

If the document you're closing has been changed since you last saved it, WordPerfect gives you the chance to save the document before closing it so that you don't lose your work. You can click on Yes (so that WordPerfect saves the document before closing it), No (so that WordPerfect closes it without saving your changes), or Cancel (so that WordPerfect abandons the idea of closing it).

Working with multiple documents

The most common reason for opening multiple documents is to refer to one document while you write another — or sometimes to rip off text (did we say that?) from one document while you write another. WordPerfect makes this technique easy: You can use all the WordPerfect cut-and-paste commands to move or copy text from one document to another.

If you wrote a truly stellar paragraph in one letter and want to use it in another letter, for example, follow these steps:

1. **Open both documents.**

   Use the usual Program⇨Open Window command.

2. **In the original letter, select the paragraph you want to copy.**

   Quadruple-click on it (if your fingers are dexterous enough) or double-click in the left margin next to the paragraph.

3. **Press Ctrl+C to copy the paragraph to the Clipboard.**

   Or choose Edit⇨Copy or click on the Copy button on the toolbar. Nothing seems to happen.

4. **Switch to the other document by choosing the Window command.**

   Or, use the mouse to click on the other document, if you can see it.

5. **Move your cursor to the point where you want the paragraph to appear.**

6. **Press Ctrl+V to paste the paragraph there from the Clipboard.**

   If you prefer, you can choose Edit⇨Paste or click on the Paste button on the toolbar.

After you get good at this kind of thing, it's amazing how much text you can recycle!

In addition to The WordPerfect Way of copying and pasting, you can use The X Window Way. (The X Window System is part of what Linux uses to display windows on your screen.) Select the text you want to copy by using the *left* mouse button. Switch to the window where you want to paste. Move the mouse pointer (not the cursor) to the spot where you want the text to appear. Press the *middle* mouse button if you have a three-button mouse or the *left and right* buttons simultaneously if you have a two-button mouse. Presto! Your text appears. This technique is an old X Window shortcut that works for almost any window with text in it, not just in WordPerfect.

Windows on Top of Windows

It can be annoying to flip back and forth between two documents, copying information or just referring to what you have written. Sometimes, seeing both documents at the same time is more convenient. Again, WordPerfect is happy to oblige.

Seeing lots of windows

You can view multiple documents onscreen in these three ways:

- ✔ Choose Window⇨Cascade from the menu bar in the program window. WordPerfect creates a little window for each document and stacks the windows like a deck of cards, as shown in Figure 12-2.

- ✔ Choose Window⇨Tile Top to Bottom or Window⇨Tile Side by Side from the menu bar in the program window. Again, WordPerfect puts each document in a little window. This time, however, it fills the WordPerfect window with the documents like a game of dominoes, as shown in Figure 12-3. Top-to-bottom tiling arranges the documents in wide, horizontal strips; side-by-side tiling arranges the documents in skinny, vertical strips. The top-to-bottom arrangement generally makes documents easier to read. If you have 4 or more documents open, WordPerfect simply arranges documents in a grid. If you have 11 or more documents open, the Tile commands are disabled. (If you're working with that many documents at one time, you have bigger problems than a disabled Tile command).

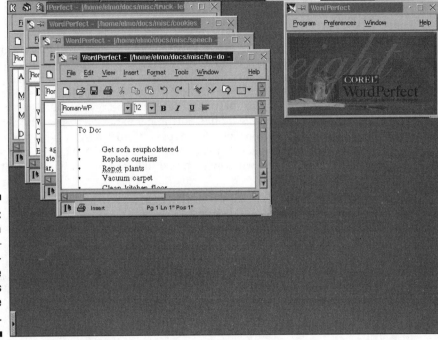

Figure 12-2:
Pick a document — any document. These windows are cascaded.

✔ If you're using KDE on your Linux desktop and you maximize one document to fill the WordPerfect window, you see three little buttons at the right end of the window title bar. These buttons work only in the active document. The first button is the Minimize button (it looks like a dot); the second is the window Restore, or Maximize, button (it looks like a recessed square); and the third is the window Close button (it looks like an X). If you click on the Restore button, WordPerfect cascades or tiles your documents, using whichever command you used last. If you're using a window manager other than KDE, the buttons may be different, although their behavior is the same.

If you minimize a document, it turns into either a bar in the KDE taskbar or an icon on the desktop if you're using another window manager, such as WindowMaker or FVWM. When you arrange the open documents by using a Tile or Cascade command, the minimized window stays minimized. You can get it if you want, although it isn't taking up space.

Each document window has its own title bar that shows the filename of the document and has its own little scroll bars. You can move around in each document by using the mouse and the cursor keys we describe in Chapter 3.

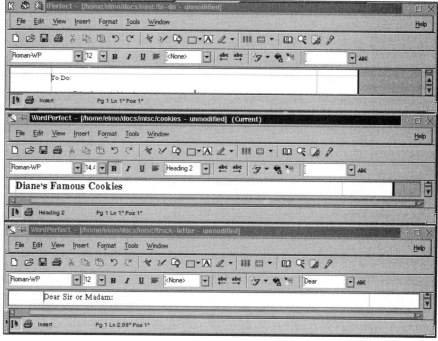

Figure 12-3:
Shuffle your documents and lay them end to end.

"I want that one!"

When you can see multiple document windows, one of them is active. The *active* document window is the one with the highlighted title bar. That document is usually on top of the other windows (no other windows obscure your view of it). The active window is the one you're editing, and your cursor is in it. The formatting commands you give affect the active window. Text you type lands in the active window.

You can switch from one window to another by clicking in the window for the document you want to use, or you can use the Window menu commands described earlier in this chapter.

Sizing your windows

Either cascading or tiling your documents is extremely unlikely to produce document windows large enough for you to get any work done. You probably will have to move them around a little, perhaps making the window for the main document you're working on large and the other document windows small. No problem.

Each document window has a border, and you can move these borders around at will, as explained in the following list:

- ✔ If you point to the left or right border of a window, the mouse pointer turns into a little left or right arrow. You can click and drag the window border to the left or right to resize it horizontally.

- ✔ When you point to the top or bottom border of a window, the mouse pointer turns into an up or down arrow, and you can drag the window border up or down to resize it vertically.

- ✔ When you point to a corner of a border, the mouse pointer turns into a diagonal arrow, and you can drag the corner around in any direction. WordPerfect adjusts the borders accordingly.

You can also move the windows around by clicking and dragging their title bars. The process is similar to moving papers around on your desk, except that they never get coffee stains on them. You can waste most of your work-day, in fact, by moving your windows around until you get them lined up just the way you want them.

Maximizing your documents

All these windows, borders, and scroll bars on your screen can become distracting. When you want to get back to work and look at just one document, you can *maximize* it so that it takes up your entire Linux desktop.

To maximize a document with KDE, look at the right end of its title bar. Click on the middle of the three buttons (it looks like a little square). Poof! All other windows on your screen are covered by this document. (All X Window managers have either a Maximize button like KDE, or a Maximize pull-down menu item. Not surprisingly in the wildly nonstandardized land of UNIX, each window manager puts this function in a different place.)

Minimizing your documents

If you click on the button with the dot on it on the KDE title bar of a document window, the window is *minimized:* It gets really small and appears as a bar somewhere on the KDE taskbar (or as an icon on your desktop). No one we know ever minimizes a document on purpose, although it happens whenever you want to maximize your document window and you click on the wrong button. Click on the bar or icon to open the document window again.

You can minimize all of your document windows at once by choosing Window⇨Minimize All.

Saving all your open documents

As you know, saving your open documents frequently is a good idea. Then, if all the air conditioners in the building kick in at the same time, the power dips, and your computer blips out, you don't lose your work.

If you have several documents open, you should save all of them. You can do that by choosing Program⇨Save All from the program window, or you can press the Save All key combination: Ctrl+Shift+S. This step saves all the open documents you have changed.

Combining Documents

As you know, each WordPerfect document lives in its own cozy little file on your disk. Sometimes, however, you want to break down the walls between your documents and get them together, throw a little party, or whatever.

One document may contain a standard description of the product you sell — chocolate-belly futures, for example. Then you create a new document in which you begin a letter to a prospective client. You realize that you want to include the product description in your letter.

Inserting one document into another one

No dirty jokes at this point, please. Let's just stick to word processing. Follow these steps:

1. **Move your cursor to the location where you want the text from the other file to appear.**

   Move the cursor to the point in your letter where you want, for example, to wax eloquent about chocolate-belly futures.

2. **Choose Insert⇨File.**

   WordPerfect displays the Insert File dialog box, which looks suspiciously like the Open File dialog box and a half-dozen other dialog boxes that have to do with files.

3. **Choose the name of the file you want to insert into the current document.**

   Choose the file that contains the standard product description, for example.

4. Click on Insert or double-click on the filename.

WordPerfect opens the file, sticks its contents into the current document right where your cursor is located, and shoves aside any text that comes after the cursor.

Another way to include information from one document in another is to open both documents and then use cut-and-paste commands to copy the information from one document to the other. The resulting combined document has the same name as the document in which you pasted the text.

You can insert more than one document into the current document. WordPerfect has no limit, in fact, to the number of other documents you can stick into the current one. Watch out, though: Don't create enormous documents unless you have to. They can become slow and unwieldy.

WordPerfect doesn't keep track of where inserted text comes from. If you want the inserted text to change with its source document, you want *linked documents*. WordPerfect can do that; you have to use the File➪Document➪Subdocument command, which we discuss in Chapter 17.

Saving a chunk of text as a separate document

You can also do the reverse of inserting text — you can save part of the current document in a new, separate file. What if you write a letter that contains a terrific explanation of how to make vegetarian chili (your specialty)? Now you want to save your recipe in its own file, as shown in these steps:

1. Select the text you want to save separately.

Chapter 4 shows you ways to select text.

2. Choose your favorite way of issuing the Save command.

Choose File➪Save, click on the Save button on the toolbar, or press Ctrl+S.

WordPerfect notices that some text is selected and displays the Save dialog box, as shown in Figure 12-4.

Figure 12-4:
Saving
some text in
its own file.

3. **To save the selected text in its own file, choose Yes.**

   WordPerfect displays the usual Save As dialog box so that you can tell it the filename you want to use for the selected text. You may name the selected text `Chili_Recipe.wpd`, for example.

4. **Choose OK in the Save As dialog box to create the new document that contains the selected text.**

   The text you selected also remains in the original document — that is, WordPerfect saves a *copy* of it in the new file.

What If the File Already Exists?

As you work in WordPerfect, opening and saving documents, you frequently type names for new files. The day will come when you type a name for a new file, little suspecting that you have *already* used that filename — probably for a document you have forgotten all about. According to the rules, you cannot have two files with the same name in the same directory.

What happens? WordPerfect asks you what the heck you want to do, that's what happens. You have a choice of saving the new file on the top of the old one or changing your mind. A dialog box like the one shown in Figure 12-5 appears.

Figure 12-5: How can you have two files in the same place at the same time?

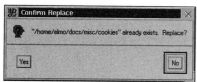

You can click one of these two buttons:

- ✔ **Yes** means "Blow away the existing file with this name and replace it with the one I'm saving now." Show no mercy.

- ✔ **No** means "Wait! I chose the wrong filename! Give me another chance to enter the right one!"

ASCII no questions, I'll tell you no lies

You can use WordPerfect to edit ASCII files. You may be called on someday to edit one of the special text files that tell Linux how to work, such as your `~/.bash_profile` or `~/.mailrc` file.

When you edit an ASCII file, you must be sure to save it again as an ASCII file, not as a WordPerfect document. To find out how to open the text file in WordPerfect, follow the directions in the section "Reading a foreign file," later in this chapter. Then edit the file, but don't use any formatting or insert any special characters. Finally, save it as an ASCII text file just as you would any other foreign file (see the section "Creating a foreign file," later in this chapter).

For most ASCII-editing purposes, using a standard UNIX editor is easier, such as Emacs, GNOME gEdit, or the KDE Text Editor. It's also safer because you won't accidentally save an important Linux ASCII file as a WordPerfect document.

Using Foreign Files

I see a foreign document in your future. It is strong, handsome, and exotic. You will travel over water.

Oops! That's not the kind of foreign thing we're talking about. A foreign file is one that isn't stored in WordPerfect 8 format.

You have several reasons to use foreign documents:

- ✔ You receive drafts of documents on disk from someone who uses FrameMaker.
- ✔ You want to give your documents on disk to someone who will edit them some more with Microsoft Word.
- ✔ You get data files (such as lists of names and addresses) from a database program such as Microsoft Access or Paradox.

WordPerfect can both read (open) and write (save) files in other formats, including the ones in this list:

- ✔ Applix Words
- ✔ FrameMaker
- ✔ HTML
- ✔ Lotus 1-2-3
- ✔ Lotus AmiPro

- ✔ Microsoft Word
- ✔ Other versions of WordPerfect
- ✔ PostScript
- ✔ Plain old ASCII text
- ✔ RTF (rich-text format, a Windows standard)
- ✔ Web pages

When you (or someone) installed WordPerfect on your computer, you (or someone) may have opted to conserve disk space by not installing all the conversion options that come with WordPerfect. If that's the case, your WordPerfect installation may choke on some of the preceding formats.

Which format should I use?

If you want to read or create a file for one of the programs listed in the preceding section, you're in Fat City. Otherwise, see whether the other program can read or write RTF or ASCII text files. If so, you should be able to communicate with WordPerfect.

The name doesn't match the face

Here's one confusing thing: After you save a file in a foreign format, WordPerfect changes the document name on the title bar to the name of the foreign file. If you save the file again by using File➪Save, Ctrl+S, or the Save button on the toolbar, WordPerfect wonders which format you have in mind and displays the Save Format dialog box.

WordPerfect suggests that you save the file in regular WordPerfect format, in the format you last used, or in some other format. If you want to use the format you used last time, just tell it what you want. If you want to save the file in WordPerfect format now, however, you have a problem. We suggest that you just press Cancel to close this dialog box and then choose the File➪Save As command instead.

The reason is that if you choose WordPerfect format, WordPerfect does indeed save the document as a WordPerfect file. Unfortunately, it still uses the filename you typed when you exported the document. Suppose that you save an important marketing report as Chocolate.wpd in WordPerfect format and then save it as Chocolate.doc in Microsoft Word format. The filename that then appears on the title bar is Chocolate.doc. You press Ctrl+S to save the document again, the Save Format dialog box appears, and you select WordPerfect format. WordPerfect saves the report in a file named Chocolate.doc in WordPerfect format.

A file that has the wrong type of file name for its contents is confusing; you can easily get bollixed up this way. Watch out! You're better off using the File➪Save As command (or pressing F3), which enables you to specify both the format and the filename.

ASCII text files contain nothing but regular old letters, numbers, spaces, and other punctuation — no formatting. They're named ASCII text files because they contain character codes defined by the American Standard Code for Information Interchange, or ASCII. The *RTF* (Revisable Form Text) format includes most of your document's formatting, unlike ASCII, which loses most formatting (refer to the sidebar "RTF: The Esperanto of file formats," later in this chapter).

Creating a foreign file

Creating a file in a format other than the regular old WordPerfect format is also called *exporting* a file. To export a WordPerfect document, follow these steps:

1. **Save the file in WordPerfect format.**

   If you want to do more editing later, you can open this file and export it again.

2. **Choose File⇨Save As or press F3.**

   You see the dialog box shown in Figure 12-6. The File Format option at the bottom usually says `WordPerfect 6/7/8`. This message is the WordPerfect way of saying that it plans to save the document in the usual WordPerfect format, which WordPerfect Versions 6, 7, and 8 can read and write, and suggesting some commonly used file extensions.

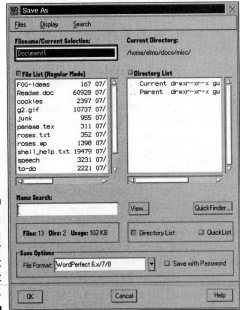

Figure 12-6:
Sending your WordPerfect document overseas.

Word processors versus food processors

Although WordPerfect does a great job of importing and exporting files in many other formats, it isn't perfect. Not that it's WordPerfect's fault — the problem is that different word processors have different capabilities and do things in different ways. Sometimes, files that have been imported or exported look as though they were mistakenly put in a food processor for a few seconds.

When you're using a foreign file, look around it before you blithely edit or print it. The formatting may be fouled up. Fonts may change mysteriously. You may find extra paragraph-ending characters (the ones you usually put in using the Enter key) where they don't belong. Some cleanup may be in order.

Chapter 13

Juggling Files on Your Disk

- -

In This Chapter

▶ Naming files

▶ Using directories

▶ Using the WordPerfect file manager

▶ Moving, renaming, copying, and deleting files

▶ Finding a file with a forgotten name

- -

*1*n the old days, Linux didn't have a file manager. As with all UNIX systems, everything you did to a file was done by typing commands in response to a cryptic prompt. Users became adept at typing cd, ls -l, pwd, cat, and about a hundred other commands whenever they wanted to look at, copy, move, delete, or rename a file. Thankfully, file managers have blossomed, and Linux has so many file managers that you could spend a week just deciding which file manager you like best. These file managers are replete with pretty icons, menus, and drag-and-drop features.

File managers have become so routine that you can now even find them inside other applications, including WordPerfect for Linux. WordPerfect has its own file manager program built in, to help you with all the file manipulating you're bound to run into. This chapter runs through the basics of the WordPerfect file manager.

We talk a great deal about *directories* in this chapter. If you're used to Windows or Macintoshes, you probably know them as *folders*. Although they're the same thing, long before anyone ever thought of the folder analogy, they were known in UNIX-land as directories, and the name has stuck. You can call them folders if you want, but then no one will ever believe that you're a UNIX guru.

WordPerfect Versus Real File Managers

Exploring the directories and files in your computer is a rather large topic. In fact, a whole chapter in *LINUX For Dummies,* 4th Edition, tells you everything about it. (Margy wrote the book with John R. Levine; it's published by — who else? — IDG Books Worldwide, Inc.) We don't do that here. Instead, we *do* tell you just enough to get your files organized.

The topic is also large enough that Linux has not one, but rather several programs that do nothing other than help you explore the directories on your computer. Most common Linux desktop environments (such as KDE and GNOME) have a file manager program, and for heavy-duty file exploration, they're just the ticket. If you want to make big changes to your files, like moving lots of files at one time or reorganizing your directories, consider learning to use the file manager that comes with your window manager. If you use KDE, for example, you can choose K➪Home Directory from the KDE taskbar at the bottom of the screen to see KDE's own file manager (which looks amazingly like the Windows 98 My Computer folder windows).

Although the WordPerfect file manager does the job of managing files, calling it a file manager may be a bit overblown. Just as one wouldn't expect a *real* file manager to excel at processing words, one shouldn't develop high hopes that a word processor should include a full-featured, supercharged file manager. For example, the WordPerfect file manager doesn't let you drag and drop files with the mouse. Despite the file manager's shortcomings, though, it's still a handy tool. The rest of this chapter describes the file management magic you can perform with the WordPerfect file manager.

Exploring Your Directories

In WordPerfect, you may have noticed that the File➪Open, File➪Save As, Program➪File Manager, and Insert➪File commands all show you more or less the same dialog box. It's where the WordPerfect file manager lives. You can also display a similar File Manager dialog box by choosing Program➪File Manager from the program window. Look at the Save As dialog box, as shown in Figure 13-1.

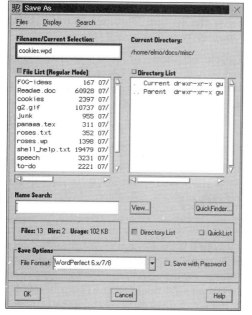

Figure 13-1:
Save As,
the Swiss
army knife
of dialog
boxes.

Like the WordPerfect window, this dialog box has several parts. Here are the most important ones:

- ✓ **Current Directory:** The directory where WordPerfect saves your document unless you tell it otherwise.

- ✓ **File List:** The documents in the current directory.

- ✓ **Directory List:** The subdirectories inside the current directory. Use the directory list to travel up and down the directory tree. On the directory list, double-click on a directory name to enter the directory. To go up one directory, double-click on the directory named `.. Parent`.

- ✓ **Filename/Current Selection:** The name of the selected file. If you select a directory, the selection box shows *, which is the wild card for "all files." Sometimes, this box is named simply Current Selection. Don't worry: It's the same box.

- ✓ **View:** Opens a preview window showing the contents of the selected file without having to open it.

- ✔ **QuickFinder:** Searches the contents of a bunch of files for a particular word or group of words. The section "Finding a File with a Forgotten Name," later in this chapter, tells you how it works.

- ✔ **Directory List and QuickList:** Shows or hides these lists. The *Directory List* shows the subdirectories inside the current directory. The *QuickList* is a list you create that contains short, easily recognizable names for directories you use often. See the section "The QuickList," later in this chapter.

Okay, now that you have the basics down, you can get to work managing files!

Creating directories

Unless you tell WordPerfect otherwise, it saves all your documents in your default document directory, which is usually either your home directory or the directory that was open when you started the WordPerfect program. If your user-name is `hpotter`, for example, your home directory would be `/home/hpotter`. You probably don't want to put all your documents in your home directory, unless you're an especially big fan of disorganization. Instead, you can easily either specify a different directory when you save your document or create a new directory. You can also change your default document directory. (See Chapter 19 for more information about changing the WordPerfect default settings).

Earlier in this chapter, we mention that directories are often called folders because they're somewhat analogous to the paper folders used in filing cabinets. They have a key difference, though. Although a supply cabinet never seems to have enough real paper folders in it, electronic folders never have that problem; you just create new ones out of thin air. Here's how to do it with the WordPerfect file manager:

1. **Open the Save As dialog box by choosing File⇨Save As, or open the File Manager dialog box by choosing Program⇨File Manager.**

   You see a dialog box that looks something like the one shown in Figure 13-1.

2. **Select the existing directory in which your new directory will be created.**

   Double-click on directory names in the Directory List to move to the existing directory you want.

3. **Choose Files⇨Create Directory from the menu bar in the Save As dialog box or the File Manager dialog box.**

   The Create Directory window appears, with the name of your current directory already in the window.

4. **Type the name of the directory you want to create.**

   To place the directory inside your current directory, just append the new directory name to your current directory, after the final slash mark. (Remember that the slash is used to separate directory names.) If you type the name of an existing directory, WordPerfect refuses to create it and complains in the form of an error message. Don't leave a space between the pathname WordPerfect provided and the additional directory name you type.

5. **Click on OK.**

   WordPerfect creates the new directory and displays it in the Directory List box.

You've created a new directory, although nothing is in it. If you're using the Save As dialog box, you can go ahead and save a document in that new directory. When you double-click on the directory name in the Directory List box, the new directory name appears in the Current Directory portion of the dialog box. Type the document name in the Current Selection box and press Enter. Congratulations!

Pathnames

When you want to talk to your computer about your files, how do you distinguish between files that have the same name? Suppose that you have two recipes, both named `cookies.wpd`. They can coexist because they're in separate directories: one in a directory named `chocolate` and the other in a directory named `oatmeal`. Pathnames are used to tell your software how to navigate the hierarchy to get to the right place. A pathname consists of the list of directories, separated by a slash (/).

A pathname to the `chocolate` directory looks like this:

`/home/hpotter/recipes/chocolate`

A pathname to the `oatmeal` directory looks like this:

`/home/hpotter/recipes/oatmeal`

If you want to be precise in telling your computer about a file, you can use the pathname with the filename and its extension. The pathname looks something like this line:

`/home/hpotter/recipes/`
`    chocolate/cookies.wpd`

Moving, Renaming, Copying, and Deleting Files

What, exactly, can you name a file? Linux filenames can be as long as you want, although you should avoid special characters (such as *, &, and !) and spaces. Not being able to use spaces can occasionally cramp the style of those used to Windows or Macintosh systems. Because Linux users get used to using periods or underscores to take the place of spaces, you often see filenames like `cookie_recipe.wpd` or `letter.to.diane.wpd`. The `.wpd` extension on WordPerfect for Linux filenames is optional, but a good idea because it helps you recognize which files are WordPerfect documents.

To move, copy, or delete a file, start with these steps:

1. **Open the File Manager (or similar) dialog box by choosing Program⇨File Manager or File⇨Save As or File⇨Open.**

2. **Find the file you want to move, copy, or delete.**

   Double-click on a directory name on the Directory List to enter a directory. Make sure that the directory name doesn't stay highlighted. If it does, double-click on . `Current` to clear the highlighting.

3. **Highlight the filename by single-clicking on it in the File List box.**

   Don't double-click on the filename; that method tries to either save or open the file, depending on which dialog box is displayed.

Follow the steps in one of the following three sections to move, rename, copy, or delete the file you selected.

Moving or renaming a file

To move a file, follow these steps after you've finished Steps 1–3 in the preceding section:

1. **Choose Files⇨Move/Rename from the dialog box menu.**

   You see the Move/Rename dialog box, with the file's current pathname.

2. **Enter the destination or new filename.**

   Type the path and filename to which you want to move the file. You can also edit the pathname that WordPerfect already displays. If you want to move the file, type the path to a different directory from the one in which the file is stored. If you want the file to keep the same name, type the same name. If you want to rename the file, type a different name.

3. **Click on OK.**

WordPerfect renames the file if you typed a different filename, or moves the file if you typed a different directory name, or both! For example, if the file is originally at the pathname /home/hpotter/spells/test1.wpd, you can rename it by changing the entry to /home/hpotter/spells/quiz1.wpd. Or, you can move it to a different directory by changing the entry to /home/hpotter/history/test1.wpd. If you try to move the file to a directory that doesn't exist, WordPerfect complains, displays a message, and refuses to move the file. WordPerfect (Linux, actually) doesn't let you move a file to a directory for which you don't have the proper permissions, either. (So much for your bright idea of moving incriminating files into your boss's home directory!)

Copying a file

Copying a file works much like moving a file. To copy a file, follow these steps after you've finished Steps 1–3 in the section "Moving, Renaming, Copying, and Deleting Files," earlier in this chapter:

1. **Choose Files⇨Copy from the dialog box menu.**

   You see the Copy dialog box, with a blank box asking where you want to put the copy of the file.

2. **Type the destination where you want WordPerfect to copy the file.**

   Type the path and filename you want to copy to. The directory must already exist. Unfortunately, WordPerfect doesn't provide a way for you to take a look at the directories you have — no little folder icon appears to the right of the box. Rats! Just type carefully.

3. **Click on OK.**

WordPerfect leaves the original file where it was and creates a copy where you indicated. You can't copy a file into a directory that doesn't exist or in which you don't have permission to write files. Linux is picky that way.

Deleting a file

To delete a file, follow these steps after you've finished Steps 1–3 in the section "Moving, Renaming, Copying, and Deleting Files," earlier in this chapter:

1. **Be really, really sure that you want to delete this file.**

   Linux is unforgiving and doesn't believe in second chances; you have no way to undelete a file!

2. **Choose Files⇨Delete from the dialog box menu.**

   You see the Delete dialog box, which asks whether you're sure that you want to delete the file.

3. Click on Yes.

WordPerfect deletes the file, and, because Linux (unlike Windows and Macs) has no Recycle Bin, you have no easy way to get it back.

Two Helpful File-Management Tools for the Forgetful Author

No matter how carefully you name your files, at some point you lose track of what's in them. (Does memo.wpd contain that memo to your boss or the memo to your sweetheart?) The WordPerfect file manager has two nifty tools to jog your memory.

The viewer window

The View button in the File Manager, Save As, or Open dialog box opens the Viewer window, showing the contents of whichever file you have selected, as shown in Figure 13-2. You can't do anything with this preview except see what's in the file; at this point, however, that's all you're interested in.

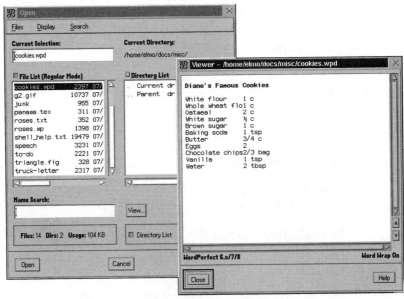

Figure 13-2: Sneak peek: Using the Viewer window to see a file's contents without opening it.

The Viewer window stays open as you pick your way through your files. If you select an unreadable file (such as a program), WordPerfect just says that it's an unknown file type. When you're all done with the Viewer window, click on the Close button.

The QuickList

Depending on how organized you are, you may find that some documents are buried several layers down in directories. For example, your business letters may be buried in the directory /home/hpotter/documents/letters/current/business, and you'll probably get tired of clicking all the way down there every time you want to open a letter.

The WordPerfect QuickList is just what you need to save all that wear and tear on your mouse button. The QuickList lets you make shortcuts to your commonly used directories.

To display the QuickList, click the QuickList button in the lower-right part of the File Manager, Save As, or Open dialog box. WordPerfect displays the QuickList pane, as shown in Figure 13-3. It's somewhat small because it's sharing space with the Directory List. (You can make the Directory List go away temporarily by clicking on the Directory List button.) The QuickList begins by displaying only one shortcut, named *Documents*.

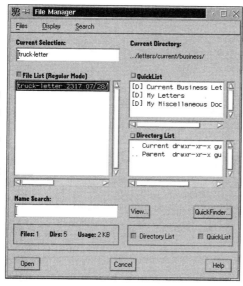

Figure 13-3: The file manager with the QuickList window active, your ticket to fewer mouse clicks.

To move to a directory listed on the QuickList, double-click on it. For example, double-clicking on the Documents shortcut takes you to the directory in which WordPerfect thinks that you store your documents.

The QuickList gets useful when you create your own shortcuts. Suppose that you want to make a shortcut to `/home/hpotter/documents/letters/ current/business`. The shortcut would enable you to switch to that directory with one quick double-click of the mouse. Follow these steps to create your own QuickList shortcuts:

1. **If the QuickList doesn't appear on the right side of the File Manager, Save As, or Open dialog box, click on the QuickList button to display it.**

2. **Click and hold down the *right* mouse button inside the QuickList pane.**

3. **When the pop-up menu appears, click on the Edit QuickList option.**

   The Edit QuickList window appears, as shown in Figure 13-4. You can add new shortcuts, delete shortcuts you don't use, and change existing shortcuts.

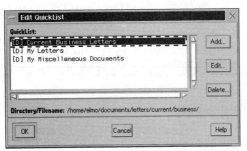

Figure 13-4: The Edit QuickList window, where your shortcuts are created.

4. **To create a new shortcut, click on the Add button.**

   You see the Add QuickList Item dialog box, in which you tell WordPerfect the name you want to give the shortcut and the directory to which the shortcut should take you.

5. **Type in the Directory/Filename box the name of the directory.**

   For example, type **/home/hpotter/documents/letters/current/business**.

6. **Type in the Description box the name of the shortcut.**

   For example, type **Current Business Letters**.

7. **Click on OK.**

`Current Business Letters` appears on the QuickList, and whenever you want to go there, you can double-click on the QuickList rather than click your way down an endless list of directories.

You can also edit shortcuts by selecting the shortcut in the Edit QuickList dialog box and clicking on the Edit key. If you never use a shortcut, get rid of it by selecting it in the Edit QuickList dialog box and clicking on Delete. WordPerfect doesn't delete the directory — only the shortcut to the directory.

Kinds of Files

WordPerfect can, and does, use many different files. Some are its own, WordPerfecty kind of files. Others are of the import–export variety, such as spreadsheets, databases, graphics, and documents from other word processing programs. You have to be slightly aware of their differences to prevent confusion when, for example, a graphics file and a document file have the same name and are stored in the same directory.

You can usually tell a WordPerfect document file when you see it listed (as in a dialog box). It usually has the three-letter wpd extension appended to its name and separated by a period (HiMom.wpd, for example), unless you deliberately gave the document a different extension when you created it (not a good idea). Documents from other word processing programs use other extensions.

Graphics files also generally have distinctive two- or three-letter extensions, although hundreds of variants exist. Some common ones are tif, eps, and jpg. These extensions are used with the Insert⇨Graphics⇨From File command and elsewhere.

Most of the time, WordPerfect knows from the type of command you're giving just which kind of file you want and displays only the right sort of file. Considering all the settings you can fool with, however, it's only a matter of time before you do something that makes WordPerfect throw up its hands and leave you to sort things out from the extensions.

Finding a File with a Forgotten Name

Boy, is WordPerfect ever glad that you want to know how to find your files. It has invested heavily in creating the *Star Wars* of file finding, the Saint Bernard of lost and stranded files, the veritable *Rescue 911* of technology-assisted document search-and-rescue. It's named QuickFinder, and it's lurking almost unseen in the File Manager, Save As, and Open File dialog boxes. QuickFinder is so muscle-bound that we don't even try to describe everything it can do; we focus instead on how it helps you find a file.

QuickFinder finds files by looking for certain text. If you want to find a letter to Ms. Tannenwald, for example, but cannot remember the name of the file, you just type **Tannenwald** in the right place in the QuickFinder.

QuickFinder then sounds the alarm; dispatches armies, navies, and air forces to execute your humble request; and comes marching back, proudly carrying in its teeth any and all files that have any hint of the word *Tannenwald* in them. This feature works for phrases and various word combinations, too.

Before you go any further, here's how to perform a simple single-word search:

1. **Choose Program⇨File Manager, Programs⇨Open Window, or File⇨Save As from the menu bar.**

   You see a dialog box that has the QuickFinder button near the lower-right corner.

2. **Click on the QuickFinder button to display the QuickFinder dialog box.**

3. **In the File Pattern box, select a file pattern for files to search.**

   To search all files in a directory, leave this entry as * (the default). To search only WordPerfect documents, you can enter ***.wpd**. (Filename extensions are useful for finding particular types of files.)

4. **In the Search For box, type a word you want to search the files for.**

   For example, type **Tannenwald**.

5. **Select the directory where you want the search to start.**

   To search in only the current directory, set the Search In box to Directory. To search the current directory and all directories inside it (and the ones inside them, and so on), set the Search In box to Subtree.

   To start the search in a different directory, either type the name of the directory or click on the little folder icon to the right of the directory name. The File Manager dialog box appears, and you can select a new directory.

6. **Click on the Find button.**

   The Find button becomes the Stop Find button while QuickFinder searches. As QuickFinder finds files, it lists them on the list of documents.

You're finished. QuickFinder has found all files that contain the word you're looking for. You can double-click on one of these files, if you selected the File⇨Open command to see this dialog box, or you can just click on the Close button in the Search Results dialog box and go about your business.

Sometimes, a single word may not be enough when you're looking for a file. You cannot just type a phrase in the Search For box; QuickFinder interprets it as a list of individual words and finds files that contain any of those words. (A space means the same as an *or* symbol in the normal mode of operation.) To tell QuickFinder that you're typing a phrase, put it in quotation marks (" "). If you want to get fancy, click on the left-pointing triangle button to the right of the Search For box and choose some QuickFinder advanced options. Then click on Find, and away you go.

Part IV

Creating Documents That Don't Just Sit There

The 5th Wave   By Rich Tennant

"It's a ten-step word processing program. It comes with a spell-checker, grammar-checker, cliché-checker, whine-checker, passive/aggressive-checker, politically correct-checker, hissy-fit-checker, pretentious-pontificating-checker, boring-anecdote-checker, and a Freudian-reference-checker."

In this part . . .

Step right this way, ladies and gentlemen. See documents with amazing snaking columns. Watch words wait upon your tables. Take a trip to the very border of civilized word processing. Most spectacular of all, see the amazing text that's captured in a box and has pictures tattooed all over it. See documents cloned from one another. Finally, from the mysterious land of ether, the spiderwoman will weave a web made entirely of WordPerfect documents. Step into the most astounding word processing sideshow on earth.

If you want to see your documents do these amazing tricks and more, you've come to the right place. In this part, we talk about getting your words exactly where you want them on the page with tables, columns, and boxes. Get ready for your productivity to skyrocket as you find out how to put pictures in your WordPerfect documents. Then make your documents multiply a thousand times, each copy with a different name and address. This part is all about these word processing tricks — plus, it's your guide to publishing your WordPerfect documents on the World Wide Web.

Chapter 14

Chasing Your Words Around on the Page

In This Chapter

▶ Borders

▶ Columns

▶ Tables

▶ Boxes

▶ Lines and arrows

The cool thing about word processors now is that you can dress up a document in ways that only a designer, typesetter, or printer could do a few years ago. The trouble is, now that people (your boss, for example) know that normal people can do this kind of thing, they begin to expect it.

The other less-than-cool thing about today's word processors is that, in giving you all this wonderful stuff, "they" have gone absolutely overboard. WordPerfect, for all practical purposes, performs not only word processing but also drawing, charting, spreadsheet-like calculating, and elements of typesetting.

The problem for the average schmo is getting around all the fancy stuff to do the basic stuff. That's what this chapter is all about. We don't give you a course in spreadsheets or computer art; we just help you get started in creating basic columns, tables, and stuff. Here's what we talk about in this chapter, and why you want to know:

- **Borders and backgrounds:** You want to know about these elements because everything you put in your document (including paragraphs of text) can have its own border and background.

- **Columns:** They're interesting only if you really want to do, er, well, columns.

- ✔ **Tables:** They're perfect for anything you want to arrange in both rows and columns. Tables are especially cool because you can do a certain amount of math in them. They help avoid embarrassing errors in memos and similar documents.

- ✔ **Boxes:** In WordPerfect, boxes — like boxes in real life — are where stuff goes. Stuff, in this case, is pretty much everything except the main text of your document. Stuff like lines and blocks of text, which we talk about in this chapter, are either *in* boxes or *act* pretty much like they're boxes. Pictures, graphs, and drawings you create, which we talk about in the Chapter 15, are also all in boxes.

Working with Borders and Backgrounds

For some reason, nothing looks as neat as having a nice, fancy border around your text. At least, that's what the folks at WordPerfect must believe because their border features are yet another case of overkill for most of us common folks. WordPerfect lets you choose from among a dizzying array of tasteful (and not so tasteful) borders. You can fill the background of your document with subtle, interesting, or downright bizarre patterns.

Some of these features can be useful if you want to create some kind of fancy document — a certificate, for example. Unless you use these features carefully, you can easily end up with an illegible mess.

Basic borders

To put a snazzy border around part of your document, first decide which area of your document you're interested in making illegible — oops, we mean fancy. Your choices are pages, paragraphs, or columns. Applying borders to pages, paragraphs, or columns does pretty much what you may expect: You get borders down the whole side of your page, borders down the side of your paragraph (and that includes each paragraph in multiple columns), or borders down the side of the entire area that's in columns.

For the basic once-over, we choose paragraphs because all border controls work in basically the same way. Choose the Format➪Paragraph➪Border/Fill command to see the Paragraph Border dialog box, as shown in Figure 14-1. (You see the same dialog box, named Paragraph Fill, if you choose the Format➪ Page➪Border/Fill command or if you click on the Border/Fill button in the Format➪Columns dialog box.)

WordPerfect displays the Paragraph (or Page or Columns) Border dialog box. Click on the big X labeled Border Style to see a box full of borders, as shown in Figure 14-2.

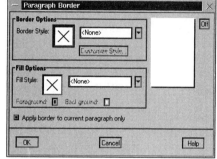

Figure 14-1: The Paragraph Border dialog box.

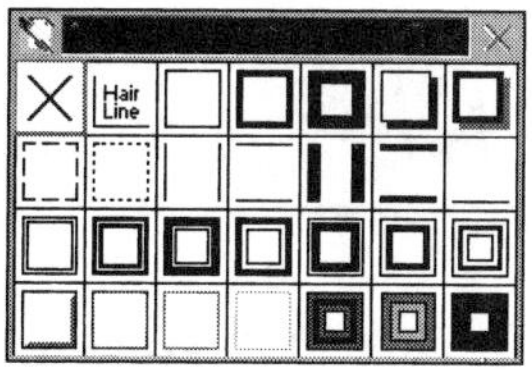

Figure 14-2: A box full of borders.

The folks at WordPerfect have wasted — er, we mean spent — a tremendous amount of time coming up with zillions of kinds of borders for your documents. You can look around the collection of border styles and find the one that suits you best. (The big X means "none.") When you see a border you like, click on it. Another way to pick a border (if you prefer descriptions to pictures) is to click the downward-pointing triangle box to the right of the box that says <None> in the Paragraph Border dialog box and choose a border from the list of borders.

If you don't find one you like, you can select a border and then click the Customize Style button to set the color, line style, and shadow direction yourself, if you don't have anything better to do.

You're not quite finished yet. In the lower-left corner of this box is a button labeled Apply border to current paragraph (or page or column group) only. If you leave this box selected, that's exactly what WordPerfect does. If you want to do a great deal of damage quickly, though, _un_select this box. All the following pages (or paragraphs or column groups) will have this border.

Phil — for all that white space behind your text

If you like borders, you'll love Phil. Phil (or, rather, Fill) shows up when you click on the big X labeled Fill Style in the Paragraph Border dialog box. (Or, click on the downward-pointing triangle button to its right.) Mostly, what this button does is make your text illegible by putting a pattern behind it. You may want to put a light-gray pattern behind something you want to have stand out. Make sure, though, that your printer and copier are up to the job of printing or copying this stuff; otherwise, you end up with a smudge rather than read-able text.

Click on OK when you have what you like. When you see what you've done to your document, you may want to remove the borders and fills. Just press Ctrl+Z to undo your changes.

Some miscellaneous thoughts about borders

"But I'm not an artist!" you cry nervously. "What am I going to do with all these borders and backgrounds, other than make my documents illegible?" This section lists some things you may want to do:

- **Put a border around your whole document.** Using the Format⇨Page⇨Border/Fill command, you can put some neat borders around certificates and posters.

- **Limit your borders to the paragraph, page, column, or whatever area the cursor is in.** In the Border dialog box, click on the box in the lower-left corner that says Apply border to current *whatever* only. Checking this box is an alternative to selecting an area of text before you issue the Border/Fill command.

- **Put lines between columns.** Place the cursor anywhere in your columns (which you can read about in the next section), choose Format⇨Column, and then click on the Border/Fill button to display the Column Border dialog box (which looks similar to Figure 14-1). Click on the downward-pointing triangle button to the right of the Border Style button. The last three borders on the list of border styles are special, and they apply specifically to columns. Scroll down the list until you see the last three: Column All, Spacing Only, and Column Between. Column Between puts a line between your columns. Spacing Only adds space for lines around your columns but doesn't put in the lines (an obscure but useful feature if you have some columns with lines and some without). Column All puts borders around your whole set of columns, including lines between your columns.

TIP

- ✔ **You can even change the way borders and lines between the columns look.** After you have selected the Column Between or Column All border from the Column Border dialog box, you can click on the Customize Style button and choose your own color and thickness for lines.

- ✔ **Don't use borders.** Use a horizontal or vertical line. We talk about them in detail in the section "Scribbling on Your Document," later in this chapter.

Working with Columns

Columns are great for newsletters, newspapers, magazines, scripts, lists, and certain charts or tables. With newspaper and magazine documents, even if you don't print the document yourself, you can use columns and the correct character and paragraph formatting to determine approximately how long your article will be when you print it.

WordPerfect can lay out columns in the following four styles (when was the last time we said that WordPerfect has only *one* way to do something?):

- ✔ **Newspaper:** Fills one column to the end of the page before beginning another column. Use this option for newsletters and long, incoherent, raving letters to the editor.

- ✔ **Balanced Newspaper:** Continuously shuffles your text to make sure that all columns are of more or less equal length. Use this style (which has nothing to do with a balanced editorial policy) when a document alternately uses a single column and multiple columns, such as when you have a long, multicolumn list in the middle of a regular document. You can also use this style for ending the last page of a multicolumn newsletter before the end of the physical page.

- ✔ **Parallel:** Creates rows across columns and creates cells of text in a manner similar to a table. When you use this style, you create a row one cell at a time by inserting a hard column break when you want to begin writing in the next cell to the right. This style is useful for scripts and contracts.

- ✔ **Parallel with Block Protect:** Similar to Parallel, but ensures that automatic page breaks don't mess things up if your rows must continue on the next page.

If all these styles sound confusing, take heart. The WordPerfect Columns dialog box shows neat pictures of which sort of columns are used for each option.

Creating columns

To turn on columns in your document, follow these steps:

1. **Place the cursor where you want columns to begin.**

   If you want your entire document to appear in two newspaper columns except for the title at the top, for example, move the cursor to the first line after the title.

2. **Choose Format➪Columns.**

   You can also use the toolbar to turn on columns. Click on the button labeled Columns; it's the one with the three little columns of parallel blue lines on it. A menu drops down. To put text in columns quickly, allowing WordPerfect to use the default column style (Newspaper) and spacing, just click on the number of columns you want and you're finished. If you want to define your columns yourself, choose Format from that menu — but then you could have chosen Format➪Columns from the main menu and ended up in the same place.

   The Define Columns dialog box appears, as shown in Figure 14-3.

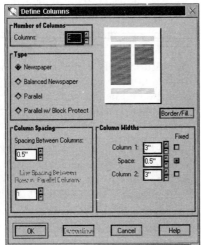

Figure 14-3:
Getting, like, totally columnar with the Define Columns dialog box.

3. **Choose the number of columns you want.**

   In the upper-left corner, in the Number of Columns section, WordPerfect suggests two columns (unless you're working with text that's already in columns, in which case it shows the current setting). Change this number by typing a number or clicking on the up and down arrows next to the Columns box.

4. Choose the type of columns you want.

In the Type section, choose one of the options (Newspaper, for example) described in the preceding section.

5. Adjust the column widths or spacing, if you want.

In the Column Widths section, WordPerfect suggests nice, even column widths with a half-inch space between them. It allows column widths to vary if you change the page margins, but it prevents the spacing between columns from changing (it keeps the spacing fixed).

To fix (or unfix) any column or space-between-columns dimension so that it doesn't vary, click on the box in the Fixed column to the right of the Column Widths setting.

To change widths, click on the width box and edit the value by typing and deleting, or click on the adjoining up-and-down (increment and decrement) arrow buttons. Use the ” symbol for inches or **mm** or **cm** for metric values.

If you want all spaces between the columns to be the same size, you can adjust the intercolumn spacing by using the Spacing Between Columns setting, next to the number of columns. Be careful, though — if you change the value in this box, *all* spaces between the columns (even ones you changed by hand) are set to the new column-spacing size.

If you made your columns look sort of like a table by using Parallel or Parallel w/ Block Protect, you can also specify the number of blank lines WordPerfect leaves between rows. Click on the up-and-down arrow buttons in the small box with the long name (Line Spacing Between Rows in Parallel Columns).

If you click on the Border/Fill button, you see the Column Border dialog box we talk about in the first section of this chapter.

6. Click on OK or press Enter when you finish (like we had to tell you that).

The hyper-observant will have noticed that the word Insert on the Application Bar (between the picture of the printer and your position on the page) has changed to indicate which column you're in, usually Col 1 at this point.

To turn off columns at some point in your document, place the cursor where you want things to go back to normal. Then choose Format⇨Columns or click on that new Col 1 button on the Application Bar. In either case, you see the WordPerfect Define Columns dialog box; click on Discontinue. Alternatively, press the Columns button on the toolbar and choose Discontinue from the menu that drops down. If you're going to turn off columns in your document, you should use Balanced Newspaper columns rather than plain Newspaper columns. Plain Newspaper columns will most likely leave an entire blank column at the place where you turn off columns.

Putting selected text in columns

Sometimes, you want to put a block of text in columns. You may put a long list of words, such as in a packing list, into several columns to save space, for example.

Begin by highlighting the block of text you want to columnate. (Columnarize? Columnify?) Next, choose the Format⇨Columns command. In the Columns dialog box, choose the style you want. The Balanced Newspaper option probably

works best, unless you want to control where the columns break, in which case you use the Newspaper option. Then click on OK. If you want newspaper columns, you can click the Columns button on the toolbar. Choose the number of columns you want and you're all set.

Using highlighted text in this way is equivalent to turning columns on, typing all the text in the block, and then turning columns off.

Bad breaks and what to do about them

Some breaks are good, and some breaks are bad — column breaks, that is. WordPerfect decides where to break your columns depending on many things, and it's different for different kinds of columns. When columns don't break where you want them to (or break where you don't want them to), you can regain some control by inserting hard column breaks.

To insert a hard column break, follow these steps:

1. **Place the cursor before the line (or word or character) where you want a column to begin.**

2. **Press Ctrl+Enter to insert a hard column break.**

Column breaks don't always do what you think they will do. It depends on which column-type option you choose: Newspaper, Balanced Newspaper, or one of the Parallel styles. The following list shows the types of columns in the column-break story:

- **Newspaper:** Column breaks begin a new column in the way you think that they should.

- **Balanced Newspaper:** A column break begins a whole new block of balanced columns; it's almost like turning columns off and then on again. This style probably isn't what you have in mind if you're trying to fix the way WordPerfect has balanced your columns. Rather than use a column break to change the balance, try regular newspaper columns.

> ✔ **Parallel or Parallel with Block Protect:** A column break moves text across the current row to the next column. The break doesn't put text at the top of a new column, as you may expect. When you insert a column break at the end of the row, you're back in the left column, in a new row.

Column breaks are invisible no matter what you do, unless you use the Reveal Codes window (refer to Chapter 9), and who wants to do that? If you want to delete hard column breaks, have faith that they're located just before the first character in a column (or just before the current cell in a parallel-type column). To delete hard column breaks, place the cursor before the first character in the column and press the Backspace key. Or, put the cursor at the end of the preceding column and press the Delete key. (Don't try to delete soft column breaks — the ones WordPerfect puts in.)

Working with Tables

When it comes to tables in WordPerfect, guess what? Yup — more overkill. WordPerfect is a word processor that swallowed a spreadsheet program. The program can perform such tasks as automatically computing sums of columns and rows. It can, in fact, automatically compute the standard deviation of the arc tangent of the logarithm of the net present value of your mortgage, over multiple random variations of the interest rate.

Fortunately, for those of us who would just as soon leave spreadsheets to the accounting department, WordPerfect also does ordinary tables. It even makes them easy to create.

Making tables with Table QuickCreate

The fastest way to create a table is to use the Table QuickCreate button on the toolbar. Follow these steps:

1. **Click on the toolbar button that looks like a little grid and hold down the mouse button.**

   As you hold it down, a little grid appears. You can use it to tell WordPerfect how big to make your table.

2. **Drag the mouse pointer down and to the right on the grid to highlight the number of rows and columns you want.**

   In tables, columns flow vertically, and rows flow horizontally. The number of columns times rows appears above the grid (for example, 5 x 2 for a table with five columns and two rows).

3. **Release the mouse button.**

   Your table is ready. Would Madame follow me? Walk this way, please.

When to use columns and when to use a table

Columns and tables both stick text into columns. How do you choose between them? The choice isn't always obvious. In many cases, either one will do.

Columns are better when you have a large amount of text and you're willing to have it move from one column to another, depending on how your page layout looks. Magazine and newspaper layouts use columns.

Tables are better when you have a smaller amount of text and it's important what text appears beside what. If you have text that must appear in specific columns, you can use parallel columns with the Block Protect option, although a table is usually easier to use. Use tables if you have lots of numbers and you want to ask WordPerfect to total them (or do other math).

One last guideline: Don't use more than four columns. If you need more than that, use a table.

To fill a table with goodies, simply click in a cell and type. You can include text, numbers, and even graphics, and you can format your text in the usual way by using the Format commands.

If you want to do special table-ish things, you'll be pleased to notice that the Property Bar now has a whole bunch of table-ish buttons on it. The Property Bar for tables is shown in Figure 14-4. Just as a graphics menu appears on the Property Bar when you're dealing with boxes, a table menu has appeared on the Property Bar. It's quite useful, as you see in this chapter.

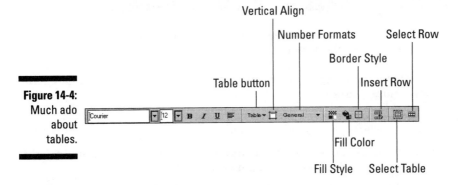

Figure 14-4: Much ado about tables.

Adding or deleting rows and columns

 To make tables larger or smaller (to increase or decrease the number of rows or columns), you use the Table button on the Property Bar — it's the button with the downward-pointing triangle to its right. When you click on the Table button, a menu of table-related commands appears.

These steps show you how to add one or more rows or columns to your table:

1. **Click on any row or column that will adjoin your new row or column.**

   Click anywhere in the bottom row, for example, to add a new row to the bottom of your table.

2. **Click on the Table button on the Property Bar and choose Insert from the menu that appears.**

   You see the Insert Columns/Rows dialog box.

3. **In the Insert section of the dialog box, click on Columns (for columns) or Rows (for rows).**

   If you want more than one new row or column, type the number in the box next to Columns or Rows or increment the number by clicking on the adjoining up and down arrows.

4. **In the Placement section of the dialog box, click on Before if you want the row to be placed above (or the column to be placed to the left) of the cell you selected in Step 1; otherwise, click on After.**

   To add a row to the bottom of your table, for example, click on After.

5. **Click on OK.**

 To quickly insert a row, click on the Insert Row button on the Property Bar (refer to Figure 14-4). Why does it have no Insert Column button? Who knows?

To delete a row or column from your table, follow these steps:

1. **Click anywhere in the row or column you want to delete.**

   For multiple rows or columns, click and drag to highlight them.

2. **Click on the Table button on the Property Bar and choose Delete to display the Delete dialog box.**

3. **In the Delete section, click on Columns or Rows.**

4. **Click on OK.**

To delete the entire table, begin by highlighting all the cells. The quickest way is by pressing the Select Table button on the Property Bar. Then, if you press the Delete key on your keyboard, the Delete Table dialog box appears. You can delete the whole table by clicking on Entire Table. Or, if you prefer (and it's kind of a nice feature), you can delete only the table contents and leave behind the table framework by clicking on Table Contents. Other weird options are available, too; ignore them. Then click on OK.

To delete the contents of a bunch of cells, highlight them and press the Delete key. Although you don't get any warning, the contents are gone. (You can always get them back by using Edit⇨Undo or Ctrl+Z.)

Changing the column width

Changing individual column widths is simple. Click on the vertical line that divides the columns and drag it. The mouse pointer turns into a little horizontal-arrow gizmo, to tell you that you're moving a column divider. When you release the mouse button, the column divider moves over so that the column on one side of the line gets wider and the other one gets narrower.

If you hold down the Ctrl key while you move the column divider, only the column to the left of the divider gets wider or narrower as you move the divider. The column to the *right* of the divider line stays the same size. The whole table gets wider or narrower to provide the space needed. The columns to the right of the divider line just *move* rather than get resized. This feature can be handy.

 Changing the width of more than one column or the entire table is not hard, although it requires that you use a slightly intimidating dialog box. Using this dialog box, you can change other aspects of a table's appearance — such as left–right justification, alignment of numbers, column margins, table left–right justification on a page, and even text-style variations by column or row. Because SpeedFormat, discussed in the following section, does such a good job with all this stuff, though, we don't go into it here.

Take a deep breath and follow these steps:

1. **To change the width of several columns, highlight the columns by clicking and dragging across them.**

2. **To change the column width of the entire table, click anywhere in the table.**

3. **Click the Table button on the Property Bar and choose Format or press Ctrl+F12 to display the Format dialog box.**

   The options across the top enable you to specify whether you want to format an individual cell, a column, a row, or the entire table.

4. **To change the column width for the entire table, click on Table.**

5. **To change the column width for an individual column, click on Column.**

6. **Change the value in the Column Width box (the box marked Width).**

   Click in the box and type a new number or click on the increment–decrement arrow buttons. If your table is set to take up the full width of the page, click on the increment-arrow button until WordPerfect doesn't increase it any more. Your columns then get as wide as they can.

7. **Click on OK or press Enter.**

Choosing borders and backgrounds with SpeedFormat

Tables look best when certain rows or columns are specially formatted with bold or italics or colored shading. The fastest and coolest way to format your table is to use SpeedFormat. (SpeedFormat has nothing to do with QuickFormat, which is described in Chapter 6, in the section about copying character formatting.) Follow these steps:

1. **Click anywhere within the table.**

2. **Click on the Table button on the Property Bar and choose SpeedFormat.**

   The Table SpeedFormat dialog box appears, as shown in Figure 14-5, displaying a list of named table styles on the left side of the dialog box.

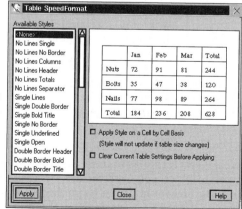

Figure 14-5:
Faster than
a speeding
format, it's
Speed-
Format.

3. **Select a style on the Available styles list.**

   SpeedFormat shows an example of how that style looks. The example in the dialog box is just that — an example. SpeedFormat doesn't actually enter things in a table for you, by typing titles or creating totals; it just formats the table with various fonts, row and column widths, alignments, and borders. You take care of typing stuff.

   To quickly look at the available SpeedFormats, click on <None> on the Available styles list. When you click down to the next style, the style is highlighted and its sample appears.

4. **Click on the Apply button.**

   SpeedFormat applies your chosen table style to the table.

If you later insert rows or columns in the table, WordPerfect automatically formats them in the same style. If you insert a column after a totals column, for example, WordPerfect formats the original totals column as an ordinary data column, and the new column takes the appearance of the original totals column. If you prefer that SpeedFormat leave its cotton-pickin' hands off your new rows or columns, click on the check box labeled Apply Style on a Cell by Cell Basis after you choose a style in the Table SpeedFormat dialog box.

Making incredibly complex spreadsheet-like tables

Spreadsheet-like tables don't have to be incredibly complex, although they certainly can get that way. Tables become like spreadsheet programs when they begin to calculate values automatically. To show you how this process occurs in WordPerfect, we focus on a simple example of summing rows and columns.

First, however, you have to keep a couple of things in mind when you're creating a spreadsheet-like table:

- Every cell in a table has a reference name that describes its row and column position. Rows use single letters, beginning with *A* in the top row. Columns use numbers, beginning with 1 in the left column. The top-left cell, therefore, is A1, and so on. Users of Lotus 1-2-3 and other spreadsheet programs should feel right at home.

- The calculations are based on formulas that are entered (in a special, invisible way) in the cell in which you want the answer to appear. To add cells A1 and B1 and put the answer in C1, for example, the formula A1+B1 must be specially stuffed into cell C1. We talk more about this subject in a minute.

Look at the simple budget shown in Figure 14-6. It has sums of columns and even a little division and subtraction to calculate the percentage change from year to year.

It's hard to tell that formulas, not numbers, are entered in the total rows and the rightmost column. The only way to tell, in fact, is to turn on the Formula toolbar, which lets you enter or see formulas, To see the toolbar, click on the Table button on the Property Bar and choose Formula Toolbar from the menu that appears. (Click on the Formula toolbar's Close button to make the bar go away.)

The white box on the left side of the top line of the bar shows which table WordPerfect thinks that you're in (such as A, B, or C, which WordPerfect uses to keep track of tables) and in which cell the cursor is located. In Figure 14-6, that location is Table A, cell C14 — the sum of the FY00-01 expenses.

The other white box shows the formula in this cell: +SUM(C8:C13). The colon means "through," so this formula means "Sum cells C8 through C13." (Does this look like a spreadsheet formula or what?)

To create this formula, click in the formula box and type the formula or click on the QuickSum button in the second row of the Formula toolbar. If you type the formula, click on the adjoining check mark button to test the formula and insert it in the cell.

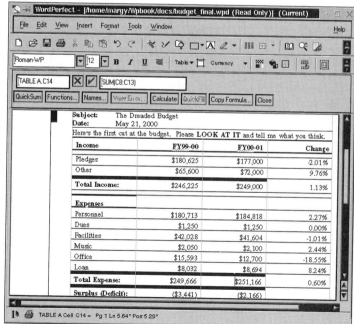

Figure 14-6:
A memo with a complicated table: The Formula toolbar appears between the Property Bar and the document.

The QuickSum button is kind of magical. It inserts a formula for the sum of cells either above or to the left of the cell in which you're putting the formula. QuickSum is intelligent about doing it correctly (it's not at all a dim sum), although sometimes it guesses wrong about what you want.

Try it. If the QuickSum button guesses wrong, you can always edit the formula in the formula box. (Don't forget to click on the check mark button when you finish.)

Values must already be in the cells for the QuickSum button to work. Put the values in first and then use the QuickSum button.

To perform multiplication and other simple calculations, such as computing the percentage change from year to year, you can use these symbols in your formulas:

* (Multiply)

/ (Divide)

+ (Add)

– (Subtract)

You can access other formulas by clicking on the Functions button on the Formula Bar, but, hey — it's all heady stuff for a mere word processing program.

Formatting the numbers in your complex spreadsheet

To get your numbers to look as pretty as ours do in Figure 14-6, with dollar signs and stuff, click in a cell you want to format, click on the Table button on the Property Bar, and choose Numeric Format (or press Alt+F12). You see the Number Type dialog box, which enables you to format an individual cell or a column or the entire table. Rather than fool with the details of how to format your numbers, WordPerfect has defined some number types, such as fixed (decimal-point numbers), scientific, currency, and accounting. Choose the number type you want and trust that WordPerfect will make your numbers look right. If it doesn't, you can always specify a different number type. In the Number Type dialog box, specify whether you want to format the cell the cursor is in, the column, or the entire table. Click on a selection in the Available Types section (check out the example in the Preview section) and then click on OK.

Working with Text Boxes

Suppose that you're reading a serious article — in *People* magazine, for example ("Tom Hanks: Does He Really Hanker After Meg?"). In the corner of the page, bordered in fuchsia, are two columns of text about some frivolous, annoying peripheral subject, such as "Tom Hanks and Cher: Separated at Birth?" Guess what? You too can make annoying sidebars such as this one in your document by using text boxes.

Seriously, you should read this section if you want to create *any* kind of boxes in your WordPerfect documents. Plain old text boxes like the one we just described, some tables, pictures, and even equations use this box stuff, so it's handy to know. All the boxes in WordPerfect work pretty much the same way. We use text boxes to introduce them.

Creating your first box

 To create a text box, choose Insert⇨Text Box or click on the Text Box button on the toolbar (it has the letter *A* on it inside a rectangle). Poof! A box appears in your document. WordPerfect decides where to put the box and what it should look like. The cursor is inside the box, so type away to your heart's content.

You can format this text by using the Format commands, just as you would format any other text. You can even put text in columns. Don't try to use the Format commands to change the border of the text box, though; all you get are boxes within boxes. Text is automatically centered between the top and bottom bars. If the text box is the wrong length or width, don't worry about it now; just type the text. You can change the box dimensions when you're finished.

You may decide that this box has a couple of problems. Two that we can think of are that it may not be exactly where you want it to be and it may not have the border outline you want. Never fear. You can change all that too. Just read on.

 Pressing Ctrl+Z doesn't undo adding a text box, and neither does choosing Edit⇨Undo, so be sure to save your document before working with text boxes.

Selecting your box

Everything we talk about in this part of this chapter requires that WordPerfect be thinking about your box, not about the *contents* of your box. If you click *in* the box, WordPerfect obliges by thinking about the contents of the box. (In this section, boxes contain text, so the Property Bar shows all its text-ish things.) If you click *outside* the box, WordPerfect obliges by thinking about the text outside the box. More text. You can select your box in one of two ways:

✔ **Click on the contents of your box:** Works if the attention of WordPerfect is focused

elsewhere and your box isn't showing its eight handles. This method doesn't work for text boxes. For those, and for boxes WordPerfect is already thinking about, it starts selecting the contents of the box rather than the box itself.

✔ **Click on the border of your box:** Works if you can see the border of your box but WordPerfect has its attention elsewhere, usually on the contents of the box.

Moving a box to more or less where you want it

Okay, you've typed a bunch of text in your box, and the box has grown to suit. It's just not quite where you want it to be. No problem. Because this box is the one you're typing in, it should have eight little square blocks, or *handles,* around it. Click and hold the mouse button anywhere along the outsides of the box *between* the handles. You know that you're in the right place when the mouse cursor turns into a four-headed arrow. After you've clicked and started to drag, that box should move anywhere you want it.

Making a box more or less the right size

This task is just about as challenging as moving the box. Find those eight handles around the outside of the box and drag one of them to resize the box. The cursor changes again to tell you that you're in the right place. In this case, you get an arrow pointing either up and down (you can make the box taller or shorter), left and right (you can make the box wider or narrower), or diagonally (you can drag the corner of the box and change both its width and height at the same time). Go wild.

Changing everything else about a box

When you select a box, notice that the Property Bar changes completely: It usually shows type fonts and sizes and the like. If you've clicked on the outline of the box and see the eight handles, however, the Property Bar starts with the word *Graphics*. It's a good thing that it does, too, because you may want to do about a million things to your box.

Getting the Property Bar to display the *box* properties, as opposed to the properties of the *text inside* the box or the *text outside* the box, can be a little tricky. If you click inside the box, the Property Bar tells you about the text inside the box. If you click outside the box, the Property Bar tells you about the text outside the box. If you click on the edge of the box itself, however, you see not only the arrow and the handles but also the box Property Bar, as shown in Figure 14-7.

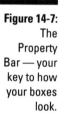

Figure 14-7:
The Property Bar — your key to how your boxes look.

Next Box ⌐ ⌐ Border Style
⌐ Fill Style
⌐ Caption   Text Wrap

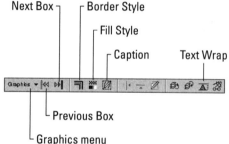

└ Previous Box

└ Graphics menu

A few of these buttons are simple:

- **Previous Box/Next Box:** While your mind is on boxes, you may want to do stuff to other boxes in your document. Rather than have to find them and click on them, let these handy buttons take you to those boxes directly. If either button is grayed out, it means that no previous or next box is in your document.

- **Border Style:** This button gets you into Border Formatting Land, which we talk about in the section "Basic borders," at the beginning of this chapter.

- **Fill Style:** This button introduces Phil, the fill guy we talk about at the beginning of this chapter, in the section "Phil — for all that white space behind your text."

The other buttons deserve a look in a little more detail.

Working with the Graphics menu

Because a whole bunch of commands are meaningful only when you have selected a box (technically, a graphics box), the folks at WordPerfect decided that it would be less confusing to have the Graphics menu appear only when a graphics box is available to edit. Rather than have the Graphics menu appear on the menu bar, where you may not notice it, they put it on the Property Bar that appears when you're editing a graphics or text box. At least that's what we figure.

You can do only two things of major importance from this menu that you *can't* do anywhere else: Set the exact size of your box and set the exact position of your box.

Moving a box exactly where you want it

Earlier in this chapter, we talk about dragging the border of the box (between the handles) to move it around. That method may be fine if you don't care *exactly* where your box is placed. If you want to specify the gory details, however, select the text box, click the Graphics button on the Property Bar, and choose the Position command. Figure 14-8 shows the Box Position dialog box.

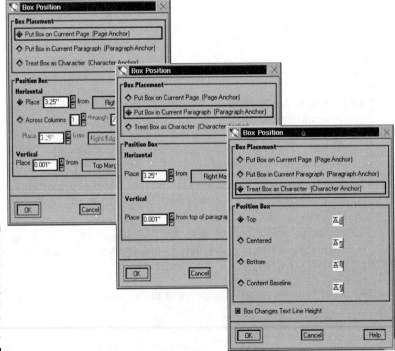

Figure 14-8:
The Box Position dialog box comes in three flavors.

Because boxes aren't part of your text, WordPerfect needs to decide where they should be placed on the page and what should happen to them if the text on the page changes. This last point, what happens when the text changes, is why the various settings all have the word *anchor* in their names: You anchor your box to some item in your document, and where that item goes, so goes your box. You can attach boxes to a page, paragraph, or character by using the Page Anchor, Paragraph Anchor, or Character Anchor settings, respectively, in the Box Position dialog box. The rest of the settings in this dialog box depend on which type of anchor you choose.

Anchoring your box to a page

Boxes attached to pages don't move relative to the page. Text can come and text can go; this box, however, always appears in the same place on the page. Ahh, but *which* page, you ask. It all has to do with codes, again. Creating a box in a document inserts another one of the secret codes we discuss in Chapter 9. The secret code moves with the text around it. If you add text, the code moves further along in the document. If you delete text, the code moves further toward the beginning of the document. Your box appears on the page where the code is, but always at the same place on the page.

If that's not what you want to have happen, that's okay; you can fix it. For example, if you want a box to appear always on page 2 and only page 2 of your document, create the box on page 2. Click the Graphics button on the Property Bar, choose the Position command to open the Box Position dialog box, and select Put Box on Current Page (Page Anchor). The dialog box contains the settings shown in the leftmost version in Figure 14-8. Now your box stays on page 2, regardless of how much text you insert in front of it or how much text you delete. In fact, if you delete all the text from page 2, you may end up with a page containing *only* the box you created. That's what you said you wanted, though, so that's what WordPerfect does.

You may think that specifying *where* your box will appear on the page would be straightforward, but this is WordPerfect — you have *many* options. To start with, you specify the horizontal and vertical position of the box. Relative to what, though? For horizontal position, you can specify that you want your box placed relative to the edges of the paper, relative to the margins of your text, or relative to columns if you have any on your page.

After you figure out what to attach your box to, you can figure out relative to where. The left or right margin or the center of the page? Or the left edge of the paper (in case the margins change)? The left column, the right column, or the center of the columns? Usually, you want to choose relative to the left or right margin. Choose relative to the left edge of the paper if your box is big enough that it may not fit between the margins. You may need to experiment until you find what you like.

Anchoring your page to a paragraph

To attach your box to a paragraph, click the Graphics button on the Property Bar, choose the Position command to open the Box Position dialog box, and select Put Box in Current Paragraph (Paragraph Anchor). The dialog box contains the settings shown in the middle version in Figure 14-8. Boxes attached to paragraphs move with the paragraph they're attached to. If you add text in front of the paragraph, your box moves down the page with the paragraph; if you remove text, your box moves up the page. Telling WordPerfect where a box should appear relative to its paragraph is simpler than telling it where a box should appear relative to a page. The horizontal options are pretty much the same. For vertical options, however, you can just specify where the box should appear relative to the paragraph. In most cases, you want boxes to be placed relative to the paragraphs they're near.

Anchoring your page to a character

Boxes can also be attached to characters. You can think of this type of box as a special character you can draw by yourself. (If you really want to draw it, look at Chapter 15.) If you just want some text to move around in your document as though it were a character, however, you're in the right place.

To attach your box to a paragraph, click on the Graphics button on the Property Bar, choose the Position command to open the Box Position dialog box, and select Treat Box as Character (Character Anchor). The dialog box contains the settings shown in the rightmost version in Figure 14-8. You have a dizzying array of options, of course, for where your box should go. Horizontally, it goes with the character right after it. Vertically, however, WordPerfect lines up the top, center, or bottom of the box with the line of text. The Box Position dialog box does a nice job of illustrating your options. Our guess is that you'll want to use the Content baseline option, even though it sounds scariest. It just means that the bottom of what's in the box should line up with the bottom of the text on the line.

Making a box exactly the right size

As you may imagine, if dragging isn't good enough for determining exactly where a box should be placed, that method probably also isn't good enough for determining how big the box should be. To complement the Box Position dialog box, therefore, WordPerfect has the not-quite-so-massively-overcomplicated Box Size dialog box, as shown in Figure 14-9. You display it by clicking on the Graphics button on the Property Bar and choosing Size. In the Box Size dialog box, you can enter an exact height and width for your box. This feature is useful because it gives you the option of maintaining the proportions of your box. When you're dragging the corners of the box around, you can stretch it like Silly Putty, which works better for some boxes than for others.

Figure 14-9:
How large a
box do you
want?

If you want to keep the original height-to-width proportions of your box, resize it by using the Box Size dialog box and then click on Maintain proportions. If you click it in the Height section, you can change the box width, and WordPerfect adjusts the height automagically. If you click on Maintain proportions in the Width section, you can probably guess what happens.

If you want a box to run the full width of the page, click on Full in the Width section. If you want the box to run the full height of the page (if you want a tasteful stripe up the page, for example), click on Full in the Height section. Don't click on Full for both height and width.

Adding captions to your boxes

Using regular document text to put a caption where you want it, such as below a box, is virtually impossible. You have to use the special Caption feature. When you click on the Caption button on the Property Bar, WordPerfect creates a little typing space below your box and may suggest a caption (*Figure 1* or whatever). If you don't like the suggestion, press the Backspace key to delete it. Alternatively, you can add your caption to the beginning or end (or both) of what WordPerfect suggests. As you type your caption, you can use any of the usual Format commands or formatting buttons, such as boldface or different type sizes. When a caption already exists, pressing the Caption button displays the caption text so that you can edit it. You could, of course, just click on the text to edit it, but that would be too easy!

You can delete a caption, although you wouldn't know it by looking around Word Perfect. To do so, the box must be selected and the Graphics menu displayed (refer to Figure 14-6). Click on the Graphics button on the Property Bar and choose the <u>C</u>aption command to display a dialog box that has more options about captions (and captions about options) than a reasonable person wants. Ignore them all and click on Reset (on the right side of the dialog box). WordPerfect warns you that you are — gasp! — about to delete your caption. If you click on Yes, you get absolutely no indication that you have deleted your caption; click on OK in the Box Caption dialog box, however, and rest assured that the caption is gone, gone, gone!

When all is said and done, we think that captions are great. It may take a little time to get them set up exactly the way you want them; after you do, though, they help people find their way around your document, and they look classy!

Text wrapping

Text wrapping is kind of like gift wrapping, with a twist. (Or is that a bow?) You have a box on your page; what should WordPerfect do with the text in your document when it gets to the box? You have a couple of alternatives:

- ✔ **Jump over the whole box, leaving white space to the right and left of the box.** That's what we've done with the figures in this book.

- ✔ **If your box isn't exactly in the middle of the page, the space on one side is smaller than the space on the other side.** (At last, a use for high school geometry!) WordPerfect is perfectly happy to figure out which side is smaller and leave it blank and then run the text down the wider side of the page. That's what WordPerfect does, in fact, unless you tell it otherwise, and it's not a bad choice.

- ✔ **Run the text around the box, assuming that a reader's eye will just skip over the box.** This choice is usually not a good idea unless your box is rather small. Otherwise, people get confused and don't know whether to read down one side of your box and then down the other or across the page, skipping the box.

 Because you're using WordPerfect, you have two ways to tell WordPerfect how you want to wrap text around your box: Click the Text Wrap button on the Property Bar or right-click on the box and click on the Wrap command to display the Wrap Text dialog box. Figure 14-10 shows the Wrap Text dialog box, which includes the WordPerfect illustration of what these different options look like. To see this dialog box, right-click the text box and choose Wrap from the pop-up menu.

Figure 14-10: Text-wrapping your box in time for the holidays.

The Text Wrap button on the Property Bar makes selecting which kind of wrapping you want easy. In case you forget, the only way to see the Property Bar for the box itself, rather than for the contents of the box, is to click on the outline of the box; you should see eight square "handles" around the edge of your box (see the section "Changing everything else about a box," earlier in this chapter). When you click on the Text Wrap button, you see a list of the options we just described, with a few additions. Don't worry about contours for now; we talk about them in Chapter 15 when we talk about pictures. You can also have your box block out the text it's sitting on top of (that's the In Front of text option) or have the text march right over your box (Behind Text). You figure out whether that may be useful sometime.

Scribbling on Your Document

In the ceaseless quest to make documents on computer screens look more and more like documents on paper, word processors feel compelled to let you scribble on your document, just like you might with a pen or pencil. This feature can be very useful if you want to emphasize something or draw a visual connection between elements of your document. WordPerfect is uncommonly accomplished in this area. You can easily draw horizontal and vertical lines in your document and, with a little more effort, draw lines and shapes anywhere you want.

Up and down and side to side

To draw a horizontal line, press Enter to make a new paragraph, place the cursor there, and then press Ctrl+F11 or choose Insert⇨Shape⇨Horizontal Line. To place a vertical line through most of your page, choose Insert⇨Shape⇨Vertical Line. You can change the length of the horizontal or vertical line and change its location by editing it. Right-click on the line to select it, which can be a bit tricky. Pass the mouse cursor *very slowly* over the line you just inserted. At some point, the cursor should turn into a right-pointing arrow. That's your cue to right-click. On the QuickMenu, you see the choice Edit Horizontal Line (or Edit Vertical Line), which displays the Edit Graphics Line dialog box, with lots of fun options. If you're tired of your line, you can delete it by right-clicking on the line and choosing Delete. When you select a line by clicking on it, black handle boxes appear, which you can use to move the line.

Lines that go any which way

WordPerfect has a more useful type of line, which it calls a draw line. *Draw lines* let you decide where a line should start and end almost anywhere on a page.

Add draw lines to your document by choosing the Insert⇨Shape⇨Draw Line command. The cursor turns into a set of crosshairs. Click *and hold down the mouse button* on the place where you want one end of the line to be and drag the line to where you want the other end to be. Because the line is in a box, all the things we mention about text boxes earlier in this chapter apply. The reason you can see the text behind your line is that the Wrapping Text option for this box is set to In Front of Text.

When a draw line is selected, the Property Bar mutates to include some new buttons. A couple are worth pointing out; the rest, we encourage you to explore. Figure 14-11 shows the graphics Property Bar.

Figure 14-11: The graphics Property Bar and the secret of arrows.

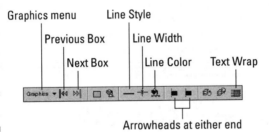

Graphics menu — Line Style
Previous Box — Line Width
Next Box — Line Color — Text Wrap
Arrowheads at either end

To transform your plain old line into a pointed arrow, click on one of the Arrowhead buttons (the fourth and fifth buttons from the right) on the Property Bar. Choose from among the pointy or feather ends of the arrow. Or, use two pointy ends. Sometimes, it takes a little doing to figure out which end gets which arrow, although you can choose as often as you want.

We said it elsewhere in this chapter, and we'll say it again: Your draw line is actually in a box. All the box tricks we introduce earlier in this chapter apply to this box, too.

Chapter 15

Say It with Pictures

In This Chapter

▶ Working with graphics

▶ Using clipart

▶ Using pictures from anywhere

▶ Drawing your own graphics

▶ Handling complicated pictures

▶ Dealing with graphs and charts

*M*ichelangelo had fewer tools for painting the Sistine Chapel than WordPerfect has for creating graphics. For art's sake, that's probably a good thing. Otherwise, Michelangelo's descendants would still be figuring out how many degrees to rotate whom and which color palette to use.

For that matter, Michelangelo probably didn't think that he was creating graphics; he probably thought that he was *painting*. You probably don't think that you're working with graphics either; you just want to put a simple picture in your document. That's okay — you probably didn't think that you were word processing; you probably thought that you were *writing*. Translating from computerese, "working with graphics" means "finding and creating pictures and stuff like that and then putting them in your documents."

We asked the Assumption Fairy (the patron spirit of mathematicians) to grant us two Simplifying Assumptions about what you may want to do. Assume that the tasks you want to do are limited to the ones in this list:

✔ Insert a picture, diagram, or chart that someone has created for you or that came with WordPerfect.

✔ Create a simple picture or chart.

When you want to save a document that contains boxes, WordPerfect (and we) can get confused about what you want to save. When a graphics box is selected and you try to save your document, WordPerfect thinks you want to save only the graphic, in a separate file! Before saving a document that contains graphics boxes (or text boxes, which we describe in Chapter 14), therefore, be sure that the box is *not* selected (doesn't have little black handle boxes around it).

Working with Graphics

You need to know a few basics before we jump in to the subject of working with graphics:

✔ **All pictures live in boxes.**

We talk a great deal about this subject in Chapter 14. If you haven't read it, take a look at the section there about working with text boxes. Pretty much everything we say about text boxes applies to all pictures also. That's why we spend so much time talking about them. Who really cares all that much about text boxes, anyway?

✔ **All boxes have borders and backgrounds.**

That's why we talk about them in Chapter 14, in the first section.

✔ **You can select boxes and the pictures that are in them in two ways.**

If you're typing along in your text and click on a box, you see black *handles* (little boxes along the borders and corners of the box) and no border around the box (unless the box itself has one). When you see black handles, as shown in Figure 15-1, the box itself is selected.

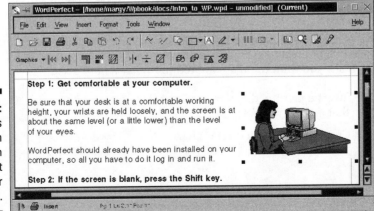

Figure 15-1: Graphics appear in boxes when you select them for editing.

Double-clicking your picture opens the WP Draw program, described in the section "Creating Your Own Graphics with WP Draw," later in this chapter.

Inserting some Corel clipart into your document

This section tells you the simplest way to insert a graphic into your document. We assume (the Assumption Fairy at work again) that you want to insert in your document one of the 200 or so *clipart* images (predrawn pictures) that Corel includes with WordPerfect. (If you downloaded WordPerfect from the Corel Web site, no clipart is included, and the /wpgraphics directory is empty.) Before you get excited about them, though, a word of caution: Although we don't claim that we've looked at every single one of them, we've found that they're mostly cartoonish pictures that are more appropriate for adding emphasis to a slide presentation than for inclusion in a serious business document. Look around — just don't get your hopes up. WordPerfect installs its clipart files in the wpgraphics subdirectory of its program directory. If WordPerfect is installed in the /usr/local directory, for example, the graphics files are in /usr/local/wpgraphics.

To use one of these clipart images, proceed as follows:

1. **Move the cursor somewhere near where you want the picture to appear in your document.**

2. **Choose Insert⇨Graphics⇨From File from the menu bar.**

   Or, click on the Clipart button on the toolbar (the one with the file folder behind the Corel hot-air balloon).

   Either way, the list of available clipart appears in the Insert Image dialog box, as shown in Figure 15-2. (WordPerfect should already know where its clipart files are stored.)

3. **Click on a filename that sounds appealing and click the View button.**

   The picture is displayed in its own little Viewer window. You can keep clicking on filenames to see the files in the Viewer.

4. **When you find the image you want, click the Close button in the Viewer window.**

   The image's filename should still be selected in the Insert Image dialog box.

5. **Click on the Insert button to put the image in your document.**

   WordPerfect places the picture in your document. If you're feeling artistic, you can double-click on the picture and edit it in WP Draw. (We talk more about WP Draw in the section "Creating Your Own Graphics with WP Draw," later in this chapter.)

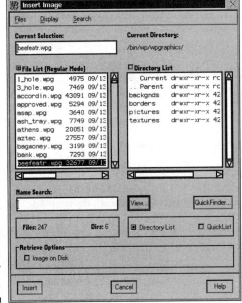

Figure 15-2:
The Insert
Image
dialog box
lets you
preview
pictures
before you
insert them
in your
document.

The cursor should now be merrily blinking at just the point where you left it, and your graphic should appear in your document. Overall, this technique isn't difficult. The document shown back in Figure 15-1 has one of the WP-supplied graphics in it.

Fooling with your picture

Because your picture is in a box, you can do the same things to a graphics box as you can do to a text box:

- ✔ **Move it** by clicking on it (so that the black handle boxes appear), keeping the mouse pointer inside the box (so that the pointer looks like a four-headed arrow) and dragging the picture around.

- ✔ **Change its size** by selecting it and then clicking on the corner black handles and dragging them around. When you "pull" on one of the handles, the box changes size and shape. The contents stretch like Silly Putty to fit the new shape of the box. Figure 15-3 shows the black handles and what can happen if you drag them to make a picture wider. (If you accidentally drag the handles, click on some text in your document. Then you can choose Edit⇨Undo to return the picture to its preceding shape.) You can also size the image to exact dimensions by right-clicking on the image and choosing the Size command from the QuickMenu that pops up.

↳ **Add a border to it** by selecting it and then clicking on the Border Style button on the Property Bar.

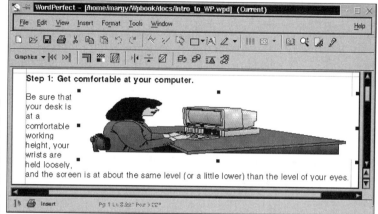

Figure 15-3:
What can
happen to
your figure if
you stretch
it.

These mysteries and more are described in loving detail in Chapter 14.

Keep in mind that the proportions you see onscreen aren't exactly the ones you see when you print. Print your document to check it.

WordPerfect provides a bunch of other commands you can use to edit a graphics box. Select the box (not its contents) by clicking on it once and then right-click on the picture. From the resulting QuickMenu, choose Image Tools. You see the Image Tools dialog box — with its set of 14 buttons. Hover the mouse pointer over a button to find out what it does. The buttons do things such as convert a picture to black-and-white, move a picture around within a box, and set picture brightness and contrast. Close the Image Tools dialog box by clicking on the X box in the upper-right corner.

How to see where you're going

To make seeing where you're positioning an image easier, zoom out to Full-Page view before you begin positioning or sizing your image. Click outside the image area, somewhere in the text. Click on the Page/Zoom Full button on the toolbar; it's the button with the magnifying-glass-and-plus/minus icon. Now start positioning and sizing.

When you finish positioning and sizing the image, click in the text somewhere and then click on the magnifying-glass button again.

Inserting a shape into your document

If you want to insert a simple picture (like a square, rectangle, circle, ellipse, or polygon), move the cursor to where you want the picture inserted and choose Insert⇨Shape from the menu bar. Then choose Polygon, Rectangle, Rounded Rectangle, Circle, or Ellipse from the menu that appears. Click to show WordPerfect the corners, ends, or other points that define the shape. WordPerfect creates a box and sticks into the box the shape you choose. To fix up the shape if it's not quite what you need, double-click on it and skip over to the section "Whipping your drawings into shape, or whipping shapes into your drawings," later in this chapter.

Inserting a picture from somewhere else into your document

You've figured out that the images supplied with WordPerfect don't do it for you. Or, you have a picture that has to do specifically with what you're writing about and you want to include the picture in your document. No problem there, either! WordPerfect is happy to insert just about any ol' image file in your document. Here's how:

1. **Make sure that the graphics file is on a hard or floppy disk in your PC (or on your network).**

   If you're getting a graphics file from a Web page, you need to save the file from your Web browser. Right-click the graphic and choose the Save Image As or Save Picture As option from the menu that appears. When the browser asks where you want to save the file, specify a directory on your hard disk.

   If you're getting your graphics file from a friend or co-worker, you need to put it on your PC. The file can be either on a floppy disk or copied in a directory on your hard disk. If you don't know how to copy the file, weasel out of the job by subtly implying to the person who made the file that it's his responsibility. If that doesn't work, dig out the ol' cookie package and go get your PC guru.

2. **Choose Insert⇨Graphics⇨From File from the menu bar.**

   The Insert Image dialog box appears (refer to Figure 15-2).

3. **Find the file.**

   Use the Directory List box to move to the directory that contains the file. You can use all the same tools (including finding files) that we describe in Chapter 13 to help you find your file.

4. **Click on the filename and click on Insert to insert the picture into your document.**

   To see a quick preview of the picture while you're using the Insert Image dialog box, click the View button.

The same rules apply for inserted graphics files as for WordPerfect clipart: The picture is in a box, it can have borders, and you can move it and resize it just like you can do with any other box.

Creating Your Own Graphics with WP Draw

If you can't find any art that suits your document or if you find some and decide that it needs a little touch-up, WordPerfect has a tool that's all set for you. *WP Draw* has a set of drawing tools that definitely help you get the basics done, and then you can waste days refining every single dot on your screen or on your paper. So what if you're not Norman Rockwell? With WordPerfect, you can still create your own home-style graphics and have them look . . . well, okay. Hey, at least staying inside the lines is easy.

Before we launch into a discussion of the WP Draw program, we need to talk a little about what's going on. When you create a WordPerfect document, you type text in WordPerfect. Simple enough. When you create a text box (refer to Chapter 14), you add to your document something that is not text: a box. What's inside the box is more text. In Chapter 14, we talk about things you can do to these boxes themselves. Because the boxes contain text, you can do all sorts of text-ish things to the text in them — the kinds of things we talk about throughout this book.

What if the box doesn't contain text? What if it contains, just to pull an example out of thin air, a picture? For that matter, what *is* a picture, in WordPerfect? Just as a document is made of text, a picture is made of *objects*. (Think back to high school geometry here because you're about to run into some acquaintances from back then.) We give you a quick rundown of what a picture can contain; then we talk in more detail about the ones you may actually want to use:

   ✔ **Dot:** A dot of color in your picture. Dots usually gather in groups, and together they're trying to be a picture of something. Pictures made entirely of dots are called, for obscure historical reasons, *bitmaps* in computerese (and in WordPerfect). Although you can insert a bitmap in your drawing from a file or from a scanner, you don't draw one.

✔ **Line:** A line or curve from one point to another. There's nothing too special here. You can draw on your picture as many lines as you want. Straight lines are simplest, although WordPerfect also knows about curved lines.

✔ **Enclosed shape:** Lines or curves that enclose some space. These shapes automatically close themselves, so if you're drawing a box, for example, you don't have to manage to click back precisely on the starting point when you finish the fourth side. The space inside the enclosed shapes can be filled with a solid color or 2-color pattern.

✔ **Text:** If you're reading this book from front to back, you know all about text; we've been talking about it for a couple of hundred pages. Each individual letter or other character inside a WordPerfect graphic, however, has two parts: the thin line around the outside and the space inside it.

Fine, you say, but you don't want dots and lines and shapes in your document; you want, for example, a map with some notes on it. Be patient. Using just these four ingredients, you can create anything!

Many Linux systems come with graphics editors you can use to create or edit graphics files. Our favorite is The Gimp (we are not making this up), which comes with Red Hat and many other versions of Linux. We used The Gimp, in fact, to capture the pictures of WordPerfect windows you see in this book.

Creating a new picture

To create a new picture, start simply. Draw a few rectangles, ovals, or freehand shapes:

1. **Use the Insert➪Graphics➪Draw Picture command to create a new graphics box, and run WP Draw to edit the picture in the box.**

   A new window opens, labeled WP Draw (in the window on the right, as shown in Figure 15-4). A separate window contains the WP Draw toolbar (in the window on the left).

2. **Use the toolbar in the WP Draw window to create your drawing.**

   Try out all the tools and add lines, text, and colors to your drawing. The tools are described in detail in the next section.

3. **When you're finished, choose File➪Update to save the drawing as part of your document.**

4. **Choose File➪Exit and Return to close the WP Draw window and get back to your document.**

   The drawing you created is displayed in your document.

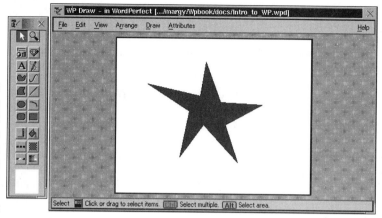

Figure 15-4:
WordPerfect
comes with
WP Draw, a
graphics
editing
program.

Editing a graphic

You can also edit a graphics box that's already in your document. When you double-click on the picture in the box, WordPerfect runs the WP Draw program so that you can edit the picture. Or, right-click on the picture and choose Edit Image from the QuickMenu that appears.

Whipping your drawings into shape, or whipping shapes into your drawings

WP Draw has far too many built-in shapes for us to describe each one in detail. We list the shapes and offer some notes on how to draw each one. At the end of this section, we talk about things that are common to all the shapes. After you have run WP Draw to edit your drawing, you can insert all of them in your drawing by choosing Draw from the WP Draw menu bar and then selecting the shape you want.

Some shapes also have selections on the WP Draw toolbar. The selected button appears in a darker gray (it must be depressed) on the toolbar, and hints about how to use the selected button appear at the bottom of the WP Draw window. In Figure 15-4, the Select (arrow) button is selected. To figure out what the buttons do, move the mouse pointer to the button without clicking: A short description of the button appears on the WP Draw window's title bar.

We assume throughout this section that you have already double-clicked on the drawing and have it displayed in the WP Draw window.

This list describes what you can do with some of the buttons on the WP Draw toolbar:

Line: Click and drag within your drawing to create a line. Double-click on the end of the line. To make a series of connected lines, click once at the end of each line and double-click at the end of the last line.

Polygon: To create a closed shape consisting of a series of line segments (like a triangle, f'rinstance), click and release the end points of each line segment. Double-click on the end of the last segment, which WordPerfect automagically connects to the first point so that the lines form an enclosed space.

Rectangle: Click and drag diagonally across the space you want covered by the rectangle.

Rounded Rectangle: It's the same as a rectangle, except with rounded corners.

Ellipse: Click and drag to make an ellipse or circle.

Elliptical Arc: Probably not the way you want to draw a curve, but you never know. Click and drag from one end of the arc. You get ¼ of an ellipse that ends at the place you next click.

Curve: Confusing but powerful. Click on one end of your curve. At the first *inflection point* (that's where you want your curve to change direction, such as at the top of a rainbow), click again. Each additional click gets you another inflection point. Double-click when you're finished.

Closed Curve: It's just like a polygon, except with curved lines.

Freehand: Click and hold; wherever you drag the mouse, you see a line. Don't forget to release the mouse button when you're finished!

When you click a shape you've drawn, it's surrounded by handles. (If clicking doesn't select the shape, right-click on it and choose Select from the menu that appears.) By pulling on them, you can reshape the object. When the shape is selected, you can also drag it to a new location in your picture. Right-clicking on the shape displays a QuickMenu with some other cool commands. Our two favorite QuickMenu picks are Edit Points (lets you change any of the points where you clicked when you drew the shape) and Rotate, which lets you, well, rotate your shape.

Before you draw a shape, you can choose what type of line will outline it and what color or pattern will appear inside it (for closed shapes). After you've chosen a line and fill style and pattern, all the shapes you draw use those settings until you change the settings again. Here are the buttons you can use:

Line Style: Sets the line type, such as dotted or solid

Line Color: Sets the color of the line

Fill Pattern Style: Sets the pattern with which closed shapes will be filled

Fill Pattern Color: Sets one color of the pattern with which closed shapes will be filled

The line and fill color and style buttons work much like the text box border and fill settings we explain in Chapter 14.

Putting text in your drawings

WordPerfect is, after all, all about words. It shouldn't be surprising, therefore, that you can type directly in your drawing, by clicking the Text button on the WP Draw toolbar. Text in a drawing appears in its own little text box inside the picture. Unlike with text in a WordPerfect document, you can change the size of text in a drawing by dragging on the handles that surround it (after you've put it in your drawing). Rather than be defined by point sizes (refer to Chapter 6), the text can grow and shrink with infinite variability.

To add text to your drawing, double-click on your drawing to edit it in WP Draw (if you don't already have it open in WP Draw) and follow these steps:

1. **Click on the Text button on the WP Draw toolbar (the button with the big *A* on it).**

   The mouse pointer turns into crosshairs in your drawing. You can use the crosshairs to create the text area.

2. **Drag the crosshairs to create a box to hold the text.**

   Your box is displayed in the WP Draw Text Editor, as shown in Figure 15-5. The box is blank because you haven't typed the text yet.

3. **Type the text in the WP Draw Text Editor box.**

   You can use the Format menu in the WP Draw Text Editor to change the text font and justification (left, right, center — you know the drill).

4. **Choose File⇨Close to close the WP Draw Text Editor and get back to your drawing.**

   The text you just typed is added to your drawing.

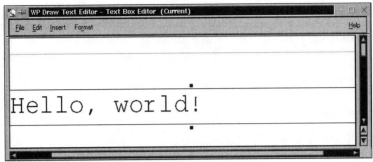

Figure 15-5:
Typing text
to appear
inside a
picture.

   5. **Click the Select button (the arrow) on the WP Draw toolbar and click on the text you just inserted.**

      The usual handles appear around the text. You can move it around or drag the handles to stretch the text.

   6. **Choose File⇨Update Document on the WP Draw menu bar to put this glorious artwork in your document.**

      That's it! To close WP Draw, choose File⇨Exit and Return and go admire your handiwork.

If you want to choose the color of your text, you can select the fill color before you start entering the text.

Creating Graphs and Charts

Using WP Draw, you can create a variety of data charts, including pie, bar, line, and other forms. Put it this way: If you filled a gymnasium with economists, gave them colored pens and rulers, locked the doors, and went back in ten years, WP Draw could have more graphing done than those guys could do during that time. (If you had fed them, they may have had a fighting chance, of course, but why pass up such an opportunity?)

Making a new chart

To create a chart in your document, choose Insert⇨Graphics⇨Chart. A chart and a *Datasheet,* with some figures in rows and columns in it, obligingly appears in a good old WP Draw window, as shown in Figure 15-6. The Datasheet is a sort of spreadsheet or table where you put the data you want to chart. WP Draw draws the chart automatically from the data.

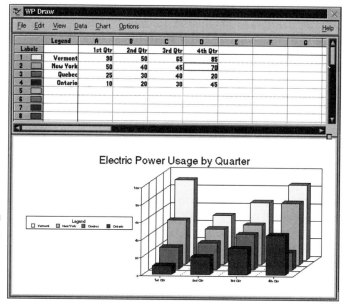

Figure 15-6:
Creating a
data chart in
WordPerfect.

Editing your chart

When you insert a new chart, WP Draw gives you a bar-chart example to begin. You can easily change to another kind of chart, if you want, and then substitute your own data for the example data.

You can learn a great deal about how WP Draw charts data by examining the Datasheet and the chart. Notice that WP Draw uses the entries in the top row of the Datasheet as labels along the horizontal axis on the chart. Also notice that each row of data in the Datasheet has its own color, which matches the color of the data on the chart. The words in the Legend column (the leftmost column on the Datasheet) appear in the Legend box on the chart.

While you're using the WP Draw charting feature, the window has its own chart-related menu bar. After you choose Insert⇨Graphics⇨Chart to create a sample chart, follow these steps to turn the sample chart into _your_ chart:

1. **Change the chart to the type you want.**

   Choose Chart from the WP Draw menu bar and select a chart type.

2. **Delete the sample data.**

   Each little rectangle on the Datasheet that contains a word or number is a _cell._ Delete the values in individual cells by clicking on them, pressing the Delete key, and clicking on OK in the Clear dialog box that appears.

To delete a rectangular group of cells, click on the cell in the upper-left corner of the data to be deleted; hold down the mouse button; and drag the mouse to extend the highlight to the lower-right corner of the data. Release the mouse button and press the Delete key on your keyboard. Click on OK again in the Clear dialog box.

3. **Click on individual cells and type your own data, legends, and labels.**

Scroll the Datasheet window, if you need to.

4. **To put your own title on the chart, choose Options⇨Titles.**

In the Titles dialog box that appears, click in the Title box, change the text there, and then press Enter.

This list shows straightforward ways of changing the graph, in case you don't want to wrestle with each and every option:

✔ **To change the chart type:** Choose Chart from the WP Draw menu and select from the list the type of chart you want. Each type of chart also has a number of possible layouts. To change the layout (for example, to change bar charts from 3-D to 2-D), choose Options⇨Layout from the WP Draw menu and select the layout you want.

✔ **To change the line color and style or the fill color and pattern:** Choose Options⇨Series from the WP Draw menu to display the Series Options dialog box, and then change the settings in the Attributes section.

✔ **To change the position and orientation of the legend:** Choose Options⇨ Legend from the WP Draw menu to display the Legend dialog box. Click on the Series Font button to change fonts displayed in the legend, or click on the Attributes button to change the border and fill that appear in the legend.

To change the size of your chart, drag the black handles while the chart is selected. WP Draw redraws your chart in the amount of space you gave it.

Putting the chart back into the document

To exit the charting feature and return to the text in your document, just close the WP Draw window and click on Yes when the dialog box pops up, asking whether you want to save changes. The chart appears in a graphics box that you can move or resize in the usual ways.

To return to the charting feature to make some more changes, double-click on the chart.

Chapter 16

Creating Your Own Junk Mail

• •

In This Chapter

▶ Creating a data file

▶ Creating a form file

▶ Merging your files

▶ Printing envelopes

▶ Printing your data file

• •

*D*on't you just *love* getting junk mail? Doesn't it warm your heart to know that some direct-mail marketing executive thinks enough of your buying (or donating) power to send you a cleverly personalized letter? "Yes, JOHN, we know that you and the entire SMITH household really enjoy getting heaps of junk mail."

Seriously, sometimes you really *want* to create junk mail. Although you may not want to create the same kind that gets sent to JOHN SMITH, you want to use the same tools.

"What on earth could you be thinking of?" you may ask. Think about the following situations:

✔ You receive a list of names or items or part numbers from someone. The other person went to all the trouble of putting the information in a computer file and maybe even in a WordPerfect document. Your job is to send a letter to each person, print a label for each item, or print a sheet for each part number. It's time to use the WordPerfect junk-mail feature.

✔ You're keeping a list of people, and you need to print the list three ways: alphabetically, by last name; as a set of mailing labels; and by the oldest child's age.

What's up with these two examples? In the first, you want to create a bunch of similar documents (letters or whatever) from information you got for someone else. You want to do it only one time, and many items are on the list. If you have more than about ten items, you probably ought to be using the WordPerfect junk-mail feature.

In the second example, you keep a small or medium number of names (or whatever), and every so often, you have to create two, three, or more kinds of lists from those names. The WordPerfect junk-mail feature — which we may as well call by its right name, *merge* — lets you keep *one* list; make all your address changes, product updates, or whatever, in *one* place; and still create two, three, or more kinds of printouts.

You should be thrilled to hear that WordPerfect can help you out. Thanks to some good engineering, the folks at WordPerfect turned what used to be a tedious, nerdy job into something most human beings can actually do.

Even better, if you want to create letters (or envelopes or mailing labels) for an address list, WordPerfect works with a variety of third-party address books. If you already have your addresses in an electronic address book, you may be able to use those existing addresses with WordPerfect. Contact your system administrator to see about getting your address book installed in WordPerfect.

How Does the Junk-Mail Feature Work?

To create personalized junk mail, you need two documents: a data file and a form file. The *data file* contains the stuff you plan to put in each of your documents; you must enter this stuff in a special format. WordPerfect helps you do that by displaying a dialog box for your data file that lets you fill in the blanks. If you have detailed information about the people on your list — the amount they owe you, name of their firstborn sons, or any other information you may want to include in a form letter — you should create your own data file. The data file is, in effect, a minidatabase. Each piece of information is a *field*. All the information about one person is a *record*. (Doncha love these technical terms?)

The *form file* contains the form letter. The form file contains, in place of a name or address, *merge codes* that tell WordPerfect to use information from the data file. One of the most useful aspects of data files and form files is that a single data file can feed several different form files. That way, the same data can appear on several different printouts. When someone's address changes, you don't have to change it on the mailing label and the address list and the telephone list, for example.

When you perform the merge, you tell WordPerfect to create one copy of the form file for each person in the data file. You can send this combined file directly to the printer or store it as a new, third document.

So far, so good. In this chapter, we step through the procedure for creating a data file and a form file and then show you how to merge them. The procedure isn't that bad, although it is a bit of work to set up.

TIP

The WordPerfect merge feature is cool, although it's not worth using unless you want to send a bunch of letters. For two or three letters (or even four or five), it's not worth the effort. For small jobs, type one letter and print it; then edit the address and print it again; and so on.

Creating a Data File

Before you begin creating a data file, you have to know which fields you want to put in it. Remember that fields are the bits of information you want to keep that will enable you to create the merged documents (the junk mail letters). Fields are such things as a person's first and last names, street address, city, state, and zip code and how much money he owes you. For a list of parts in inventory, fields may be part numbers and prices. For a list of relatives, fields may be family member names, parents, and children.

To make the rest of the process much smoother, take some time to figure out which information you need. For a list of people, you may want to have separate First Name and Last Name fields so that your letter can begin with *Dear Joe* and mention *the Bloggs family* later. Other fields may be something like the amount each family donated last year in response to a church-donations letter or the child's name and the school's start date for a letter from a day-care center.

When you have a list of fields jotted down on a piece of paper, you're ready to get started creating your WordPerfect merge data file. Figure 16-1 shows the fields we figured out that we would need in order to create form letters to students in a (hypothetical) daycare center.

Figure 16-1:
Which
pieces of
intrusive
personal
information
do you want
to include in
your form
letters?

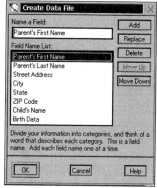

Begin creating your merge data file by choosing Tools⇔Merge or pressing Shift+F9. WordPerfect displays the dialog box shown in Figure 16-2. To create the data file (the list of people, for example), you click the Data button. To create a form file with the codes for a form letter or mailing labels, you click the Form button. After you've created the data file and form file, you click the Merge button to merge the data into the form and create a finished junk mail document!

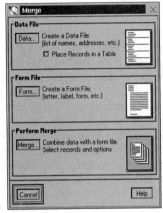

Figure 16-2:
The Merge dialog box serves as Mission Control for creating personalized junk mail.

Clicking on the Data button lets you type from scratch the list of people (or whatever's on your list). What if your data is already in a file, though? What if someone has delivered a data file to you, in some nice, fancy format that made sense to her, but has nothing to do with a WordPerfect merge data file? All may not be lost. The (rather long) following section, "Turning a document full of text into a data file," may be able to help you hack your way out of this situation. If you're lucky, however, and you're staring at a desk full of paper whose information you now intend to enter into WordPerfect, skip the following section and rejoin us at the section titled "Creating a data file from scratch."

Turning a document full of text into a data file

You're not supposed to need to do this task. You're supposed to get your merge data file all set up and then enter data into it. In real life, you often start with a document full of data you want to use for merging. It can happen in many ways, although typically you typed all your data and only then decided to read this chapter and find out how to use that stuff in a merge document. Or maybe somebody gave you a file and asked, "Can you create a bunch of labels for these things?" Or maybe you just can't follow instructions. No matter. If your data is already in a WordPerfect document (or a document WordPerfect can read), it *can* be turned into a merge data file. Although the job isn't easy, it can be done.

No mechanical process really works for all data files. Instead, we take you through one example of how you can change a document into a merge data file. (You have to adapt these steps to your situation.) Before you get started working on your data, you still have to figure out how you want to divide it up — that is, which fields you have in your document. Take a look back at Figure 16-1 to see what we figured we would need for our daycare center.

Figure 16-3 shows what a sample file may look like that contains the information we need. It's a typical way that someone (certainly not you) may enter data into a WordPerfect file. The file contains the data you need for form letters; it's just not laid out as WordPerfect merge data.

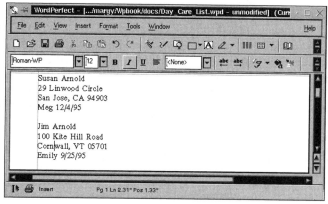

Figure 16-3: A typical document you want to use as a merge data file. The document needs a little work!

The way the data in Figure 16-3 is typed doesn't have much to do with the way WordPerfect is expecting it to look in a merge data file. We can help you fix that, by showing you how to replace the blank lines between the records with ENDRECORD codes and replace the spaces between the fields with hard carriage returns and ENDFIELD codes. Follow these steps:

1. **Save your file.**

   We could assume that you've already done this step, although it never hurts to remind you. It's an especially good idea to save files right before you embark on a project like this one that requires a great deal of finding and replacing, because you can do lots of damage to your document very quickly this way if something goes wrong. A word to the wise. . . .

2. **Make sure that you have a blank line (or something) between each record.**

   Remember that a *record* is a collection of data about any one thing — in this case, about a prospective daycare student. In this example, as is usually the case, a blank line is between records.

3. **Choose Edit⇨Find and Replace or press F2.**

   The Find and Replace Text dialog box appears. You're about to venture into deepest, darkest Find and Replace territory. If you need a refresher course, take a look at Chapter 4. Right now, we show you how to replace the blank line between each record with a code telling WordPerfect that this is the end of a record.

4. **Enter two end-of-line codes in the Find box.**

   Refer to Chapter 4 if you need help with this step. (***Hint:*** Choose Match⇨ Codes to enter the codes [HRt][HRt]. Click the Insert button to insert the codes. Then close the Find Codes dialog box.) If something other than a blank line appears between your records, type that something instead.

5. **Enter the [HRt] and end-of-record codes in the Replace With box.**

   Click in the Replace With part of the Find and Replace Text dialog box. Choose Replace⇨Codes to display the Replace Codes dialog box, insert one [HRt] code, and then check the Display Merge Codes Only check box. The code you're looking for is ENDRECORD. Insert one ENDRECORD code and close the Replace Codes dialog box. The Replace With box should say [HRt][Mrg:ENDRECORD].

6. **Choose the Options command on the Find and Replace Text dialog box menu and make sure that the Begin Find at Top of Document option is selected.**

   That way, you know that WordPerfect will replace all the blank lines with ENDRECORD codes, regardless of where you are in the file.

7. **Click on Replace All and click on OK when WordPerfect tells you how it did.**

   WordPerfect replaces all blank lines between the records with ENDRECORD codes. Don't leave the Find and Replace Text dialog box; you have more to do.

8. **Enter a space in the Find box.**

   Replace the contents of the Find box with a single space. Each of your fields must be on a line by itself. You have no good way to make that happen, other than to replace *some* spaces in your document with WordPerfect end-of-line codes. (Those codes are discussed in Chapter 4.) Also, isn't it annoying that WordPerfect doesn't type anything when you put a space in the Find box? You just have to know that you typed a space there.

9. **Enter** [HRt] **in the Replace With box.**

Just click in the Replace With box, choose Replace⇨Codes, and scroll through the list until you see HRt. Click on Insert and then on Close. Alternatively, you can just delete the [Mrg:ENDRECORD] code, leaving the [HRt] code from Step 5.

10. **Replace just the right spaces with** [HRt] **codes.**

Pretty helpful instructions, huh? You need to look at your document as WordPerfect finds each space in turn. *You* decide which spaces ought to be [HRt] codes: You need an [HRt] code between each field and the next.

To replace only the spaces that separate fields, click on the Find Next button to find the first space. Decide whether what *follows* is the beginning of a new field. In our daycare example (take a look at Figure 16-3 again), the first space WordPerfect finds is the one between Susan and Arnold. You *do* want to replace this space with [HRt] because you want to separate first and last names into two different fields in the data file. (Glance back at Figure 16-1.)

To replace a space with [HRt], click on the Replace button. WordPerfect replaces the space and automatically finds the next one.

In our example, WordPerfect would next find the space between 29 and Linwood. We would *not* replace this space with [HRt] because both 29 and Linwood are part of Address (refer to Figure 16-1 again).

To skip a replacement (to *not* replace a space with [HRt]), just click on Find Next to find the next space.

If the Find and Replace Text dialog box gets in the way of your document, move it out of the way by dragging its title bar with the mouse.

Keep going on, and on, and so on . . . until you get all the way through the document. WordPerfect lets you know when you get to the end by displaying a dialog box that says Text not found and asking you to click on OK. Although each field is now on a separate line, you still have to insert codes between the fields. Do not close the Find and Replace Text dialog box. You have one more replacement to make.

11. **Enter an end-of-line code in the Find box. Double-click in the Find box to make sure that you get rid of that pesky invisible space you typed in Step 8. Leave the** [HRt] **code.**

Next, you change all [HRt] codes in the document to end-of-field codes.

12. **Enter in the Replace With box an end-of-field code followed by an end-of-line code,.**

Refer to Step 5 for an example of how to do this step. You should see [Mrg:ENDFIELD][HRt] in the Replace With box.

13. **Click on Replace All. Click on OK when WordPerfect has made all the replacements.**

This time, close the Find and Replace Text box.

14. **Use the File⇨Save As command to save your file with a new name.**

You just did all this work to your file; it looks pretty much right. Save it so that if something happens to the power, you don't lose all this work. Save it with a different name so that if you realize later that something has gone wrong, you can start over. We like to include the word *data* in the filename.

Phew! — we didn't say that it would be easy. Figure 16-4 shows what the document we start with in Figure 16-3 looks like after all that finding and replacing. You may need to do a little cleanup by hand. For example, we had to delete the commas that appear after the town names. Look through your finished data file carefully to see that each field is on a separate line and nothing looks strange.

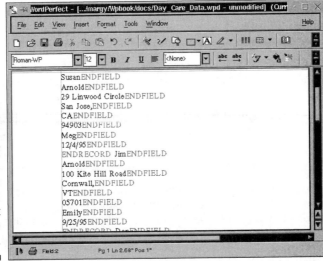

Figure 16-4: Our document full of data on its way to becoming a WordPerfect merge data file.

You're not done yet; you still have to tell WordPerfect the names of those fields in each record. You do that just as though you were creating a merge data file from scratch, though, so read on.

Creating a data file from scratch

Follow these steps to make a data file:

1. **Choose Tools➪Merge or press Shift+F9 to display the Merge dialog box (refer to Figure 16-2).**

2. **Click on the Data button.**

   If you see the Create File dialog box, skip to Step 3.

   If anything is in the document you're editing, WordPerfect first displays a dialog box labeled Create Merge File. If it does, you have a choice of two options: Use File in Active Window and New Document Window. Unless you've just converted an existing file full of data to a merge file, you should select New Document Window so that WordPerfect creates a new document to contain your list of records. If you've just survived our conversion instructions in the preceding section, by all means select Use File in Active Window to finish turning that file into a merge data file.

3. **Decide which pieces of information (fields) you want to store about each person (record).**

   If you've read the section "Creating a Data File," earlier in this chapter, refer to the list of fields you jotted down there. Look back at Figure 16-1, which shows the fields we use to send letters to some (hypothetical) daycare clients displayed in the Create Data File dialog box.

4. **Enter the names of the fields.**

   For each field, type the name in the Name a Field box. When you click on Add (or press the Enter key), the field name appears on the Field Name List.

5. **Click on OK in the Create Data File dialog box when you finish naming fields.**

WordPerfect does three things to prepare the data file for your use:

- ✔ **Puts information about your field names at the beginning of the document:** You see special merge codes, which are visible even though you aren't using the Reveal Codes window. You can see FIELDNAMES and ENDRECORD codes at the top of the document window.

- ✔ **Obscures your view of the document with a fill-in-the-blanks *data-entry* screen:** (That's computerspeak for a dialog box that has blanks for each field you created.) Figure 16-5 shows the Quick Data Entry dialog box WordPerfect created for our hypothetical daycare center.

- ✔ **Displays another row of buttons — in this case, the Merge toolbar:** (Sounds like a swinging singles joint, doesn't it?) We talk more about the merge bar in the following section.

Now you're ready to enter data if you're creating a new file or enter and edit data if you're converting an old file.

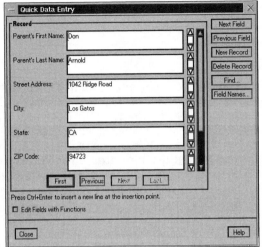

Entering the data at last

Before you can get WordPerfect to fill in the blanks and generate tons of let-ters, labels, address lists, or whatever, you have to tell it what to use to fill in the blanks. If you're following along on our junk-mail saga in this chapter, you should see the Quick Data Entry dialog box that appeared when you finished specifying the fields in your data file. If you converted a text file that already had data in it, you should see your data in the form already. If you're entering the data from scratch, follow these steps:

1. **If the data file isn't already open, open it.**

   If you just created the data file, it's still open.

2. **If the Quick Data Entry dialog box isn't visible, display it.**

   Click on the Quick Entry button on the Merge toolbar, which is the row of buttons just above the top of your document.

3. **Fill in a value for each field to create one record.**

   Click on the First button to see the first record. Wherever you are, you can fill in or review all the facts about one person (or record). To move down a field, press Tab, press Enter, or click on Next Field; to move up, click on Previous Field.

4. **Click on New Record to start the next record (the next person).**

   When you get to the last field in a record, pressing Enter is the equiva-lent of clicking on this button.

5. When you finish entering all the facts (field data) about all the people (record data), click on Close.

WordPerfect asks whether you want to save the changes to disk. Unless you have been typing names just to see your fingers move, answer Yes. If you're editing a file that was already saved to disk, WordPerfect updates it. If you started with a blank document, WordPerfect then displays the Save File dialog box so that you can enter the filename. In that case, enter a filename and click on OK.

When you enter information in a data file, be sure to enter it as you want it to appear in your letters.

When you close the Quick Data Entry dialog box, you should see the data you entered with each field on a separate line. Between one record and the next are an ENDRECORD merge code and a page break. At the end of each field is the word ENDFIELD (another merge code).

If you don't like your screen cluttered with these long merge codes, you can display them as little blobs. Click on the Options button (the button on the right) on the Merge toolbar. A menu that appears probably has the Display Codes command selected, which indicates that WordPerfect is displaying the names of merge codes in your document. If you choose Display As Markers, the code names are replaced by little red diamonds — much more tasteful.

If you choose Hide Codes, the code names disappear; this idea is usually a bad one, though — in case you edit the records in the document, you should be able to verify that the ENDFIELD codes remain at the end of each field.

Making corrections

If your life is like our lives, soon (rather than later) you have to fix up the addresses you entered or (in our example) delete the names of people whose children have decided not to attend your daycare center. You can edit the data file as though it were a normal document, although you have to be careful not to mess up the ENDFIELD and ENDRECORD merge codes. A better way to make all your corrections is to use the Quick Data Entry dialog box, which you display by clicking on the Quick Entry button on the Merge feature bar.

While you're using the Quick Data Entry dialog box, you can do the following things:

✔ To find a record, click on the Find button. (It doesn't matter which field your cursor is in when you do this; WordPerfect looks for the information in all the fields.) You see a Find dialog box that looks and works much like the familiar Find and Replace Text dialog box. (Refer to Chapter 4 if you don't recognize it.)

✔ To move from record to record, click on the First, Last, Next, and Previous buttons on the right side of the Quick Data Entry dialog box.

✔ To delete the record in the dialog box, click on the Delete Record button. Watch out, though — WordPerfect doesn't ask for any confirmation before blowing away the record. Click with care!

✔ To add more records, click on New Record.

✔ To update the information in a record, find the record, move your cursor to the field you want to correct, and edit it.

When you finish using the Quick Data Entry dialog box, click on Close. WordPerfect asks whether you want to save your work. Click on Yes. When you close the Quick Data Entry dialog box, the additions and corrections also appear in the document.

Creating a Form File

After you create a list of recipients for your form letter, you can type the letter. The document that contains the form letter is the form file. A *form file* is a regular old WordPerfect document. You enter — in place of the name and address at the top of the letter, however — funky-looking merge codes, as shown in these steps:

1. Choose Tools⇨Merge, and click on the Form button.

If the current document is blank, skip to Step 3. If the current document contains anything, WordPerfect wants to know whether you want to create a new document to contain the form letter or to use the document that's onscreen.

2. Select New Document Window and then click on OK.

If you have already typed the letter, and if that letter is the current document, choose Use File in Active Window instead.

You see the Create Form File dialog box. WordPerfect asks which data file will provide the data for this form letter. You create the form file by using the Create Form File dialog box, as shown in Figure 16-6.

3. In the Create Form File dialog box, enter the name of your data file and then click on OK.

You can click on the little file folder button at the right end of the box, which allows you to select the filename and directory. If WordPerfect can't find your file, click on that button and browse around for the file. (Refer to Chapter 13 for more information about how to find a file in the directories on your disk.) If you haven't created the data file yet, select None. Click OK after you've decided where your data will live.

Figure 16-6: Which document contains the names and addresses for this form letter?

WordPerfect opens a new document and displays the Merge toolbar just above it. When you're editing a form file, the Merge toolbar contains different buttons than it does when you're working on a data file.

4. **Type any information you want to appear before the date and the name of the addressee.**

   Type the text for your letterhead, for example, if you'll be printing on blank paper. For a normal letter, the next thing you want to see is today's date.

5. **Click on the Date button on the Merge toolbar.**

   WordPerfect inserts a colorful DATE code in your document. When you merge this form file with a data file, the current date appears here.

6. **Press Enter to start a new line and press Enter again to leave a space before the name and address.**

7. **Click on the Insert Field button from the Merge toolbar.**

   WordPerfect displays the Insert Field Name or Number dialog box, as shown in Figure 16-7. The dialog box lists all fields you defined in the data file associated with this form letter.

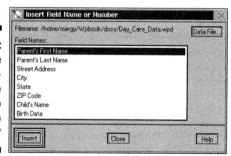

Figure 16-7: Which piece of information from the data file do you want to use?

8. **Select from the data file the first field that will appear in the form letter and then click on Insert.**

Select the First Name field, for example, and then click on the Insert button. WordPerfect inserts FIELD(First Name) in color. You're looking at a WordPerfect merge code, which displays each person's first name when you print the form letters. The dialog box is still visible, which is nice because you have to use it a few more times.

9. **Click in the document, type a space (to appear between the First Name and Last Name fields), select Last Name in the dialog box, and click on Insert again.**

    Codes for the First Name and Last Name fields now appear in the form letter.

10. **Click in the document and press Enter to start a new line.**

    Continue in this vein by inserting codes and typing spaces, pressing Enter, or doing whatever between the codes, until you have laid out the entire address. Check out Figure 16-8 for an example. You don't have to use all the fields from the data file — use only the fields you want to appear in the letter.

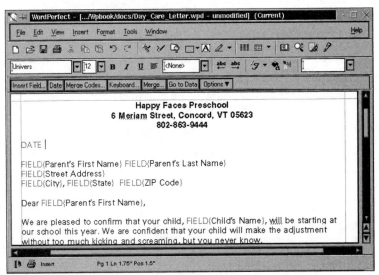

Figure 16-8:
Creating a
form file.

11. **Type your letter.**

    You can use all the usual formats, fonts, and margins you use in a normal letter. You can even include the contents of merge fields (first name, for example) in the body of the letter for that personalized touch. Don't go overboard, though — you know how tacky computer-generated letters can be.

12. **Save the document.**

Choose File⇨Save As and give the letter a filename.

You can create several form files for one data file. If your data file contains a list of people who owe you money, for example, you can make one form file that contains a polite letter requesting payment. A second form file can contain a letter using firmer language, and a third form file can contain the letter that tells your pal Vinnie whose legs to break. For the hypothetical daycare center we show you how to create earlier in this chapter, you can create a telephone list and address list and invitations for an open house.

When the time comes to print, you can print envelopes to go along with your letters. You can even print envelopes but no letters, although that job is a little more complicated. In the following section, we explain how to do both.

What if you choose the wrong data file for this form letter? Or, what if you create a new data file and want to use an existing form file? No problem. To associate a different data file with your form file, look on the Merge toolbar and click on the Insert Field button. WordPerfect displays the Insert Field Name or Number dialog box. Click on Data File and specify a new data file or a new address book and click on OK.

Merging Your Files

After you have a data file and a form file, you're ready to merge. We know, folks, that this explanation is taking awhile if you're following along with all the procedures we show you in this chapter; if you have a large number of letters to send, though, it's worth it. Here we go.

Call the post office and tell them to stand back before you follow these steps:

1. **Choose Tools⇨Merge and then click on the Merge button.**

WordPerfect displays the Perform Merge dialog box, as shown in Figure 16-9.

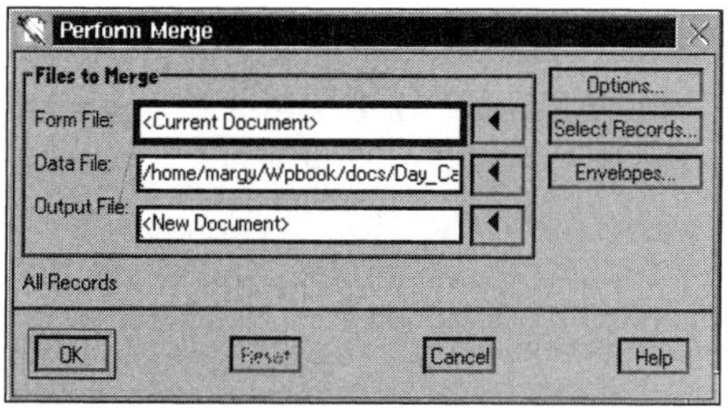

Figure 16-9: Making junk mail from a data file and a form file.

Perform Merge

Files to Merge

Form File: <Current Document>

Data File: /home/margy/Wpbook/docs/Day_Ca

Output File: <New Document>

All Records

OK   Reset   Cancel   Help

Options...
Select Records...
Envelopes...

2. **Enter the name of the form file.**

   Click on the little triangle at the right end of the Form File box and pick Select File. WordPerfect enables you to select the filename and inserts the complete pathname of the form file (/usr/wpbin/threat1, for example). If the form file is the open document, you can leave the Form File box set to <Current Document>.

   As soon as you enter the name of the form file, WordPerfect enters the name of the associated data file in the Data File box. If no associated data file exists, you have to specify the name of the data file to be used in the merge.

3. **Tell WordPerfect where to put the resulting form letters.**

   Click on the little triangle button to the right of the Output File box and choose from the menu that appears. We recommend the following choices:

   - <New Document>: (It's our favorite.) WordPerfect makes a new document and sticks all copies of your form letter in it for you to review before printing them.

   - <Printer>: Choose this option to print the form letters without reviewing them. This choice is the "go for the gold" approach. You can waste lots of paper this way, however, if your form file has a typo.

4. **If you also want to print an envelope for each person on your list, click on the Envelopes button. If not, skip to Step 11.**

   WordPerfect gives you the option of tacking a bunch of envelopes to the end of your form letter. This option is useful if you plan to mail your letters. You see the Envelope dialog box, as shown in Figure 16-10. You have to enter merge codes in the Envelope dialog box to tell WordPerfect how to arrange the fields on the envelope.

5. **Type the return address in the Return Addresses box.**

   If you unselect the Print Return Address box, WordPerfect skips this part — useful if you have preprinted envelopes.

6. **Click in the Mailing Addresses box and enter the merge codes to print the first field from your data file.**

   Click on the Field button at the bottom of the dialog box to display the list of fields in your data file. Select the first field from the data file to appear on the envelope (First Name, for example); then click on Insert. For this example, WordPerfect inserts FIELD(First Name).

7. **Type a space (to appear between the First Name and Last Name fields); then click on Field, select Last Name, and click on Insert.**

8. **Press Enter to start a new line.**

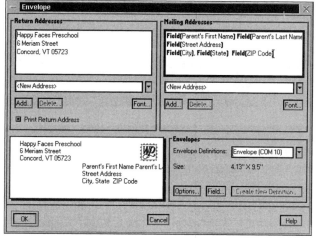

Figure 16-10:
Creating
envelopes
for your junk
mail.

9. **Continue inserting codes and typing spaces, pressing Enter, or doing whatever between the codes until you have laid out the entire address, as shown in Figure 16-10.**

10. **Click on OK in the Envelope dialog box.**

    If you look carefully, you see that where the Perform Merge dialog box used to say `All Records` (refer to Figure 16-9), it now says `All Records; Envelope` in the lower-left corner. This line means that every time you do a merge with this form file, WordPerfect adds envelopes to the end of the letters it creates. If you change your mind, click on the Envelopes button again and select Cancel Envelope.

11. **Click on OK in the Perform Merge dialog box.**

    WordPerfect makes one copy of your form file for each record in your data file and puts the results where you told it to put them.

    Figure 16-11 shows a letter to our hypothetical daycare center clients from the example we create earlier in this chapter. All the letters are in this one new document, one per page. If you selected envelopes, all the envelopes come after all the letters.

12. **If your merged letters are in a new document, print the document.**

    If you added envelopes to your merge document, this step can be a little tricky unless you have a printer with a separate bin you keep stocked with envelopes or a printer clever enough to ask for envelopes when it needs them. For the rest of us mortals, skim down through your document until you see the first envelope. Click on the envelope and note the page number (15, for example) on the Application Bar. Print all pages up to the first envelope (pages 1 through 14, in our example), put envelopes in the printer, and print pages 15 through 28, which are the envelopes. Chapter 11 has all the gory details on how to do this step, if you need a refresher.

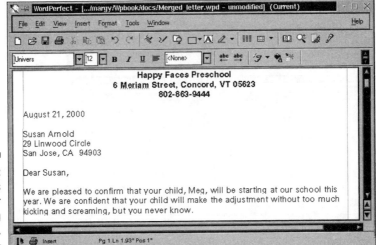

You can look through the letters first to make sure that they look appropriately personal. You can even make changes in them so that they really are personalized. ("P.S. As you requested, we have added bars on the windows of our classrooms so that little Frederika will be sure to stick around.")

After you print your form letters, you can save the document that contains them or close it without saving it. You can always create the letters again, after all, by repeating these merge steps.

Printing Your Data File

If you want to print an address list of the people to whom you sent letters, you can print the data file.

To hide the merge codes, click on the Options button on the Merge toolbar and then choose Hide Codes. To print the file, click on Options and choose Print.

Chapter 17

Recipes and Templates for Popular Documents

•••

In This Chapter

▶ Templates

▶ Letters

▶ Memos

▶ Faxes

▶ Envelopes

▶ Mailing labels

▶ Booklets

▶ Books and other big documents

•••

*T*here's no point in reinventing the wheel. For years, the Great Minds of Word Processing have been contemplating the best ways to create many popular types of documents. The fruits of their contemplation are available to you in the form of templates that come with WordPerfect. WordPerfect also comes with *ExpressDocs,* which are fancy templates that ask you questions and tailor the document based on your answers. In this chapter, we do two things: talk about what a template is and look at some of the ExpressDocs you can use for whipping up crowd-pleasing documents.

What Are Templates?

Templates are prototypes for different types of documents. WordPerfect includes more than 60 kinds of templates that are predesigned; you can also design and use your own. Templates are sort of like blank forms. They don't necessarily contain text, though. A template can contain only a collection of the particular fonts and format styles for a particular type of document, or it can contain all the text of your boilerplate contract.

Whenever you create a new document, WordPerfect uses a template. The blank document you see when you start WordPerfect is (unknown to you) based on a standard template — WordPerfect has to have some default settings to use for margins, fonts, and all the other elements that make up your document. Whether you create a new document by clicking on the New Blank Document button on the toolbar (the one that looks like a blank page with the corner turned down) or choosing File⇨New, WordPerfect again uses that standard template.

If you don't care for the WordPerfect prebuilt templates, you can create your own. You may want your letters to use a template that specifies, for example, a 10-point Times Roman font. A template for product announcements may use 14-point Helvetica for titles and 12-point type for other text. A template for a newsletter, however, may also contain title text, a logo graphic, and 3-column formatting, in addition to specified fonts.

For most practical purposes, though, you cannot do much more with a template than you can do by creating an ordinary document as a prototype, reusing it (opening it and changing the text) every time you want to write a similar document, and being careful to use the Save As command to save your new documents with new names. As the care and feeding of templates has become rather convoluted as WordPerfect has evolved, templates have gotten all tied up with projects and experts. In fact, unless you're an expert (and in that case, what exactly are you doing reading a ...*For Dummies* book?), we recommend that you stick with this save-the-prototype-document-file method.

Not a Template but Just As Good: Making a Document Uneditable

We like making our own prototype documents so much that we want to share a trick with you.

If you make up an ordinary document you reuse rather than a template, you can tell WordPerfect not to allow you to write on top of it. That way, whenever you customize the document and forget to use Save As (and use the Save command instead), WordPerfect complains that you aren't allowed to write on your prototype document. Those of us who are a little absent-minded find this reminder very useful. Linux lets you set a file as *read-only* so that you can't edit or replace it.

After you've saved a file you don't want to be able to edit later, you can change the file *mode* to read-only. In the Save As or Open dialog box, click on the name of the file in the File List box. Choose Files⇨Change Mode from the dialog box's menu to display the Change Mode dialog box, as shown in Figure 17-1. Click on the Write box in the User (first) row of boxes to unselect the box, thereby making the file uneditable by you. Then click on OK.

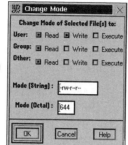

Figure 17-1:
You can set
a file to be
uneditable.

Using Templates

Even if you don't create your own template, you may want to use the WordPerfect template. Talking about using templates is, in fact, like talking about using air: It's not like you have much choice in the matter. All documents use templates. As we mention earlier in this chapter, you use something called the *standard template* every time you create a new document. The standard template doesn't have much in it — at least, not much as it comes out of the box from WordPerfect. (You can change the template, though.) The standard template contains mostly the initial paragraph, character, and page formatting that WordPerfect uses for your documents. If you're having to change your fonts and other formatting every time you create a new document, you probably should create your own template; see the sidebar "Creating your own templates," later in this chapter.

Here's how to use a template other than the standard one:

1. **Choose File⇨ExpressDocs in a WordPerfect document window.**

   The first time you use this command, you see the Personal Info dialog box. If you (or someone else using your computer) has used this command before, skip to Step 3.

2. **Fill in the fields in the Personal Info dialog box.**

   You have to do this step only the first time you use ExpressDocs; WordPerfect remembers what you type and uses it to personalize your documents automagically when you use some preprogrammed templates. When you click on OK, you see the WordPerfect ExpressDocs dialog box, as shown in Figure 17-2. The documents are listed alphabetically, by description. If you want to change your personal information later, click on the User Info button in the ExpressDocs dialog box.

Creating your own templates

You can create your own templates, although they won't be as fancy as the WordPerfect ones with dialog boxes and stuff; if you decide to spend an inordinate amount of time on them, though, you could end up with something more useful than a prototype document. Briefly, here's how:

1. **Proceed as though you're creating a new document.**

   Create your template as you would a regular document. If you have a prototype document you like, you can start with it and make changes or include it by choosing the Insert⇨File command.

2. **When your template looks the way you want it, save it in the templates directory with the filename extension .wpt.**

   Choose File⇨Save As and (here's the important part) save your file in the wpexpdocs subdirectory of the WordPerfect program directory. If WordPerfect is installed in /usr/local, for example, store your template in the /usr/local/ wpexpdocs directory. For the filename, include .wpt as the filename extension. Click on OK to save the document as a template.

   You may not have permission to write files in that directory. (Linux, which is designed

to be a multiuser system, keeps track of who has permission to do what in which directory.) If not, save the file in your own document directory and then ask your local Linux guru to move the file to the wpexpdocs directory.

3. **Choose File⇨ExpressDocs to display the ExpressDocs dialog box.**

   The template appears at the top of the Document Template list, with the name *****.

4. **With the ***** file selected, click on the File Info button to see the ExpressDocs Template File Info dialog box.**

   The name of the file you just created appears in the Template Filename box with ***** in the Template Description box.

5. **Type a description in the Template Description box and click on OK.**

   Your very own template appears on the ExpressDocs list! (Because ExpressDocs are listed alphabetically, by description, you may have to scroll down to see your file.)

The next time you want to create a document based on this template, choose File⇨ExpressDocs, and it will be there.

3. **Select a template from the Document Template list and click on Select.**

   WordPerfect opens a new document window (unless you unselected the Open New Document Window box in the ExpressDocs dialog box) and creates a new document using the template. The template may prompt you to enter information: if you select the Monthly Calendar template, for example, WordPerfect asks for the month and year for which you want a calendar.

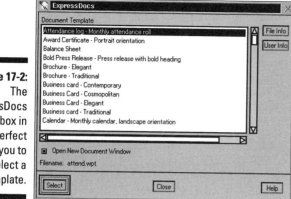

Figure 17-2:
The
ExpressDocs
dialog box in
WordPerfect
asks you to
select a
template.

4. **If WordPerfect prompts you for information, enter it and click on OK.**

   You're ready to start entering text. If the template includes your name or address, the information you entered in the Personal Info dialog box appears in the template automatically. (Way cool!)

When you save the new document, you have to give it a name, just as though you were saving a document you wrote from scratch.

Letters

Unless everyone you know has switched over to e-mail, chances are that you do a great deal of letter writing with WordPerfect. What's a word processor for, after all, if not to make tasks like that one quick and easy? Word processing should let you concentrate on your sterling prose and not on the position of the inside address. Look through the following pointers on how to get WordPerfect to lay out a letter the way you like it. Then save all this work so that you have to do it only once.

Getting WordPerfect to write your letter for you

We used to say that, with all the wonders of word processing, you still have to pick what words you want to process. (We used to call that *writing;* but it's a new millennium.) You can let WordPerfect set up the letter for you, however, so that you have nice headers and footers with things like the date and page numbers in them. You can then modify the letter to suit your fancy. Here's how to get WordPerfect to do the writing and formatting for you:

1. **In a document window, choose File⇨ExpressDocs from the menu bar.**

   (If no document window is open, open one by choosing Program⇨Open Window from the program window.) WordPerfect shows you its list of templates.

2. **Scroll down the list of templates until you see** Letter — Traditional centered company name at top **on the list of templates.**

   We use the traditional letter for this discussion, although in real life it doesn't matter which one you pick. They work pretty much the same way.

3. **Double-click on the kind of letter you're creating.**

   As usual, you can single-click on your choice from this list and then click on Select. In either case, be patient because WordPerfect has a great deal on its mind for you. For example, it needs to know the name of the recipient of your letter, and it prompts you for this information.

4. **Type the recipient's name in the dialog box and click on OK or press Enter.**

   WordPerfect asks all the questions it needs in order to create the letter. Fill in each dialog box as it appears and click on OK or press Enter to go to the next dialog box. After gathering all the needed information, WordPerfect displays your letter.

5. **Type the information you want in the body of the letter.**

   Hey, WordPerfect can't do everything! You still have to type the message you want to send. When you're done, save and print the letter as usual.

Congratulations: You've composed a letter (with a little help from WordPerfect). Take a look at the tips in the following section to tweak your letter so that it's just right.

Printing your own letterhead

If you're looking at a tasteful letter (and you should be, if you're following along in this chapter), you may decide that you want WordPerfect to print a letterhead directly on your letter for you. That way, you can write letters from each of your ten split personalities and not have to invest in preprinted letterhead for each one. Using the many fonts, lines, boxes, and other effects in WordPerfect, you can create a snazzy letterhead; you can even include graphics. Take a look at Chapters 14 and 15; most of what's in those two chapters makes good material for letterhead. Remember to save early and often while you're getting your letterhead to look the way you want it. After you create a letterhead you like, save it as a template (see the section "Saving your letter as a prototype document," a little later in this chapter) so that all your letters can include it automatically.

Skipping space for the letterhead on stationery

If you're printing on stationery, you have to leave a bunch of space at the top of the letter so that your text doesn't print on top of the letterhead. Follow these steps:

1. **Get out a ruler and measure how far down the page you want your letter to start.**

   That place is where you want the first piece of text (usually, the date) to appear.

2. **Make sure that the guidelines (margin lines) are turned on and appear on your editing screen.**

   Use the View➪Guidelines command if you're not sure. Some of us like to have all the guidelines on all the time so that we can see what WordPerfect thinks that it's doing to our documents.

3. **Click on the guideline at the top of the page and drag it down to where you want the first bit of text to appear.**

This method works fine for 1-page letters. What if you're creating a letter that's two or more pages long, however? You don't want all that white space at the top of the second and subsequent pages; that would just waste space. No problem! Using the quick I'm-using-this-document-only-once approach, you drag the guideline back up to where you want it when you get to the top of the second page. We don't like this solution, however. If you use this technique, sooner or later you edit a letter, and all the spacing gets messed up.

Here's a better way to skip space for a letterhead on the first page of your letters: Tell WordPerfect that the spacing on the first page is different from the spacing on the second page. To do that, use the WordPerfect Advance feature. With the cursor at the top of the first page, choose Format➪Typesetting➪Advance. (Don't ask us what advancing down the page has to do with typesetting.) WordPerfect displays the Advance dialog box. For the Vertical Position option, select From Top of Page and fill in the Vertical Distance box with the number of inches (or centimeters) you want to move down the page. When you click on OK, WordPerfect inserts an Advance code (VAdv) that moves down to the position you specified. This code affects only the page it's on, which means that the spacing at the top of subsequent pages is unaffected.

Dating your letter

Be sure to make WordPerfect enter the current date rather than type it yourself; press Ctrl+D.

Numbering the pages

For multiple-page letters, page numbers add a touch of class. Use the page-numbering, header, or footer feature in WordPerfect (described in Chapter 8). Be sure to tell WordPerfect *not* to number the first page.

Saving your letter as a prototype document

You don't want a letter you've created in WordPerfect to disappear out the door with a stamp on it — especially if you've done all the work we describe in the preceding few sections! By all means, print your letter and save it for reference. Be sure to save a copy to use the next time you want to write a letter. You can do a couple of things to make this process easier.

First, delete all the text from the letter. Unless you're saving it as a particular kind of letter (an order confirmation, for example), you want to type new text every time. Second, delete the name of the person to whom you sent the letter. To keep the formatting of the address, don't just delete it. Instead, highlight it and type something like **<Address goes here>** to remind yourself to enter the address there. Third, do the same thing for the salutation. Nothing is more embarrassing than sending a letter to Helen with the salutation *Dear Fred*. Highlight the *Dear Fred* salutation and replace it with something like **<Salutation goes here>**. (You just have to remember not to send out the letter saying *Dear <Salutation goes here>*.)

That's all there is to it. You're ready to use the File⇨Save As command to save your prototype letter for future use.

Don't forget the trick we mention earlier in this chapter. After you've saved your prototype, make it read-only so that you can't foul it up later. (The details are in the section "Not a Template but Just as Good," earlier in this chapter.) Better yet, save the document as a template, as described in the sidebar "Creating your own templates," earlier in this chapter.

Memos

Everything we say in this chapter about letters goes for memos, too. If you don't use preprinted memo paper, check out the ready-to-use templates in WordPerfect. Choose File⇨ExpressDocs and select one of the memo templates from the list. Fill in all the information WordPerfect asks for and type the message you want to send, and you have your memo.

Faxes

If you have a boring, old-fashioned fax machine into which you feed boring, old-fashioned pieces of paper, we don't have much to suggest. You may want to look at the WordPerfect templates for fax cover sheets; these templates are trendy and designerish. Using larger-size type when you're printing a document to be faxed is also a good idea because a faxed document is rarely as clear as the original. Don't use a font size smaller than 12 points.

Envelopes

After you write the world's most clear and cogent letter, you need an envelope to put it in. (We have stooped to using window envelopes because we're too lazy to print envelopes, although we suspect that you haven't fallen that far.) If your printer cannot accept envelopes (most printers can), skip this section.

The folks at WordPerfect created a command that formats a document (or one page of a document) as an envelope. Wow — we're talking *convenience.* Word processing takes a major step forward.

Printing the address on the envelope

To print an address on a regular #10 (U.S. business size) envelope, follow these steps:

1. **If you have already written the letter that goes in the envelope, open that document.**

   If not, no big deal.

2. **Choose Format⇨Envelope.**

   WordPerfect displays the Envelope dialog box, as shown in Figure 17-3. (It may tell you instead that no envelopes are defined for the current printer and ask whether you want to create an envelope definition; if so, see the following section.) If the current document contains a letter in a fairly normal format, WordPerfect — get this — *finds* the name and address at the top of the letter and displays them in the Mailing Addresses box. This feature is really cool; you don't have to type the address again.

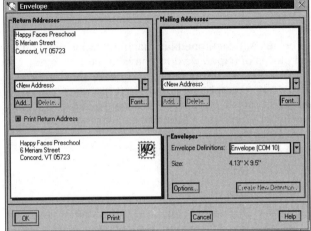

Figure 17-3:
Creating an
envelope.
You don't
even have
to type the
address!

If the address at the beginning of the letter is your *own* address, this feature backfires. Not a problem: Click on Cancel, open the letter if it's not already open, select the lines that contain the address to which you want to address the envelope, and choose Format➪Envelope again. The selected address appears in the Mailing Addresses box.

3. Enter your address in the Return Addresses box.

If you have used this dialog box, WordPerfect remembers the address you entered the last time — a nice touch. (Strangely, WordPerfect doesn't use the information you may have typed in the Personal Info dialog box you see when you open a template.)

4. To print the envelope now, click on Print.

Depending on how your printer works, you may be prompted (by a cute little dialog box) to insert an envelope. For some printers, you may have to edit the paper definition, paper size, and orientation settings; click on Create New Definition.

Or, to print an envelope as part of your document, click on OK.

WordPerfect adds the envelope as a separate page at the end of your document, along with all the formatting you need in order to make it print correctly. This feature is useful when the current document is the letter that goes inside the envelope. Whenever you print the letter, you print an envelope, too.

Printing bar codes

If you want to make the U.S. Postal Service happy (and who wouldn't?), you can print a USPS POSTNET bar code. (It will impress your friends, too.) Click on the Options button in the Envelope dialog box to display the Envelope Options dialog box. Under USPS Bar Code Options, select Include and Position Above or Below Address. Click on OK to close the dialog box. WordPerfect looks around your address for what looks like a zip code and prints it above or below your address (depending on what you selected in the Envelope Options dialog box). When you print the envelope, a tasteful row of little vertical lines appears above or below the address. Some machine at the post office must know what the lines mean.

Tips for printing envelopes

When you choose Format➪Envelope, WordPerfect may demand that you create an envelope definition. That's bad news; it means that WordPerfect isn't familiar with printing envelopes on your type of printer. You have to tell WordPerfect the length and width of your envelopes, the margins — the works. You may want to get some help for this task.

On most laser printers, you insert envelopes face up, with the right end of the envelope entering the printer first. You may have to do mechanical things to your printer, too; check the manual's "Envelopes" section. If your printer has a platen (most impact printers do), stick the envelope in upside down, with the front facing away from you so that it's right side up, facing toward you, after it comes up under the platen. Most inkjet printers have special envelope-feeding buttons; check your printer manual.

Depending on your printer, WordPerfect may know how to print more than one envelope size. In the Envelope dialog box, check out the Envelope Definitions setting. If you click on it, you may find that several sizes and shapes are available.

Mailing Labels

Zillions of kinds of labels exist — sheets of mailing labels, continuous rolls of mailing labels, disk labels — you name it. This section shows you how to print addresses on them. Luckily, WordPerfect can handle an amazing variety of formats.

Printing addresses on mailing labels

To print addresses on mailing labels, follow these steps:

1. **Begin with a new, blank document.**

   Your first step is to tell WordPerfect which kind of labels you're using. In technical jargon, you're providing a *label definition*.

2. **Choose Format⇨Labels to display the Labels dialog box, as shown in Figure 17-4.**

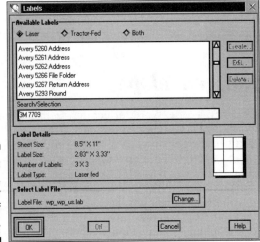

Figure 17-4: Sheets, rolls, or stacks of labels.

WordPerfect already knows about an amazing variety of labels, including most of the ones Avery manufactures. Most label definitions listed in the Available Labels section of the dialog box are identified only by their Avery part number. This number is useful because most label manufacturers now include the equivalent Avery number on their packages.

3. **Select the type of labels you have.**

   In case you're not sure which kind you have, WordPerfect displays a little diagram of the labels you selected. Avery 5159 Address labels, for example, come in sheets of 2 labels across and 7 rows per page. The Label Details section of the dialog box describes the size and shape of the sheets and individual labels you selected.

4. **Click on OK.**

   The dialog box closes, and your document now looks truly weird. An area the size of a label stays white (or whatever background color you use for WordPerfect documents; refer to Chapter 19), and the rest of the page is draped in shadow, as shown in Figure 17-5.

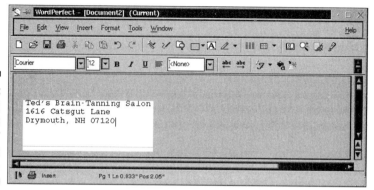

Figure 17-5:
Typing
addresses
for your
mailing
labels.

5. **Type the addresses.**

   Or, type whatever it is you want to print on the labels. WordPerfect lets you enter only as much information as fits on a label.

   To move to the next label, press Ctrl+Enter. After you enter a bunch of labels, you can press Alt+PgUp and Alt+PgDn to move from label to label. (If you cannot remember these arcane key combinations, just use your mouse.)

6. **Save the document.**

7. **Print the labels.**

   Put the labels in your printer. If you have a sheet-fed printer, be sure to insert the label sheet so that you print on the front, not on the back.

Selecting which labels to print

You don't have to print an entire page of labels at a time. To print selected labels, you can refer to them by number. WordPerfect thinks of each label as a separate miniature page. On the Application Bar, in fact, the Pg number is the number of the label.

When you know which labels you want to print, choose File⇨Print and select Multiple Pages in the Print Selection part of the dialog box. When you click on OK, you see the Multiple Pages dialog box. In the Page(s) box, select which labels you want to print. Enter **3** to print the third label, for example; **5-12** to print a range of labels; **2,14,23** for several labels; or **15-** for all the rest of the labels, beginning at label 15.

Tips for printing labels

You can use all the usual formatting for labels — select a nice font, make the zip code boldface, or whatever.

The WordPerfect list of label definitions is awfully long. To make it shorter, select Laser or Tractor-Fed at the top of the Available Labels section of the dialog box. WordPerfect lists only labels of that type.

If you have used the WordPerfect merge feature to enter a list of addresses for creating junk mail (refer to Chapter 16), you can print the same addresses on mailing labels. Create a new *form file* (the merge term for the document that contains the form letter) and choose Format⇨Labels to format it for labels. On the first mailing label, enter merge codes for the parts of the address. Then choose Tools⇨Merge to fill in the labels.

If you're using a type of label that WordPerfect doesn't know about, you can create your own label definitions. Click on the Create button in the Labels dialog box and tell WordPerfect all about the size and arrangement of your labels.

Booklets

A common typing job is a pain in the neck with most word processors: a little booklet that consists of regular sheets of paper folded in half, like the one shown in Figure 17-6.

Wait! — WordPerfect has a special booklet feature for making just this kind of document. This cool feature makes us want to take back (almost) all the snide things we've said about WordPerfect.

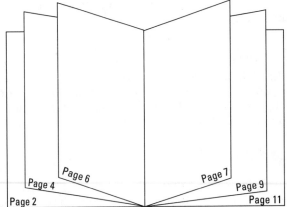

Figure 17-6:
A typical
booklet —
commonly
used and a
pain to
create,
except in
WordPerfect.

Creating a booklet document

These steps show you how to make a 5½-by-8½-inch booklet that consists of folded sheets:

1. **Type the text for your booklet.**

   Do all the character and line formatting you plan to use, including fonts, boldface, and centering. Set up page numbering, headers, and footers as you want them.

2. **Tell WordPerfect to print sideways (*landscape* orientation) on the page by choosing File⊏>Page Setup⊏>Page Size.**

   You see the Paper Size dialog box. Select the landscape version of the paper you're using. If you're using U.S. letter-size paper, for example, change the selected paper from Letter (Portrait) to Letter (Landscape).

   If your printer handles *duplex* printing (prints on both sides of the paper in one pass), choose File⊏>Page Setup⊏>Two-Sided Printing and turn on duplexing.

3. **Save your document and press Ctrl+Home to move the cursor to the beginning.**

   Whatever else happens, having to type the text again would be a pain!

4. **Choose File⊏>Page Setup⊏>Subdivide Page.**

   WordPerfect displays the Subdivide Page dialog box, as shown in Figure 17-7.

   Make sure that the cursor is at the beginning of the document when you perform this step so that the formatting affects the entire document.

   Your document looks like a booklet, with two pages per sheet of paper.

Figure 17-7: How many booklet pages print on each piece of paper?

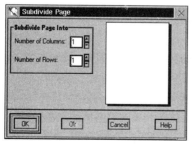

5. **In the Number of Columns box, type 2 or click on the up and down arrows until you see 2 in the box. Leave the number of rows set at 1 and click on OK.**

Your text moves around big-time. It appears in two columns, as it will be printed in the booklet. Subdividing a page into columns works like regular columns (described in Chapter 14), although WordPerfect knows that you want to treat the columns like separate pages. Way cool!

If you don't see your text in two columns, choose <u>V</u>iew➪<u>P</u>age.

6. **Set your booklet's margins.**

If you didn't set them earlier, you should set them now, to see how your text looks on these small pages. You may want to move your graphics, lines, boxes, and headings around a little to fit into the smaller columns of text.

7. **Create a front cover, if you want one.**

At the beginning of the document, enter the title or other material you want to appear on the cover. Press Ctrl+Enter to insert a page break between the cover text and the next page. You can center the cover text on the page by choosing the Fo<u>r</u>mat➪<u>P</u>age➪<u>C</u>enter command.

8. **Save your document — it looks great!**

Printing your booklet: The magic part

You're ready for the tricky part of printing a booklet: telling WordPerfect to shuffle the pages so that they're in the right order when you fold the booklet in half. Luckily, WordPerfect does almost all the work. Just follow these steps:

1. **To print, choose <u>F</u>ile➪<u>P</u>rint to display the Print dialog box and then click on the Output Options button.**

You see the Output Options dialog box.

2. **Select Booklet Printing and click on OK.**

This step tells WordPerfect to switch the order of the pages so that when the sheets of paper are folded, the booklet pages are in order.

3. **Click on OK in the Print dialog box.**

WordPerfect thinks about the job for a moment. If your booklet is long, the moment may be rather long. After all, WordPerfect is reshuffling the entire document. Then your printer fires up and spews out the booklet. All you need now is one of those $35 staplers so that you can staple your booklet in the middle.

Tips for creating booklets

If your printer doesn't print in *duplex* mode (on both sides of the paper), you can click on the Output Options button in the Print dialog box and tell WordPerfect to print only odd pages (click to select the Print Odd/Even Pages box and then select Odd). Depending on which printer you use, this option may be unavailable. (You can tell because it appears in a ghostly gray.) WordPerfect prints the odd-numbered pages. Then reinsert the pages so that the first sheet of paper that was printed last time is the first page printed this time — make sure that the blank side is set to print. Choose File⇨Print again, click Output Options, and print only the even pages. This procedure can get a little confusing because you must be sure to insert the right page, the right way around, at the right time.

Unless you're printing in color, you may find it simpler to print everything on one side of blank sheets of paper and then photocopy them. You probably want more than one copy, anyway.

To insert a page break and move to the top of the next page, you press, as usual, Ctrl+Enter. When you have subdivided your pages, you move to the next booklet page, not to the next sheet of paper. To move to the next or preceding booklet page, press Alt+PgUp or Alt+PgDn.

Reports, Books, and Other Big Documents

These days, people use word processing programs for much more than writing letters. You may want to use WordPerfect to typeset a book, for example. This idea isn't as stupid as it sounds; WordPerfect can handle large documents, and it can even create tables of contents and indexes.

The secret is not to store the entire book (or report or whatever) in one big document; instead, break it up into chapters or sections — one per document. Then create a master document to connect all the parts.

What's a *master document?* (We're so glad that you asked.) It's a WordPerfect document containing secret codes that link it to other documents. These other documents are *subdocuments*. When you're writing a book (to pick a wild hypothetical example), each subdocument may contain one chapter. The master document contains a secret code for each chapter document, in addition to introductory text, the table of contents, and the index.

To go about creating a really big document, such as a book or long report, create the subdocuments first. Then create the master document. Finally, set up the table of contents. Don't worry: We step you through the process.

Creating a master document and its subdocuments

To create a master document and its subdocuments, you have to get the text of the book organized. Follow these steps:

1. **Create a document for each chapter.**

   Because you want all chapters to be formatted the same way, consider creating a template that contains the formatting. Alternatively, create a prototype chapter with some section headings and other elements you expect to use in each chapter. Don't worry about page numbering, headers, or footers in the subdocuments; those elements are controlled by the master document. Give the documents names such as Chapter1 and Chapter2.

2. **Type the text in each chapter document or copy it from existing documents.**

3. **Create the master document.**

   Open a new document and type the title page and other front matter. Skip the table of contents for now. (We get to it in the following section.) If the introduction and preface (or whatever) are short, you can include them in this document; if they're long, store each one in its own document, as you do with chapters. Save the document with a name such as Book or Report.

4. **For each chapter, create a secret code in the master document.**

   Move the cursor to the spot in the master document where you want the chapter to appear. If you want the chapter to begin on a new page, insert a page break by pressing Ctrl+Enter. Then choose File⇨ Document⇨ Subdocument to display the Include Subdocument dialog box. Type the filename of the chapter (or click on the little folder button and select the filename from the Select File dialog box) and click on OK. In Figure 17-8, we include Chapter 1 in our master document.

 Not much happens at this point. In Page view, you see a little subdocument icon in the left margin of your master document. In Draft view, you see a Subdocument code that looks like Subdoc: Chapter 1 or whatever the filename of the subdocument is. (It looks something like Figure 17-8.) We prefer to work in Draft view so that we can see the filenames of our chapters all the time.

 In Page view, to find out which document the little subdocument icon refers to, click on it.

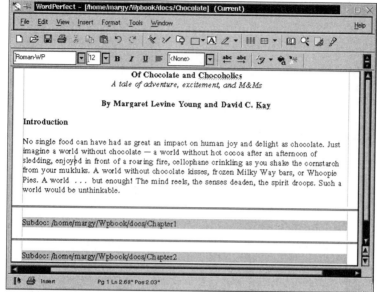

Figure 17-8:
The master
document
and its sub-
documents.

A faster way to issue the File⇨Document⇨SubDocument command is to use a QuickMenu. Right-click in the left margin of the document and then choose Subdocument from the QuickMenu.

Expanding a master document

WordPerfect can display (and store) a master document in either of two ways: expanded or condensed. When a master document is *expanded,* WordPerfect retrieves the text of each subdocument and sticks it in the master document, right where it belongs. When a master document is *condensed,* the text of each subdocument is stored — you guessed it — in its separate file, and you see only subdocument icons.

To expand a master document, choose File⇨Document⇨Expand Master (or double-click on one of those subdocument icons or codes). WordPerfect displays the Expand Master Document dialog box, as shown in Figure 17-9, which lists all your subdocuments. To expand them all, click on Mark All and then click on OK. To skip expanding a subdocument, click on its little box so that it isn't selected.

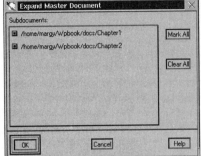

Figure 17-9:
Expand, oh
master!

When you expand a master document, you still see the subdocument icons
or codes. You see twice as many, in fact — they appear at the beginning and
end of each subdocument, as shown in Figure 17-10. (Because the chapters in
our sample book are extremely short, more than one fits on the screen.)

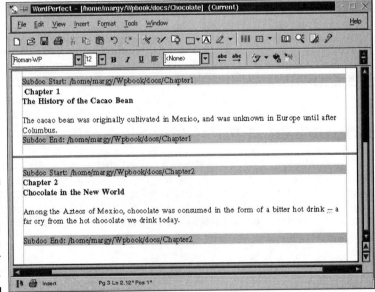

Figure 17-10:
Your sub-
documents
appear in
the master
document.

When you're working on a master document, you're probably safest not to
open any of its subdocuments in other windows. Some versions of WordPerfect
get upset when you save a master document if any of its subdocuments are
also open.

Saving a master document

When you save a master document, WordPerfect wants to know two things about each of its subdocuments:

✔ Do you want to *save* the text of the subdocument back in the subdocument's file?

✔ Do you want to *condense* the subdocument so that only its icon appears in the master document?

You answer both these pithy questions in the Condense/Save Subdocuments dialog box. When you want to save your master document, follow these steps:

1. **Choose File⇨Save, press Ctrl+S, or click on the Save button on the toolbar.**

   If you haven't expanded your master document, or if you have condensed it, WordPerfect saves the document with no comment.

   If your master document is expanded, however, WordPerfect displays the message `Document is expanded. Condense?`.

2. **Click on No to save the document as is.**

   WordPerfect saves the master document with the text of all the expanded subdocuments, too. It *doesn't* save the text of the subdocuments back in the separate subdocument files. If you edit the text of your chapters in the master document, therefore, your edits aren't saved in `Chapter 1`, `Chapter 2`, and so on — only in `Chocolate`.

   Or, **click on Yes to save each subdocument in its own separate file.**

   WordPerfect displays the Condense/Save Subdocuments dialog box, as shown in Figure 17-11. Each subdocument is listed twice: once so that you can condense it (remove the text from the master document) and once so that you can save it in its own file. We always leave all the boxes checked. Go for the gold, we say.

3. **Click on OK.**

   WordPerfect saves and condenses as you indicated.

You can also condense a master document by choosing File⇨Document⇨Condense Master.

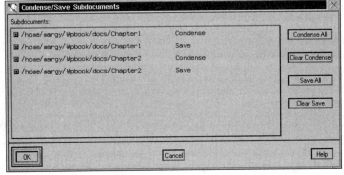

Editing a master document

After you have set up a master document, what do you do when you want to edit a chapter of your book? What if you get new information about early uses of chocolate among the Aztec nobility, for example, and you want to include it in Chapter 2?

You have these two choices:

- ✔ **Edit the chapter file.** In this case, make sure that your master document is condensed to ensure that the text of your chapter is stored in the subdocument file, not in the master document. Make your changes and save the chapter file. The next time you open and expand the master document, the updated chapter appears.

- ✔ **Edit the master document.** In this case, make sure that your chapter file is closed. Open the master document and expand the subdocuments (or at least the one you want to edit). Make your changes and save the master file. You probably want to save the changes back to the subdocuments when WordPerfect presents the Condense/Save Subdocument dialog box, as we just described.

This process can get rather confusing when you try to remember where the text of your chapters is *really* stored. We recommend that you always do your editing the same way and always store your master document the same way (either expanded or condensed).

Creating a table of contents

"What good is a table without contents?" we always ask (when we're sitting down to dinner). WordPerfect can automatically generate a table of contents for your book (or any document) by using the headings in the file. You can also use small-Roman-numeral page numbers for the table of contents pages — just like a real book! These steps show you how:

1. **Open your master document and expand it.**

   You want to be able to see all your lovely chapters so that you can decide which ones should appear in your table of contents.

2. **Choose Tools➪Reference➪Table of Contents.**

   More lovely buttons appear, mostly named Mark, as shown in Figure 17-12. This thing is (what else?) the Table of Contents toolbar.

Figure 17-12:
The Table of Contents toolbar.

3. **Mark the lines of text (headings) you want to use in the table of contents.**

   Your table of contents can have several levels (chapters and sections within chapters, for example). To mark each heading, select it and then click on the appropriate Mark button on the Table of Contents toolbar. (Where else?) Mark each chapter title by using Mark 1, for example, and each section within the chapters by using Mark 2, for example.

   When you perform this step, nothing seems to happen. WordPerfect inserts secret codes at the beginning and end of each selected heading (the `Mrk Txt ToC` code, if you were wondering).

4. **Create a new page where you want the table of contents to appear.**

   For most books, you want the table of contents to be on a page by itself, right after the title and copyright pages. Press Ctrl+Enter to insert a page break.

5. **Tell WordPerfect to number the pages with small Roman numerals, beginning with the first page of the master document.**

   Most books number the front matter (including the table of contents) with Roman numerals and then start the page numbers again with Arabic numerals at the beginning of the introduction or first chapter. You can do that, too. (Won't your document look just like a real book?)

Move the cursor to the beginning of the master document and choose Format➪Page➪Page Numbering➪Numbering. Set the Position option to Alternating Top or Alternating Bottom so that the numbers appear on the right side of left pages and on the left side of right pages. Click on the Options button and set the Page box to one of the Roman numeral options (iv, -iv-, IV, or -IV-). Then click on OK to finish page numbering.

You may want to suppress page numbers on the title pages and some other front-matter pages. To do so, choose Format➪Page➪Suppress.

6. Go to the first page of the introduction or Chapter 1 and reset it to be page number 1, in Arabic numerals.

With the cursor at the top of the page you want to be page 1, choose Format➪Page➪Page Numbering➪Numbering. Click on Options and set the Page box back to Numbers. Then click on OK. Click on Value, set the page number to 1, and click on OK. We go through this technique in gory detail in Chapter 8.

WordPerfect now knows which page numbers should appear on every page. You're ready to create the table of contents (and not a moment too soon!).

7. Move the cursor to the location where you want the table of contents to appear and click on the Define button on the Table of Contents toolbar.

WordPerfect displays the Define Table of Contents dialog box, as shown in Figure 17-13.

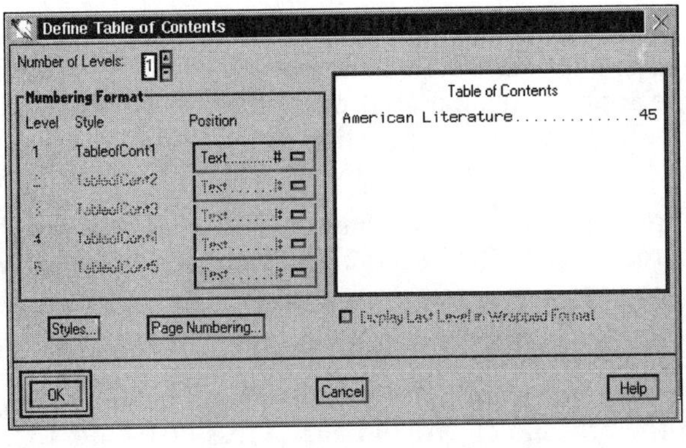

Figure 17-13: Telling WordPerfect how your table of contents should look.

8. Tell WordPerfect the number of levels and which style to use for each level (whether to include page numbers and dot leaders); then click on OK.

For a table of contents that lists one level of headings (for example, chapter titles) using regular numbers, leave everything in this dialog box alone. If you want an additional level of headings in the table of contents, change the Number of Levels box to the number of levels of headings you want. (For example, type **2** to include chapter titles and section headings within chapters.) For each heading level, you can set the position — where the number appears and whether it's preceded by a row of dots.

When you click on OK, WordPerfect inserts an invisible code and the text `<<Table of Contents will generate here>`. Don't worry: WordPerfect does better than that in a minute.

9. **Click on the Generate button on the Table of Contents toolbar.**

   The Generate button is at the right end of the Table of Contents toolbar; you may have to make the WordPerfect window wider to see it. When you click on the button, WordPerfect displays the Generate dialog box.

10. **Click on OK.**

    Some messages flash by. Then, poof — you have a table of contents.

"No big deal," you may say. "It would have been faster to copy the chapter titles by hand." Here's the nice thing, though: If you update your book and make chapters shorter or longer, when you click on the Generate button again, WordPerfect updates the table of contents and corrects the headings and page numbers.

After you finish fooling with the table of contents, click on the Close button on the Table of Contents toolbar. To get the toolbar back, you can always choose <u>T</u>ools⇨Referen<u>c</u>e⇨<u>T</u>able of Contents.

Chapter 18

Spinning Web Pages

. . . .

In This Chapter

▶ "What is all this Internet stuff, and what is it doing in my word processor?"

▶ What is hypertext?

▶ Your own personal, mini deskwide Web

▶ The World Wide Web

▶ WordPerfect and HTML: Markups for free

▶ Your very own Web pages

▶ Turn documents into Web pages

. . . .

*O*ne little-known provision of the U.S. Communications Reform Act of 1996 made marketing any piece of software in the United States illegal unless the software could connect to the Internet. Thus, we have Internet-enabled word processors, databases, spreadsheets, and toaster ovens.

Okay, it's not really a law, although it may as well be. Let's call it a trend. WordPerfect hasn't been immune to this trend. In this chapter, we do several things to help you get started in your World Wide Web experience. First, we talk a little about what the Internet and the World Wide Web are. If you're planning to create a Web page, you need to know this stuff. Of course, one of us wrote a whole book about that subject (*The Internet For Dummies*, 6th Edition, by John Levine, Carol Baroudi, and Margaret Levine Young, published by IDG Books Worldwide, Inc.), although we don't go into it here.

Second, we talk about hypertext links and bookmarks. They're the WordPerfect way of creating Web pages: linking information from one document to another. Using WordPerfect bookmarks and links is a good way for you to get started creating Web pages. You don't have to worry about all the Web parts of the process. Instead, you can concentrate on the content you want to communicate to people and the way you plan to organize that content.

Finally, we talk about creating Web pages in HTML (we explain what that is, too) and putting them on the World Wide Web. As you can tell, this topic is rather large; in fact, books have been written about the subject. We know because one of us wrote one of them. If you find this teaser tantalizing, check out *WordPerfect Web Publishing For Dummies,* which Dave wrote (IDG Books Worldwide, Inc.).

Hypertext, the Internet, and the World Wide Web

The World Wide Web is built on two basic concepts: hypertext and the Internet. When you combine these two concepts, as often happens, you end up with something that has had much more impact than either has had on its own. Understanding the World Wide Web is much easier if you at least know what the concepts are that make it work. Read on!

What is hypertext?

Hypertext is something that appears not only on the World Wide Web but also in lots of places in computer software. It's just like regular text, except for one thing: When you click on certain words or phrases, you're magically transported to different text, in either the same document or another document. Although the concept sounds very space-age, it's simple. You can follow related ideas in a way that would be difficult if you had to skip around from page to page in a book or from book to book.

You may be familiar with hypertext; in fact, you may have used it. Where? In the online help systems used by many programs in Linux and Windows. Help screens are sprinkled with little icons just enticing you to click on them; they're hypertext links to other parts of the help system. When you click on one of those links, another screen of information appears; most of us find this feature really useful. If you use KDE, try out some hypertext by clicking on the K button and choosing KDE Help from the menu.

The Internet

Once upon a time, computers were big and lonely. They lived in glass houses and were surrounded by acolytes in white coats. Later, these big computers were connected to lots of dumb terminals, like Gulliver tied down by the Lilliputians. Sometimes, the computers even spoke to one another — sort of like whales at a great distance. As computers got smaller and smaller, they became more and more social — kind of like ants. Millions of computers, large and small, are now connected — some via telephone, some via Local Area Networks within an office, and some via high-speed telephone links. Rather than try to keep all these computers rigidly organized, people have discovered that you can get a message from any computer to any other by asking a computer to pass the message to some computer that may know the recipient. *That's* the Internet: a whole bunch of computers playing whisper-down-the-lane.

The World Wide Web

For years, people used this network of computers pretty much the way they used the Gulliver-and-the-Lilliputians computer networks: All the small computers asked the big computers to do something for them. In 1990, a charming English guy named Tim Berners-Lee, at the European Particle Physics Laboratory (CERN), realized that the information could be anywhere, and he developed a way for any computer to ask (almost) any other computer connected to the Internet for some information. The way he linked all that information was with hypertext. He called it the World Wide Web.

A *Web page* (a document that forms part of the World Wide Web) looks like a regular word processing document onscreen, except that some words are underlined. Amid all the hype and all the fanfare about the Web, one fact is frequently overlooked: All those Web pages must have something on them. The pages must have *content,* and that content has to be written with some tool. Because the folks at WordPerfect already had a tool that could produce tables, boldface text, italics, outlines, and even hypertext links, WordPerfect was reborn as a Web page creator.

You probably didn't know that even normal WordPerfect documents can use hypertext. (If you did, it's not because *we* told you — at least, not yet!) Most people don't give a hoot about it because they're creating paper documents, not electronic documents. Because you're now creating electronic documents for the Web, however, it's time to give the matter some attention.

Hypertext Links and Bookmarks

The WordPerfect *bookmark* feature enables you to link one piece of text to another, in the same document or another document. You don't really need to use bookmarks to create Web pages. You ought to know about them, though, for three reasons. First, the tools you use to create a link *to* a bookmark are the same ones you use to create a link to another page on the World Wide Web. Second, as you're looking through your documents, you should be thinking about the links among them: places *from* which it make sense to help the reader jump *to* some other place in your documents, and places they should be jumping *to*. Third, it's pretty easy.

Creating a bookmark: A place you jump to

Bookmarks within a single document work pretty much the way their name implies — they let you mark a position in a document and go back to it quickly. Suppose that you're working on your epic *Of Chocolate and Chocoholics,* a 500-page masterpiece with 30 chapters. You've created a master document and a subdocument for each chapter (as explained in Chapter 17), and you're working on the master document in Expanded view (so that all the chapters appear in the document). If you're working on Chapter 23, "Ceremonial Uses of Chocolate," and want to check what you said about that topic in Chapter 1, "A History of Chocolate," you have several options (of course you do; this is WordPerfect):

✔ Press the PgUp key on your keyboard until you get to Chapter 1. This method makes your finger sore and takes a long time.

✔ Choose Edit⇨Find and Replace to search for the text *A History of Chocolate.* The problem with this method is that WordPerfect stops at every occurrence of *A History of Chocolate* in the entire book to this point. This method also takes a long time.

✔ Use a bookmark. After you set a bookmark in the text of *A History of Chocolate,* you can get back there at any time by displaying the Go To dialog box and selecting the name of the bookmark. No matter how far away you are, WordPerfect takes you there as though you were on a magic carpet. After you check out what you want to see, you can use Go To again to return to your last position in Chapter 23.

Setting bookmarks and moving to them may seem to be a great deal of work, and it is; it's worth the trouble only if you plan to go back to that bookmark often or use some of the *really* obscure features of WordPerfect. (That's why we haven't explained bookmarks until now.) With the advent of hypertext and the World Wide Web, bookmarks become really useful.

To create a bookmark, follow these steps:

1. **Move the cursor to the location you want to be able to jump to quickly. Highlight the text you want the bookmark to jump to.**

   For what you're doing here, it doesn't matter how much of your text you highlight. For example, you may highlight the chapter title, "A History of Chocolate."

2. **Choose Tools⇨Bookmark.**

   The Bookmark dialog box appears, as shown in Figure 18-1.

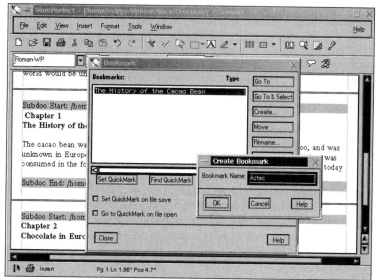

Figure 18-1:
Creating a
bookmark.

3. **Click on the Create button.**

   A little Create Bookmark dialog box (also shown in Figure 18-1) appears; if you selected text in Step 1, the Bookmark Name box contains that text as the name for your bookmark. If you didn't highlight some text, type a name for the bookmark. The Bookmark dialog box and the Create Bookmark dialog boxes are both shown in the figure.

4. **Click on OK to create the bookmark.**

   Poof! Nothing happens. Well, the dialog boxes go away — nothing looks different in your document, however. Now the fun begins!

When you create a bookmark, WordPerfect inserts a Bookmark code in your text. Chapter 9 explains how the WordPerfect codes work.

Now that we've shown you how to create a bookmark, we show you how to let people jump *to* it.

If you're extremely observant, you will have noticed that the right end of the Property Bar changes when a word or other block of text is selected. The rightmost button changes to look like a spider web wearing a pince-nez (the kind of glasses Teddy Roosevelt used to wear). Click on this button and you see a little 2-item menu; click on Insert Bookmark and you see the Create Bookmark dialog box.

Jumping to a bookmark

After you've created a bookmark, jumping to it is easy. From anywhere in your document, press Ctrl+G (or choose Edit⇨Go To), click on the Bookmark option, and choose the bookmark name from the list. When you click on OK, you zip right to the location of the bookmark.

This trick is great if you're looking at the document onscreen, but useless for the reader of the printed document.

Creating a hyperlink — a way to jump somewhere

If you plan to read your document on the screen, or allow others to do so, you can create *hyperlinks* in the text that help the reader jump to related text. Consider Chapter 23, "Ceremonial Uses of Chocolate," in the tome we're writing in this chapter. In a traditional book, you may say something like "The first known ceremonial use of chocolate occurred in Aztec society long before the European discovery of America (see Chapter 1)." The reader then flips to Chapter 1 and skims it to see whether it says anything about Aztecs. This method works fine on paper but is a little awkward on a computer screen, especially the flipping part. We can create a link, therefore, directly to the specific paragraph in Chapter 1 in our tome on chocolate.

Follow these steps:

1. **Create a bookmark at the place *to which* you want your reader to be able to jump in whatever document you're writing, and then save the document.**

   In Figure 18-1, we just finished creating a bookmark on the word *Aztec* in the document Chapter1.

2. **Open the document that contains the place *from which* you want your reader to be able to jump.**

   In this case, it's Chapter23.

3. **Highlight the words you want a user to be able to click on.**

   In this case, we may select a reference to the Aztecs at the beginning of Chapter 23.

4. **Choose Tools⇨Hyperlink.**

   The Create Hypertext Link dialog box appears, as shown in Figure 18-2. In this box, you tell WordPerfect what you want to have happen to the person who clicks on the link you're creating. Right now, we just create a link back to the *Aztec* bookmark in Chapter 1.

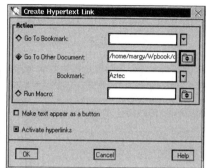

Figure 18-2:
Creating a
link to a
WordPerfect
bookmark.

5. **Select the Go To Other Document box and type the name of the document to which you want to link.**

In this case, it's `Chapter1`. If you're lazy or (like us) can't remember, click on the little file-folder button. You see the WordPerfect standard file-browsing dialog box, and you can select the file there.

6. **In the Bookmark box, type the name of the bookmark you want WordPerfect to take the user to.**

In this case, it's **Aztec**. If you've forgotten the names of the bookmarks in the document you just selected, you can click on the down arrow at the end of this box. You see a list of all bookmarks in that document. You don't have to specify a bookmark. If you leave it out, WordPerfect just takes the user to the beginning of the document.

7. **Click on OK.**

This time, you see a change in your document. The word (or phrase or character) you highlighted is now underlined and in blue.

Do yourself a favor: Save the document now. Congratulations! — you've created your own hyperlink. Creating hypertext is nothing more than creating lots and lots of these links.

Oh, you want to see whether your hyperlink *does* anything? Easy — just click on the blue, underlined text. You jump to the related text. Strangely, if the document with the related text is already open, WordPerfect opens a second copy.

The Hyperlink Tools Property Bar

Following a link is easy — just click on it. Editing the links in a document is easy, too. You can fool with hyperlinks endlessly after you've created them, and WordPerfect provides a Property Bar full of buttons you can use to work with your hyperlinks. To see the Hyperlink Tools Property Bar, position the cursor on the hypertext link (that's the word in blue) — don't click on the link because that action takes you to the bookmark to which the link is linked (Chapter 1, in our example in this chapter). Instead, click *near* the link and press the cursor-movement keys to move the cursor to the link. Look at the Property Bar: It changed. Figure 18-3 shows the Property Bar when its mind is on hyperlinks.

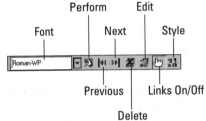

Figure 18-3:
The
Hyperlink
Tools
Property
Bar.

Because the Property Bar is the easiest way to care for and feed your hypertext links, getting to know its buttons is worth your time:

Font-selection box: Sets the font for the link. Strangely, the font is a property of your hyperlink even though its other text properties, like bold and italics, aren't. We prefer to format our text by choosing the Format⇨Font command.

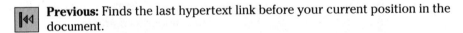

Perform: Follows the link, the same as clicking on a link, although links don't work when they've been deactivated (see the Links On/Off entry, later in this list). The Perform button works regardless.

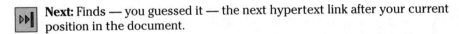

Previous: Finds the last hypertext link before your current position in the document.

Next: Finds — you guessed it — the next hypertext link after your current position in the document.

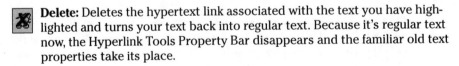

Delete: Deletes the hypertext link associated with the text you have highlighted and turns your text back into regular text. Because it's regular text now, the Hyperlink Tools Property Bar disappears and the familiar old text properties take its place.

Edit: Displays the Hyperlink Properties dialog box, in case you want this link to go somewhere else. It's the same as choosing the Tools⇨Hyperlink command.

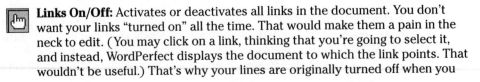

Links On/Off: Activates or deactivates all links in the document. You don't want your links "turned on" all the time. That would make them a pain in the neck to edit. (You may click on a link, thinking that you're going to select it, and instead, WordPerfect displays the document to which the link points. That wouldn't be useful.) That's why your lines are originally turned off when you create them and the Links On/Off button isn't pressed in. The only way to "follow" a hyperlink is to click the Perform button we just described. If you click the Links On/Off button, the cursor changes to a little hand whenever you pass the cursor over a hyperlink in your document. If you click on the link, you follow it to its destination.

 Style: Helps you change the way links are displayed. For more information, take a look at Chapter 10.

Now you have all the tools you need to create hypertext documents — like Web pages.

Creating Your Own Web Pages

Creating your own Web page is pretty much like creating any other WordPerfect document. Web pages are a little more structured than your average document. That is, they're all supposed to have a title and headings and some information about who prepared the page. As the World Wide Web has grown, however, some conventions have become less and less universal, until a Web page now can be pretty much anything. You're still constrained, though, by some of the original ideas about what *ought* to be on a Web page. We explain in more detail when we show you the Property Bar for editing Web pages. Figure 18-4 illustrates a simple Web page with some text on it.

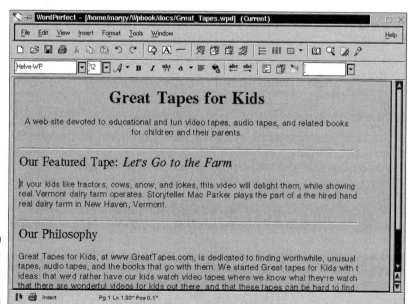

Figure 18-4:
A simple
Web page.

To get started with a Web page, follow these steps:

1. **Choose File⇨Internet Publisher.**

   It doesn't matter whether a document is onscreen when you issue this command. You see the Internet Publisher dialog box, as shown in Figure 18-5.

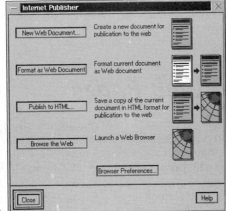

Figure 18-5:
Internet
Publisher
helps you
get started
with a Web
page.

2. **Click on New Web Document.**

   Stop drooling over those other options. We talk about the Publish to HTML option in the section "Converting Your Documents to Web Pages," later in this chapter; the Browse the Web option is just another way to start your Web browser. If you're with the program, you see a new document with a gray background, in a new window.

All the familiar WordPerfect editing tools appear in this new document window; all you have to do is type normally. If you want to copy text from another document, open the other document in a separate window (by choosing Program⇨Open Window in the program window) and copy the text from the other document to your new one.

Text formatting on Web pages

In addition to showing a sample Web page, Figure 18-4 illustrates how the Property Bar and HTML toolbar appear when you're editing a Web page. The following list describes the items on the Property Bar and HTML toolbar that you should know about when you're creating Web pages and points out how we used some of them for the sample Web page shown in Figure 18-4:

✔ **Font:** The font selector box is ho-hum news when you're editing regular WordPerfect documents, although the ability to select your own font on a Web page is rather new. Specifying a font on a Web page generally isn't a good idea because you have no guarantee that a person's computer displaying your Web page halfway around the world has ever heard of the font you picked. If you pick a font the person's computer doesn't know about, the computer guesses and tries to pick something that it thinks is reasonable, although it may guess wrong. Stay away from this setting when you're making Web pages.

✔ **Font Size:** Most of the same considerations apply for font sizes as for fonts: Let the viewer's Web browser pick them for you. To tell the browser what you want, click the button we describe next, Heading/Style, and Font Attributes, later in this list.

✔ **Heading/Style:** Click this button to display a list of the headings and styles Web pages understand. These styles (and that's what they are) apply to the whole paragraph for which they're selected. (If styles aren't familiar to you, check out Chapter 10.) Styles enable the Web to get around the fact that different computers and Web browsers have different capabilities. Web browsers know how to do only what HTML tells them to do, and it has no way of saying, "Format the following text in a spiral, using ornamental pumpkins in small caps." The text styles HTML knows about are listed when you click on this button. Most of the document shown in Figure 18-4 was created using the Normal style. The "Great Tapes for Kids" heading uses the Heading1 style, and the featured tape and philosophy headings use Heading2. The contact information at the bottom of the page uses the Address style.

✔ **Bold:** At least some things work the same way they always did. This button makes text bold on your Web document and on the viewer's Web browser.

✔ **Italic:** Thankfully, this one works the same as the Bold button: It just works.

✔ **Monospaced Font:** Unless you're into typesetting, fixed-space text looks ugly. If your Web page is about technical stuff, however, you may want to use a fixed-space font. Most computer books say, somewhere near the beginning, "Text you should type to the program appears like this: `sample command`."

✔ **Font Attributes:** At the beginning of this list, we suggest that you not use absolute text sixes to format your text. This button lists all the different font attributes HTML knows about and gives you a convenient place to try them out. Bold and italics here are the same as the Bold and Italics buttons on the Property Bar.

The rest of the Property Bar buttons work pretty much the way they do in the rest of WordPerfect, or they do things so heinously technical that you shouldn't bother with them. A couple of useful new buttons are on the toolbar, however:

✔ **Horizontal Line:** This button draws a horizontal line across the screen. That's how we drew the lines in the document shown in Figure 18-4.

✔ **Launch Your Internet Browser:** Launch your Web browser with this button. We figure that you probably have about ten other ways of launching your browser, so why do you need this one in WordPerfect? There it is, though. If we didn't tell you what it does, we figured that you would ask.

✔ **View in Your Browser:** Here's a useful button. No matter how hard WordPerfect tries, your document will look different in your Web browser than it does in WordPerfect. Using this button, you can take a quick look at what your page will look like in your Web browser. Be sure to close the browser afterward, or else the next time you view a Web page from WordPerfect, you end up with a second Web browser on your desktop, and then a third, and then a fourth — you get the idea.

✔ **Save Document As HTML:** We talk more about this button later in this chapter, in the section "Converting Your Documents to Web Pages."

✔ **Create or Edit Hyperlink:** With this button, you can display the Create Hypertext Link dialog box we talk about when we show you how to create links to other WordPerfect documents. We talk about it in more detail in the section "Creating a link to another Web page," just ahead.

Okay, you have a fairly boring Web page. Now you can begin to fancy it up; start by adding a picture, as explained in the following section.

Adding a picture to a Web page

As you do with any WordPerfect document, you add a picture to a Web page by inserting in your document the file that contains the picture. Follow these steps:

1. **Move to the place in the document where you want the picture to appear.**

   Many Web pages have pictures at the top to provide a little visual interest while a reader looks over the text. In our case, because we wanted to put a picture of the box from our video beside the video's description, we positioned the cursor just before the words *If your kids like tractors.*

2. **Choose Insert➪Graphics➪From File to display the Insert Image dialog box.**

3. **Select the file that contains the picture you want to insert.**

   It doesn't matter where on your computer the file that contains the picture is, relative to where your Web page is stored. You can browse all over the place (even to other computers) to find the file. We talk in a minute about where these pictures need to go; for now, however, just find the picture you want.

4. Click on Insert to insert the picture in your document.

You may see a message about a "conversion in progress," depending on how WordPerfect feels about the kind of picture you clicked on. Notice that the text after the picture appears below the picture, leaving blank space to the right of it. You probably would prefer the text to flow beside the picture. Unfortunately, you can't use the WordPerfect wrap feature to tell the text how to flow around this picture because it's a Web page. When we finished inserting a picture in our Great Tapes Web page, it looked like the one shown in Figure 18-6.

Figure 18-6: The WordPerfect rendering of a Web page with a picture on it.

If you're keeping an eagle-eye on the Property Bar, notice that it has, with the addition of our picture, transformed itself into the graphics Property Bar we talk about in Chapter 15, with, of course, a few additions and deletions because the graphic is on a Web page. This graphics/Web version of the Property Bar appears when the graphics box is selected (when little blue handle boxes appear around it).

5. Click on the Graphics button on the Property Bar and choose the Position command from the menu that appears.

The Box Position dialog box appears, looking somewhat like the Box Position dialog box we talk about in Chapter 14. This dialog box is the key to making text flow around a picture on a Web page.

6. In the Box Position dialog box, select Put Box in Current Paragraph (Paragraph Anchor) and then set to Left Margin the Horizontal Place setting in the Position Box section.

The Box Position dialog box is shown in Figure 18-7.

7. **Click on OK to get rid of the dialog box, and then save the document.**

The text on your Web page moves up next to the picture, as shown in Figure 18-8. That looks much better!

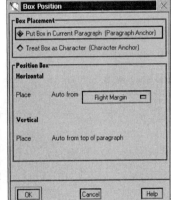

Figure 18-7: Where exactly do you want that picture?

Figure 18-8: A Web page with a picture and some text beside it.

Now may be a good time to see how your page looks in a real Web browser rather than in WordPerfect. Click on the View in Your Browser button on the toolbar. (We identify this button in the section "Text formatting on Web pages," earlier in this chapter.) Wait and listen to all the whirring and clicking going on inside your computer. In due course (that is, whenever your computer feels up to it), a Web browser appears onscreen with its rendition of your Web page. Which Web browser appears depends on which one you have installed; if no browser is installed, you may see the Browser Preferences dialog box, in which you can enter the filename of the browser program you use. Most Linux installations include Netscape Navigator, an excellent Web browser.

Creating a link to another Web page

The distinguishing hallmark of the World Wide Web is the linking from page to page that enables you to explore the connections between different pages as you discover them. For now, our page has no links on it.

While you're editing Web pages, WordPerfect makes adding a link to a Web page on the World Wide Web easy. All you have to do is type the Web address of the page you want to link to; for example, our Internet Gurus Web site, at `net.gurus.com` or the Great Tapes for Kids site, at `www.greattapes.com`. WordPerfect recognizes what you type as a Web address and automatically turns it into a link to that address. This trick is rather neat. It works for Web addresses that start with `http:` or `www` (both are links to other Web pages) and e-mail addresses that start with *somethingorother@*. What if you want a link, however, that doesn't look like a Web address? For example, we have a page that has more information about the *Let's Go to the Farm* video. Rather than put the Web address of that page onscreen for users to see, we want them to see a phrase that says, "We have more information about this charming video." Users can click on the words *this charming video* to follow the link, just as you may have clicked on the word *Aztec* earlier in this chapter. Figure 18-9 illustrates the steps we used to create a link from this page to another page on our computer:

1. **Select the text the user should see as a link.**

   In this case, we used the words *this charming video*. Alternatively, we could insert a little graphic (maybe a picture of a More Info button) and select the graphic box with the picture — pictures can be links, too.

 2. **Click on the Create or Edit Hyperlink button on the toolbar and select Create Link from the little menu that appears.**

   You see the Create Hypertext Link dialog box (refer to Figure 18-2).

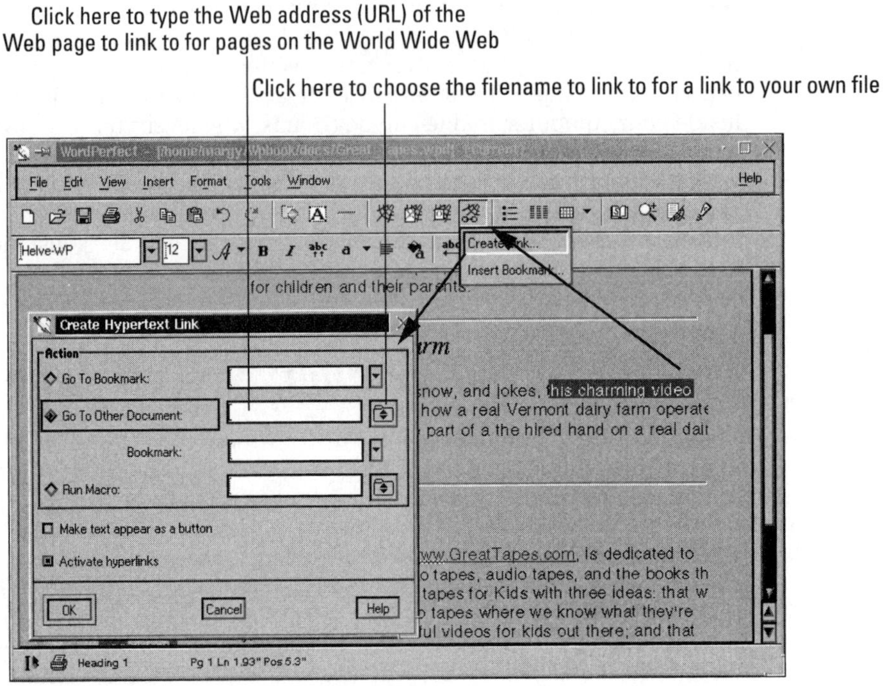

Click here to type the Web address (URL) of the
Web page to link to for pages on the World Wide Web

Click here to choose the filename to link to for a link to your own file

Figure 18-9:
Creating a
link to
another
Web page
on your
computer.

3. Select the Go To Other Document option.

You want a link to somewhere that's not in the current document —
another document you created or a page on the World Wide Web.

4. If your link will be to a document you have stored on your computer, click on the file folder to the right of the box, select the file to which you want to link, and click on Apply. If not, skip to Step 5.

In the Insert File dialog box, select a document on your computer as the
link's destination. This file is probably a Web page you created with
Internet Publisher and saved as an HTML file. At the end of this chapter,
we talk about saving HTML files.

5. If your link will be to a page out on the Web, type the URL of the page in the Go To Other Document box.

You can link to any page on the entire World Wide Web — that's one of
the beauties of the Web! If you don't want to type the Web address, display the page in your Web browser (Netscape Navigator, for example),
and copy-and-paste the Web address into the box.

6. Click on OK.

The Create Hypertext Link dialog box goes away, and the words or picture you selected in Step 1 are underlined and highlighted in blue —
they're a link.

To remove the formatting codes that make a link, select the link and click the Create or Edit Hyperlink button again. This time, choose Remove Link from the menu that appears.

Changing the look of your page

So far, the background color of your Web page is gray, the traditional color for old-fashioned Web pages. If you want to switch to a different color, choose Format⇨Text/Background Colors from the menu. In the Background Color/Wallpaper section of the Text/Background Colors dialog box, as shown in Figure 18-10, click on the Background Color setting, which looks like a little gray box. A small, untitled dialog box appears, containing zillions of colors to choose from. Click on one (we like white, which appears in the upper-right corner). Then click on OK. The background color of your Web page changes!

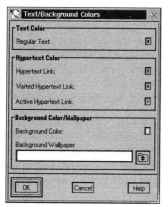

Figure 18-10: You can change the background color along with the color of your text and links.

Congratulations! That's all it takes to create a fairly complete Web page. Although you have created a document that's ready to become a Web page, you have one more step — saving the document as an *HTML* file, the standard format for all Web pages. We describe this task in the following section.

Converting Your Documents to Web Pages

One of the most useful things about the WordPerfect capability to create Web documents is that you can use those documents on the World Wide Web. (What else would you do with them?) You probably already have a bunch of WordPerfect documents. Presto — instant content for your Web site.

The only problem is that the documents aren't formatted as Web pages; they probably also use all sorts of features that don't work on Web pages.

WordPerfect comes to the rescue. The Format As Web Document button in the Internet Publisher dialog box (we tell you how to use it in a minute) removes all non-Web-page formatting from your document. What you see onscreen after using this dialog box is the result of this button's labors.

Depending on how much formatting you did in your document, you'll be more or less pleased with the result. If your document looks destroyed, you have two options:

- Reformat the document as a WordPerfect document, using only the features that work in Web documents.
- Fix the Web version by hand.

The option you pick depends on how you intend to maintain your document:

- To keep both a WordPerfect version of your document (for printing on paper) and a Web version for people to look at, pick the first option. Although this option involves a little more work, you keep the document up-to-date in only one place. Every time you change the WordPerfect version, you can convert it to a Web page again. Although you can't make it a fancy WordPerfect document, maybe that's okay.

- If you're converting your documents for use on the Web, fix the Web version by hand, which is just a matter of using the available formatting features. The better you make a document look as a Web document, the more it differs from the original. That's okay, although keeping two versions of the same document up-to-date with one another is usually difficult.

You can also add to your document some HTML features that WordPerfect has no idea about. Simply type the HTML codes in your document, highlight them, and choose Format⇨Custom HTML. (This command is available only when you're editing a Web page.) To do so, you have to know something about HTML. Get a copy of *HTML For Dummies,* 3rd Edition, by Ed Tittel and Steve James (IDG Books Worldwide, Inc.).

You have two — count 'em, two — ways to save your Web pages in WordPerfect. This fact shouldn't surprise you because WordPerfect gives you a bunch of ways to do everything. In this case, however, it's important to know when to use each one.

Saving your Web page as a WordPerfect document

Here's the confusing part: After you convert your WordPerfect document to a Web page, it's still a WordPerfect document. It's just a WordPerfect document with some magic codes which tell WordPerfect that only the Web page features work. Because the document is a WordPerfect document, you should save it as a WordPerfect file, with the file extension wpd, which is exactly what WordPerfect does if you choose the File⇨Save As command. After you convert your document, you'll notice that it still has the same name. If you're not careful, therefore, you can end up saving the Web page version (which, we assume, has lost a great deal of formatting) right on top of your beautiful WordPerfect version. You don't even get a warning.

We don't think that this situation is good. Our recommendation is that you use _web at the end of your filename so that you know that it's a Web page version of your file. Our Chapter1.wpd document, therefore, would become Chapter1_web.wpd. If you use this naming convention, at least you know what's what.

To save the Web page as a WordPerfect document, choose the File⇨Save As command or click on the Save button on the toolbar. The document isn't really a Web page, and you can't upload this file to the Internet for use on the Web. Instead, the file is an intermediate version of your Web page that you can use when you're editing the page later.

Saving your Web page as an HTML document

To convert a Web page to an HTML file for use on the Web, follow these steps to run the WordPerfect Internet Publisher:

1. **Choose File⇨Internet Publisher from the menu bar.**

   You see the Internet Publisher dialog box (refer to Figure 18-5).

2. **Click on the Publish to HTML button.**

   The Publish to HTML dialog box appears, as shown in Figure 18-11. WordPerfect suggests a filename that's the name of the WordPerfect file with .html tacked on the end.

Figure 18-11:
WordPerfect
saves your
document
as an HTML
file, for
publishing it
on the World
Wide Web.

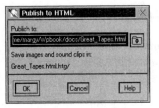

This filename may be a fine name for a Web page; it's not, however, if the name includes spaces or punctuation other than hyphens, underscores, and dots. You should edit the filename to remove them. Most browsers don't deal well with spaces in Web addresses, and some punctuation marks have special meanings on the Web. Delete the .wpd part, too because this file is *not* in WordPerfect document format.

You also see the name of the directory in which WordPerfect plans to copy the graphics files (and sound-clip files, if you use any): Later in this section, we tell you what that's about.

3. Edit the filename as needed and click on OK.

WordPerfect converts your document to HTML format. At last! A real, live Web page!

If you used the File⇨Save As command to save your Web page as a WordPerfect document and the File⇨Internet Publisher command to save it as an HTML file, you now have two files on your disk — two versions of the same document. You can open either one in WordPerfect (by choosing the usual File⇨Open command) and edit the document. You may also have a third version — the one you started with before beginning the process of converting it for the Web!

When you open your HTML file, WordPerfect displays the Convert File dialog box and asks from which format you want your file to be converted. WordPerfect suggests Internet Document (HTML), which is, after all, the right answer. Go ahead and click on OK. Knowing that an HTML file is just a text file, however, may be useful. If you want to look at the file as a text file (and see all the HTML codes in it), tell WordPerfect to convert it from ASCII text format. The guts of your Web page will be revealed to you. Yikes! Don't worry: Just close the file without making any changes.

Putting your pages on the World Wide Web

Although we talk a great deal elsewhere in this chapter about preparing your pages for the World Wide Web, we don't say what you have to *do* to get your pages on the Web. That's because the process varies from location to location. You generally have to find a *Web server* — a computer that's always connected to the Internet (or the intranet, if you're interested in distributing information only around your organization). Then, it's just a matter of putting your HTML files in the right place on the Web server.

If you use an Internet Service Provider (ISP) for your Internet account, it may give customers some space on its Web server. To transfer files to a Web server, you usually need a file transfer program (FTP). Contact your ISP for help. If you work at an organization that has an *intranet*

(internal web), contact your system administrator for help. Otherwise, you can still put your pages on the Web, by using one of many free Web-hosting services. Try GeoCities, at `http://www.geocities.com`, and follow the instructions on its Web site.

In all likelihood, a local computer-systems junkie will have to do it for you because companies are (or should be) careful about how their computers connect to the rest of the world. We've thought a great deal about this subject, and Dave even went so far as to write a whole book about it. If you want to know more, check out his book *WordPerfect Web Publishing For Dummies* (IDG Books Worldwide, Inc.). You may also want to invest in *The Internet For Dummies*, 6th Edition (IDG Books Worldwide, Inc.), which Margy co-authored.

In addition to saving your Web page as an HTML file, Internet Publisher does two useful favors for you:

- ✔ **Collects in one directory all the images (graphics files) and sound-clip files (if you know how to include audio files in the Web page) that appear on your page:** This capability is useful because one Web page can include images from all over your computer. If you have to upload your Web page to a Web server, finding and copying the various graphics files can be a pain.

- ✔ **Makes the published version of the Web page look in the directory where it just collected the images:** Otherwise, the codes in your Web page refer to the *old* locations of the graphics files. When you upload the page to the Internet, you see error messages rather than graphics!

The WordPerfect Internet Publisher tells you where it's copying the files: The directory name appears in the Publish to HTML dialog box, just below the filename for the HTML file.

Stuff You Can Do in WordPerfect That You Can't Do on a Web Page

Despite the nice job the folks at WordPerfect have done in tying Web features to the rest of WordPerfect, you should know some things about handling Web pages. Because HTML and Web browsers are just evolving, whereas WordPerfect has been around for years, you can do many things in WordPerfect that you can't do on a Web page, at least not this week. The whole Web browser market is changing so fast that any of this information could be different by the time you read this book.

As you look at the WordPerfect menus while you edit a Web document, notice that most commands on the Format menu have disappeared because most of them can't be used on a Web page. The following lists describes the features that don't convert to a Web page, in roughly the order in which we think you may care about them:

- **Tabs:** Yes, that's tabs, as in the Tab key — something so simple that you probably don't even think about it. We're sure that lots of technical reasons exist for tabs not being a part of HTML as we know it today; the fact remains, however, that they aren't. If you used tabs to create a table, reformat the text by using the WordPerfect table feature, which converts things nicely to HTML tables.

- **Margins (left or right):** Web pages specify their margins by using the size of the user's browser window.

- **Page numbering:** What's a page? Numbered relative to what? We're talking about onscreen hypertext here.

- **Columns:** Although WordPerfect tries to do something with columns, you probably won't enjoy the results. Newer Web browsers are moving toward the use of columns; these browsers just aren't part of the mainstream yet.

- **Headers and footers:** These elements don't apply to Web pages.

- **Indents:** Indents aren't critical to most documents and don't even exist in HTML documents.

- **Drop caps:** The absence of drop caps is a shame because they can be nice-looking. WordPerfect turns them back into regular text. If you still want your Web page to look artsy, replace drop caps with graphics.

- **Fill (shading behind text):** Use your page background for this effect.

- **Vertical lines:** Use tables again, if you can.

- **Watermarks:** Watermarks should be part of your page's background.

Part V

Oh, Help!

"WE SHOULD HAVE THIS FIXED IN VERSION 2."

In this part . . .

Is all going well with your word processing experience? No? You've run into a snag? Well, you've come to the right place.

This part of the book solves a number of thorny problems. You find out how to make the behavior of WordPerfect more socially acceptable. If you run into big trouble, run (do not walk) to Chapter 20 for solutions to the most common WordPerfect problems.

Chapter 19

Training WordPerfect to Act Your Way

In This Chapter

▶ Seeing information about your documents

▶ Setting the font you usually use

▶ Zooming around in your documents

▶ Setting your settings

▶ Changing the way WordPerfect looks

▶ Controlling the ruler, toolbar, Property Bar, and Application Bar

▶ Controlling your zooms

▶ Determining where WordPerfect stores your files

▶ Assigning different meanings to keys (yikes!)

*Y*ou know how software can be — badly behaved, saving files in the wrong folders, displaying incomprehensible things on the screen, and being generally rude. It's time for some lessons in deportment. You can teach WordPerfect to behave more like the kind of gentleman or lady with whom you like to be seen.

A nifty WordPerfect quality is that it lets you customize so much about the way it works. In this chapter, you find out how to display information *about* your documents, how to zoom in on the text of your document for a close-up look, how to control which buttons appear on the Property Bar and toolbar, how to control where WordPerfect stores things (in which folders on your disk), and how to set other preferences.

If you're happy with WordPerfect just the way it is, you can skip this chapter. On the other hand, if you're really, *really* happy with WordPerfect, you may want to see a shrink. Leaving WordPerfect to behave as it does out of the box is not such a bad idea. One advantage of this approach is that your WordPerfect will work just like everyone else's (unless they have customized *their* copies), so getting help from your WordPerfect-savvy friends is easier.

Seeing Information About Your Documents

You can enter information about your document in the Document Summary dialog box. To display it, choose File➪Properties➪Document Summary. The spaces for all the kinds of stuff you may want to know about a document don't fit in the dialog box; you can use the little scroll bar to slide down to see the rest.

The information you enter in the document summary is stored along with your document. You can view or edit it at any time.

Although you may not want to tell WordPerfect a great deal about your document, WordPerfect has a great deal it wants to share with you. Choose File➪Properties➪Document Info, and WordPerfect gives you a mini-analysis of how you write: number of characters in your document and number of words, lines, and paragraphs, for example. So see what WordPerfect has to say.

What if you don't want to enter something in the Descriptive Type box? (What if you don't even have the faintest idea what a descriptive type might be? We don't.) What if you want to keep track of the document's version number instead? Wow — WordPerfect lets *you* choose which blanks appear in the Document Summary dialog box. To change the facts included in all summaries you create, click on the Configure button in the Document Summary dialog box. WordPerfect displays the Document Summary Configuration dialog box and lets you choose from among a long list of possible facts about a document, including Authorization, Checked By, Document Number, Project, Status, and Version Number. Does this stuff sound official, or what?

Setting Your Favorite Font

Have you ever gotten annoyed at WordPerfect for always suggesting the same font whenever you create a new document? Particularly when it's as ugly as Courier? We have. Enough with Courier, already — we're in the mood for Helvetica!

The following list provides some solutions to this problem:

- **Use templates.** Templates allow you to predefine all the styles you use for the kinds of documents you usually create. You can make one template for letters, one for memos, and one for faxes, each with the proper fonts selected.

- **Tell WordPerfect the name of your favorite font.** WordPerfect then uses this font for all new documents unless you select another one.

For instructions about using the first approach, refer to Chapter 17, where we talk about templates and commonly used documents in general. These steps show you how to use the second approach:

1. **Choose File⇨Document⇨Default Font.**

   WordPerfect, ever ready to pop open another dialog box, displays the Document Default Font dialog box.

2. **Choose your favorite font, size, and style.**

   Show some restraint here — no one can read your polished prose if you print it in WingDings.

3. **Make sure that the Set as Printer Initial Font check box is selected.**

   Otherwise, this step sets the font for only the current document.

4. **Click on OK or press Enter.**

   You have just told WordPerfect to use your favorite font whenever you create a new document to be printed on the selected printer. Unless you use several different printers, you're all set.

If you use several printers, choose File⇨Print, click on the Select button and then on the Printer Create/Edit button, and choose a printer. Click on the Setup button and then on the Initial Font button, and set the font in the Printer Initial Font dialog box.

Refer to Chapter 6 to find out how to change fonts within a document.

Zooming Around in Your Documents

Maybe we're just getting old. Or, the lightbulb in the desk lamp may be getting dim. Or, it may be our monitor — its phosphors are probably running down, or something. Anyway, when we edit documents in 10-point type, we used to press our noses to the screen to read the teeny-tiny letters WordPerfect uses. After a few visits to the chiropractor, we realized that something had to be done.

Then we found WordPerfect's Zoom feature. You can blow up the text on your screen as much as you want without changing its size on the printed page. These steps show you how:

1. **Choose View⇨Zoom.**

   WordPerfect displays the Zoom dialog box.

2. **Choose one of the percentages listed in the dialog box.**

   The larger the percentage, the bigger the text looks onscreen (as though you were sticking your face closer to it). If you don't like any of the options WordPerfect offers, click on Other and enter the percentage you want (we like 120 percent).

3. Choose OK.

 If you prefer the toolbar to the menu bar, click on the Zoom button, which displays some percentages; then click on one of the selections on the list that drops down.

In addition to numerical percentages, the Zoom dialog box contains these four options:

✔ **Margin Width:** Blows up the text until it fills the window from side to side, with the left margin against the left edge of the window and the right margin against the right edge. This option automatically zooms the document to the maximum percentage that allows you to see the full width of your text.

✔ **Page Width:** Blows up the page until it fills the window from side to side, including the left and right margins. The left edge of the paper is just inside the left edge of the window, and the right edge is just inside the right edge. You see a little space between the edge of the paper and the edge of the window. This option always gives you a smaller zoom percentage than Margin Width does.

✔ **Full Page:** Shrinks the page until it fills the window from top to bottom. The top edge of the paper is near the top edge of the window, and the bottom edge of the paper is near the bottom edge of the window. If you use normal paper in its normal orientation so that the paper is taller than it is wide, Full Page produces a rather small (not to say unreadable) image, although it gives you the overall effect of the page.

✔ **Other:** Allows you to set any zoom percentage you want to use (up to 400 percent, anyway).

 If you use zooming to increase the size of the text on the screen and you still cannot read it, save your document (or documents); then get a clean damp handkerchief and wipe all the dust off the front of your monitor. Something about the way computer screens work creates static electricity that attracts dust from all over your house. There! Isn't that better?

 There's one problem with using a large zoom percentage: a zoom percentage bigger than what you get with the Margin Width option. Most documents get so wide that you cannot see an entire line of text. Having to scroll left and right to read each line of the document is annoying. Here's an alternative to using Zoom percentages: Set the Zoom to Margin Width, and at the beginning of your document, switch to a large font size, such as 12 or 14 points. WordPerfect reformats the document (at least, up to the next font-size code) by using larger characters, and it wraps the text to fit within the margins.

Now you can read it just fine. When you print the document, on the other hand, the text is enormous. To fix it, delete the font-size code you just added. (Refer to Chapter 9 to find out how to use the Reveal Codes window to delete a formatting code.)

Setting Your Preferences

The process of teaching WordPerfect how to behave is generally simple: You tell WordPerfect your preferences, and it whips into line. Wouldn't it be nice if everyone worked this way (especially your teenager)?

You tell WordPerfect what you want by using the Preferences command (over there in the little WordPerfect program window), which displays the Preferences dialog box, as shown in Figure 19-1.

Figure 19-1: Wow! A dialog box with lots of little pictures?

This dialog box has nifty little icons — rather than the dull, boring boxes and buttons you see in most dialog boxes — for the different types of preferences you can express:

- **Display:** What WordPerfect displays onscreen, including what the ruler includes; how the Reveal Codes window looks; and whether you want to see symbols where your spaces, tabs, and returns are. We describe these settings in detail in the section "Changing the Way WordPerfect Looks" later in this chapter.

- **Environment:** Miscellaneous stuff that didn't fit into any of the other preference categories.

- **Files:** Where WordPerfect stores your documents, templates, macros, and other files; and whether you want it to keep backups of your files. This stuff is described later in this chapter.

- **Summary:** How document summaries work and when you want to see them (if ever).

✔ **Application Bar:** What information to display along the bottom of each document window, in addition to the font and general appearance you prefer. Read on for more information.

✔ **Keyboard:** Change what each of the keys on your keyboard does.

✔ **Font:** Change some font attributes, such as the sizes of Small and Large fonts.

✔ **Convert:** Some advanced settings that tell WordPerfect how to convert graphics files, ASCII delimited-text files, and other formats.

✔ **Colors:** Change the colors of the text, background, menus, and dialog boxes.

✔ **Print:** A few miscellaneous print settings (most notably, number of copies, print quality, and print color).

Yikes! This list presents an unbelievable number of things to think about. The scary part is that you can control how all these things work. Does that give you a feeling of power? It gives us a feeling of stark terror — think of all the things we could break!

To use the Preferences dialog box to express your preferences, click on the icon of your choice; it displays one or more dialog boxes. When you dismiss the dialog boxes, you return to the Preferences dialog box. When you finish fooling with WordPerfect's innards, click on the Close button in the Preferences dialog box.

The rest of this chapter explains how to change some of the settings in the Preferences dialog box and why you would want to. Don't worry — you can always change them back.

Changing too many things at the same time is a bad idea. When you're fooling around with settings, make one or two changes and then close all dialog boxes. Look around in WordPerfect to see what you have done.

Changing the Way WordPerfect Looks

As you have noticed, WordPerfect displays a zillion gizmos onscreen. These steps show some things you may want to change and instructions for changing them. All these settings appear in the Display Preferences dialog box, which you display by following these steps:

1. **Choose Preferences in the program window to display the Preferences dialog box.**

2. **Click on the Display icon.**

   You see the Display Preferences dialog box, as shown in Figure 19-2.

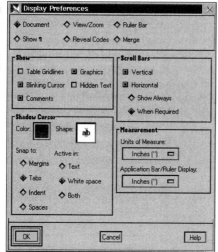

Figure 19-2:
Click on a
setting at
the top of
the Display
Preferences
dialog box
to control
what the
rest of the
dialog box
displays —
then pick
your
preferences.

WordPerfect has so many categories of display settings that it displays a box at the top of the dialog box for each type. If you choose Document, Show ¶, View/Zoom, Reveal Codes, Ruler Bar, or Merge, the rest of the dialog box changes to show settings that pertain to that subject.

Zooming

We always end up zooming in our documents a little because the usual 100 percent display is a tad too small for us to read comfortably. How annoying to have to do that every time we open a document! Instead, you can tell WordPerfect once and for all which zoom percentage you want to use. While you're at it, you can tell WordPerfect which view you usually want to see: draft or page.

Follow these steps to tell WordPerfect how you want to zoom:

1. **Choose Preferences in the program window and click on the Display icon.**

   WordPerfect shows you the Display Preferences dialog box.

2. **Click on the View/Zoom option at the top of the Display Preferences dialog box.**

   WordPerfect shows two groups of settings: Default View and Default Zoom.

3. **Choose a Default view (Draft or Page).**

4. **Choose a Default zoom.**

   You see the same options listed earlier in this chapter.

5. **Click on OK and then click on the Close button to escape from the world of dialog boxes.**

When you close the Preferences dialog box, WordPerfect changes the zoom of the current window to the one you just specified. Whenever you open a document or create a new one, WordPerfect uses this zoom percentage. You can still change the zoom for individual documents as necessary.

Displaying spaces, tabs, indents, and returns

Seeing exactly which characters are in your text can be useful. After all, spaces, tabs, and indent characters all leave blank spaces in your text, although they behave very differently. If you want to be nosy about this stuff, you can ask WordPerfect to display little gizmos where your spaces, tabs, indents, and returns appear.

To see the characters in your text, follow these steps:

1. **Choose Preferences in the program window and click on the Display icon.**

   WordPerfect shows the Display Preferences dialog box.

2. **Click on the Show ¶ option.**

   WordPerfect displays options for showing nonprinting symbols.

3. **If you want to see gizmos for these characters all the time, choose Show Symbols on New and Current Document.**

   If you get sick of them, you can always turn off the symbols by choosing View⇨Show ¶.

4. **Unselect the boxes next to items for which you don't want to see symbols.**

   To unselect a box, click on the setting on the Symbols to Display list. Displaying a special symbol for each and every space in your document, for example, can look ridiculous. (We turn off the display of spaces.)

5. **Click on the OK button and then click on the Close button in the Preferences dialog box.**

   Your document is suddenly littered with little arrows, paragraph marks, and other gizmos. (If you didn't choose Show Symbols on New and Current Documents in Step 3, you must choose View⇨Show ¶ to display this effect.)

Alternatively, you can use the Reveal Codes window to see all your codes —
not just the spaces, tabs, indents, and returns. Refer to Chapter 9 for details.

Changing your colors

WordPerfect normally displays your documents in a realistic but potentially
eye-tiring black-on-white color scheme. It also uses a conservative gray color
for its menus and windows background. Nothing is wrong with that setup,
although perhaps you would rather have something more lively (and probably
distracting), like fuschia. You may be glad to hear that you can change these
colors.

To change screen colors, follow these steps:

1. **Choose Preferences in the program window and then click on the
   Colors icon.**

   WordPerfect displays the Color Preferences dialog box, as shown in
   Figure 19-3 (the colors look much nicer on the screen). At the top of the
   dialog box is a list of *color schemes,* predefined sets of colors that some
   color-challenged person at WordPerfect thought looked good. WP Grey
   is the scheme we show in the figures in this book.

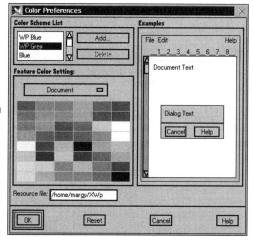

Figure 19-3:
Choose the
colors for
the various
parts of the
WordPerfect
windows.

2. **Choose a color scheme by clicking on one of the names on the Color
   Scheme List.**

   To show you what the color scheme looks like, the right side of the dialog
   box shows a miniature window that illustrates the colors in the scheme.

   Look at the color schemes to see which one you dislike least.

You can make your own color schemes, too: click on an item in the picture of the miniature window (the name of the item you clicked on appears in the Feature Color Setting section) and use the color grid to choose a color for the item. If the situation and the screen get ugly, you can always click on Cancel.

3. **Click on OK to leave the Color Preferences dialog box.**

   WordPerfect displays a dialog box telling you that your color changes will take effect after restarting WordPerfect.

4. **Click on the OK button and then click on the Close button in the Preferences dialog box.**

To see your new colors, exit WordPerfect and rerun it. You can spend all day getting your screen colors just right (and many people have). The key consideration is how your eyes feel at the end of the day.

Where Does WordPerfect Put Your Files?

You have a hard disk, and heaven knows how many files are on it. Through the miracle of directories (described in Chapter 13), you don't have to look at all of them whenever you decide to pop open a document. The vast majority of files on your disk probably are program files, which you would just as soon never see.

Telling WordPerfect about directories and backups

To tell WordPerfect where you want to store your documents in general (you can always choose different directories for some documents) as well as when to make automatic backups of your documents, follow these steps:

1. **Choose Preferences in the program window and then click on the Files icon.**

   WordPerfect displays the Files Preferences dialog box, as shown in Figure 19-4. The Documents/Backup box is selected, so the dialog box shows the settings that have to do with documents and backups.

2. **To indicate where you want your documents stored, enter a directory name in the Default Directory box.**

   If this box is empty, the default is your Linux home directory. You can type a directory name here or click the little folder icon on the right side to access the File Manager dialog box. The file manager helps you browse through your directories to find the one you're looking for.

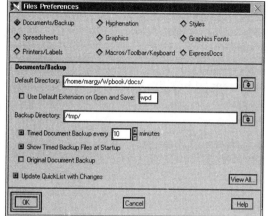

Figure 19-4:
Where do
you want to
store your
WordPerfect
files?

3. **To tell WordPerfect that you want all new documents to have the file extension** wpd, **select the Use Default Extension on Open and Save option.**

   WordPerfect suggests the extension wpd, and we do, too. You can change it, though.

4. **To make a backup copy of your open documents at regular intervals, choose Timed Document Backup every nine minutes.**

   This step tells WordPerfect to save copies of all open documents every so often. If the power goes out or you kick the computer's plug out of the outlet, this option is a godsend. To find out how to get these files back if you need them, see the section "Getting back your timed backups," later in this chapter.

   You can change the number of minutes in the box between the words every and minutes. This number specifies how often WordPerfect makes the backups.

5. **To prevent WordPerfect from accidentally replacing good files with bad ones, choose Original Document Backup.**

   If this option is selected when you save a document, WordPerfect renames, rather than deletes, the old version. The program renames these backup documents by using the file extension bak.

   If you mess up a document irretrievably and then compound your error by saving it, this setting prevents WordPerfect from deleting the preceding version of the document. You can close the document without saving it again and then open the bak version of the document.

6. **If you use templates, click on the ExpressDocs button at the top of the dialog box.**

You can change the directory in which WordPerfect looks for your templates. (Refer to Chapter 17 for a description of using templates.) If you want to use the WordPerfect built-in templates, which are stored in the default template directory, you may want to leave this setting alone.

7. **If you use graphics or macros, click on the Graphic or Macros/Toolbar/Keyboard box to change the default directories.**

   You probably are better off leaving them alone, though. Why mess with success?

8. **Click on the OK button and then click on Close to get rid of all these dialog boxes.**

   WordPerfect puts your changes into effect (invisibly).

Getting back your timed backups

If WordPerfect crashes and you use timed backups as described in the preceding section, listen up. The next time you run WordPerfect, it notifies you if timed backup files are lying around. If you had several documents open, you may have several of those files.

WordPerfect displays a Timed Backup dialog box with the message that a backup file exists. The Timed Backup dialog box offers two choices:

- **Continue:** Ignores the backup file, but does not delete it. It's still there, and the Timed Backup dialog box reappears the next time you start WordPerfect.
- **File Manager:** Opens the File Manager dialog box with the backup file shown.

If you choose File Manager, you have the opportunity to decide what to do with the backup file. In the File Manager dialog box, highlight the backup file by clicking on it. At this point, you have three choices — wait a minute. First, you have two choices: Continue or File Manager. If and only if you choose File Manager, you have three more choices:

- **Open:** Your best choice; opens the backup file in WordPerfect. You can look at the file to determine whether you want it or whether it's an incomplete version of a document you saved before the crash. You may want to open the copy you saved in the regular way, compare it with the backup, and see which version you want to keep. If you want to save the file, choose File➪Save or File➪Save As to save it under a specific name in a specific folder. If you don't want to save the file, choose File➪Close.

▶ **Rename:** Tells WordPerfect to store the backup files in an out-of-the-way place (usually in your /tmp directory) with a name you specify.

▶ **Delete:** The option to choose if you're sure that you don't want the backup file. It's hard to imagine why you would want to choose this option, though. Why not open the backup file, just to be sure?

If you choose to open the file or if you rename it and then open it, see whether it's the latest version of the document; you may have done some additional work on it after it was saved. Timed backups are usually made every ten minutes, so you may have done nine minutes' worth of editing since the backup was saved. You have to do that work again.

If more than one document was open when WordPerfect bit the dust, repeat the procedure for each file.

Some Cool Environment Preferences

The environment settings are worth looking at — they let you tell WordPerfect how to select words, and (via one of our favorite features) tell it to open documents automatically. Figure 19-5 shows the environment settings you can control.

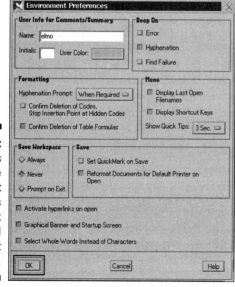

Figure 19-5:
The settings in the Environment Preferences dialog box tell WordPerfect how to work.

Finding where you left off

WordPerfect gives you two ways to easily find where you left off:

- ✔ Create a bookmark where your cursor is when you save a document.
- ✔ Save the entire workspace, including multiple documents and cursor positions, which are restored the next time you open WordPerfect.

To tell WordPerfect to create a *QuickMark,* a special bookmark, at the spot where your cursor is when you save a document, follow these steps:

1. **Choose Tools⇨Bookmark.**

   You see the Bookmark dialog box we introduce in Chapter 18. Two check boxes are at the bottom of this dialog box.

2. **Make sure that the Set QuickMark on file save box is checked.**

   Every time you save a document, WordPerfect creates a special book-mark (the QuickMark) at the place you were typing when you saved the document. This step isn't tremendously useful unless you also complete Step 3.

3. **Make sure that the Go to QuickMark on file open box is checked.**

   Now you've done something useful: Every time you open your docu-ment, you're right back where you were when you saved it. Nice feature.

You can tell WordPerfect to save your entire workspace (all the documents you had open in WordPerfect and their arrangement). (We talk all about this subject in Chapter 12.) You do this trick from the Environment Preferences dialog box. WordPerfect has another nifty feature that opens WordPerfect to look exactly like it did when you exited. You can have multiple documents open, with the cursor where you left it in each document when you exited.

To turn this feature on, follow these steps:

1. **Choose Preferences in the program window and click on the Environment icon.**

   The Environment Preferences dialog box appears (refer to Figure 19-5).

2. **In the Save Workspace section, change the setting to Always.**

   If you prefer, you can change the setting to Prompt on Exit, which means that WordPerfect asks every time whether you want to save your workspace.

3. **Click on OK to close the dialog box and Close to close the Preferences dialog box.**

From now on, WordPerfect always opens the documents you had open when you last closed it. In each document, the cursor is where it was when you closed WordPerfect.

Controlling mouse selection

You may have noticed that WordPerfect assumes that when you're selecting text with the mouse, you want whole words. So, the selection often jumps to include the whole word when you really want only part of it. For most people most of the time, this feature is useful — although it may drive you bonkers. Here's how to turn it off:

1. **Choose Preferences in the program window and click on the Environment icon.**

2. **Clear the Select Whole Words Instead of Characters box.**

3. **Click on OK and then on Close.**

Assigning Different Meanings to Keys

WordPerfect has been around a long time. (The first versions of WordPerfect were before Linux, before Windows, and even before DOS. Not before UNIX, though.) As the world of software settled on certain standards for what all the keys on the keyboard should mean, the folks at WordPerfect were in a quandary. Older versions of WordPerfect had always used the F3 key to display online help, for example, and WordPerfect users the world over were used to it. Now the world of software, especially the world of Windows users, agrees that F1 — not F3 — is the key to use. What to do?

The answer: Wimp out and try to please everyone. WordPerfect gives you the opportunity to tell it which set of keyboard meanings you want to use: the old-fashioned WordPerfect meanings (WPDOS) or the newfangled standard meanings (called XWP8). These sets of meanings are stored as keyboard definitions.

Keyboard definitions don't usually affect most keys on the keyboard. The Q key on your keyboard put a Q on the screen, regardless of which keyboard definition you use (unless you create your own definition and get really perverse). The keyboard definition, however, controls the meanings of the function keys and which keys do what when you hold down Ctrl and Alt.

As we mention in the introduction of this book, all instructions in this book assume that you're a modern, 20th century kind of person and that you're using the newfangled standard meanings of the keys (the WPWin keyboard definitions). The following steps show how you can check this out:

1. **Choose Preferences from the program window and click on the Keyboard icon.**

   WordPerfect displays the Keyboard Preferences dialog box, as shown in Figure 19-6. Seven keyboards are listed: the EquationEditor (forget about this one unless you're a mathematician), WPWin8 (useful if you're used to Windows keyboard conventions), and five other keyboard layouts. The most useful is named XWP8; it's also the default keyboard. The one that's highlighted is the one you're using.

Figure 19-6: Which keyboard layout do you prefer?

2. **Click on the Cancel button to leave your keyboard setting alone and click on the Close button in the Preferences dialog box.**

   Get the heck out of this dialog box before you change anything!

Most people use the XWP8 keyboard because it makes the keys use UNIX-standard meanings. This list shows some reasons to use some of the more old-fashioned keyboards:

- ✔ You have upgraded from an older version of WordPerfect and don't want to learn any new habits. (Who does?)

- ✔ You work in an office with lots of people who use the WPDOS or WPWin keyboard, and you want to be able to swap WordPerfect techniques with them.

- ✔ You love pain.

Chapter 20

Don't Panic! Read This Chapter!

. . . .

In This Chapter

▶ "Where's WordPerfect?"

▶ "Where's my document?"

▶ "Where am I?"

▶ "The entire document is boldface!"

▶ "The screen looks weird!"

▶ "My document isn't printing!"

▶ "Yikes! I didn't mean to delete that!"

▶ "They can't open my document!"

▶ "WordPerfect's not listening to me!"

▶ "Timed backup files exist?"

. . . .

A s long as you have this trusty book by your side, nothing should go wrong while you're using WordPerfect. The IRS should never audit your tax returns, of course, and your toast should never burn.

So much for living in a perfect world. This chapter describes some things that just may, once in a while, perhaps, happen to you or to someone you know.

"Where's WordPerfect?" (Part 1)

"Hmm. . . . I know it was here yesterday. Where is WordPerfect on my menus or on my desktop?"

WordPerfect usually hangs out on the menu your window manager displays when you click the button in the lower-left corner of the screen (equivalent to the Windows 98 Start button). Exactly *where* it appears on those menus depends on how you or your Linux guru installed WordPerfect. Nose around the menus — if it isn't there, ask your Linux guru to help you find it.

If you always run WordPerfect when you use your computer, you may want to tell Linux to run it automatically when your window manager starts. Exactly how it all works depends on your window manager — again, ask your local Linux wizard to set it up for you.

"Where's WordPerfect?" (Part II)

Another way for you to lose WordPerfect is for it to vanish before your very eyes. You're working away and you click on something — probably something in the upper-right corner of the WordPerfect window. Blammo — without so much as a puff of smoke, the entire WordPerfect document window disappears and takes your document with it.

You probably clicked on either the Minimize button or the Close button.

In KDE, the Minimize button is the leftmost of the three tiny buttons in the upper-right corner of the WordPerfect document window; the button has a little dot at the bottom of it. Clicking on this button freeze-dries WordPerfect into a button, which appears somewhere along the top of the screen. If you see the WordPerfect button, click on it to bring WordPerfect back to life. Is it still breathing? Pulse steady? Whew!

The Close button is the rightmost of the three tiny buttons in the upper-right corner of the WordPerfect document window; in KDE, the button has an X on it. Clicking on the Close button is just as easy as clicking on the Minimize button. If WordPerfect disappeared without protest, however, you must have just saved your open document before you closed it up by mistake. If you mistakenly closed your document window, the WordPerfect program window should still be on your desktop or on the taskbar. Simply switch to the WordPerfect program window and reopen your documents; they should be on the list of recently opened documents, at the bottom of the Program menu.

If you click on the Close button in the WordPerfect program window, the whole program stops running and WordPerfect closes any document windows you have open (after asking whether you want to save any documents you've edited). Run WordPerfect again, open your documents, and you're ready to roll!

"Where's My Document?" (Part I)

Uh-oh. You want to open that important report so that you can do some more work on it and you see no sign of it on your disk. Looks as though it ran off with that cute little memo you wrote yesterday. Call in the bloodhounds.

First, however, try looking around. You probably saved the document with a different name or in a different directory. Try the tricks in this list:

- Click on the Program menu in the WordPerfect program window, and see whether the document you want is at the bottom of the menu. (It may be if you used it recently.)

- Use the File⇨Open command in a document window or the Program⇨ Open Window command in the program window, and look in the directory in which you thought you left the document. Oh, yeah . . . you probably already tried this trick.

- While you're in the Open dialog box, look in some other directories you use.

- Consider the possibility that you used the wrong name when you saved the document. You never know when a brain spasm may strike.

- Use the QuickFinder button in the Open dialog box. This feature can look in all files on your hard disk (or in selected directories) and search for some text that you know is in your document. For directions, see the section in Chapter 13 about finding a file with a forgotten name.

- Use the Linux `find` command. This option is for only the strong of heart because the `find` command is one of the most confusing in Linux. Briefly, if you know how to open an xterm window so that you can enter Linux ("shell") commands, type a command like this:

```
find /home/margy -name zucchini-bread -print
```

This command tells Linux to start searching in the `/home/margy` directory, looking at the names of the files, for a file named `zucchini-bread`. Don't forget the *–print* at the end or else Linux doesn't display the filenames it finds. Linux also searches the subdirectories of the directory you specify. You can use an asterisk (*) in the filename as a wildcard character; if you do, however, enclose the filename in single quotes, like this:

```
find /home/margy -name 'zucchini*' -print
```

"Where's My Document?" (Part II)

Here's another twist on losing a document. You open the document and work on it diligently. Then you click on something (you're not sure what), and zip — your document vanishes.

You may have minimized your document accidentally. WordPerfect, as part of its capability to edit multiple documents at the same time, lets you temporarily shrink your document to the size of a postage stamp while you work on other documents, by using the Minimize button in the document window. See the section "Where's WordPerfect? (Part II)," earlier in this chapter.

"Where Am I?"

You click on something and find yourself in the unexplored reaches of your document. Where are you, and how do you get back to where you were?

Luckily, WordPerfect has a "go back to where I was a minute ago" command; it's in the Go To dialog box. Follow these steps to go back to where you were:

1. **Press Ctrl+G.**

   You see the Go To dialog box, described in the section "Go To Where?" in Chapter 3.

2. **Click on Last Position on the Position list.**

   This location is the "where I was a minute ago" place.

3. **Click on OK.**

   WordPerfect zips your cursor back to where it was just before the last search or Go To command.

If this technique doesn't work, try searching for a word or phrase that appears near where you were editing. Choose the Edit➪Find and Replace command or press F2 to display the Find and Replace Text dialog box. (Chapter 5 describes searching in detail.)

"The Entire Document Is Boldface!"

Or, it's in italics or in a weird font. The WordPerfect character-formatting commands can get out of hand sometimes. The usual way to format some text (as we explain in Chapter 6) is to select the text first and then do the formatting. This method tells WordPerfect to insert a secret code to start the special formatting at the beginning of the selected text and to insert another code at the end of the selected text to turn off the formatting.

If your codes get bollixed up, your carefully chosen formatting can be applied to the entire document rather than to just a small selection of text.

Use the Reveal Codes window (by choosing View➪Reveal Codes) to check for the code or codes that turn on the formatting. (Chapter 9 explains how to use the Reveal Codes window.) When you find the offending code, delete it. Then try applying your formatting again.

"The Screen Looks Weird!"

The WordPerfect window usually looks weird, and so does Linux, so it's nothing to worry about. If the screen looks even weirder than normal, this list shows some things you can try:

- Choose View⇨Zoom, and select a reasonable zoom size. (Chapter 19 describes zooming, for you zoom freaks.)

- Use the Reveal Codes window (choose View⇨Reveal Codes) to check for bizarre codes that may have arrived from outer space (refer to Chapter 9). If you see a code you don't like the looks of, delete it. (Saving your document under a different name first is a good idea.)

- Close your document and open it again. Maybe it will feel better.

- Exit WordPerfect, and run it again. This step may exorcise the cooties that inhabited it.

- Exit your window manager, or even Linux itself, and run it again. This step is necessary only when the situation is serious. To exit KDE, press Ctrl+Alt+Backspace or click the K button in the lower-left corner of the screen and choose Logout from the menu that appears.

- Exit Linux and go out for a walk. Who knows — maybe your eyeballs flipped out and need a rest.

- Sell your computer and go into another line of work, such as flower arranging.

"My Document Isn't Printing!"

You click on the cute little Print button on the toolbar or use some other method to tell WordPerfect that you want it to arrange some ink tastefully on some paper. Is that such an unreasonable thing to ask?

In the world of computers, arranging ink certainly can be complicated. Chapter 11 describes the sometime tortuous path your document can take from WordPerfect to your printer.

Here's the key thing: If the printer doesn't print anything, don't just try printing again. Your document may still be en route to the printer (especially if you used extensive formatting or graphics). If you issue another Print command, you probably will end up with two copies. Instead, figure out where your document got stuck.

This list shows some things to try when your document doesn't print:

- Make sure that the printer is on and online.

- Tell Linux to cancel printing the document so that you can start over. How this process works depends on your window manager. In KDE, click on the Printer icon on the desktop. You see a window with a list of print jobs that are waiting to print or actually printing. (Refer to Chapter 11 for more information.)

- If you use a network, the problem undoubtedly can be blamed on it. Ask other computer users in your office whether they can print on the printer you want to use. You may have to talk to your network administrator. Ask such questions as "How can I tell whether my print job is in the queue?" and "Can you make sure that my system is attached to the right printer?" Who knows — the joke memo you just finished writing may be printing on the fancy printer in the executive suite!

- It's worth checking into silly, pedestrian problems, such as the printer cable's falling out the back of either the printer or the computer. If the cable has detached itself, you should shut down WordPerfect, the window manager, Linux, the computer, and the printer before reconnecting the cable. Electricity is your friend, although you may as well play it safe.

"Yikes! I Didn't Mean to Delete That!"

The finger is quicker than the brain, especially when it's heading straight for a key that deletes something. In WordPerfect, as in all powerful word processing programs, blowing away hours or weeks of work is horrifyingly easy.

If you have just deleted some text, you can bring it right back by pressing Ctrl+Z. (Choosing Edit⇨Undo works, too.) If you've done some things since you deleted your text, you may have to press Ctrl+Z a number of times. You can always do your edits again, however. Reconstructing deleted text from memory can be trickier.

If you just deleted an entire document by selecting it in the Open or Save dialog box and then pressing Delete, you have a more serious problem. Few Linux systems have a way to undelete a file. This list shows some approaches to take after you delete something accidentally:

- Your system may have a trashcan or recycle bin where deleted files go to wait for final deletion. If you see a Trash or Recycling icon on your desktop, click on it and see what happens. In KDE, clicking on the Trash icon displays the Desktop/Trash directory stored in your home directory. The directory may contain the file you deleted. If it does, undelete your document by moving it back into the directory where you want it. (Refer to Chapter 13 to find out how to move files.)

✔ If you told WordPerfect to keep the preceding version of your documents, you can retrieve it and enter all the changes you made since you saved that version. This process is tedious but better than typing everything again. Chapter 19 tells you how to tell WordPerfect to keep backups. Backups of your documents have the same names as the documents, although they use the file extension BAK.

✔ If you told WordPerfect to make timed backups of documents you're editing and if you were just editing the document you deleted, the timed backup may still be around. Choose File➪Open and go to the folder where WordPerfect has been putting your backup files (usually \tmp; Chapter 13 explains how to move to a different directory). Look for a file named something like wp_bk1.637_margy (if your name were Margy, anyway) and open it immediately. If it's the file you want, save it in another directory and use another filename. If it isn't the file you want, try files that have a different number in the filename.

✔ In the worst case, dredge around in your wastepaper basket and find the last version of the document you printed. Typing the document all over again is a tremendous waste of time, although we usually find that in the process, we improve it considerably. (Maybe we should have deleted all the files that contained the chapters of this book!)

"They Can't Open My Document!"

You create a marvelous document and copy it to a disk to give to your co-worker Fred. Because Fred also uses WordPerfect, you figure that he should be able to open the file right up and edit it. (Not that it needs any editing, of course — your prose is too pristine and luminescent to be improved.)

You hear, rather than oohs and ahhs, gnashing and grinding of teeth emanating from Fred's office. "This WordPerfect document is no good," he reports. No good? That document is Pulitzer-prize material, you think. It turns out that Fred never even got to lay his eyes on your finest prose to-date because his version of WordPerfect refused to open your document.

Back in the bad old days, every version of WordPerfect stored documents in its own, slightly idiosyncratic format. Luckily, newer versions of WordPerfect can *always* read the formats of earlier versions. Beginning with Version 6, WordPerfect for DOS and WordPerfect for Windows use the same format, and WordPerfect Versions 7, 8, and 9 have continued the trend so that all versions of WordPerfect starting with WordPerfect 6 use the same format. (Tell that to your friends who use Microsoft Word, which seems to use a new format for each new version of the program!)

You can run into a problem if you give one of your WordPerfect documents to someone who uses an older, inferior version of WordPerfect, such as WordPerfect 5.1 or 5.2. To prevent problems, you can save your document in a format that one of these older programs can read.

To save your document in an older format, choose File⇨Save As or press F3. In the Save As dialog box, type a new filename so that you don't replace the version you saved in regular WordPerfect 6/7/8 format. In the File Format box, down in the Save Options part of the dialog box, select WordPerfect 4.2, WordPerfect 5.0, or WordPerfect 5.1/5.2. Then click OK. If you want to be able to give the document to someone who uses Microsoft Word or another word processor, select Rich Text Format (RTF).

Now you can give this new document — in a moldy old WordPerfect format — to your friend Fred and see what else he can find to complain about!

"WordPerfect's Not Listening to Me!"

You try choosing a command from a menu. Nothing happens. You try clicking on a button on the Property Bar or toolbar. Nothing. You click the right mouse button. No QuickMenu. Hmmm. WordPerfect must be deliberately and maliciously ignoring you. Maybe it's taking its afternoon siesta.

If you cannot get WordPerfect's attention, your first inclination may be to pound on the keyboard, shout at it, or slap it around. For technical reasons too complex to explain here, we recommend the shouting approach (assuming that you're responsible for paying for a broken keyboard and that you're not interested in breaking your hand on the side of the monitor).

After you get your frustrations out, follow these steps:

1. **Try talking to your window manager.**

   Try switching to another program by clicking on a button on the window manager's taskbar. Or, click in the window of another program. Or, click your window manager's "start" button (the K button if you use KDE). If no menu appears, your window manager is incommunicado. (This situation occurs *much* less frequently — hardly ever — in the Linux world than in Windows.) Try exiting your window manager (press Ctrl+Alt+ Backspace in most window managers) and logging back in.

2. **Make sure that your mouse and keyboard cables are securely connected.**

3. **If nothing else works, wait about five minutes.**

   Maybe some part of your computer system is so busy doing something that it hasn't had a chance to respond to you. You never know.

If talking to your window manager doesn't help, even after five minutes, it's time for serious violence. Time to bash some bits! Unfortunately, this technique blows away WordPerfect and the documents you opened. With luck, you saved your documents recently or you use timed backups (refer to Chapter 19). If you can switch to other applications, close them now in the traditional way. Unlike Windows, Linux lets you kill one "console" and the programs you're running there, without having to restart Linux entirely.

Follow these steps when WordPerfect is out to lunch:

1. **Press Ctrl+Alt+F1 to switch to a Linux shell.**

   Many versions of Linux support *multiple consoles,* so you can be logged in as several people at the same time. To switch among the various consoles, you press Ctrl+Alt, and a function key: For example, Ctrl+Alt+F1 switches you to the first console. Only one console can run a window manager, which is the seventh console, at Ctrl+Alt+F7.

2. **Press Ctrl+Alt+Del to shut down Linux.**

   Turning off your computer without shutting down Linux can confuse it seriously, so it's important to press Ctrl+Alt+Del before you give up on your computer and press the Reset button. Ctrl+Alt+Del runs the shutdown program, and you see lots and lots of messages about programs shutting down. Then your computer restarts and Linux comes back to life.

3. **Log back in, run WordPerfect, and see what it looks like.**

   If WordPerfect keeps backups of your files, you may not lose *too* much of your work. Refer to Chapter 19 to find out whether WordPerfect is configured to keep backups.

"Timed Backup Files Exist?"

If WordPerfect crashes (or another program crashes and takes WordPerfect with it) or if you turn off your computer while WordPerfect is running or if lightning strikes your house and causes a temporary blackout, WordPerfect doesn't get a chance to do the housekeeping chores it usually does when you exit. One of these chores is deleting the timed backup files it creates (assuming that you use timed backups; refer to Chapter 19).

The next time you run WordPerfect, you see the Timed Backup dialog box with the message that WordPerfect has discovered the timed backup copy of one or more of your documents — probably one of the documents you were editing when WordPerfect went west.

These timed backup files can be a godsend if you did a bunch of editing and didn't save your document before disaster struck. See the section in Chapter 19 about getting back your timed backups to find out how to use timed backup files to recover from these types of disasters.

Part VI
The Part of Tens

The 5th Wave By Rich Tennant

"MY GOD, YOU'VE DONE IT! MILLIONS OF MICROSCOPIC SLINKY TOYS MOVING ACROSS CIRCUITS AT THE SPEED OF LIGHT FORMING THE FIRST SLINKY OPERATING SYSTEM!"

In this part . . .

Y ou would think that humanity by now would have gotten beyond its fascination with tens. Yes, it's an utterly amazing fact that we have ten fingers and ten toes. Big deal. If you count on your fingers in base 2, you can count to 1,023, but do you see "1,023 Ways to Please Your Spouse" in *Reader's Digest*? No.

So, because we seem to be stuck with ten, here's The Part of Tens. This part provides more-or-less useful facts so small that they would get lost if they didn't have a place of their own. We easily could have named the tens "1,023 Ways. . . ." Our environmental sensitivities, however, don't allow us to waste that many trees. So take off your mittens and count along with us as we explore the fascinating world of WordPerfect trivia.

Chapter 21

The Ten Commandments of WordPerfect

In This Chapter

▶ Tell WordPerfect what you have in mind

▶ Do not use extra spaces or tabs

▶ Do not keep pressing Enter to begin a new page

▶ Do not number your pages manually

▶ Save early and often

▶ Save before using the Edit⇨Find and Replace command

▶ Back up your work

▶ Do not turn off your PC until you log off from Linux

▶ Turn on the printer before printing documents

▶ Always keep printer supplies on hand

*O*kay, you unbelievers. You don't have to follow the rules explained in this chapter — just don't blame us if lightning strikes you (or, more likely, strikes somewhere near your office and knocks the power out, destroying your valuable documents)!

Tell WordPerfect What You Have in Mind

You have to tell WordPerfect what you want for your document. If you want multiple columns, use the WordPerfect Columns feature. If you want wide margins, tell WordPerfect to widen them by dragging the margin guidelines around or by using the Format⇨Margins command. Don't think that these types of tasks would be easier to do if you skip all that and just use extra hard returns, spaces, or tabs to put text where you want it. This method always means extra work in the long run when you edit your text.

The WordPerfect word-wrap feature, for example, enables the program to begin a new line whenever it sees you getting perilously close to the right margin. In the mind of WordPerfect (such as it is), a bunch of text that ends with an Enter is a paragraph, so type your paragraphs like that and let WordPerfect do the rest of the work. Don't press Enter until you get to the end of a paragraph (refer to Chapter 1 for more information).

Do Not Use Extra Spaces or Tabs

In high school, your typing teacher taught you to type two spaces after each period. Other than that, you should never type more than one space consecutively (with rare exceptions). If you want to move across a line and leave some white space, use tabs. (Refer to Chapter 7 to find out how to set tab stops and use different types of tabs.)

In the world of typesetting, which includes proportionally spaced fonts, it's considered good form to type only one space after each period. Somehow, after text is typeset, it looks fine. We can understand, though, if your ingrained two-space habits are too hard to break. WordPerfect is willing to help you out here. Choose the Tools⇨QuickCorrect command and click on the Format-As-You-Go box at the top of the QuickCorrect dialog box. In the End of Sentence section, you see some correction options, including one named Change two spaces to one space between sentences. If you check that option, WordPerfect deals with all this space nonsense for you.

Incidentally, if you're using tabs to create something that looks like a table, adjust the tab stops so that you use one tab for each column. This technique enables you to press Tab just once between entries (refer to Chapter 7). Better yet, use the WordPerfect Table feature (refer to Chapter 14); remember the first rule.

Do Not Keep Pressing Enter to Begin a New Page

When you decide to begin a new page, tell WordPerfect so in no uncertain terms: Press Ctrl+Enter. Don't pussyfoot around the issue by pressing Enter repeatedly until you fill the current page with blank lines. This technique is another example of the first commandment in action — if you want a page break, say so. (Chapter 8 explains why the Ctrl+Enter method works best.)

Do Not Number Your Pages Manually

WordPerfect can number pages for you and place the page numbers in the left, center, or right corner of either the top or bottom of the page. What more could you ask? Don't type page numbers yourself; they become a mess if you edit your document and the page breaks move around. Chapter 8 tells you how to number your pages and print other information in headers and footers.

Save Early and Often

Be prepared for disaster! Every time you squirm around in your chair, scratch your foot, or take a sip of coffee, press Ctrl+S to save your document. 'Nuff said. Yes, a timed document backup helps (refer to Chapter 19); are you really willing, though, to lose your past ten minutes or so of work?

Save Before Using the Edit⇨Find and Replace Command

The WordPerfect find-and-replace feature (described in Chapter 5) has awesome power, either to make lots of wonderful updates throughout your document or to trash it big-time. What if you mean to replace *Smith* with *Smythe,* for example, and you type a space by mistake in the Find box just before you click on Replace All? Poof — all the spaces in your document are replaced by *Smythe*. Your important letter has just been transformed into performance art.

Just in case, save your document before you use the Edit⇨Find and Replace command or before you use any other command that makes Big Changes to your document.

Back Up Your Work

Saving is good. Saving your documents on your hard disk doesn't help, however, if your hard disk dies. We don't mean to sound alarmist here, but it can happen. Talk to someone in your office about setting up a backup system for you by using either disks or backup tapes. At least you can use the file manager that comes with your window manager to copy your important documents to floppy disks occasionally. Ask your local Linux guru how to "mount" and "unmount" them: Linux must be told explicitly whenever you stick a floppy disk in your disk drive.

Do Not Turn Off Your PC Until You Exit Linux

Oops — you're running late. Time to go! Don't just turn off your computer. If you turn it off while Linux is still running, you can cause problems. Leave the computer on (just turn off its screen). Many newer computers, in fact, sport the U.S. Department of Energy's EnergyStar logo. Those computers are designed so that they never have to be turned off. Instead, they turn off parts of themselves (or go to sleep, as it's sometimes described) when they're not in use. If you have an EnergyStar screen to go with your EnergyStar computer, you can just walk away without giving it a thought. We do recommend saving your document first, though.

If you prefer to turn off your computer, you have to shut down Linux first. (If you work in an organization, please check with your system administrator so that she can try to talk you into leaving your system on instead.) Log off from Linux by pressing Ctrl+Alt+Backspace. If you're still logged in, you see a Linux prompt. Type **exit** to log off. (On some systems, you can also press Ctrl+D.) Then ask your local Linux guru how to shut down Linux and when it's safe to turn off your computer.

Turn On the Printer Before Printing Documents

If your document refuses to print and you see strange error boxes onscreen, the first things to check are whether your printer is on, whether the online light is on, and whether paper is in the tray. If those checks don't fix things, refer to Chapter 11.

Always Keep Printer Supplies on Hand

Ooh — how does the printer know when you're about to print the final draft of something big? It does somehow, and that's the moment when the ink cartridge runs empty or the toner cartridge ejects its last hiccup of toner. Rats!

Be sure to have extra printing supplies on hand so that you can foil the printer when these things happen. If you use toner cartridges, you can sometimes get a few more pages out of them by removing the cartridge from the printer, dancing around with it wildly (to shake up the toner inside), and putting the cartridge back in. Your officemates will enjoy the show, too.

Chapter 22

Ten Awesome Tricks

In This Chapter

▶ Dragging and dropping text

▶ Returning to where you were

▶ Using QuickMarks and bookmarks

▶ Reopening an earlier document

▶ Inserting the date

▶ Using unbreakable hyphens and spaces

▶ Inserting bullets

▶ Converting tabs to tables

▶ Sending WordPerfect documents by e-mail

▶ Using QuickCorrect to type long phrases automatically

*W*ordPerfect has more awesome tricks than a troupe of acrobatic elephants. Because personal taste varies, however, when it comes to "awesome," we picked out ten tricks that one person may find fabulously useful and another may find completely stupid.

Dragging and Dropping Text

The fastest way to move text within a document is just to highlight it, click on it, and drag it somewhere else.

If you want to move or copy text from one document to another, copy it or cut it to the clipboard by pressing Ctrl+C (for copy) or Ctrl+X (for cut), move to the document and location where you want the text to appear, and press Ctrl+V to paste. You can paste as many copies as you want.

Unlike in Windows and on the Mac, not all X programs share the same clipboard. You can't always use cut and paste commands to copy or move information to or from another program. It's worth a try, though!

Returning to Where You Were

If you're moving around a great deal between two places in your document, being able to switch easily is a nice feature. To go back to where you were, choose the Edit⇨Go To command (or press Ctrl+G). Click on Last Position in the Go To dialog box and then click on OK.

Going Back to the Old Same Place

If you want to keep returning to one important place in your document, try using a QuickMark. Click in that important place and press Ctrl+Shift+Q (or choose Tools⇨Bookmark from the menu and click the Set QuickMark button). Now you can go back there at any time by pressing Ctrl+Q.

If you're dancing around several places in your document, you might try using bookmarks. Highlight a word or phrase unique to that place, such as "little grass shack" (this phrase serves as a name). Choose Tools⇨Bookmark to display the Bookmark dialog box and then click the Create button. Click on OK in the Create Bookmark dialog box to accept the highlighted text as a name. We talk more about this topic in Chapter 18.

To go back to your little grass shack, press Ctrl+G to display the Go To dialog box, select Bookmark, select the name in the Bookmark box, and then click on OK. You can have several bookmarks in a document.

Reopening an Earlier Document

WordPerfect keeps track of the last nine or so documents you worked on. To reopen them, click in the WordPerfect program window (the one with the WordPerfect logo), click on Program on the menu bar, and then click on any document listed at the bottom of the drop-down menu.

Inserting the Date

WordPerfect gives you two — count 'em, two — ways to put today's date in your document. Choose a method:

✔ **Insert today's date as though you had typed it.** Press Ctrl+D, or choose the Insert⇨Date/Time command and click on the Insert button. This command inserts the text of today's date.

✔ **Insert a secret date code that changes to the current date every time you open the document.** Press Ctrl+Shift+D or choose the Insert⇨ Date/Time command, click on the option labeled Keep the inserted date current, and click on the Insert button.

Using the Insert⇨ Date/Time command lets you specify the format of the date. The Date/Time dialog box, as shown in Figure 22-1, lets you choose any format, from European to American to Martian. This command also lets you insert the time, with or without the date.

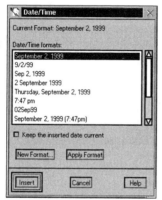

Figure 22-1: Choosing the format of a date and whether the date is updated auto-magically.

Using Unbreakable Hyphens and Spaces

Normally, when you insert a hyphen, WordPerfect takes that action as a license to break the line there, if necessary. This breaking capability is inconvenient for compound terms, such as "Figure 1-17" or phone numbers, such as 555-1212, which should always appear unbroken. For these types of things, you should insert unbreakable *(hard)* hyphens by pressing Ctrl+–. Likewise, you can also insert hard spaces, which prevent a line break between two words, by pressing Ctrl+spacebar.

Chasing Speeding Bullets

To "bulletize" a bunch of paragraphs, select them and choose Insert⇨Bullets & Numbering. You see the Bullets and Numbers dialog box. Select the bullet style you want from the Style list. Then click on OK. Your paragraphs have tasteful (or not so tasteful, depending on what you picked) bullets in front of them.

If you want new paragraphs to be bulleted also, move the cursor just after the last word in the last paragraph that has a bullet on it. Press Enter, and the next paragraph receives a bullet. If you want to see what's really happening, check out the hidden codes, as described in Chapter 9.

You may also notice that your paragraphs are indented. The Bullets and Numbers dialog box has applied a style to your paragraphs. You can edit this style. Use the Insert➪Bullets & Numbering command to bring up the Bullets and Numbers dialog box again. The Edit button on the right side of the box lets you change the formatting of the bullet style you selected. Go crazy. The key to editing styles is in Chapter 10.

Converting Tabs to Tables

Sometimes you wish that you could create a table the old-fashioned way: by using plain old text with tabs in it rather than by choosing the Insert➪Table command and filling in the cells. This capability is also valuable when you're importing unformatted text from some other program, so WordPerfect doesn't know that the text is supposed to be a table.

WordPerfect helps you create a real WordPerfect table from tabular text. Each row of the table-to-be must be a line that ends with a *hard return* (the HRt secret code; refer to Chapter 9). To insert a hard return at the end of a line, place the cursor there and press the Enter key. Within each line, separate columns by pressing the Tab key. Use only *one* tab character: If the columns don't line up, use the ruler to move the tabs around until the columns look right.

Be sure to save your document just before converting text to a table — the Undo command doesn't reverse this process!

Highlight all lines in the entire table-to-be. When you press F12 (which is the same as choosing Insert➪Table), a Convert Table dialog box appears, as shown in Figure 22-2. Click on Tabular Column and then on the OK button. Zap! You're "tableized." The last column is probably a little too large, stretching all the way to the right margin. To reduce its width, move the mouse pointer over the right edge of the column until it changes form; then click and drag this edge to the left until the column is the width you want. You can also drag any of the column divider lines to change the widths of the columns. You may also find that you have a blank row at the end of your table. If you want to get rid of that line, click in the row, click the Table button on the Property Bar, and choose the Delete command to delete the row.

Figure 22-2:
Converting a
tab-based
table to a
real table.

Sending Your Document By E-Mail

Attaching a WordPerfect document to an e-mail message couldn't be easier!
Choose File⇨Send to⇨Mail from the menu bar to display the Send UNIX Mail
dialog box, as shown in Figure 22-3. (WordPerfect may prompt you to save
your document.) Address the message by typing the address in the To box,
enter a subject in the Subject box, and type in the Message box a message to
accompany your file.

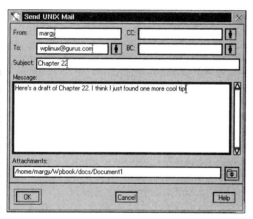

Figure 22-3:
Attach a
WordPerfect
document to
outgoing
mail with
one easy
command!

When you click on OK, WordPerfect composes an e-mail message with the
information you specified, including attaching the current document. If your
computer isn't connected to the Internet, nothing happens, of course. If you're
on a LAN with a connection to the Net, however, the mail goes through!

Type It Again, Sam!

Sometimes, you need to type a long name or address over and over. To relieve your fingers, think of an abbreviation for the long name and then tell the WordPerfect QuickCorrect feature to replace the abbreviation — whenever you type it — with the long name. For example, if you frequently have to type *IDG Books Worldwide, Inc.,* you can tell WordPerfect to replace *IBW* with the full name. To set up a QuickCorrect entry, choose Tools⇨QuickCorrect to display the QuickCorrect dialog box. Type the abbreviation (for example, *IBW*) in the Replace box and type the full name or phrase (for example, *IDG Books Worldwide, Inc.*) in the With box. Then click on Add Entry and click OK. For more information about QuickCorrect, see the section in Chapter 5 about seeing words change as you type them.

About the CD

On the CD-ROM
- Some fonts for use with WordPerfect
- Corel WordPerfect 8 For Linux
- Language modules to customize WordPerfect for your country

*T*he version of WordPerfect that's on the CD in back of this book is the same product you can download from the Corel Web site (http://linux. corel.com). We're just saving you some time by including it on the CD!

System Requirements

Make sure that your computer meets the following minimum system requirements:

- **X86 processor; 486 DX 33 or higher:** An Intel Pentium processor or higher is recommended. This version of WordPerfect doesn't work on Sparc, Mac, or other non-Intel X86 computers.
- **Linux:** You must have Kernel release 2.0.*x* or higher and ibc5 properly installed.
- **X Window System:** KDE, GNOME, or other.
- **At least 9MB of total RAM installed on your computer**: If your system has more than one user, you need more memory. (Corel suggests another 2.5MB per user.)
- **87MB hard disk space:** During the installation, you may need more space than that. While both the installation file and the program are on your hard disk, you need more like 116MB of free space.
- **CD-ROM drive**

For basic Linux information, read *Linux For Dummies,* 2nd Edition, by Jon "Maddog" Hall, and *UNIX For Dummies,* 4th Edition, by John R. Levine and Margaret Levine Young (IDG Books Worldwide, Inc.).

How to Use the CD

The CD is designed to be accessed with a Linux system. You cannot install WordPerfect For Linux on Windows or Mac systems. To install the program, you have to be able to type commands at the Linux command prompt, or *shell* prompt. You also have to be able to log in to your version of Linux as root (the administrative account). If you don't have permission to work as root, ask the administrator of your system for help. (You can probably talk her into doing the whole installation.)

Installing WordPerfect

When you install WordPerfect, you log in to Linux as either root (the administrator) or as another user. You should install WordPerfect as the root user so that you can give all the commands that only the root user can give and so that the files and directories you install belong to the root user. Although you can install WordPerfect even if you can't log in as root, you need someone who *can* to help you.

Note: The capitalization and slash marks (/) look different in the Readme file on the CD. It doesn't matter — just follow along with what we tell you here.

If you have a choice between using a regular console and a terminal-emulation program (like xterm or Terminal) under KDE, GNOME, or another desktop environment, choose the terminal-emulation program. The prompts look nicer.

Follow these steps to install the WordPerfect program:

1. **Log in to Linux as** root.

2. **Create a directory in which to install the program.**

   The directory should be in the /usr/local directory, where most application programs live. For example, type the following commands to create a directory named /usr/local/wp, and press Enter after each command line:

   ```
   cd /usr/local
   mkdir wp
   ```

3. **If you're planning to install WordPerfect as a user other than the root user, give the other user permission to write files in the directory you just created.**

For example, type the following command and press Enter to make the user margy the new owner of the /usr/local/wp directory, with permission to write files in it:

```
chown margy /usr/local/wp
```

4. **Insert the CD into your computer's CD-ROM drive.**

After a moment, your computer spins the CD up to speed.

5. **When the light on your CD-ROM drive goes out, go to the command prompt and type the following command to *mount* the CD (tell Linux that a CD is in the drive), and then press Enter:**

```
mount /dev/cdrom /mnt/cdrom
```

(The names of the CD-ROM device and the mount directory may be different on your system from the ones we use here, which are the Linux standard names.) Linux warns you that the CD is read-only (that is, you can't store your own data on it). The contents of the CD now appear in the directory /mnt/cdrom.

6. **Type this line to move to the CD-ROM directory and then press Enter:**

```
cd /mnt/cdrom
```

Not much seems to happen, except that your shell prompt may change to include the new directory name.

7. **To install WordPerfect as a user other than** root, **log out now and log back in as the other user.**

8. **Create a temporary directory in which to copy the installation program.**

The /var/tmp directory is a popular place to use: Type the command **mkdir /var/tmp/wp** and press Enter to make a wp directory in the /var/tmp directory.

9. **Copy the file GUILG00.GZ from the GUILG directory on the CD to the directory you just created.**

For example, type this command and press Enter:

```
cp /mnt/cdrom/GUILG/GUILG00.GZ /var/tmp/wp
```

Note: Capitalization counts. The directory and filenames on the CD are capitalized (which is strange in the world of Linux). The two characters at the end of the filename are zeroes, by the way, not capital *O*s. The file-copying takes a moment because the file is big (23.7MB).

10. **Use the Linux-standard gunzip and tar programs to "unzip" (uncompress) the file into its constituent files. Type these commands, and press Enter after each one:**

```
cd /var/tmp/wp
gunzip GUILG00.GZ ; tar -xvf GUILG00
```

This line actually contains two commands: the gunzip command that handles the first step in uncompressing the files, and the tar command that finishes the job. Be sure to capitalize the letters exactly as shown here. These commands replace the GUILG00.GZ file with a bunch of new files.

11. **Take a look at the Readme file, just in case something interesting is in there, by typing** more Readme **and pressing Enter.**

   If you see instructions for installing the downloaded version of WordPerfect, don't worry — keeping reading this appendix.

12. **To run the installation program, type this command and press Enter:**

```
./Runme
```

   This step runs the installation program Runme, which you just uncompressed.

13. **The installation program asks whether you unzipped and "tarred" the files you downloaded: Press Y.**

   That gunzip and tar command you typed in Step 10 did the trick. The real, live installation program *really* starts running now.

14. **Follow the instructions onscreen.**

   When the program asks where to install WordPerfect, type the directory name you created in Step 2 (probably **/usr/local/wp**). Choose which installation you want (everything, standard, or minimum). When the program asks whether it can update your /etc/magic file, go ahead and let it. You are asked what kind of printer you have and what Linux calls it. Although Linux usually calls your printer lp, you may have to ask a Linux guru for help at this point. After you answer all the questions, the program installs WordPerfect.

The installation program creates a subdirectory named wpbin in the directory you specified and copies the WordPerfect program files into that directory. The WordPerfect program is named xwp, so if you installed WordPerfect in the /usr/local/wp directory, the pathname of the program is /usr/local/wp/wpbin/xwp. (Sounds redundant, but there it is!)

After you install WordPerfect, save disk space by deleting the temporary installation files (the ones you put in /var/tmp/wp). Type the commands **cd /var/tmp/wp** and **rm *** to delete the files.

Running WordPerfect

Before you run WordPerfect, run your window manager (KDE, GNOME, or another desktop environment). Then run WordPerfect by opening a terminal window and typing the directory name in which you installed the program (/usr/local/wp, if you followed our instructions), followed (with no space) by /wpbin/xwp. For example, type **/usr/local/wp/wpbin/xwp** and press Enter.

The first time you run the program, it asks for a license key, which you can get for free from Corel's Linux Web site (http://linux.corel.com). Follow the links to see information about Corel WordPerfect 8 for Linux, and then click the Register Now link. After you fill in your personal information and click the Submit button, Corel displays your license key. Type this long string of characters just as they appear (remember that punctuation and capitalization count!).

You don't have to enter a license key the first time you use WordPerfect; You have 90 days before the program refuses to run without a license key.

Installing the language modules

If you use a language other than American English, you can install a "language" module for another language. The modules are stored on the CD-ROM in the following files:

Canadian English	GUILGCE/GUILGCE0.GZ
Australian English	GUILGOZ/GUILGOZ0.GZ
U.K. English	GUILGUK/GUILGUK0.GZ
Canadian French	GUILGCF/GUILGCF0.GZ
French	GUILGFR/GUILGFR0.GZ
Dutch	GUILGNL/GUILGNL0.GZ
Spanish	GUILGES/GUILGES0.GZ
German	GUILGDE/GUILGDE0.GZ
Italian	GUILGIT/GUILGIT0.GZ

To install a language module, first install WordPerfect itself by following the instructions in the section "Installing WordPerfect," earlier in this appendix. Then follow Steps 9 through 12 in the same section, substituting the name of the language module (for example, GUILGUK/GUILGUK0.GZ for U.K. English) in place of the WordPerfect program file (GUILG/GUILG00.GZ).

After installing the language module, you can tell WordPerfect to use the module by starting the program with the command **xwp –lang XX** (replacing *XX* with the two-letter abbreviation for the language, from the last two letters of the name of the CD-ROM directory that contains that language module). To add the language to the spell-checker, choose Tools⇨Spell Check in the WordPerfect document window, choose Dictionary⇨Main, and click Add to choose the dictionary for the language. To select a language for the current document, choose Tools⇨Language⇨Settings. To select a language for all new documents, choose File⇨Document⇨Current Document Style, choose Tools⇨Language⇨Settings, and select the language.

Adding WordPerfect to your KDE menus, panel, and desktop

Note: The instructions in this section are for the KDE window manager: if you use another window manager, like GNOME, consult your window manager's help files or manual.

The KDE Personal menu

The WordPerfect installation program doesn't get around to adding WordPerfect to the menu that appears when you click the K button (the Application Starter button) in the lower-left corner of the KDE screen. You can fix this problem by adding WordPerfect to your Personal menu, which appears when you choose K⇨Personal. (You click the K button and choose Personal from the menu that appears.) Follow these steps:

1. **Choose K⇨Utilities⇨Menu Editor to run the keditmenu program.**

   You see the Menu Editor window, with your Personal menu on the left and the standard KDE menus for your Linux system on the right. (Unless you're logged in as root, you probably can't edit the menus on the right.) Your Personal menu may be empty — that's okay!

2. **Right-click on the Personal menu and choose New from the menu that appears.**

   You see the keditmenu window, showing information about a new entry on your Personal menu.

3. **In the File Name box, type wp.kdelnk as the name of the file to contain the information about this new menu entry.**

4. **In the Name box, type WordPerfect or whatever you want to appear on the menu.**

5. **In the Execute box, type the pathname of the WordPerfect program file.**

The pathname of the WordPerfect program file is the directory name you created when you installed WordPerfect, followed by wpbin/xwp. For example, if you installed WordPerfect in the /usr/local/wp directory, type **/usr/local/wp/wpbin/xwp**.

6. **Click on the large icon on the right side of the window, and pick the icon you want to use for WordPerfect.**

   The Corel WordPerfect icon isn't among your options, although you have some nice icons from which to choose!

7. **Click on OK to close the keditmenu dialog box.**

   You return to the Menu Editor window, and your Personal menu now contains an entry for WordPerfect.

8. **Close the Menu Editor window by clicking on its Close (X) button and choose Yes to save your changes.**

To test your new menu entry, choose K⇨Personal and see whether WordPerfect appears on the menu! If it does, choose WordPerfect and see whether the WordPerfect program runs.

If you need to change an entry on your Personal menu, run the Menu Editor again, right-click on the entry, and choose Change from the menu that appears. To get rid of a Personal menu entry, right-click the entry in Menu Editor and choose Delete from the menu that appears.

The Panel

You can add WordPerfect to the KDE panel that appears along the bottom of the screen, too. Choose K⇨Panel⇨Add Application⇨Personal⇨WordPerfect (or whatever you called your menu entry for the WordPerfect program). If you add an extra icon to the panel, delete it by right-clicking it and choosing Remove from the menu that appears.

The KDE Desktop

You may like to have a WordPerfect icon on your desktop, too. The easiest way to create a new icon for WordPerfect is to display the WordPerfect pro-gram directory (probably /usr/local/wp/wpbin) in the File Manager. When you see the xwp file, drag it to your desktop. Choose Link from the small menu appears.

The resulting icon has the unglamorous name of xwp. To rename it, right-click the icon, choose Properties from the menu that appears, and change the File Name option.

If You Have Problems (Of the CD Kind)

For more information about WordPerfect 8 For Linux, see the Corel Web site about the program, at

```
http://linux.corel.com/linuxproducts_wp8.htm
```

A mailing list named `wordperfect8` exists for WordPerfect for Linux users to discuss their experiences and answer each other's questions. To subscribe to the mailing list, start at the Corel Web page we just mentioned, click on the Support link, and click on the List Server link. You see instructions for subscribing to the list.

You can also discuss WordPerfect for Linux in the Usenet newsgroup `corelsupport.wordperfect-linux`, hosted at the new Corel server, `cnews.corel.com`. You can use any Linux newsreader program (trn, tin, nn, or Netscape for example) to read newsgroup messages.

If you still have trouble installing the items from the CD, please call the IDG Books Worldwide Customer Service phone number: 800-762-2974 (outside the United States: 317-596-5430).

Index

• Symbols •

¶ (paragraph symbol), 45

• A •

About Corel WordPerfect, Help, 49
active windows, 209
addresses
  envelopes, 301–303
  mail merge, 290
  mailing labels, 303–309
alignment. *See* justification
All justification, 117
Alt key, 44–45
anchoring text boxes, 255
appearance of screen, 363
Application Bar
  document window, 17, 18
  Preferences dialog box, 348
  Typeover mode, 77
Applix Words files, 214
applying styles
  character styles, 174–175
  document styles, 184
  paragraph styles, 174–175
arrow keys, 55–56
ASCII files, 214, 215
autohyphenation, formatting codes, 158
automatic word selection, 64

• B •

background, 235
  SpeedFormat, 247–248
  Web pages, 335
Backspace key, 56, 76
backups, 373–374
  timed, 353–355, 367
bad breaks, columns, 242–243
bar codes, printing, 303
bitmaps, 267
block protect, 136
  columns and, 239
blocks, text. *See* text blocks
blue underlined words, 86–87
bold text, 3, 98–99
  formatting codes, 158
  HTML toolbar, 329
booklets, 306–309
Bookmark dialog box, 322–323

bookmarks, 321–323, 378
  moving to, 321
Border Style button, Property Bar, 253
borders, 235–239
  graphics boxes, 262, 265
  lines between columns, 238
  paragraphs, 236
  SpeedFormat, 247–248
  text boxes, 253
bottom margins, 132
Box Fill button, Property Bar, 253
box on menu commands, 35
Box Position dialog box, 254–256, 257
boxes. *See* graphics boxes; text boxes
browser, launching, 330
built-in styles, 176–178
  heading, 176–177
  InitialStyle, 177
bullets, 379–380
Bullets & Numbering command, 379–380
buttons
  command buttons, dialog boxes, 38
  custom, toolbar, 41
  mouse, 32–33
  Property Bar, 42–43
  toolbar, 16

• C •

calculations, tables, 248
Cancel button, dialog boxes, 38–39
capitalization, 108
Caps Lock, 19
Caption button, Property Bar, 257
captions, text boxes, 257–258
cascading windows, 207
case sensitivity, filenaming, 23
CD-ROM, 6
cells in tables, 248
center tab, 122
centering
  center justification, 117
  top/bottom, 137–138
CERN (European Particle Physics
    Laboratory), 321
chaining styles, 184
Change Mode command, 294–295
character formatting, 97
  bold text, 98–99
  copying, 107–108
  emphasizing text, 98–99
  fonts, 101–103

character formatting *(continued)*
  formatting codes, 98
  italic text, 98–99
  Property Bar, 100
  QuickFormat, 107–108
  typefaces, 101
  underlined text, 98–99
  undoing, 158
character formatting codes, 152, 157–159
character styles, 172
  applying, 174–175
characters, text boxes, attaching, 256
charts, 272
  documents, 274
  editing, 273–274
check boxes, dialog boxes, 37
circles, 266
clipart. *See also* graphics; images; pictures, 263–264
  Insert Image dialog box, 263–264
Close box, windows, 38
Close button, windows, 360
Closed Curve button, WP Draw toolbar, 270
closing windows, 205–206
codes. *See* formatting codes; merge codes
color preferences, 351–352
columns, 235, 243
  bad breaks, 242–243
  block protect, 239
  creating, 240–242
  Define Columns dialog box, 240
  lines between, 238
  newspaper columns, 239
  parallel columns, 239
  spacing, 241
  tables, 245–246
  tables comparison, 244
  Web pages, 340
  width, 241, 246–247
Columns dialog box, 242
combining documents, 211–213
command buttons, dialog boxes, 38
commands, 35
  box on menu, 35
  Change Mode, 294–295
  Convert Case, 108
  Copy, 71
  Cut, 72
  diamond on menu, 35
  Draw Picture, 268–269
  ellipsis (...), 35
  Flush Right, 118
  Go To, 57
  Hyperlink, 324
  Insert File, 211
  Internet Publisher, 328
  key combinations, 35
  keyboard selection, 46–47
  Language Hyphenation, 119
  Line Tab Set, 123

  Match Case Sensitive command, 82
  Match Whole Word, 82
  Merge, 278
  mouse and, 33–35
  mouse buttons, 39
  New Window, 205
  Open Window, 204
  Paste, 71
  Position, 254–256
  QuickMenus, 39–40
  Redo, 78
  right-pointing triangle on menu, 35
  underlined characters, 37
  Undo, 77, 78–79
  Undo/Redo History, 78
  Update Command, 272
  View Show, 46
computer, turning off, 374
condensed master documents, 311
Contents box, Styles Editor, 182
Contents, Help, 48
context-sensitive help, 50
conversion options, 215
Convert Case command, 108
Convert File dialog box, 217–218
converting
  documents to Web pages, 335–339
  files, 26
  tabs to tables, 380
Copy command, 71
copying text, 70–71
  between documents, 71, 206–207
  character formatting, 107–108
  drag and drop, 377
  files, 227
  X Clipboard and, 71–72
Corel clipart, 263–264
crashes, 15
Create Form File dialog box, 286
Create Merge File dialog box, 283
Ctrl key, 44–45
  arrow keys and, 56
current directory, Save As dialog box, 223
cursor, 17, 52
  lost, 59, 362
  moving, 52
  returning to one point, 378
  ruler and, 43
  shadow cursor, 53
Curve button, WP Draw toolbar, 270
customization, 343–358
Cut command, 72
cutting, X Clipboard and, 72–73

• *D* •

dark edges, document window, 17
Data button, Merge dialog box, 278
data entry screen, mail merge and, 283

data files, mail merge, 276
  creating, 277–286
  creating from scratch, 282–284
  document as, 278–282
  editing, 285–286
  entering data, 284–285
  printing, 292
Data sheets, charts and, 272–273
date
  headers/footers, 145–146
  inserting in document, 120, 378–379
  letters, 299
Date/Time command, 378–379
decimal tab, 122
Define Columns dialog box, 240
Delete button, Hyperlink Tools Property Bar, 326
Delete key, 70, 76
Delete Table dialog box, 246
deleting
  accidental, 364–365
  files, 227–228
  formatting codes, 156, 168
  headers/footers, 149
  styles, 186
  tab stops, 124
  tables, 246
dialog boxes, 36–39
diamond on menu commands, 35
dictionaries, Spell Checker, 91
directories, 221, 222–225
  creating, 224–225
  current, 223
  home directory, 21
  naming, 224–225
  pathnames, 225
  QuickList, 229–231
  Viewer window, 228–229
disks, printing to, 200
Display icon, 350
Display Preferences dialog box, 347–352
doc file extension, 27
document
  formatting, undoing, 160–161
Document Default Font dialog box, 106–107
Document Info command, 344
document styles, 183–184
Document Summary, 344
document window, 15–18
documents, 20
  active window, 209
  borders around it, 238
  charts in, 274
  clipart in, 263–264
  closing, 205–206
  combining, 211–213
  converting to Web pages, 335–339
  copying text between, 71, 206–207
  data files from, 278–282
  enclosed shapes, 268
  formatting, 106–107

inserting to another document, 211–212
  large, 309–317
  linked, 212
  locating, 360–361
  location, 18
  marking place in, 356–357
  master documents, 309
  maximizing, 210
  new, 205
  opening, 25–27, 378
  opening multiple, 204–205
  printing, 27–28, 192–194
  protecting, 294–295
  read-only, 294–295
  retrieving styles from, 185
  saving, 20–24
  saving all open, 211
  saving Web pages as, 337
  saving, filename exists, 213–214
  sending in e-mail, 381
  shapes in, 266
  starting new, 27
  subdocuments, 309
  switching between open, 205
  templates, 293–294
  text bocks, saving as, 212–213
dot leader tabs, 122
dots, pictures and, 267
double spacing, 127
double-sided printing, 197–199
downloading clipart, 263
draft view, 138
drag and drop, 377
dragging margin lines, 112–113
dragging text, 70
draw lines, 260
Draw Picture command, 268–269
drawing. *See also* pictures, 259–260, 267–272
  text in drawings, 271–272
drop caps, Web pages, 340
duplex printing, booklets and, 307

• *E* •

e-mail, sending documents, 381
Edit button, Hyperlink Tools Property Bar, 326
editing
  ASCII files, 214
  charts, 273–274
  data files, mail merge, 285–286
  formatted text, 158–159
  graphics, 269
  master documents, 314
  text, 19
editors, graphics editors, 268
Ellipse button, WP Draw toolbar, 270
ellipses, 266
ellipsis (...) on commands, 35
Elliptical Arc button, WP Draw toolbar, 270

emphasizing text, 98–99
enclosed shapes, documents and, 268
End key, 55, 57
end of line, formatting code, 158
Enlightenment window manager, 12
Enter key, 20, 45, 372
  dialog boxes, 37
  styles and, 175
entering data in data files, mail merge, 284–285
entering text. *See* typing
Envelope dialog box, 291
envelopes, 301–303
  bar codes, 303
  mailing labels, 303–309
environment preferences, 355–357
  Preferences dialog box, 347
Esc key, dialog boxes, 38
existing styles, modifying, 182–183
exiting
  Linux, 374
  WordPerfect, 28–29
expanding master documents, 311
exporting files, 216–217
ExpressDocs, 293, 295
  Personal Info dialog box, 295
extending text selections, 68–69
extensions, filenames, 24, 27

• F •

F1 key (Help), 34
F2 key (Find and Replace), 34
F5 key (Print), 34
F10 key (Save), 34
faxes, 301
Field Codes, Reveal Codes and, 155
fields, mail merge, 276, 287–288
  data files, 277
file extensions, 231, 296
  htm, 27
  Save As dialog box, 216–217
  wpt, 296
File List, Save As dialog box, 223–224
file managers, 221, 222
filenames, 23–24, 213–214
  extensions, 24, 27
  foriegn files, 215
files
  ASCII, 214
  backups, 353–355
  conversion, 26
  copying, 227
  deleting, 227–228
  exporting, 216–217
  foreign, 214–219
  formats, 214–219, 231
  graphics, 266–267
  importing, 217–218
  merging, 289–292

opening, 25–27
preferences, 352–355
renaming, 226–227
RTF, 218
saving documents, 20–21
searches, 231–232
types, 231
Viewer Window and, 228–229
Files option, Preferences dialog box, 347
Files Preferences dialog box, 352–353
Fill Pattern Color button, WP Draw toolbar, 271
Fill Pattern Style button, WP Draw toolbar, 271
fills, 238, 271
  text boxes, 253
  Web pages, 340
Find and Replace
  formatting codes, 85, 161–165
  saving and, 373
  text, 79–80, 83–85
Find and Replace Text dialog box, 80
fixed-space fonts, 102
Flush Right command, 118
folders, 221
Font dialog box, 103–107
fonts, 101–103, 344–345
  documents, 106–107
  formatting codes, 158
  HTML toolbar, 329
  hyperlinks, 326
  Preferences dialog box, 348
  proportionally spaced, 372
  serifs, 102
  size, 100–101, 104
  templates and, 344
footers. *See* headers/footers
foreign files, 214–219
  creating, 216–217
  reading, 217–218
Form button, Merge dialog box, 278
form files, mail merge, 276
  creating, 286–289
form letters. *See* mail merge
Format-As-You-Go, 372
formats, files, 214–219, 231
formatting codes. *See also* Reveal Codes, 98
  block protect, 136
  centering, 138
  character codes, 152
  character formatting, 157–159
  deleting, 156, 168
  deleting and, 76
  editing formatted text, 158–159
  end of line, 158
  Find and Replace, 161–165
  finding and replacing, 85
  hard, 156
  headers/footers, 149
  hyphenation, 158
  indent, 116
  information about, 155, 169

justification, 119
margins, 132
modifying, 155
Open Style, 157
page breaks, 134, 157
paired, 152
replacing, 165–168
revertible codes, 152
single codes, 152
soft, 156
soft page break, 157
suppressing headers/footers, 148
tabs, 127, 157
undoing, 159–161
formatting. *See also* styles
documents, 106–107
emphasizing text, 98–99
fonts, 101–103
line formatting, 110
QuickFormat, 107–108
reformatting, 20
removing, 99, 362
ruler, 110–111
styles, 108
text blocks, 104
text boxes, 251
troubleshooting, 362
Web page text, 328–330
Formula toolbar, 249
formulas, tables, 248
FrameMaker files, 214
Freehand button, WP Draw toolbar, 270
full justification, 117
function keys, 34
FVWM Window manager, 12

GNOME panel, 14
Go To command, 57, 324, 378
Go To dialog box, 57–58
Grammar-As-You-Go, 89
Grammatik, 93
graphics boxes, 262
borders, 265
handles, 262
moving, 264
selecting, 262
sizing, 264–265
graphics editors, 268
Graphics menu, 254
graphics. *See also* clipart; pictures, 254, 262–267
creating, 267–272
editing, 269
Insert Image dialog box, 263–264
inserting from files, 266–267
graphs, 272–274
Guidelines dialog box, margins, 112
guidelines, margins, 112

handles
graphics boxes, 262, 264
text boxes, 252
hanging indents, 116
hard codes, formatting codes, 156
hard page breaks, 133
formatting code, 157
hard return formatting code, 157
headers/footers, 142–149
deleting, 149
discontinuing, 148–149
page numbering and, 139
printing, 147–148
suppressing, 147–148
three-part header, 145
Web pages, 340
Headers/Footers dialog box, 143
heading styles, built-in, 176–177
headings
HTML toolbar, 329
keeping with text, 136–137
marking for table of contents, 315
height-to-width proportions, text boxes and, 257
Help, 48–50
context sensitivity, 50
PerfectExpert, 49–50
searches, 48
hiding/showing
formatting codes. *See* Reveal Codes
headers/footers, 143
paragraph marks, 46
ruler, 34
home directory, 21
Home key, 55, 57
How to Use This Book, 2–3
htm file extension, 27
HTML
documents, Web pages saved as, 337–338
files, 214
toolbar, 328–329
Hyperlink command, 324
Hyperlink Tools Property Bar, 325–327
hyperlinks, 321, 324–325
to other Web pages, 333–335
hypertext, 320
hyperlinks, 321
hyphenation, 119–121
formatting codes, 158
nonbreaking, 379

iconifying, 13–14
icons, 6–7
Display, 350
printer icon, 18

Remember, 7
tab set, 123
WordPerfect, 359–360
importing files, 217–218
indents, 116
    displaying, 350
    first line of each paragraph, 125–127
    paragraphs, 46
    Web pages, 340
initial capitalization, 108
InitialStyle style, built-in, 177
Insert File command, 211
Insert Image dialog box, 263–264
Insert key, 77
Insert mode, 77–78
    application bar, 18
inserting
    clipart in documents, 263–264
    date, 378–379
    documents into documents, 211
    graphics from files, 266–267
    shapes in documents, 266
insertion point, 52
    ruler and, 43
installed printers, 190–192
Internet, 320–321
    browser, launching, 330
Internet Publisher command, 328
Internet Publisher dialog box, 328
ISP (Internet Service Provider), 339
italic text, 98–99
    formatting codes, 158
    HTML toolbar, 329

• *J* •

junk mail. *See also* mail merge, 275–292
justification, 116–119

• *K* •

KDE (K Desktop Environment)
    closing windows, 206
    directores, 222
    hypertext, 320
    window manager, 3, 12
    window sizes, 208
keeping text together, 134–137
key combinations, 35
keyboard
    Alt key, 44–45
    arrow keys, 55
    Backspace, 56
    command selection, 46–47
    Ctrl key, 44–45
    Delete key, 70
    End, 55, 57
    Enter, 45
    function keys, 34

Home, 55, 57
navigating documents, 55–57
navigation keys, 67
numeric keypad, 19, 55
Page Down, 55, 57
Page Up, 55, 57
Preferences dialog box, 348
programming, 357–358
Shift key, 44–45
text selection, 67–68
keyboard shortcuts
    copying text, 72
    cutting text, 72
    formatting text, 98
    pasting, 72
    selecting text, 73

• *L* •

Labels dialog box, 304–305
landscape orientation, 130
    booklets and, 307
Language Hyphenation command, 119
large documents, 309–317
leader tabs, 122
left justification, 117
left tab, 122
letter spacing, 117
letterhead, 298–299
letters, 297–300
    automated, 297–298
    dates in, 299
    multiple, 275–292
    page numbering, 300
    saving as prototype document, 300
    templates, 297–298
libraries, styles, 185–186
Line button, WP Draw toolbar, 270
Line Color button, WP Draw toolbar, 271
line formatting, 110
line spacing, 127–128
Line Style button, WP Draw toolbar, 271
Line Tab Set command, 123
lines
    between columns, 238
    draw lines, 260
    drawing, 259
    pictures and, 268
    Web pages, 340
linked documents, 212
Links On/Off button, Hyperlink Tools Property
    Bar, 326
Linux For Dummies, 2
Linux versions, 3
list boxes, dialog boxes, 37
location in document, application bar, 18
lost pointer, 59
Lotus 1-2-3 files, 214
Lotus AmiPro files, 214

• M •

mail merge
  addresses, 290
  data files, 276, 286
  data files, creating, 282–284
  data files, from documents, 282–284
  entering data in data files, 284–285
  envelopes, 291
  fields, 276
  form files, 276
  form files, creating, 286–289
  merge codes, 276
  merging files, 289–292
  records, 276
  saving form letters, 290
mailing labels, 303–309
margin strip, ruler, 111
margins
  dragging to set, 112–113
  entire document, 114–115
  guidelines, 112
  indents, 116
  justification, 116–119
  paragraphs, 115–116
  ruler, 44, 110
  setting, 112–116
  top/bottom, 132
  Web pages, 340
  Zoom and, 346
Margins dialog box, 113–114, 132
marking
  headings for table of contents, 315
  place in document, 356–357
master documents, 309
  condensed, 311
  editing, 314
  expanding, 311
  saving, 313–314
  subdocuments, 310–311
Match Case Sensitive command, 82
Match Whole Word command, 82
maximizing windows, 210–211
memos, 300
menu bar
  dialog boxes, 38
  document window, 16
  mouse, 33, 34–35
  text selection, 66–67
menus
  mouse buttons, 39
  pull-down, 34
  QuickMenus, 39–40
  underlined characters, 37
merge codes, mail merge, 276
Merge command, 278
Merge dialog box, 278
merging files, 289–292

minimizing windows, 13–14, 210–211, 360
misspelled words
  QuickCorrect, 87–89
  red underlined, 85–86
  Spell Checker, 89–93
modifying existing styles, 182–183
modifying formatting codes, 155
monitors, sleeping, 374
mouse
  buttons, 32–33, 39
  commands and, 33–35
  controlling selection, 357
  menu bar, 33–35
  pointer, 17, 52
  pull-down menus, 34
  QuickMenus, 39–40
  scroll bar and, 54–55
  text selection, 62–67
  X Window System and, 22
mouse pointer, 52–55
  lost, 59
  shadow cursor, 53
moving
  cursor, 52
  files, 226–227
  graphics boxes, 264
  in documents. *See* navigating documents
  tab stops, 123–124
  text, 70
  text boxes, 252, 254–256

• N •

naming
  directories, 224–225
  files, 23–24, 213–214, 226
  renaming files, 226–227
  styles, 174, 181
navigating documents, 51–59
  Go To dialog box, 57–58
  keyboard, 55–57
  mouse, 52–55
  page by page, 55
  quickly, 56–57
  scroll bar, 53
  top of the page, 58
  unseen document areas, 53
navigation keys, 67
new documents, 27, 205
New Window command, 205
newspaper columns, 239
Next button, Hyperlink Tools Property Bar, 326
nonbreaking hyphens, 379
numbering pages, 139–142, 373
  Web pages, 340
numbers in dialog boxes, 38
numeric keypad, 19, 55

• O •

OK button, dialog boxes, 38–39
online help, 49
Open button, toolbar, 25
Open dialog box, 26
Open Style code, 157
open styles, 183
Open Window command, 204
opening
  documents, 378
  files, 25–27
order of pages for printing, 195
organization of book, 4–6
orphans, 134–135

• P •

page breaks, 133, 372
  bad breaks, 134
  booklets, 309
  formatting codes, 157
  widows and orphans, 134–135
Page Down key, 55, 57
page formatting, undoing, 160–161
page numbering, 139–142, 373
  changing numbering, 142
  letters, 300
  positioning numbers, 140
  Roman numerals, 141–142
  table of contents and, 315–316
  Web pages, 340
Page Numbering dialog box, 139–140
page setup
  centering top/bottom, 137
  margins, 114
  page breaks, 133
  page size, 130–131
page size, setting, 129–131
Page Up key, 55, 57
page view, subdocuments and, 138, 310–311
paired formatting codes, 152
paired styles, 183
paper
  printers, 190
  size, 129–131
  types, 131
Paragraph Border dialog box, 236–237
Paragraph Format dialog box, 125–126
paragraph formatting, 159–160
paragraph styles, 173
  applying, 176
  QuickStyle, 175–176
paragraph symbol (¶), 45
paragraphs
  borders, 236–237
  Enter key, 20, 45
  fills, 238
  indents, 46

  selecting, 65
  spacing between, 128
  splitting, 20
  text boxes, attaching, 255, 256
parallel columns, 239
Paste command, 71
pasting
  drag and drop, 377
  X Clipboard and, 71–72
pathnames, 225
PerfectExpert, Help, 48, 49–50
Perform button, Hyperlink Tools Property Bar, 326
Perform Merge dialog box, 289
Personal Info dialog box, 295
pictures. *See also* clipart; drawing; graphics
  dots in, 267
  lines, 268
  shapes, 269–271
  text and, 268
  text in, 271–272
  Web pages, 330–333
point-and-click, mouse, 32
  text selection, 92–67
pointer, 17
  returning to one point, 378
  ruler and, 43
points, font size, 100
Polygon button, WP Draw toolbar, 270
polygons, 266
portrait orientation, 130
Position command, text boxes, 254–256
Position, Go To dialog box, 59
PostScript files, 215
preferences, 347–348
  color, 351
  environment, 355–357
previewing printing, 190
Previous Box/Next Box button, Property Bar, 253
Previous button, Hyperlink Tools Property
  Bar, 326
Print button, toolbar, 28
print preview, 190
printer daemon, 201
printer icon, application bar, 18
printers, 189–190
  installed, 190–192
  networks, 192
printing. *See also* page setup, 27–28
  basics, 189–190
  booklets, 306–309
  canceling print jobs, 201–202
  copies, 199–200
  data files, mail merge, 292
  entire documents, 192–194
  headers/footers, 144, 147–148
  letterhead, 298–299
  mailing labels, 305–306
  order of pages, 195
  Preferences dialog box, 348
  printer supplies, 375

random pages, 196
ranges of pages, 195–196
specific pages, 195
text selections, 194
to disk, 200
troubleshooting, 363–364
turning on printer, 374
two-sided printing, 197–199
working while printing, 193
program window, 15–17
Proofread command, 89
properties, 17
Property Bar. *See also* toolbars, 40, 42–43
   Border Style button, 253
   Box Fill button, 253
   Caption button, 257
   document window, 17
   draw lines and, 260
   font size, 100
   formatted text, 99
   formatting and, 159
   Hyperlink tools, 325–327
   justification and, 118
   Previous Box/Next Box button, 253
   Select Styles list, 173
   tables and, 244
   text boxes, 253
   Text Wrap button, 258
proportionally spaced fonts, 102, 121, 372
protecting documents, 294–295
pull-down menus, mouse, 34

● Q ●

Quick Data Entry dialog box, 284
QuickCorrect, 382
   Format-As-You-Go, 372
   misspelled words and, 87–89
QuickFinder, 224
   searches, 231–232
QuickFormat, 107–108
QuickList, 229–231
QuickMarks, 356
QuickMenu, 39–40
   shapes, 270
   text selection, 66
   X Clipboard and, 73
QuickStyle, 173–174
   document styles, 183
   paragraph styles, 175–176
QuickSum button, Formula toolbar, 250

● R ●

random pages, printing, 196
ranges of pages, printing, 195–196
read-only documents, 294–295
reading foreign files, 217–218

records, mail merge, 276
Rectangle button, WP Draw toolbar, 270
rectangles, 266
Recycle bin, 364–365
Red Hat Linux, 3
red underlined words, 85–86
Redo command, 78
reformatting, 20
Remember icons, 7
renaming files, 226–227
replacing formatting codes, 165–168
replacing text, 77–78, 84–85
returning to one point, 378
returns
   displaying, 350
   hard return formatting code, 157
   soft return formatting code, 157
reusing styles, 184–186
Reveal Codes. *See also* formatting codes,
      152–154
   closing, 154
   column breaks, 243
   removing formatting, 362
   window, 153–154
revertible codes, 152
right justification, 117
right tab, 122
right-pointing triangle on menu commands, 35
Roman numerals, page numbering, 141–142
Rounded Rectangle button, WP Draw toolbar, 270
rows, tables, 245–246
RTF (Rich Text Format) files, 215, 218
ruler, 43–44, 110–111
   hiding/showing, 43
   margins, 110
   tab stops, 43–44, 110, 121
   uses, 111
runaround, text, 258

● S ●

sans serif fonts, 102
Save As dialog box, 22, 216–217, 223–224
Save button, toolbar, 21–23
saving, 373
   all open documents, 211
   before closing documents, 206
   documents, 20–24
   filename exists, 213–214
   Find and Replace command, 373
   master documents, 313
   text blocks as documents, 212–213
   Web pages as HTML documents, 337–338
   Web pages as WordPerfect documents, 337
   workspace, 356–357
screens
   appearance, 363
   sleeping, 374
   splash screen, 15

scroll bar, 53
  document window, 17
  mouse, 54–55
searches, 81–83
  files, 231–232
  find and replace, 79–80
  Help, 48
  refining, 82–83
  wildcards, 83
Select Styles list, Property Bar, 173
selecting text
  automatic word selection, 64
  deleting, 76
  extending selections, 68–69
  keyboard, 67–68
  menu bar, 66–67
  mouse, 62–67
  nose and pickle, 68
  printing selections, 194
  QuickMenu, 66
sentences
  formatting, undoing, 159–160
  selecting, 65
serifs, fonts, 102
shadow cursor, 17, 53
  application bar and, 18
shapes
  curves, 270
  ellipses, 270
  enclosed shapes, 268
  in documents, 266
  polygons, 270
  QuickMenu, 270
  rectangles, 270
  WP Draw, 269–271
Shift key, 44–45
single formatting codes, 152
single spacing, 127
size, text, 100–101
sizing
  graphics boxes, 264–265
  text boxes, 252, 256–257
  windows, 154, 209–210
sleeping monitors, 374
soft codes, formatting codes, 156
soft page break formatting code, 157
soft return formatting code, 157
spacebar, 45–46
spaces, 372
  displaying, 350
spacing, 119
  columns, 241
  line spacing, 127
  paragraphs, 128
  unbreakable, 379
special characters, file naming, 23
SpeedFormat, 247–248
Spell Checker, 89–93
Spell-As-You-Go, 89
splash screen, 15

spreadsheet-like tables, 248–250
  formatting numbers, 250
standard template, 295
starting WordPerfect, 14–15
stationery, letterhead and, 299
sticky selections, 82
Style button, Hyperlink Tools Property Bar, 327
Style List dialog box, 177–179
Styles Editor, 177
  Contents box, 182
  options, 179–180
Styles QuickCreate dialog box, 173–174
styles. *See also* formatting, 108, 171–186
  applying character styles, 174–175
  applying document styles, 184
  applying paragraph styles, 174–175
  built-in, 176–178
  chaining, 154
  character styles, 172
  creating, 173–174
  creating from scratch, 181–182
  defined, 172
  deleting, 186
  document styles, 183
  Enter key and, 175
  existing, modifying, 182–183
  headings, 176–177
  InitialStyle, 177
  libraries, 185–186
  names, 174
  open, 183
  paired, 183
  paragraph styles, 173
  paragraph styles, QuickStyle, 175–176
  QuickStyle, 173–174
  retrieving from other documents, 184–185
  reusing, 184–186
  turning off, 184
Subdivide Page dialog box, 307
subdocuments, 309
subscript text, 105
superscript text, 105
suppressing headers/footers, 147–148

Tab Set dialog box, 123
tab set icon, 123
tab stops, 111, 121–125
  creating, 124–125
  deleting, 124
  moving, 44, 123–124
  ruler, 43
  setting, 121–123
  types, 44, 122
tab strip, ruler, 111
table of contents, 315–317
Table of Contents toolbar, 315
Table QuickCreate, 243–244

Table SpeedFormat dialog box, 247
tables, 235, 243–250
  calculations, 248
  cells, 248
  column width, 246–247
  columns comparison, 244
  columns, adding/deleting, 245–246
  converting from tabs, 380
  deleting, 246
  formulas, 248
  numbers, formatting, 250
  Property Bar, 244
  rows, adding/deleting, 245–246
  spreadsheet-like, 248–250
tabs, 45–46, 372
  converting to tables, 380
  displaying, 350
  formatting codes, 157
  ruler, 110
  Web pages, 340
Technical Stuff icons, 4, 6
templates, 293–294
  creating, 296
  customization and, 344
  letterhead, 298–299
  letters, 297–298
  memos, 300
  prototype documents, 300
  standard template, 295
terminal window, starting WordPerfect, 14
text
  bold, 98–99
  drag and drop, 377
  drawings, 271–272
  emphasizing, 98–99
  formatted, editing, 158–159
  headings, keeping together, 136–137
  hypertext, 320
  italics, 98–99
  keeping together, 134–137
  pictures and, 268
  Reveal Codes window, 153
  size, 100–101
  styles, 98–99
  underlined, 98–99
  Web pages, 328–330
text blocks, 61–73
  deleting, 76–77
  extending selections, 68–69
  formatting, 104
  mouse, selecting, 62–67
  protecting, 135–136
  saving as documents, 212–213
text boxes
  anchoring, 255
  borders, 253
  captions, 257–258
  characters, attaching to, 256
  dialog boxes, 37
  draw lines and, 260

  formatting, 251
  Graphics menu, 254
  handles, 252
  height-to-width proportions, 257
  moving, 252, 254–256
  paragraphs, attaching to, 255, 256
  Position command, 254–256
  Property Bar, 253
  runaround text, 258
  selection, 252
  sizing, 252, 256–257
  width, 26
  wrapping text, 258–259
text copy, 70–72
text deletion, 19, 70, 75–78
  Backspace key, 76
  blocks, 76–77
  Delete key and, 76
text edit, 19
text replacement, 77–78, 84–85
text runaround, text boxes, 258
text selection, printing selections, 194
text wrap, 20
Text Wrap button, Property Bar, 258
text wrap, text boxes, 258–259
The Gimp, 268
Thesaurus, 94
three-part header, 145
tiling windows, 207
timed backups, 367
  copies, 353–355
Tip icons, 6
title bar, document window, 16
toolbars. *See also* Property Bar, 40–41
  document window, 16
  Formula, 249
  hiding/showing, 41
  HTML toolbar, 328–329
  Open button, 25
  Print button, 193
  Save button, 21–23
  Table of Contents, 315
  WP Draw, 268, 270–271
top margins, 132
top of the page, moving to, 58
top/bottom centering, 137–138
Trash bin, 364–365
triangles in ruler, 111
troubleshooting, 359–367
  cursor location, 362
  deletions, accidental, 364–365
  document location, 360
  formatting, 362
  locating WordPerfect, 359–360
  no response, 366–367
  opening documents, 365–366
  printing, 363–364
turning off computer, 374
turning off styles, 184
turning on printer, 374

two-sided printing, 197–199
txt file extension, 27
typefaces, 101
Typeover mode, 18, 77–78
typing, 19
  editing text, 19
  ending lines, 372
  Grammar-As-You-Go, 89
  header/footer text, 145–147
  QuickCorrect, 87–89, 382
  Spell-As-You-Go, 89

• U •

underlined characters in commands, 37
underlined text, 98–99
  blue, 86–87
  red, 85–86
Undo, 47–48, 78–79
  character formatting, 158
Undo command, 77, 78–79
Undo/Redo History command, 78
Update Document command, 272

• V •

View Show command, 46
Viewer window, file contents and, 228–229
viewing codes. *See* Reveal Codes
views, documents, 138

• W •

Warning! icons, 7
watermarks, Web pages, 340
Web Page view, 138
Web pages, 215, 321
  background color, 335
  columns, 340
  converting documents to, 335–339
  creating, 327–335
  drop caps, 340
  fills, 340
  formatting text, 328–330
  headers/footers, 340
  hyperlinks to others, 333–335
  indents, 340
  lines, 340
  margins, 340
  numbering pages, 340
  pictures, 330–333
  publishing to Web, 339
  saving as HTML documents, 337–339
  saving as WordPerfect document, 337
  tabs, 340
  watermarks, 340
white space, 46

widows, 134–135
width, columns, 241
wildcards, searches and, 83
window managers, 11–13
  Enlightenment, 12
  FVWM, 12
  KDE, 12
  WindowMaker, 12
WindowMaker window manager, 12
windows, 15–17
  active, 209
  borders, dragging, 210
  cascading, 207
  Close button, 360
  closing, 205–206
  iconifying, 13–14
  maximizing/minimizing, 210
  minimizing, 13–14, 360
  multiple, 207–211
  Reveal Codes, 153–154
  sizing, 154, 209–210
  tiling, 207
Word files, 215
word spacing, 117
word wrap, 20
WordPerfect
  crashing, 15
  disappearing, 360
  exiting, 28–29
  icon, 359–360
  locating, 359–360
  not responding, 366–367
  starting, 14–15
words, selecting, 65
workspace, saving, 356–357
World Wide Web, 321
WP Draw, 267–272
  charts, 272–274
  graphics, 272–274
  shapes, 269–271
  toolbar, 268, 270–271
wpt file extension, 296
wrapping text, 20

• X-Y-Z •

X Clipboard, 70
  copying and, 71–72
  cutting and, 72
  pasting and, 71–72
  QuickMenu and, 73
X Window System, 11
  copy and paste, 207
xterm windows, starting WordPerfect, 14
xwp command, 14

Zoom, 345–347
  preferences, 349–350
zooming, graphics boxes and, 265

IDG Books Worldwide, Inc., End-User License Agreement

READ THIS. You should carefully read these terms and conditions before opening the software packet(s) included with this book ("Book"). This is a license agreement ("Agreement") between you and IDG Books Worldwide, Inc. ("IDGB"). By opening the accompanying software packet(s), you acknowledge that you have read and accept the following terms and conditions. If you do not agree and do not want to be bound by such terms and conditions, promptly return the Book and the unopened software packet(s) to the place you obtained them for a full refund.

1. **License Grant.** IDGB grants to you (either an individual or entity) a nonexclusive license to use one copy of the enclosed software program(s) (collectively, the "Software") solely for your own personal or business purposes on a single computer (whether a standard computer or a workstation component of a multiuser network). The Software is in use on a computer when it is loaded into temporary memory (RAM) or installed into permanent memory (hard disk, CD-ROM, or other storage device). IDGB reserves all rights not expressly granted herein.

2. **Ownership.** IDGB is the owner of all right, title, and interest, including copyright, in and to the compilation of the Software recorded on the disk(s) or CD-ROM ("Software Media"). Copyright to the individual programs recorded on the Software Media is owned by the author or other authorized copyright owner of each program. Ownership of the Software and all proprietary rights relating thereto remain with IDGB and its licensers.

3. **Restrictions on Use and Transfer.**

   (a) You may only (i) make one copy of the Software for backup or archival purposes, or (ii) transfer the Software to a single hard disk, provided that you keep the original for backup or archival purposes. You may not (i) rent or lease the Software, (ii) copy or reproduce the Software through a LAN or other network system or through any computer subscriber system or bulletin-board system, or (iii) modify, adapt, or create derivative works based on the Software.

   (b) You may not reverse engineer, decompile, or disassemble the Software. You may transfer the Software and user documentation on a permanent basis, provided that the transferee agrees to accept the terms and conditions of this Agreement and you retain no copies. If the Software is an update or has been updated, any transfer must include the most recent update and all prior versions.

4. **Restrictions on Use of Individual Programs.** You must follow the individual requirements and restrictions detailed for each individual program in the "About the CD" appendix of this Book. These limitations are also contained in the individual license agreements recorded on the Software Media. These limitations may include a requirement that after using the program for a specified period of time, the user must pay a registration fee or discontinue use. By opening the Software packet(s), you will be agreeing to abide by the licenses and restrictions for these individual programs that are detailed in the "About the CD" appendix and on the Software Media. None of the material on this Software Media or listed in this Book may ever be redistributed, in original or modified form, for commercial purposes.

Installing the CD

The *WordPerfect For Linux For Dummies* CD contains the most appropriate possible program — WordPerfect for Linux, from Corel Corporation! To install WordPerfect from the CD to a Linux system, follow these steps:

1. **Log in to your system as** `root` **and display a shell prompt.**

   If you don't know how to type shell commands or don't have permission to log in as `root`, ask your Linux system administrator for help with installing WordPerfect.

2. **Type the Linux** `mount` **command to tell Linux that a CD is in the drive, like this:**

   ```
   mount /dev/cdrom /mnt/cdrom
   ```

3. **Move to the directory where new software is installed (usually** `cd/usr/local`**) by typing**

   ```
   cd /usr/local
   ```

4. **Create a new directory named** `wp` **in which to install WordPerfect by typing**

   ```
   mkdir wp
   ```

5. **Create a temporary directory into which to copy the installation file by typing**

   ```
   mkdir /var/tmp/wp
   ```

6. **Copy the file GUILG00.GZ from the GUILG directory on the CD to the directory you just created by typing**

   ```
   cp /mnt/cdrom/GUILG/GUILG00.GZ /var/tmp/wp
   ```

7. **Uncompress the installation program files by typing these commands:**

   ```
   cd /var/tmp/wp
   gunzip GUILG00.GZ ; tar xvf GUILG00
   ```

8. **Run the installation program by typing**

   ```
   ./Runme
   ```

   This command asks whether you unzipped and "tarred" the files: Answer **Y**. The installation program runs.

9. **Follow the instructions onscreen.**

   When the program asks where to install WordPerfect, type the directory name **/usr/local/wp** (or whatever directory you created in Step 4).

For more information about installing WordPerfect from this CD, see the appendix, which also includes directions for adding WordPerfect to your KDE desktop, Personal menu, and panel.

IDG BOOKS WORLDWIDE
BOOK REGISTRATION

Register
This Book
and Win!

We want to hear from you!

Visit **http://my2cents.dummies.com** to register this book and tell us how you liked it!

- Get entered in our monthly prize giveaway.

- Give us feedback about this book — tell us what you like best, what you like least, or maybe what you'd like to ask the author and us to change!

- Let us know any other ...*For Dummies*® topics that interest you.

Your feedback helps us determine what books to publish, tells us what coverage to add as we revise our books, and lets us know whether we're meeting your needs as a ...*For Dummies* reader. You're our most valuable resource, and what you have to say is important to us!

Not on the Web yet? It's easy to get started with *Dummies 101*®: *The Internet For Windows*® *98* or *The Internet For Dummies*®, 6th Edition, at local retailers everywhere.

Or let us know what you think by sending us a letter at the following address:

...*For Dummies* Book Registration
Dummies Press
7260 Shadeland Station, Suite 100
Indianapolis, IN 46256-3917
Fax 317-596-5498

...FOR DUMMIES™

BESTSELLING
BOOK SERIES